Rerum familiarium libri i–viii

Francesco Petrarca

Rerum familiarium libri
I–VIII

TRANSLATED BY ALDO S. BERNARDO

ALBANY, NEW YORK, 1975

STATE UNIVERSITY OF NEW YORK PRESS

Published with assistance from
the University Awards Committee
of State University of New York

Rerum familiarium libri I–VIII
First Edition
Published by State University of New York Press
99 Washington Avenue, Albany, New York 12210
© 1975 State University of New York
All rights reserved
Printed in the United States of America

Library of Congress Cataloging in Publication Data
Petrarca, Francesco, 1304–1374.
  Rerum familiarium libri I–VIII

  A translation of the first 8 books.
  Bibliography: p.
  I. Title.
PQ4496.E29E23   1975   851'.1 [B]   75-2418
ISBN 0-87395-295-2
ISBN 0-87395-296-0 (microfiche)

To Claudia

Contents

Book III

Book IV

Book V

Book VI

Book VII

Preface

This translation is the result of a casual conversation held with the director of a computer center in 1968. In discussing ways and means of making the computer useful to humanistic research our discussion turned to how the computer might assist in the preparation of translations. I confessed my reluctance to undertake a project which I nevertheless felt was essential for a firmer grasp of those two cultural movements marking the beginning of modern times, Humanism and the Renaissance. I had just completed a seminar on Humanism and had found appalling the inability of students to read certain Latin prose works of Petrarch. The obvious worsening of the situation in the study of Latin had convinced me that the only practical solution to the problem was to translate such works as were obviously basic documents in the history of such important cultural movements. Since very few of Petrarch's Latin works had been translated into English in their entirety, the prospect of future scholars undertaking such translations appeared dim indeed considering the excessive length of such works as the collections of letters.

As our discussions continued, it became clear that there was a variety of ways in which the computer could assist in the preparation of such translations. The one that appealed to me most was the use of the computer to prepare a Latin-English word list of Petrarch's letters that would start with the first word of the first letter and end with the last word of the last letter. This would mean that I would have at my disposal a printout that, if carefully prepared, would provide me with the basic and perhaps only tool needed to proceed most rapidly with the translation, that is, by simply dictating it into a dictaphone.

Since I had already started work on a book about Petrarch's Laura in anticipation of the six hundredth anniversary of his death in 1974, I determined to seek funding for the necessary computer assistance that would allow me to initiate the translation of the *Familiari* and by 1974 to carry it at least to the end of the eighth book which, as we shall see, was the original terminal point for Petrarch in the first stages of forming his collection. I was fortunate to win a large grant from the Research Foundation of the State University of New York without which the costs of the project would have been prohibitive. Most of the computer time was kindly donated by our computer center, while all other costs were defrayed by the grant.

The job of keypunching the entire text was begun almost at once, and by the summer of 1969 an alphabetical word list of unique forms was ready and awaited the inclusion of the English meanings. A team of five Latinists and I worked through the summer entering on special printout sheets from one to seven meanings of each word. By the winter of 1969 all entries were completed, and the computer next provided the desired chronological dictionary of all twenty-four books of letters. Circumstances prevented me from starting the translation until the following summer. Between the fall of 1970 and the winter of 1971 I was able to complete the translations of the first eight books. All translations were dictated on belts which were transcribed by a bevy of secretaries and student help.

Meanwhile we found that our computer program could also produce as a kind of by-product, a concordance of the entire collection. This was done almost at once, in the spring of 1970. The concordance ran to 288,000 forms, and should also see publication in 1975. Perhaps even more exciting is the prospect of preparing a dictionary of Petrarch's Latin which might eventually be expanded into a dictionary of Renaissance Latin.

The assumption that the computer's crude list of individual meanings could be transformed into idiomatic English proved to be fallacious, and the original translation was extremely stilted and awkward despite the translator's sense of its correctness. Fortunately my distinguished colleague, Bernard F. Huppé, agreed to polish this rough draft in which he sensed an almost diabolical mechanical touch. My hope had been to render the original Latin turn of expression as precisely as possible, but Professor Huppé convinced me that there were simply too many pitfalls in such an approach. I feel confident, barring some real computer voodoo, that as I proceed with the remaining books and with the *Senili* I shall be able to produce a truly idiomatic translation even in the first draft.

The decision to start this translation series with the *Familiari* was based on the fact that it is the only Latin work completed by Petrarch for which we have a definitive edition.[1] The monumental edition by V. Rossi and U. Bosco was transcribed into the computer verbatim and with its pagination and paragraphing. Original plans called for a facing translation with the exact Latin text of the definitive version. Prohibitive costs made it imperative to exclude the Latin. However, the translation retains the original paragraphing so that despite its rather awkward appearance to an English reader, it does allow him to refer readily to the definitive edition by using the beginnings of paragraphs as flagging devices.

With very few exceptions, the entire translation is my own. I have made minimal use of the outdated and rather impressionistic Italian translation by Fracassetti and only for the purpose of double-checking particularly difficult passages.[2] The recent Italian translation of the first four books by Ugo Dotti came to my attention too late to be of any use.[3] I refrained from using the many Italian fragments contained in the anthology of Petrarch's prose works edited by G. Martellotti.[4] I diligently avoided the English translations by Robinson and Rolfe and by Morris Bishop which are limited to a select group of letters.[5]

In order to avoid burdensome notes, I have identified only the correspondents to whom the letters were addressed. For the identification of specific allusions, whether proper names, events, or other references contained in the text of letters, the reader is referred to the exceptionally detailed, though in some cases outdated, notations appended to Fracassetti's translations. Dotti's notes to the first four books are also helpful.

For identifications of citations from classical and other authors the notes to the Rossi edition are more than ample, as are its subject-matter and name indices. All verse citations are rendered in prose and are incorporated into the text.

Names of authors cited in the text are given in the form in which they appear (Maro, Naso, Publius, etc.). The same holds true of the dates appended to most of the letters. As I shall explain in detail in the Introduction, any attempt to arrive at an exact date overlooks the fact that large numbers of letters, especially in the opening books, are fictitious, and were inserted by Petrarch at the time he organized the collection. The most useful guide to the letters for the identification of dates, correspondents, and of places of writing is Ernest H. Wilkins, *Petrarch's Correspondence* (Padua, 1960).

In addition to Professor Huppé, without whose assistance and advice the present translation would not have been possible, other persons to whom I owe a debt of gratitude include the director of our computer center at State University of New York-Binghamton, Robert Roberson; his assistant for special projects, Alfred Lynn; the Research Foundation of State University of New York whose generous support made it all possible; my secretary, Mrs. Dorothy Huber; my daughter, Adele; and especially my wife whose patience throughout the endless days and nights of hearing the steady pounding of typewriter keys never faltered.

Binghamton, N.Y.
January 1973

1. *Le familiari*, vols. 1–3 ed. V. Rossi, and vol. 4 ed. Rossi and U. Bosco (Firenze, 1933–1942).
2. *Lettere di F. Petrarca*, trans. G. Fracassetti, vols. I–IV (Firenze, 1863–1866).
3. *Francesco Petrarca, Le Familiari, Libri I–IV* (Urbino, 1970). New edition, vol. I, *Libri* I–IV; vol. II, *Libri* VI–XI (Urbino, 1974).
4. *Francesco Petrarca, Prose*, ed. G. Martellotti *et al.* (Milan, 1955).
5. James Harvey Robinson and Henry Winchester Rolfe, *Petrarch, the First Modern Scholar and Man of Letters* (New York, 1914); *Letters from Petrarch*, trans. Morris Bishop (Bloomington and London, 1966).

Introduction

This translation, when completed, will for the first time make available to English readers Petrarch's earliest and perhaps most important collection of prose letters written for the most part between 1325 and 1366, and organized into a collection of 24 Books between 1345 and 1366. The collection represents a portrait of the artist as a young man seen through the eyes of the mature artist. Whether in the writing of poetry, or in being crowned poet laureate, or in confessing his faults, or in writing to Pope or Emperor, Petrarch was always the consummate artist, deeply concerned with creating a desired effect by means of a dignified gracefulness. As early as 1436 Leonardo Bruni wrote in his Life of Petrarch: "Petrarch was the first man to have had a sufficiently fine mind to recognize the gracefulness of the lost ancient style and to bring it back to life." Bruni was confirming a view widely held by humanists of his day that the true father of the new devotion to *humanitas* had been Petrarch. Though greatly influenced by Augustine, Boethius and Ambrose, he was recognized by subsequent generations as the first man of letters to have "approached literature and the *studia humanitatis* in the full knowledge of their significance and of the value which an education of the mind through conversation with the great masters of antiquity was bound to have for the whole of mankind." [1] It was indeed the very style or manner in which Petrarch consciously sought to create this impression that was responsible for the enormous impact he made on subsequent generations.

This first, carefully organized collection of his prose letters mirrors "the most remarkable man of his time; and . . . one of the most remarkable men of all time." As a principal actor in the cultural life of the fourteenth century, and as one of the greatest interpreters of the general political ideas of a very complex period, "he was and is remarkable for his awareness of the entire continent on which the drama of European life was being enacted . . . for his awareness of the reality of times past and times to come." But perhaps what makes him most remarkable is, again in the words of E. H. Wilkins, "the fact that we know far more about his experiences in life than we know about the experiences of any human being who had lived before his time." [2] Or in the words of Morris Bishop: "he gives his correspondents—and posterity, his more remote correspondent—the most complete picture in existence of the inner and outer life of a medieval man." [3] These are the letters of a man of action and of contemplation addressed to a circle of intimate friends who have been called the first *cenacle* of Italian and European intellectuals.

The first eight books of the *Familiari* encompass the most crucial years of Petrarch's life, years that extend from his life and enamorment in Provence, to his crowning in Rome, and finally to the relentless loss of his dearest acquaintances. As we have noted, Book VIII was a natural stopping point in the evolution of the collection, a point that was reached in 1356. From the letters of Book I, which were obviously contrived to project the image of a wise young man dispensing time-honored wisdom to personal friends, to the letters of Book VIII, where he tries unsuccessfully to form a community of scholars from those few who had survived the great plague of 1348, one senses the maturing artist and intellectual. In between we see his growing intimacy with the powerful Colonna family with a stirring assurance to one of its members of Laura's existence (II, 9); his dedication to Rome as *caput mundi* (VI, 2); his adherence to the principle that both the active and contemplative life are equally effective in achieving salvation (III, 12); his ravenous hunger for books (III, 18); his sensitivity to eloquence and music (I, 9; III, 22); his famous comparison of life to a mountain climbing expedition (IV, 1); his dramatic reception of the laurel crown in Rome (IV, 3–8); his consolations and bereavement at the frequent deaths of prominent friends and acquaintances (IV, 12; V, 1); his reaction to conditions in Naples (V, 6); his advice to a Pope on the unreliability of physicians (V, 19); his advice to ruling princes (III, 7, 16; VII, 15); his short-lived enthusiasm for Cola di Rienzo (VII, 5, 7); his view of a proper education of the young (VII, 17); and impressive character sketches (IV, 14; V, 8, 9).

But perhaps the most important letters in these first eight books are I, 1 and I, 9 which provide significant insights into Petrarch's concern for form and style. Many scholars have indeed considered I, 9 a most revealing document because of the evidence it affords of Petrarch's crucial role in the evolution of Humanism. Despite its focus on the importance of eloquence for the thinker and writer, it goes beyond the mere revival of rhetoric and philology to a new vision of nature, of man, and of history.[4] For Petrarch *studia humanitatis* meant the cultivation of the mind through the careful cultivation of speech, *sermo*, which is the ultimate measure of mind's worth. The essential value of human speech, however, lies in its power to disseminate knowledge to others. Internal dialogue is of little value; speech must be outer-directed, it must serve the good of others, of one's neighbors. Even if it employs techniques borrowed from the pagans, it must contribute to the spread of Christian *caritas*.[5]

Human speech is the basic instrument for the process that can be called "authentically humanistic." It is capable of traversing and fusing the most distant epochs and spaces with truths that are eternal. As *Fam*. I, 9 states: "Let thousands of years flow by, and let centuries follow upon centuries, virtue will never be sufficiently praised, and never will teachings for the greater love of God and the hatred of sin suffice; never will the road to the investigation of new ideas be blocked to keen minds. Let us therefore be of good heart; let us not labor uselessly, and those who will be born after many ages and before the end of an aging world will not labor in vain. What is rather to be feared is that men may cease to exist before our pursuit of humanistic studies breaks through the intimate mysteries of truth."

Such then is the mission that Petrarch envisions for human

discourse. In the name of charity its voice echoes antiquity and sounds the future. It teaches the *studia humanitatis* which are intended to nurture the mind through the constant assimilation of the loftiest products of the human spirit from ancient and modern times. The Christian world has perfected the instruments with which to recapture and enrich classical values. The purpose of such studies is truth and not vainglory. If glory does accrue, it must rest with future generations and must serve as incitement for the good.[6]

Fam. I, 1, the dedicatory letter, was in all probability also written in 1350, the same year as I, 9, with the specific purpose of serving as introduction to the collection.[7] It describes the extreme pains taken by Petrarch in trying to give the collection an air of unity by including letters of an appropriate tone and character in order to avoid the deformity of a strict chronological ordering. It touches upon such other details as his search for the best title to give the collection and his careful avoidance of excessively personal matters. Petrarch's concept of stylistic unity reflects a strong, manly style in the opening and closing of the collection, leaving the weakest part for the middle portion. Ultimately the collection was to appear "woven with multi-colored threads."

If we were to combine the spirit of *Fam.* I, 1 and I, 9 with the content of II, 9 in which Laura, St. Augustine and St. Jerome are discussed with equal seriousness; of IV, 1 which describes the famous ascent of Mt. Ventoux; and of IV, 4–8 which describes the poet's critical decision on whether to be crowned poet-Laureate in Paris or Rome, we would see reflected in these first eight books the principal foci of the new humanistic vision.

Turning now to the collection as a whole, the *Rerum familiarium libri XXIV* is one of the three collections of Petrarch's Latin prose letters prepared by Petrarch himself. It contains twenty-four books of letters written to various people presumably between the years 1325 and 1366. The number of letters in the several books varies from eight in Book XIV to twenty-two in Book III. The collection as a whole contains 350 letters.

The great majority of the letters are addressed to definite

persons ranging from obscure priests and monks to the Emperor Charles IV and even to a number of famous writers of antiquity. In many of the letters the name of the correspondent is not indicated. With the exception of the last book, of which ten of the thirteen letters are addressed to illustrious ancients, all the designated correspondents are contemporaries. This last book also contains two letters in verse.

Among the correspondents having ten or more letters addressed to them are Giovanni Boccaccio; Philippe de Cabassoles, Bishop of Cavaillon, a small town in Provence; the Emperor Charles IV; Cardinal Giovanni Colonna; Francesco Nelli, a Florentine prior to whom Petrarch dedicated his second extensive collection of prose letters, the *Senili;* Guido Settimo, whose friendship with Petrarch extended back to their childhood days; and the Flemish Ludwig van Kempen, a learned musician and member of the Colonna circle for whom Petrarch had great respect and admiration, and to whom he dedicated the *Familiari*.

Each letter is introduced by a rubric announcing the subject matter and the addressee if any. The addresses use the form *Ad* with the accusative.

A good number of the letters of the first twenty-three books end with some indication of the date and, less often, place of composition. In these books the date is always indicated in the Latin form and never includes the year. However, eight of the thirteen letters of the last book, most of which are addressed to ancient authors, terminate with a *subscriptio* indicating the place of writing and the complete date, including the year.

As already mentioned, the first letter of the first book is a dedicatory letter to Petrarch's close friend, Ludwig van Kempen, whom, out of respect for his learning and wisdom, he always calls Socrates. The last letter of the last book is also addressed to him.

The individual missives vary in length. In the *Edizione Nazionale* (in octavo) the letters run from less than a page to a maximum of thirteen pages. The form of the letters is generally a running Latin prose except for the two verse letters of the last book, one addressed to Horace and the other to

Vergil. Throughout there are many quotations in prose or verse taken from classical or church writers.

The contents of the collection are extremely heterogeneous. To cite but two extreme examples, Letter IX, 4 deals with a "Revocatio amici a periculosis amoribus," while X, 1 is an exhortation to the Emperor Charles IV to descend into Italy. As Petrarch himself states in the dedicatory letter: "you will find many things in these letters written in a friendly style to a number of friends including yourself. At times they will deal with public and private affairs, at times they will touch upon our griefs . . . or still other matters that happened to come along. In fact I did almost nothing more than speak about my state of mind or any other matter of interest which I thought my friends would like to know."

In his study *Petrarca letterato* (Rome, 1947), Giuseppe Billanovich traces the history of the collection. Since this is considered the latest authoritative view on the matter, I am summarizing it here. The idea of forming a collection of his letters came to Petrarch in Verona in May of 1345 as he feverishly copied Cicero's epistolaries *Ad Atticum* and *Ad Quintum Fratrem,* and the apocryphal letter to Octavian, which he had then discovered. As he then envisioned it, his collection was to comprise letters in both prose and verse. It was not long, however, before he showed a decided preference for the prose form since it meant competing with Cicero, Seneca and the Church Fathers who appealed to him more than did Horace and Ovid. Quite naturally, the series of letters to the ancients, which were to constitute the bulk of Book XXIV, was among his first projects. In fact, he started immediately with a letter to Cicero written at Verona in those very days.

Once the idea of a personal epistolary had taken a firm hold in his mind, it became necessary to return to Provence, where the bulk of his library was located as well as copies of his letters. Having returned there in the summer of 1345, he wrote a second letter to Cicero and began going through the massive correspondence he had on file. The initial stages of the project were slow, what with the necessary listing, selecting, gathering all possible exemplars of classical collections, deliberating on the fundamental canons of epistolary technique (from form of address to date), fixing the number of books and the average size of each and arriving at a possible title. The collection, following the example of the *Aeneid* and the *Thebaid*, was originally to be in twelve books. The first book was to contain twelve letters. The last book was to be reserved for the letters to the ancients and introduced by the two letters to Cicero. The work was to be dedicated to his close friend Socrates. But the constant interruptions caused by other works which he was then in the process of writing (*Bucolicum Carmen, De vita solitari, De otio religioso*), as well as a trip to Italy, slowed the work considerably.

While at Parma in the summer of 1348, Petrarch composed another letter to another great ancient—Seneca. This was inevitable since, next to Cicero, the author of the *Letters to Lucilius* represents an influential model.

It was during Petrarch's first residence in Padua between 1349 and 1351 that the collection really began taking shape. A letter to Varro was added to those to Cicero and Seneca. The dedication and the first letter of the *Epystolarum ad diversos liber*, as the work was first called, were also written during this period and were sent to Socrates in Provence with the date January, 1350. A few weeks before Petrarch's departure from Padua at least six of the ten letters to the ancients (XXIV, 3–6, 8, 10) had been finished, and Boccaccio, who had been sent to Petrarch by Florence to recall its long lost favorite son, was permitted to copy them. Upon leaving Padua, Petrarch took the manuscript with him, and on the first stop at Vicenza en route through Venetia and Lombardy to Provence he read the two letters to Cicero to his traveling companions who discussed them at length as dusk settled. A few days later, he sent *ex itinere* copies of the two letters—introduced by what was to become XXIV, 2—to the poet Enrico Pulice da Costozza.

On his return to Provence in the summer of 1351, Petrarch was able to show to his beloved Socrates only a very incomplete piece of work—the two letters that Socrates had already received, a few other opening ones, plus those to the ancients that Boccaccio had copied. But between the summer of 1351 and August of 1353, he did a great deal of work on the collection. By the spring of 1353, he was able to send a friend (presumably Socrates) as a gift the transcription of the first three books and a fragment of the fourth with the letters arranged in an order that was to be kept intact in subsequent transcriptions and in a form which was to undergo but few substantial changes.

From the summer of 1353, when we find Petrarch taking residence in Lombardy, the progress of the collection continued unabated for many years. In May of 1353, he promised the Venetian Chancellor, Benintendi Ravignani, a copy of the collection and even permitted him to transcribe some of the letters to the ancients, but we find Ravignani still asking for his prize on January 27, 1356. It was not until late that year that the promise was kept and the Chancellor received a copy extending to Book VIII, 9.

Even before this, however, Petrarch had decided that he could not limit himself to a collection of twelve books, and he resolved to increase the number of books to twenty—after the model of Seneca's twenty books of letters to Lucilius and Cicero's total of twenty to Atticus, to his brother Quintus and to Marcus Brutus (a fact discovered by Petrarch at Verona). By September of 1356, he decided that it would be best to compile a separate collection of the letters of his later years: this was to be the *Rerum senilium libri*.

This expansion to twenty books would admit correspondence from the years of the composition of the *Secretum* (1341–42). Petrarch had been enlarging and polishing these letters all the while and then placed them into the second part of Book V and the beginning of Book VI without regard to chronological ordering.

After the embassy to Charles IV in 1356, Petrarch was able to develop the collection much more rapidly, for he was entering those letters which were written after the year 1349 with an eye to inclusion in the collection. In fact, some of the most notable and best constructed letters of the work, found in Book X and Book XI, were composed between 1349 and 1351. Between the early autumn of 1356 and the beginning of 1357 the transcription of letters into the manuscript had gone from Book VIII to at least Book X.

In 1358, Petrarch secured the services of a competent scribe and the collection proceeded rapidly and smoothly. At about the same time, together with Boccaccio and others, he had been introduced to the works of Homer through the translation of Leonzio Pilato. So by 1359 he had decided to increase once again the number of books of the collection, this time to twenty-four, following the example of Homer. During the few following years, Petrarch continued selecting suitable items from his correspondence. Finally, with the completion of the letters to the ancients, another scribe, Gasparo Scuaro dei Broaspini, was charged with the transcription of Books XX–XXIII shortly after March 1363. But this was intended only as a draft to evaluate literary and structural merits. It was not until the years between 1363 and 1366 that Petrarch's favorite scribe, Giovanni Malpaghini, was able to transcribe the definitive form of the last five books.

A vexing problem regarding the nature of the collection is that of identifying the fictitious letters that doubtless are scattered throughout. Vittorio Rossi, the editor of the definitive edition, was among the first to detect the presence of such letters. He believed that Petrarch had to amplify and revise his personal moral, political, and literary views in the letters. Furthermore, artistic exigencies required "fill-ins" if, as is stated in the dedicatory letter, the collection as a whole was to reflect a distinctive tone. Using evidence that emerged as he prepared the definitive version of the *Familiari*, Rossi identifies five letters as fictitious. These are: IV, 1; VII, 11; and XII, 14–16.

It was, however, Giuseppe Billanovich in *Petrarca Letterato*, pages 3–55, who first indicated the extensiveness of the fictitious letters. In his opinion, all those in the first book, with the exception of I, 1, were invented by Petrarch between 1340 and 1351. After indicating how, as a mature artist, Petrarch destroyed many works written in his youth because they no longer satisfied his higher standards, Billanovich maintains that among these must have been his early letters which, as a novice, he had written following closely the rules set by the *dictamina* and with the cadences of the *cursus*. Billanovich marshals persuasive evidence to support his view that Petrarch invented his early letters in the course of a few months.

Turning first to the dates that Petrarch appended to the letters Billanovich indicates how the twelve letters of Book I may be divided into two parts, with the months represented in each part perhaps inadvertently repeating a yearly cycle. Thus the month sequence of the first six letters is January, April, May, June, August; while that for the last six is March, April, May and December.

Billanovich next points out that throughout the Book may be found borrowings from classical writers with whom Petrarch is known not to have come in contact until the period 1350–51, especially Plautus, Quintilian and Horace. We thus find Letters 7, 8 and 9 representing a scholastic trilogy apparently derived from Quintilian's *Institutiones Oratoriae*. All three letters are addressed to Tommaso da Messina and form, as it were, a short tractate introduced by a polemic preface: "contra senes dyaleticos, de inventione et ingenio, de studio eloquentie." Since it is known that Petrarch received a copy of Quintilian's work as a gift in 1350, Billanovich imagines that Petrarch must have written this group of letters shortly after his return from his Jubilee pilgrimage to Rome. Other details singled out by Billanovich on this point are: (1) that Petrarch must have read right through the *Institutiones* and somewhat hurriedly since the citations derived therefrom are taken from a variety of books of the classic work and from well-advanced ones; (2) that in his copy of the *Institutiones* Petrarch made frequent favorable notations in the margins of that portion of the work dealing with Quintilian's invectives against dialecticians; and (3) that no borrowing from Quintilian can be found in the first six letters of Book I nor in the initial five letters to classical authors which represent the beginning of the collection.

Fam. I, 10, which follows upon these three letters, is nothing more than an elaboration of a long citation taken from the *Aulularia*. It, too, introduces an obvious trilogy (I, 10–12) addressed to Tommaso di Messina, except that this time the citations and the styles are derived from Plautus and Horace.

The subjects of these three letters are: *descriptio avari senis, descriptio famelici parasiti,* and . . . *ex reliquiis concertationes sopra posite cum dyaletico sene garrulo.*

Of the twelve letters of this first book, seven are addressed to Tommaso da Messina. Having identified the anachronistic nature of the last six, Billanovich tries to do the same with I, 2. He shows that Petrarch had carefully selected the argument in order to win praise of maturity in an age of immaturity, and that every paragraph contains evidence of its having been written later than Petrarch would like us to believe (the too harmonious eulogy of King Robert; the *quadrato canone* of Church fathers—Augustine, Jerome, Gregory and Ambrose; constant citations from works read or encountered later than the residence at Bologna, which the *subscriptio* presents as the presumable place of origin). Billanovich, therefore, concludes that these seven letters to Tommaso as well as the two others addressed to him in the collection (III, 1, 2) are nothing more than "gentili offerte di fama a quel rimpianto compagno di studi e della prima clientela presso i Colonna," and "si rivelano manifeste esercitazioni su lati e spesso usuali temi retorici." The single letter to Raimondo Subirani might also be similarly classified, according to Billanovich.

Proceeding with his argument, Billanovich then presents his conviction that it is precisely because the letters of Book I are fictitious missives (except, of course, for the very first one) that they are addressed exclusively to friends who had died before 1350. This plus the fact that subsequent descriptions of trips were to be addressed to Cardinal Colonna, prompted Petrarch to address the fictitious letters I, 4 and 5 to the Cardinal. Billanovich presents the following points in support of his thesis:

1. It could not have been mere chance that no Gamma (original or closest to the original) form has been found for any of the eleven letters in question (I, 2-12), especially since there is one for the very first letter of Book II. (He admits, however, the possibility that *Fam.* I, 6 to Bishop Giacomo Colonna is a re-working of a real missive since an echo of it is to be found in the late *Sen.* II, 5.)

2. Other letters beyond Book I, which are rhetorical exercises similar to those in Book I, seem more genuine because of the "accenni pratici e precisi che le costellano, particolarmente nell'aperture e nel commiato." In the second part of Book II the *consolatoria* and *hortatoria* after the manner of Seneca and Cicero show "vivace varietà," and in Books III and IV may be found "una serie quasi integra di reale corrispondenza."

3. A comparison with the opening portions of Petrarch's other collection of prose letters, the *Rerum senilium*, will show that the two were compiled by different methods: the latter systematically files real epistles. In the *Familiari*, "le convenzionalità di scuola minacciavano di sormontare," but in the *Senili*, "i casi e i doveri quotidiani stringono troppo."

Billanovich also disputes the authenticity of *Fam.* IV, 1 and 3 by exploring the relations between Petrarch and Boccaccio. He establishes the fact that the Augustinian Father Dionigi da Borgo San Sepolcro had started Boccaccio on the road to becoming "il più grande discepolo" of Petrarch. In Naples in 1338–39 he permitted Boccaccio to copy a verse letter (*Metr.* I, 4) and a prose letter (*Fam.* IV, 2) that had been sent to Dionigi by Petrarch. Billanovich asks why Dionigi did not also show Boccaccio the famous *Fam.* IV, 1 which had presumably also been addressed to him and which Boccaccio would certainly not have failed to include in his collection of Petrarch's writings. In like manner, he wonders why *Fam.* IV, 3 to King Robert never reached Boccaccio, who would certainly have received a copy of it from court friends of Petrarch. Indeed why did not Petrarch himself offer Boccaccio a copy of *Fam.* IV, 1 when the two met in 1351, since the letter was addressed to their closest common friend? Never does Boccaccio allude to the two letters, not even in those works in which one would certainly expect such allusions, the *De vita et moribus domini Francisci Petracchi* and Letters X, 3 and 4 in which affectionate mention is made of Petrarch's *fratello monaco* Gherardo, who figures so heavily in *Fam.* IV, 1. There is little doubt that Boccaccio also would have considered the letter the epistolary masterpiece of his master. It is natural, therefore, for Billanovich to conclude that these two letters are also fictitious and were composed in 1352 or early 1353 when Petrarch was ordering the first part of Book IV:

> . . . accorgiamoci finalmente che anche queste due lettere sono fittizie: secondo un costume abituale nella parte piu antica dei *Rerum familiarium,* formate dopo la morte del re e di quel confidente spirituale; non scritto nel '36 e nel '40; neppure pronte nel '51: composte nel '52 o all'inizio del '53, quando il Petrarca, verso la conclusione dell'ultima dimora in Provenza, ordinava la prima parte del quarto libro dei *Rerum familiarium* (p. 194).

He then shows how *Fam.* IV, 1 in particular points to late composition. Like Rossi, Billanovich doubts that the letter could have been written before Gherardo's unexpected conversion and entrance into a monastery in 1343. In the allegorical interpretation of the letter it is the devout Gherardo who has little trouble reaching the summit of the mountain, whereas Petrarch encounters innumerable difficulties. It is Billanovich's opinion that the idea for the letter came to Petrarch "da due entusiasmi di lettore appassionato" (p. 195): first from the image of King Philip standing atop Mt. Emo to gaze upon the two seas in Livy's *Ab urbe condita;* and then from contemplation of the vanity of man who probes into the mysteries of nature and the universe without scrutinizing his own soul, an idea derived from Saint Augustine's *Confessions.*

As for the date of the letter, it was prompted by an "obbedienza a ingegnose convenzioni." In the letter, Petrarch relates that in his thirty-second year Saint Augustine was converted by a sentence from Saint Paul's letters which he had read by chance in the shade of a "fico salutare." (Petrarch also alludes to a similar incident in the life of Saint Anthony.) The ostensible date of the letter, which is 1336, and the reference to the *Confessions* create the analogy between the humanist and the Church father. The first part of the date, which gives the month and the day, was simply a happy expedient that enabled Petrarch to establish in well-rounded figures another milestone in his life: for that day marked exactly the tenth anniversary of his departure from the University of Bologna.

Billanovich brings further evidence of the fictitious nature of IV, 1. A glance at the biography of Dionigi shows that in 1336 he was in Avignon. Therefore Petrarch did not need to communicate with him by letter. And, if he did, there was no reason for trying to make it appear as though Dionigi were in Italy at the time Petrarch wrote: "inextimabilis me ardor invasit et amicum et patriam revidendi."

Billanovich collated posterior texts of the beginning portions of the collection with those presented to the friend from Avignon (presumably Socrates) to transcribe between 1352 and 1353. Such a collection, involving the first three books and the first three letters of Book IV, shows the majority of variants occurring in these three letters. The most natural explanation for this, in the opinion of Billanovich (pp. 194–197), is that these were the letters that had been either written at the time of transcription (IV, 1 and 3) or extensively retouched (IV, 2).

After devising the structure of Book III, Petrarch had to extract from his papers the letter that he had sent to Dionigi shortly after the latter's transfer to Naples (*Fam.* IV, 2). Nostalgic recollection of and sincere respect for the Augustinian father, who had nourished his spiritual life and introduced him to King Robert's circle, prompted Petrarch to build around this missive a small nucleus of letters which would represent for the reader of the *Familiari* the battles and anguishes of his soul, followed closely (as though to preserve the pattern of eternal oscillation found in his *Secretum*) by a dramatic account of his coronation. *Fam.* IV, 2 falls between the description of the ascent of Mount Ventoux and a supposed answer to an imaginary letter whereby King Robert of Naples was presumably to have offered Petrarch the laurel crown.

Billanovich believes that careful examination of *Fam.* IV, 2 reveals how it too underwent definite, though minor, modifications in order to fit within the new framework. The very last sentences are anachronistic if written in 1339. Since the ideas of these closing sentences are echoed in the subsequent letter to King Robert (IV, 3), it then follows that this one must have been fictitious as well. There are also indications that IV, 2 was modified to fit in with IV, 1: a Vergilian quotation that had been part of IV, 2 in its original form was transferred to IV, 1 and a paraphrase substituted.

Billanovich also casts a doubting glance at letter III, 1. We have already seen him labeling all the letters of the first book addressed to Tommaso da Messina "manifeste esercitazioni su lati e spesso usuali temi retorici." He now includes in this same category the "lontana peregrina dissertazione 'de Thule insula famosissima sed incerta', ostentamente offerta in testa al terzo libro con accademica esultanza per l'erudizione costipatavi." He bases his argument on a misspelling in the definitive as well as earlier versions of the letter which he maintains resulted from Petrarch's consulting a manuscript of Pliny's *Naturalis historia* in the Papal Library at Avignon in 1352 when he presumably began work on Book III of the *Familiari*.

In my unpublished Harvard dissertation I also adduce evidence to cast doubt on the authenticity of III, 8, 19; IV, 17–19; V, 9, 13, 15; and IX, 3.[8] In a chapter later published in *Speculum* XXXIII (1958), I show how Petrarch's practice of splitting excessively long letters into two or more separate epistles (for example, *Fam.* VIII, 7–9) belies the authenticity of some letters in the *Familiari*.

It is, therefore, essential that the reader of this translation bear in mind that a good portion of the collection, especially in the first eight books presented here, is composed of fictitious letters that were added to the collection to produce a desired effect—that of a learned man desirous of providing his friends and contemporaries with wise lessons derived from the best minds of all times and passed on by a devotee of letters who wished to revive in his correspondence the spirit of Cicero, Seneca and Augustine.

1. Eugenio Garin, *Italian Humanism*, trans. Peter Munz (New York, 1965), pp. 18, 19. Page 18 gives a full bibliography in support of the contention.

2. All 3 quotes from Ernest H. Wilkins, *Life of Petrarch* (Chicago, 1961), p. v.

3. *Letters from Petrarch* (Indiana, 1966), p. v.

4. Hans Baron, *La crisi del primo rinascimento italiano* (Firenze, 1970), p. xvi.

5. See *Fam.* II, 9 in which Petrarch explains that the reason he had

abandoned Jerome in favor of Augustine was because of Jerome's reluctance to turn to the pagans, and especially to Cicero.

6. E. Garin, *Italian Humanism*, pp. 19–20; U. Dotti, *Le Familiari*, pp. 5–14.

7. E. H. Wilkins, *Petrarch's Correspondence* (Padua, 1960), pp. 49–50.

8. A. S. Bernardo, *Artistic Procedures Followed by Petrarch in Making the Collection of the "Familiares"* (Cambridge, Mass., 1949).

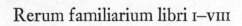

Rerum familiarium libri I–VIII

Fam. I, 1.

To his Socrates.[1]

What are we to do now, dear brother? Alas, we have already tried almost everything and no rest is in sight. When can we expect it? Where shall we seek it? Time, as they say, has slipped through our fingers; our former hopes are buried with our friends. The year of 1348 left us alone and helpless; it did not deprive us of things that can be restored by the Indian or Caspian or Carpathian Sea. It subjected us to irreparable losses. Whatever death wrought is now an incurable wound. There is only one consolation in all this: we too shall follow those who preceded us. How long our wait will be I do not know; but this I do know, that it cannot be long. And however short the wait may be, it cannot avoid being burdensome.

But we must desist from complaining, at least for now. I do not know what your preoccupations or what your thinking may be. For me, I am arranging my belongings in little bundles, as wanderers are wont to do. I am considering what to bring with me, what to share with friends, and what to burn. I have nothing to be put up for sale. Indeed I am richer, or perhaps I should say more hampered than I thought, because of the great number of writings of different kinds that lie scattered and neglected throughout my house. I search in squalid containers lying in hidden places and pulled out dusty writings half destroyed by decay. I was attacked by a bothersome mouse and by a multitude of highly voracious worms; and the spider, enemy of Pallas, attacked me for doing the work of Pallas. But there is nothing that unyielding and constant labor cannot overcome. Therefore, beset and encircled by confused heaps of letters and formless piles of paper, I began a first attack by determining to throw everything into the fire, thereby avoiding a thankless kind of labor. Later, as thought followed upon thought, I found myself saying, "What stops you from looking behind

1. The Flemish Ludwig van Kempen, chanter in the chapel of Cardinal Giovanni Colonna, whom Petrarch first met in France in 1330.

like a tired traveler from a vantage point after a long journey and slowly recalling the memories and cares of your youth?" This thought finally dominated, and while the work involved did not appeal as a grand undertaking, neither did trying to recall the thoughts and memories of times past seem too unpleasant. But when I began turning over the papers piled at random in no particular order, I was astonished to notice how varied and how disordered their general aspect appeared. I could hardly recognize certain ones, not so much because of their form but because of the changed nature of my own understanding. Other things, however, did come back to mind with considerable delight. Part of the writing was free of literary niceties, part showed the influence of Homeric control since I rarely made use of the rules of Isocrates; but another part intended for charming the ears of the multitude relied on its own particular rules. This last kind of writing, which is said to have been revived among the Sicilians not many centuries ago, had soon spread throughout Italy and beyond, and was once even popular among the most ancient of the Greeks and the Latins, if it is indeed true that the Attic and Roman people used to employ only the rhythmic type of poetry. Thus, this sizeable and varying collection of writings kept me busy for several days and made me concentrate with delight and attachment on my own creations, and especially on those major works that had been interrupted for a considerable time despite the expectation and anticipation they had created in many. But the recollection of the brevity of life overcame me. I feared indeed an ambush, for what is more fleeting, I ask, than life, and what more determined than death? I reflected on the foundation that I had established, on what remained of my labors and on my few lingering years. It seemed rashness, indeed madness, to have undertaken so many long and demanding works in such a brief and indefinite period of time, and to have directed my talents which would hardly suffice for limited undertakings to so great a variety of writings, especially since, as you know, another project awaits me which is the more striking because actions are more praiseworthy than words. What more need I say? You will now hear a thing perhaps incredible but true. I committed to Vulcan's hands for his correction at least a thousand and more of all kinds and variety of poems and friendly letters, not because nothing in them pleased me but because to sort them would have required more work than pleasure. I am not ashamed to admit that I did this with a certain tenderness and with many sighs; just as an overweighted boat in deep waters can be lifted above the billows by discharging overboard even its most precious cargo so it was necessary to render assistance, no matter how drastic, to my preoccupied mind. In any event, while these were burning I noticed lying in a corner, a few others which had been saved, not consciously but by mere chance, or perhaps indeed because they had been transcribed earlier by scribes. All of these had somehow resisted the ravages of time. I say they were a few, but I fear that they may appear too many to the reader and too long to the scribe. To these I was more indulgent than the others and permitted them to live not because of their merit but as a consolation to my labor. Actually they seemed not to require much revision. So, weighing carefully the nature of my two dearest friends, it appeared best to divide the writings in such a way that the prose works would be dedicated to you and the poetic ones to our Barbato.[2] This I remembered that you had both once wished for and I had promised. Thus while all these things were being destroyed as I came across them, and—in the mood I was in—being disinclined to spare even these, the two of you appeared to me, one on the left, the other on the right, and grasping my hand, affectionately urged me not to destroy my promise and your expectation in a single fire as I had determined to do. This above all is what saved all those writings; otherwise, believe me, they would have burned with the rest.

Therefore these that are coming to you from among the manly portions of the remains, of whatever sort they may be, I am certain you will be reading with understanding and even with eagerness. I dare not refer to what Apuleius of

2. Barbato da Sulmona, member of the court of King Robert of Naples, whom Petrarch first met in 1341, and to whom he was to dedicate his collection of *Epistolae metricae*.

Madaura once said: "Oh reader, pay attention, you will enjoy yourself"; for where can I find so much confidence that I could promise my reader both amusement and pleasure? But nonetheless read these things, my dear Socrates, and since you are very kind to your friends, perhaps you will enjoy them, for if you approve of the writer's mind you will enjoy his style. What does an attractive figure avail if it is to be subject to the judgment of a lover? It is useless for a woman to beautify herself if she is already pleasing. If any of these pieces are appealing to you I must say that they are so not because of me but because of you. They are all testimonials of your friendship rather than samples of my talent. Indeed nothing among them required great power of speech; this I do not possess and if I did, to speak honestly, I would not use it with this style. Cicero himself did not use such a style in his letters although he was most distinguished in it, nor in those books that required an "equable" style, as he called it, and "a temperate type of speech." And so in his orations we find him using that unique kind of power and a lucid, rapid, and almost torrential kind of eloquence. Such style did Cicero use an infinite number of times on behalf of his friends, often against his enemies and those of the Republic; as did Cato often in behalf of others and forty-four times for himself. I myself am untried in this style, for to begin with I am free from all cares of state, and furthermore my fame, though perhaps provoked at times by the blandishments and threats of critics (with their soft murmurings or hidden hissings), has thus far not had to avail itself of vengeance or evasion, and thus avoided the wounds inflicted by legal actions. Nor indeed has it been our profession to use the power of the word to the detriment of others. Nor, endowed as I am with a deeply resisting and reluctant nature that made me a lover of silence and of solitude, and being an enemy of the forum, and a disdainer of wealth, have I striven for courtroom, judicial or political power or to lease my tongue. It was fortunate indeed that I did not feel the need for such things since perhaps my nature would have deprived me of them had I felt such need. Therefore, you will enjoy, as you have my other writings, this plain, domestic and friendly style, forgetting that rhetorical power of speech which I neither lack nor abound in and which if I did abound in I would not know where to exercise. And as a faithful follower you will find words that we use in ordinary speech proper and suitable for expressing my ideas. But surely all my judges will not be like you. Nor will they all feel or love in the same manner. But in what manner can I please everyone when I have always striven to please a few? Indeed there are three poisonous obstacles to genuine judgment: love, hate and envy. Be careful lest by loving me excessively you may be publicizing something that would best be hidden, for just as love would impede your judgment thus might something else impede the judgment of others. Between the blindness produced by love and that produced by envy there may be a great difference in point of cause, but there is no difference in effect. As for hatred which I had listed as second, I neither deserve it nor indeed fear it. It may happen that you could receive these trifles, read them and then call to mind nothing more than past events in our lives and those of our friends. This would make me very happy since your request will not seem neglected and my fame will be safe. I will not fool myself into thinking any differently. How can we believe that a friend, unless he is another me, could read all these things without aversion or boredom since so many of them conflict and are contradictory because of their uneven style and uncertain goal? Indeed, according to the variety of subject matter, I was often inspired to seek effects that rarely led to a joyful tone and often to a sad one.

Epicurus, a philosopher unpopular with the multitude but considered great by wise men, wrote letters to three of his friends: Idomeneus, Polienus and Metrodorus. Cicero did likewise with Brutus, Atticus and other Ciceros, namely, his brother and his son. Seneca wrote very few except to Lucilius. To know the mind and heart of one's interlocutor is not a difficult art and assures greatest success. To be accustomed to the personality of only one person, to know what he likes to hear, and what you should say, is a good quality in a writer. My fate unfortunately has been completely different. I have spent all my life, to this moment, in almost constant travel. Compare my wanderings to those of Ulysses. If the reputation of our name and of our achievements were the same, he indeed traveled neither more nor farther than I. He went beyond the borders of his fatherland when already old. Though it may be true that nothing at any age is long-lasting, all things are very brief in old age. I, begotten in exile, was born in exile, with so much labor undergone by my mother, and with so much danger, that she was considered dead for a long time not only by the mid-wives but by the doctors. Thus I experienced danger even before being born and I approached the very threshold of life under the auspices of death. Arezzo, not an ignoble city of Italy, recalls all this. It was there that my father, expelled from his native city, fled with a large number of good men. From there, in my seventh month I was taken and carried throughout Tuscany on the arm of a strong young man. Since I enjoy recalling for you these first labors and dangers of mine I might add that he carried me hanging at the end of a rod after having wrapped me in a linen cloth so as not to hurt my tender body just as Metabus had done with Camilla. While crossing the Arno, having fallen as a result of his horse slipping, while trying to save the bundle that had been entrusted to him, he almost perished in the violent current. Our Tuscan wanderings ended in Pisa whence I was once again snatched, this time at the age of seven, and transported by sea into France. We were almost shipwrecked by winter winds not far from Marseilles and once again I was not very far from being denied a new life on its very threshold. But where am I being led, forgetful of my purpose? Since that time to the present I have had either no opportunity or a very rare one to abide anywhere or to catch my breath. As for how many kinds of dangers and fears I have encountered on my trips no one knows better than you except myself. I have enjoyed recalling some of this for you so that you might remember that I was born in danger and have grown old under the same conditions, provided I have now grown old and that even more painful things are not reserved for me in my old age. Such misfortunes, although common to all who enter upon life (for man's life on earth is not only like military service but like actual warfare), vary with each individual as do the battles; and while particular burdens may weigh upon each person, the fact is that the actual burdens differ considerably from one man to another. Therefore in these storms of life, to return to the point, not throwing my anchor for any length of time in any port, and making a number of ordinary friends but unsure of how many true ones (being uncertain of their status and not really having very many), I struck an acquaintance with countless famous ones. I thus had to correspond a great deal with many of them who differed considerably in character and station. As a result, the letters were so different that in rereading them I seemed to be in constant contradiction. Whoever has had a similar experience must confess that to be contradictory was my only expedient. Indeed, the primary concern of a writer is to consider the identity of the person to whom he is writing. Only in this way can he know what and how to write, as well as other pertinent circumstances. The strong man must be addressed in one way, the spiritless one in another, the young and inexperienced one in still another, the old man who has discharged his life's duties in another, and in still another manner the person puffed up with good fortune, the victim of adversity in another, and finally in yet another manner must be addressed the man of letters renowned for his talents, and the ignoramus who would not understand anything you said if you spoke in even a slightly polished fashion. Infinite are the differences between men nor are their minds any more alike than the shapes of their foreheads. And as one particular sort of food not only does not appeal to different stomachs but does not even appeal always to a single one, so it is impossible to nourish a single mind at all times with the same style. Thus, writing entails a double labor: first to consider to whom you have undertaken to write, and then what his state of mind will be at the time he undertakes to read what you propose to write. These difficulties compelled me to be very inconsistent, but I have in part escaped the censure of hostile critics by availing myself of the benefits of fire, and in part by turning to you in the hope that you would accept these letters in secret and without revealing the name of the writer. If you cannot hide them from the few friends that remain (since friendship has the eye of a lynx and nothing can be kept from the sight of friends), urge those who may still have copies of these letters to destroy them forthwith, lest they become upset at the changes I have made in the content or in the style. For I never suspected that you would request, or that I would consent, to gather these things into a single collection; and so, avoiding hard work, what I had said in one letter I would often repeat in another to avail myself of what was mine, to quote Terence. When recently they all were collected together at one time and in one place, after having been written over many years and sent to various regions of the world, the deformity of the collection could be easily discerned though it was hidden in individual letters. Thus a word that had been happily used once in a particular letter being repeated too often throughout the collection began being troublesome. Therefore, I had to see to it that while it was retained in one letter it was eliminated from the rest. Similarly many things having to do with personal matters while perhaps considered a worthy insertion when first written now appear unwarranted, notwithstanding the anxious reader's interest. Seneca chided Cicero for this very thing although I must confess that I shall for the most part follow the example of Cicero more than that of Seneca in these letters. As you know, Seneca collected in his letters all the morality that he had intersperced in almost all his books; Cicero restricted his philosophical concerns to his books and included in his letters accounts of the highly personal, unusual and varied goings-on of his time. What Seneca might feel about Cicero's letters is a personal matter. As for me, I must confess, I find them delightful reading; for such reading is a change from having to deal with difficult matters, and is a source of delight if done intermittently but a source of unpleasantness if done continuously.

Therefore you will find many things in these letters written in a friendly style to a number of friends including yourself. At times they will deal with public and private affairs, at times they will touch upon our griefs which supply plenty of subject matter, or still other matters that happened to come along. In fact I did almost nothing more than to speak about my state of mind or any other matter of interest which I thought my friends would like to know. In this I agreed with what Cicero says in his first letter to his brother, that the true characteristic of an epistle is to make the recipient more informed about those things that he does not know. This I might add was also the source of my title. After some thought on the matter, I initially concluded that the name "Epistles" would be suitable to them. But because many ancients had used that title, and because I myself had done so (for various metrical pieces that I had directed to my friends, as I said previously), I did not want to use the same title twice, and liking the idea of a new one, I decided to call the collection *Familiarium rerum liber*. In it you will find very few letters that can be called masterpieces, and many others written on a variety of personal matters in a rather simple and unstudied manner, though sometimes, when the subject matter so requires, seasoned with interspersed moral considerations, an approach observed by Cicero himself. I must confess that writing so much about so little was prompted by my fear of caustic critics who, while writing nothing noteworthy themselves, make themselves judges of the talents of others. One can avoid such impudent rashness only through silence. It is indeed an easy matter to applaud from the shore in trying to determine the skill of a helmsman. Against such impudence defend these unpolished and improvidently released pieces at least by hiding them. That other work I have been polishing with great care, though not a Phidian Minerva, as Cicero asserts, but a true portrait and likeness such as it is of my talent if ever I shall be able to give it the last touches, that work, I say, when it reaches you, you may set up without concern at the summit of whatever stronghold you please. But enough of that.

Another matter which I would gladly remain silent about must be mentioned. A serious disease is not easily hidden since it breaks out and becomes visible through its own peculiar features. I am ashamed of a life fallen into excessive softness. The very order of my letters will testify to this. My style was strong and sober in the early years, an indicator of a truly strong mind, of the type which was a source of comfort not only to myself but often to others. With the passage of time it became weaker and more humble and seemed to lack strength of character. It is that style especially that I beg you to try to conceal. What can one expect others to say when I myself blush at rereading those portions? Could it be that I was a man in my youth and a youth in my old age? Unfortunate and cursed perversity! My intention was either to change the order or to make entirely unavailable to you those letters which I now condemn! Neither expedient could have deceived you since you possess copies of the more doleful ones and the exact date of all of them. I, therefore, take refuge in the power of excuses. Fortune exhausted me with long and serious battles. As long as my spirit and courage lasted, I resisted it and urged others to do the same. When the enemy with her strength and attacks began to make my spirit and resistance waver, the grand style perished and I found myself descending to these lamentations which now displease me. Perhaps the devotion of my friends will excuse me. Just knowing of their safety was sufficient to prevent me from groaning at the wounds of fate. All these friends, however, in no time at all were destroyed in almost one stroke, and when the whole world seemed to be dying it appeared inhuman rather than manly not to be moved by it. Before this time whoever heard me complain about exile or disease or litigation, about elections, or about any of the public upheavals? Whoever heard me complain about my place of birth, about ill fortune, about diminished glory, about wasted money, or about the absence of friends? In such adversities Cicero revealed himself so weak that while I take pleasure in his style I often feel offended by his attitude. I feel the same about his contentious letters and the many quarrels and abuses that he directs against famous men upon whom he had not long before lavished praise. And I feel the same about the casualness with which he does all this. When I read his letters I feel as offended as I feel enticed. Indeed, beside myself, in a fit of anger I wrote to him as if he were a friend living in my time with an intimacy that I consider proper because of my deep and immediate acquaintance with his thought. I thus reminded him of those things he had written that had offended me, forgetting, as it were, the gap of time. This idea became the beginning of something that made me do the same thing with Seneca after rereading after many years his tragedy entitled *Octavia*. Him also I reproached and thereafter, as occasion arose, I similarly wrote to Varro, Virgil and others. Some of these letters I have placed in the last portion of this work. I say this here so that the reader will not be filled with undue wonder when he comes upon them. Many of them I also threw in that bonfire of which I spoke. Just as Cicero played the role of a man in his sorrows, so did I, Today, however, so that you may know my present state of mind (nor can it be called envy if I should appropriate for myself what Seneca often says about the unskilled), I have become stronger out of that very state of despair. After all, what can frighten someone who has struggled with death so many times? "The only salvation for the vanquished is not to hope for any salvation." You will see my actions daily become more fearless and my words more bold. And should any worthy cause require a stronger style you will see style itself become more vigorous. Without question a great number of subjects will present themselves but I welcome this because for me writing and living are the same thing and I hope will be so to the very end. But although all things must have their boundaries or are expected to, the affection of friends will allow no end to this work which was begun haphazardly in my earliest years and which now I gather together again in a more advanced age and reduce to the form of a book. For I feel impelled to answer and to correspond with them constantly, nor does the fact that I am so terribly busy serve as an excuse for avoiding this responsibility. Only then will I no longer feel this obligation and will have to consider this work ended when you hear that I am dead and that I am freed from all the labors of life. In the meantime I shall continue along the path I have been following, and shall avoid any exits so long as there is light. And the sweet labor will serve for me almost as a place of rest. Furthermore as the rhetoricians and military leaders are wont to place their weakest parts in the middle, so I shall give to the work both a beginning and an end consisting of the most manly kinds of advice, all the more because as I grow older I seem to become stronger against the blows and injustices of fortune. Finally how I fare in the trials of life remains to be seen, for I dare not try to make any promises. This much is true, however, that right now my spirit is such that I shall never succumb to anything further. "If the world slips into destruction, the crumbling ruins will find me fearless." I want you to know that it is thus that I proceed armed with the advice of Maro and Horace, advice I formerly read about and often applauded but now, at last, in the final days of my life, I have learned to make mine because of the necessities of unavoidable fate.

This discourse with you has been most pleasant for me and I have drawn it out eagerly and as though by design. It has kept your face constantly before me throughout a great number of lands and seas, as if in my presence until dusk, though it was with the early morning light that I had taken up my pen. But the end of the day and of this letter is now in sight. These letters, therefore, woven with multi-colored threads, if I may say so, are for you. However, if I were ever to enjoy a steady abode and the leisure time that has always escaped me, something that begins to appear possible, I would weave in your behalf a much more noble and certainly a unified web or tapestry. I should like to be numbered among those few who can promise and furnish fame; but you shall step forth into the light through your own merits. You shall be borne on the wings of your genius and shall need none of my assistance. If indeed, among so many difficulties I should manage to enjoy a measure of success, I shall make you my Idomeneus, my Atticus and my Lucilius. Farewell.

To Tommaso da Messina,[1] *on untimely appetite for glory.*

No wise man advertises his complaints. There are enough, indeed too many, personal complaints to worry about at home. But do you believe that no one does this? You are wrong; there are very few who do not. The writings or deeds of anyone who is still alive are hardly ever pleasing; death lays the foundations for the praises of men. Do you know why? Because with the body dies envy, just as it lives with the body. You may say "but the writings of many are praised, which if one may boast. . . ." You do not proceed further, but instead as is the custom with angry men, you omit the sermonizing and leave the mind of your listener in suspense. Indeed in my own mind I follow the fleeting truth; I know what you mean; "the writings of many are praised, writings when compared to yours deserve no praises or even readers; while in the meantime none seem to be turning to yours." Recognize in my words your own indignation which would be justified except that you have appropriated for yourself something belonging to the common crowd, and especially to those who are victims or will fall under the spell either of the love or the disease of wanting to write. You must first of all consider whose writings are being praised. Search for the authors: you will certainly find that they have been dead many years. Do you want yours to be praised also? Then you must die. Human favor begins with the death of a man; thus the end of life is the beginning of glory. Should it begin earlier, it would be a most unusual and untimely phenomenon. I shall tell you even more: while any of your contemporaries survive, you will not fully enjoy what recognition you seek; when a grave encloses all of them, there will come those who judge you without hatred and without envy. Therefore let the present age judge us as it will; if the judgment is just, let us accept it with equanimity; if it is unjust, since we cannot turn to

1. Tommaso Caloiro da Messina whom Petrarch knew since his student days at Bologna. Little is known about his life beyond the fact that he too wrote love poetry in the vernacular as can be seen in Petrarch's specific reference to him in the *Triumph of Love* IV, 59–60.

others, let us appeal to the more equitable judges of posterity. Perpetual conversation is a most delicate activity: it is offended at the smallest provocation; and one's presence is always an enemy of glory. Familiarity detracts a great deal from the admiration of fellow men as does repeated intimacy. Have you not observed pedants, that species of men who have become slovenly through wakefulness and fast? Believe me, there is nothing that outdoes them in hard labor and nothing that is more flexible in rendering judgment. While they may read many things most industriously, they really ponder nothing; and whatever substance may be in anything, they disdain to seek it out when they feel they know the writer personally. Therefore there is a single law that applies generally: all the writings of those authors whom these men have seen even once are boring to them. You may say, "such things happen to small minds; the truly great and powerful ones make their way through whatever obstacles." Return Pythagoras to me and I shall deliver to you the despisers of his talent. Let Plato return to Greece, let Homer be reborn, let Aristotle live again, let Varro return to Italy, let Livy appear again, let Cicero flourish again, and we will find a few sluggish praisers of them but also biting and even spiteful detractors, for all of them met with them in their own day. Who greater than Virgil does the Latin language have? Yet you would discover those who said that he was not a poet, but a plagiarizer and translator of the inventions of others. And yet he himself, relying on the faith and judgment that Augustus had for his talent, disdained in a manly fashion the words of his detractors. I am aware that you also are highly conscious of your talent; but where will you find an Augustus as a judge, who we know protected the talents of his day most strenuously and in every possible way? Our kings are able to judge tasty dishes and the flights of birds, but not men's talents. Should they presume to do so, their puffed pride would not allow their eyes to open or to turn and contemplate the truth. And in order not to appear interested in their own age, they admire the ancients whom they disdain to become acquainted with, so that the praise of the dead is not entirely free from insult to the living. It is our lot to live and die among such judges, and, what is even harder, to be silent. For as I said, where do we look for a judge like Augustus?

Italy does have one, indeed the entire world has only one, Robert, the King of Sicily. Oh fortunate Naples whose good fortune has given you the incomparable happiness of having the only ornament of our age. I say fortunate and enviable Naples, most venerable home of letters, which if you appeared to Maro attractive in his day, how much more attractive would you seem now being the place where the foremost judge of talent and learning lives. Let whoever honors talent take refuge in you; and let him not postpone doing so, for all delay is harmful. He is well advanced in age and the world can lose him very quickly. He is worthy of superior kingdoms, and I worry lest I am preparing for myself cause for late repentance by too much delay. Deferring admirable things is shameful and similarly any prolonged deliberation in accomplishing the good becomes dishonest. The occasion must be seized, and one must quickly accomplish what could not be accomplished earlier. Insofar as I am concerned I intend to hasten and to act quickly, "so that," as Cicero says about Julius Caesar, "I am directing all my energies to that. In fact I shall do so most enthusiastically, and perhaps I shall accomplish what often happens to wayfarers when they hasten. If they happened to get started later than they wished, by hurrying they accomplish what they set out to do more rapidly than if they stayed up nights. The same holds with me since I have so sluggishly cultivated this man that I am trying to compensate for my tardiness by hastening." Thus did Cicero write. You however must act through the intercession of friends inasmuch as you are kept from approaching that king not so much because of the intervening straits but because of war. Your country, which none loves more than yourself, lies in the hands of a hostile king. I would say "tyrant" but for my not wanting to offend you. But these matters are very complicated and cannot be determined by our pens but by swords. Therefore I return to the beginning.

If these examples taken from the most famous men do not suffice, I can point to others of a different type and of more recent times and famous for their sanctity. How many rivals did Augustine, Jerome or Gregory have until such time as their respected virtue and their divine and astonishing abundance of writings overcame envy. Hardly any one of these enjoyed any public fame until the day of his death. I find written that only one was fortunate enough to have no rivals and detractors, only one was honored by rich and deserved praise. This was Ambrose, whose fame could not be affected by bitter envy during the course of his life. But perhaps this may be ascribed to the pure simplicity of his doctrine which avoids all ambiguity. The fact remains that in the works of Paulinus who wrote the *Life of Ambrose* we read both the names of his detractors and of the vengeance inflicted upon them by divine judgment. Therefore, bear without lament what you see befalling to the greatest men of talent.

However, you seem to complain in a certain part of your letter about the fact that many men achieved renown during their lifetime. This too, if you would listen to me, you would disregard with confidence. Surely you know to whom this happens; exclusively to those who defend their fame through clamor since they certainly know not how to write. Consider those who like to dress in purple and who with loud outcries draw to themselves the attention of the people. They wish to be known as wise men and are called such by the multitude which assigns swarms of wise men to each city. Compare this to that once flourishing mother of studies, Greece, that gloried in having not more than seven such wise men, a reputation that seemed even to posterity a sign of arrogance. But those who try to justify them say that the reputation fell to them not because of their personal judgment, but through the judgment of the people. Throughout the centuries Epicurus dared to declare himself a wise man, an intolerable arrogance indeed or rather a ridiculous madness to which Cicero refers in the second book of his *De finibus bonorum et malorum*. Today that madness has become common amidst the swarms of our courtiers. Just consider those who spend every minutes of their life in debates and dialectical scoffing and who are constantly stirred up by inane trifling questions. Observe them well and believe my prediction about all of them: the fame of all of them will disappear with their deaths and a single grave will suffice for their bones and their names. When death compels their cold tongues to remain still, not only must they be silent, but there will also be silence about themselves. I could produce examples in abundance and make you yourself a witness to many more—how many garrulous magpies do we know who take delight in squawking before the eyes of the mad multitude and whose voices have suddenly become silent. I refrain from doing so because my enumeration would be superfluous and perhaps even odious to some people. But we spoke about these and many others often in the past and now we must turn to the matter at hand. The purpose of my discussion was not to speak against them but to reply to you satisfactorily, your situation being completely different from theirs. Your reputation will resound when you will no longer be able to speak. Moreover, to be disturbed by a brief period of waiting is a sign of much too impatient a mind. Wait a little while; your wishes will be answered when you cease being an obstacle to yourself. Perhaps a long absence may answer your wishes in part, but death alone will really answer them for you. Recall the famous men of all times; Romans, Greeks, barbarians whose fame was not hurt by their own presence. Perhaps more historical examples will come to your mind since your memory is fresher. Only of Africanus, I recall, could it be said that he was extraordinary through reputation but even more through his presence. The same tribute was paid to Solomon in sacred scripture. Think of another, but I doubt that you will. Virgil, through his excessive zeal to embellish his Aeneas, tried to endow him with this kind of glory, but the truth is unshakable; and too many excuse him by maintaining that he was describing not Aeneas but under his name the strong and perfect man. In the same way that orator who could more truthfully have usurped the reputation for himself attributed it to only one other. I speak of course of that most illustrious prince of orators, Marcus Tullius, who did the same with only one poet, namely Aulus Licinius Archias. But I am afraid that he paid such a compliment to his teacher, a man of mediocre talent, because his love distorted his judgment, for he did not do the same with Homer nor would he have with Virgil.

Returning to you, there is nothing in all that I have said that could cause you to become upset. The only one who cannot bear to be surpassed by one or by a few is that person who stubbornly abrogates for himself preeminence and fame. Let fortune dispose of the destiny of your talent and of your name as it does with all other things. Did you think that her power extended only over wealth? She is the mistress of all human affairs except virtue; and often she even attacks virtue but never does she succeed in overcoming it. Fame, than which there is nothing less stable, she easily overthrows and causes to revolve with shifting favors, transferring it from those who are worthy to those who are not. For this reason nothing is more inconstant and unjust than the judgment of the people on whom fame rests. That such judgment is constantly shaky is not surprising, therefore, since it is supported on such weak foundations. Thus, fortune has power only over the living; death frees man from her. As a consequence such nonsense ceases and, whether fortune likes it or not, fame follows virtue like a shadow follows a solid body. Therefore, dear friend, unless I am mistaken, you have more cause for celebration than for anger if indeed your fate is similar to almost all the outstanding and famous men of the past. And that you may be even more reassured, I shall restore to his proper place the very Africanus whom I had seemed to separate from this company. As I said, although very unusual, his presence did not harm his reputation, yet like other men, envy, despite his many virtues, he could not avoid. In fact his very virtues en-flamed and fanned envy. It angers me when I recall that he was harmed by excessive socializing and by contempt bred from excessive familiarity. You will ask where I get such in-formation. I do not want you to suspect that I am transforming the truth. I shall cite the very words of Titus Livy, a very famous writer who, describing a disagreement between Scipio Africanus and Titus Flaminius concerning merit and esteem, reports that Scipio yielded and says, "the glory of Scipio was greater but for that very reason more subject to envy." And immediately afterward he adds, "Moreover, Scipio Afri-canus had been in public view constantly for almost ten years, something which makes great men less venerable because of excess." This too does Livy say. Therefore you, to bring this letter to a close, should consider yourself fortunate to be a member of such company and you will mark time more calmly recalling the old saying found in Horace that time improves poetry just as it does wine. And somewhat before him Plautus said, "I consider wise men those who use old wine as well as those who enjoy old stories with pleasure." I suspect Horace like you became angered at the thought that so much reverence was shown to the past that he had to defend himself in a long sermon of the "crime" of having criticized Lucilius. In conclusion, think of why we seem to torment ourselves so much. The fame we seek is but a breeze, smoke, a shadow: it is nothing. Therefore it can very easily be scorned by a clear and fearless judgment. But if by chance—since this pestilence usually pursues noble minds more relentlessly—you cannot eradicate this appetite because it is too deeply rooted, at least hold it in check through the power of reason. One must yield to the times and to circumstances. Finally, to summarize my thought most briefly, cultivate virtue while you are alive and you will find fame after your death. Farewell.

Bologna, 18 April.

Fam. I, 3.

To the venerable elder Raimondo Subirani, Attorney at Law,[1] on the fleetingness of life.

You fear, and perhaps rightfully, that, as happens to almost all young people, I have been beguiled by the flowering of my age. I do not promise you, O father, a firm and stable mind free from all vanity, which in this age of ours I consider very difficult to attain and to result from divine grace rather than human power. But I do pledge a mind by no means ignorant of its condition. I feel myself, believe me, while I seem to be in the very flowering of my life, beginning to wither. But why use slow words when referring to a very rapid occurrence? Indeed, I feel myself hastening, running, and to speak most clearly, flying. As Cicero says, "life does indeed fly." He then adds that "the time of this life is really nothing more than a race toward death." And according to Augustine, "no one is permitted to remain a short while or to delay in his progress while on earth, but all are driven equally in different ways. Nor indeed were days any faster for him whose life was shorter than for him whose life was longer. But rather an unequal number of moments were snatched from both. One travelled nearer and another further, but with equal speed. For to travel over a road further is one thing and yet another to travel more slowly. Thus the one who travels to his death over a longer expanse of time does not advance more slowly; rather he covers more of the road." That is what two such famous men have to say concerning the rapidity of mortal life, one asserting that it flies and the other that it runs. Indeed how often did Virgil say that time flies? And even if all were silent on the matter or even tried to deny it, would it fly or hasten more slowly? Please do not think that I speak of such matters somewhat blithely, or, as is the custom among my contemporaries, that I go about plucking gems from the gardens of authors. This habit Seneca called ugly in older people but is considered permissible for us younger ones. In fact nothing seems more becoming to youth. I do not deny that

1. A highly respected resident of Avignon and close friend of Petrarch.

I often read the *sentences* of great writers. I do so to use them among older people should the occasion arise; but just as I hope to arrive at welcomed old age with deserved praise, I consider such things much more important for the sake of leading the good life than for the sake of eloquence. And although I do delight in the study of eloquence, according to my custom, my talent, my bent and my age; nevertheless whenever I consider the wise sayings of others and whenever I produce something of particular eloquence, I view both experiences as useful to life and helpful against the evils of youth rather than as a temptation towards the fancy language of my juvenile discourse. One must indeed be mad to attempt excellence in something which one will probably never achieve and which comes to a few only, and which, were one even to achieve it, would be of limited benefit, and perhaps even harmful—at the same time neglecting what is intended for everyone, useful to everyone, and can never be harmful. However, we know, through the authority of great men and through experience, that eloquence is reserved for the few, while a good life is possible for all. Nevertheless more people seek the former and flee the latter. Such is the nature of men to seek what is difficult and pursue with great desire those things requiring greater toil. As for me, though my age may diminish my credibility, nevertheless I can assert in good confidence that I read not that I may become more eloquent or more witty but a better man, and I apply to all things what Aristotle said about moral philosophy. Yet, if both benefits do accrue, I would not deny that my attempts would indeed be fortunate. I do thank you, however, dear father, for warning me in such a fatherly manner, and I pray that you continue to do so. But rest assured that from this moment I have begun to understand my proper course and to recognize the perils that beset me. I also know a number of very old men who adhere to things of this earth more deeply, more fixedly, and more tenaciously than I. I was deeply touched by what the emperor Domitian said when already grown old: "there is nothing more pleasing than elegance but nothing more ephemeral"; and by what Tullius has Cato the Elder say: "Who is so foolish, though he be young, as to believe that he will live until evening?" Similarly by what Virgil said most seriously and maturely though still very young: "Oh maiden, gather roses while the buds are new and you are still fresh and young, and be mindful that your life hastens as quickly." I am mindful of these things, and although I cannot weigh them fully, yet I do as best I can, and strive harder each day. I do not consider what I seem to others but what I am, and I am aware that this age of mine, my bodily endowments, and whatever else belongs to me—the envy perhaps of others—were given to me as a venture, as a trial, as toil. In sum, I know that I ascend to descend, blossom to wither, grow up to grow old, live to die. Farewell.

Avignon, the calends of May.

Fam. I, 4.

To Giovanni Colonna,[1] *Cardinal of the Roman Church, description of a journey.*

Recently I traveled through France for no particular purpose, as you know, except for the youthful desire of seeing as much as possible. At one point I reached Germany and the shores of the Rhine River carefully viewing the customs of the people and delighting in the sights of an unknown country, comparing each thing to ours. And though I saw many magnificent things on both shores, I nevertheless did not repent being an Italian. Indeed to tell the truth the further I travel the greater is my appreciation of my native soil. And if Plato expressed his gratitude to what he called his immortal gods, among other things, for having been raised in Greece and not in another foreign land, what prevents us from expressing the same gratitude and recognizing our God as the author of our birthright? Unless, of course, it is more noble to be born a Greek than Italian; but whoever says this would also say that a slave is more noble than a master. But no ordinary Greek would dare say this, however great, impudent and imprudent he might be, when he recalls that long before the founding of Rome and before the birth of the empire on its foundations of valour, in short before "the Romans who were masters of the world and toga-wearing people," a certain portion of our country, which at that time was forsaken and deserted, was occupied by Greeks and called Magna Grecia. If it was considered great at that time how huge, how much greater would it have seemed after the overthrow of Corinth, after the devastation of Aetolia, and after the overthrow of Argos, Mycenae, and the other cities, and after the capture of the Macedonian rulers, and the subduing of Pyrrhus and after Thermopylae had been steeped in Asiatic blood a second time! I believe that no one would deny that it is considerably more noble to be Italian than Greek. But I shall speak of these things perhaps at another time. Let us now return to France. I entered Paris, the capital of the kingdom which claims Julius

1. An elder of the powerful Colonna family to which Petrarch was indebted for many benefits.

Caesar as its founder, with the same kind of attitude shown by Apuleius while visiting Ipatea, a city of Thessaly. Similarly, in suspense and in thoughtful anticipation, viewing everything carefully, desiring to see and to discover whether what I had heard about that city was truth or fiction, I spent considerable time in it. When the light of day was spent I devoted my nights to the visit. At last, ambling around and gaping, I observed enough of it to discern the truth about it and the fiction. But since this would be a long story which cannot be satisfactorily told here, I must postpone it until you can hear me recount everything personally. Not to mention the cities in between, I also saw Ghent which is proud of having the same founder as Paris, a magnificent and opulent city. I also saw the wool spinners and weavers of Flanders and of Brabant. I saw Liège, famous for its clergy; I saw the abode of Charles, Aix, as well as his tomb in a marble shrine, frightening to the barbarians. There from the clergy appointed to the shrine I heard a rather amusing story which they showed me as it had been written and which afterward I read in a more discreet form as recounted by modern writers. I should now like to tell it to you also provided, however, that you do not seek verification of it from me but, as they say, from those authors to whom it belongs.

They recount that King Charles, whom they dare equate to Pompey and Alexander by giving him the surname of "the Great," loved a certain ordinary woman desperately and immoderately. Overcome by her flattery and forgetful of his reputation which he was accustomed to cultivate carefully, and neglecting also the responsibilities of his position, and forgetful of all other cares and even of himself, for a long time he devoted himself exclusively to the caresses of this woman despite the indignation and sorrow of his people. When finally there seemed to be no hope since his mad love had closed his royal ears to all advice, an unforeseen death struck the woman who had been the cause of so much evil. As a result a wide-spread joy at first spread throughout the kingdom. This however was followed by an even more serious concern than the former one when the people saw their king overcome by a frightening illness, for his madness was not mitigated by death but instead became transferred to the foul and bloodless cadaver which had been treated with balsam and perfumes, weighed down by jewelry and covered with a purple shroud. Charles began strangely fondling it night and day in an attitude of sadness and longing. It is unnecessary to explain how unbecoming and unpropitious it is for a king to be a lover, for opposites can never be joined without serious consequences. What is a kingdom if not a just and glorious reality? By the same token what is love but foul and unjust slavery? Therefore when embassies, governors and other officials came to the lover or rather to the insane king to discuss very important affairs of the kingdom, he, wretched in his small bed, and with his doors shut and bolted, clung to the loved body, addressing his mistress repeatedly as if she were breathing and able to answer. He would relate to her his cares and labors, whisper blandishments, suffer nocturnal sighs and shed upon her constantly his tears of love. So this king who otherwise, as they say, was most wise, chose this dreadful consolation for his distress. The story adds something which I neither believe could have happened nor really think I should recount. It says that at that time there was in that court a bishop from Cologne, a man outstanding for his sanctity and wisdom, and indeed a primary counselor to the king. Having seen the pitiful state of his lord, and having noted that there was nothing that could be done by human means he turned to God and began praying constantly. He placed his trust in Him, and tearfully sought from Him an end of misfortune. When he had done this for some time and seemed ready to continue indefinitely, one day he found relief through a miracle which became widely known. As he was offering his usual mass and after his very devout prayers and tears which fell copiously on his breast and on the altar, a voice was heard echoing from heaven saying that the cause of the king's madness lay under the tongue of the dead woman. Joyful at this news and following the completion of the sacrificial offering he hurried to the place where the body was. He gained admission through a right granted him through his friendship with the king, and secretly with his finger he felt inside the dead woman's mouth and found a jewel encased in a very small ring under the cold stiff tongue. He then hastened away. Shortly thereafter when Charles hurried according to his custom to the dead woman, he was shaken by the sight of the withered cadaver. He appeared chilled and horrified at the contact with it and ordered it to be removed as quickly as possible and buried. Then turning to the bishop he began to love him, honor him, to embrace him daily more and more, and finally to do nothing unless it was approved by him. He also refused to be separated from him either night or day. When the good and wise man sensed what was happening, he determined to abandon a situation which, while perhaps desirable to most men, seemed burdensome to him. Being worried lest it fall into the hands of others or that it be destroyed by fire, or that it bring to his master any danger, he threw the ring into the deep ravine of a nearby marsh. At that time the king by chance happened to be living at Aix with his chief men, and from that moment that seat of government became preferred above all other cities. And no marshland became more pleasing to him than those waters beside which he sat and which he viewed with pleasure. Even the smell of the place came to please him very much. Finally he transferred his abode there, and in the middle of the marsh at an immense cost he built a palace and a church so that nothing, either human or divine, could draw him away from there. There he spent the remainder of his life, and there he was buried after having carefully ordered that there his successors be crowned and there they begin to rule. This tradition still continues and will continue as long as the reins of the Roman empire are in Teutonic hands.

I have taken more time in telling the story than I intended. But my extensive journey depriving me of the consolation of books, and my constant moving about making it easier to contemplate many things rather than great things, and being unable to fill my letter properly with serious things, I have crammed it as you can see with whatever was ready at hand. Farewell.

Aix, 21 June.

To the same correspondent, on the same subject.

Having left Aix, but not without first having been wet by the luke-warm waters reminiscent of Baia—whence it is believed that the city gets its name—I arrived at Cologne which is located on the left bank of the Rhine and which is famous for its location, its river, and its people. I was astonished to find so much civility in a barbarous land. I was equally surprised by the appearance of the city, the seriousness of its men, the cleanliness of its women. I arrived, as it happened, on the eve of the feast of St. John the Baptist when the sun was about to set. Without delay and on the advice of friends—for I had won friends there through my fame rather than merit—I was taken from the inn to the river to see a remarkable spectacle. Nor was I disappointed. The entire shore was covered with a huge and remarkable crowd of women. I stood there astounded. Good God, what beauty, what costumes! Anyone could have fallen in love were his heart free. I stood on a somewhat higher location in order to understand what was going on. There was a remarkably controlled crowd. The women were cheerful, part of them girt with fragrant flowers, with their sleeves folded back above the elbows as they washed their white hands and arms in the water and conversed in attractive though foreign whispers. I never understood more clearly what Cicero liked about the ancient proverb that "among the known languages everyone is to some degree deaf and dumb," but I did have the comfort of very gracious interpreters. You will be astonished to hear that those heavens rear poetic spirits, so that while Juvenal was astonished that "eloquent Gaul taught British orators," he would have been equally astonished that "learned Germany rears lively prophets." However, lest you misunderstood me, keep in mind that there is no Virgil here but many Ovids. (You might say that there was truth in the prediction made at the end of the *Metamorphoses* where he maintained that, depending on the good graces of posterity or on his own talent, wherever the power of Rome or indeed wherever the Roman name became established after conquering the world, he would be read with applause by a favorable public.) I made use of these writers and friends as though they were my tongue and my ears whenever it was necessary to answer or understand. As I admired what I saw without knowing what it was, I inquired of one of the persons near me by means of that short verse of Virgil, "what is the meaning of the rush to the river? What do those souls seek?" I was told that it was a very old ritual of the people, widely accepted, especially by the women. They believed that any calamity that might befall throughout the year could be avoided by their washing in the river on that day and that therefrom more joyful things would happen. Thus the ritual had become an annual affair, cherished and cultivated with great enthusiasm. Smiling at this I cried, "Oh happy inhabitants of the Rhine whose afflictions are cleansed by it! Our miseries neither the Po nor the Tiber were able to cleanse. You send your ills across to the Britons by means of the Rhine; we would gladly send ours to the Africans and Illyrians. But we realize that our rivers are more lazy." After a good laugh, we departed rather late.

On the following several days I went about the city from morning to night with the same guides. It was a pleasant enough experience, not so much because of what I witnessed, as from the recollection of our more renowned leaders who had left such illustrious monuments of Roman virtue so far from the fatherland. Among the first that came to mind was Marcus Agrippa, the founder of Cologne, who, although he had built outstanding things at home and abroad, considered that city the most worthy of all to bear his name. He was a builder and distinguished warrior, worthy of having Augustus choose him as a son-in-law from throughout the world, as husband of his only daughter whom always he venerated and held dear. While there I also saw thousands of bodies of the sacred virgins and, dedicated to those magnanimous women, the soil which, so they say, rejects the remains of degenerates. I saw a Capitoline which was an imitation of ours; except that whereas deliberations of peace and law are heatedly held in the Senate in Rome, here in the evening handsome young men and girls together sing the praises of God in

alienation of your mind, accomplished not by some outrageous act, not by some harsh word, not by heavy arrogance, but by means of a silent departure. If you intended to test or inflame, take care lest you choose too subtle a game for a feeble mind. But perhaps the reason was more kind. I imagine that you wanted to spare me trouble, fearful that I might be unequal to the roughness of the journey by sea, and, since you also had to make a journey through parched Apulia, that I would be unable to withstand the summer sun. But I ask you, doesn't this judgment of yours do more harm to my reputation? How did I deserve this opinion? What hardship ever crushed me or frightened me? The mere joy of observing has led me through unknown foreign countries: I trust that the proper necessity would have led me through Italy. Try to recall without embarrassment with how much prayer and flattery you once overwhelmed me so that I would be your companion on a trip to the Pyrenees. To be truthful about it, however, I confess that I followed you almost more eagerly than you dragged me. Now, then, did I not deserve to be your companion to the Apennines? But perhaps that journey revealed my laziness. And yet you daily expressed your astonishment at my endurance of toil though nourished and brought up in the peaceful pursuit of literature, especially since the time of year was bad, the road was rough, and the region was uncultivated. But what distressed us most was that our conversation was difficult and very foreign to our normal ways. But perhaps, since reason leads to truth slowly, we cannot now do what we were able to do once, for time may give, but it also takes away. That journey occurred four summers ago and I am now three years older. Such a period of time suffices not only to change the shaky body of mortal man, but to overthrow empires and cities on a large scale. As you can see, I am jesting; but sometimes great sorrow turns to jest when lamentations fail. I must confess that it is indeed true that each day is a step toward death and the whimpering child in his cradle grows old by growing up. But I am not yet of an age which may feel natural defects. I have not yet indeed reached maturity. And so I carry on with the increasing years, and I become stronger in my limbs and in my mind daily although I do not ignore what is to follow. The higher a wayfarer ascends, the closer he comes to his descent. To put it differently, by ascending he in a certain way descends. The same is happening to me; but meanwhile I am ascending.

The situation being as it is, you probably know the proper cause for your action. I am searching for it trembling and do not find it. I understand only this, that I do love you because it is the way of lovers to be shocked by the first offenses. Then when they cannot extinguish the flame, they seek recourse in the remedies of excuses; and they either express sadness at what has been done, or they deny that it has been done at all, if that is possible, or they say that it was done with good intentions. I am, therefore, doing this so that, if possible, I may seem to have been forsaken rightfully. I wish I could persuade myself of this! Indeed it could be that you did not want to hinder my departure or could have awaited my return. And when as I was leaving you freed me from your embrace while I was in tears, you did not wish to add further to my unhappiness. I wish you had been unmerciful with me, for your devotion produced the opposite effect. Nothing is more painful than an unexpected enemy, and untimely things of any kind always hurt more. If I could not avoid tears, it would have been better to cry then, since it is more natural for those departing to shed tears than for those returning. Thus, I beg you to think about defending yourself as soon as possible with that eloquence you used at my departure. What you say does not have to be really true, only likely. For one who is prepared to believe, there is no ineffectual argument. Meanwhile I shall more easily be tempted to forgive your fault than my ill fortune. Farewell and do not forget me.

Lyons, 9 August.

Fam. I, 7.

To Tommaso da Messina, against aged dialecticians.

It is rash to clash with an enemy who seeks not so much victory as conflict. You write that a certain aged dialectician, violently moved by my letters as if I were condemning his craft, is complaining publicly, and in his letters has threatened our studies; however, for many months you have awaited these letters in vain. Do not wait for them any longer. Believe me they will never come. Let this much modesty remain in him, either out of shame for his style or as a confession of ignorance. Unappeasable in their speech such dialecticians do not contend with a pen. They do not wish to have anyone see how frivolous are the weapons with which they are armed. Therefore in the fashion of the Parthians they practice a retreating kind of battle, and, hurling around swift words, they commit their weapons to the winds. As I said, to try to battle with such men is rash. They get the greatest pleasure out of strife and set out not to find truth but to quarrel. As Varro's saying goes, "the truth is lost in excessive disputation." Do not be troubled by the possibility that they may descend openly into the field of writing and disputation. They are the ones about whom Quintilian in his *Institutes of Oratory* spoke: "You may find them wonderfully expert in disputations, but when they depart from their sophistry they can no more hold their own in any serious activity than those small animals that are very active in narrow places but are easily overtaken in the open." They therefore rightfully fear the open. And thus that same truth holds for them, that "the byways and digressions afford support for their weakness, so that those who are not successful in the straight raceway avoid it by taking winding paths." And so I wish to say this one thing to you, my friend: if you pursue virtue and truth, avoid that kind of man. But where will we flee from the presence of these madmen if even the islands are not safe from them? Can it be that neither Scylla nor Charybdis kept the passage of this plague from Sicily? Indeed it has now become a pestilence peculiar to the islands that to the ranks of British dialecticians is now being added the swarms of new Cyclopes from Aetna. Did I not read in the *Cosmography* of Pomponius that Britain is very similar to Sicily? Indeed I used to think that this similarity lay in the position of the lands and the nearly triangular shape of each and perhaps even in the perpetual collision of the surrounding seas. I never gave any thought to the role of the dialecticians. I had heard that the Cyclopes first and afterward the Tyrants had both been fierce inhabitants; I knew nothing of the arrival of a third kind of monster armed with split enthymemes and more blustering than the violent shore of Taormina. One thing only I had observed, and now you warn me about it; that they protect their sect with the brilliance of Aristotle's name, saying that Aristotle used to debate the way they do. Following the footsteps of famous leaders is, I confess, an excuse of sorts. Cicero said that, if necessary, he would not be unwilling to fall into error provided he could have Plato on his side. But they are wrong. Aristotle, a man of glowing talent, alternately debated and wrote about lofty matters. Otherwise whence came so many volumes of his prepared with so much study and over so many wakeful nights, and among the serious projects of so many disciples, especially of that fortunate one,[1] and over a lifetime which can hardly be considered long? As we know, death overcame him when he was about sixty-three, a time of life considered infamous among writers. So why do these dialecticians depart so radically from their leader? Why I ask do they enjoy being called Aristotelians and are not rather ashamed to be called so? Nothing is more unlike that great philosopher than a man who writes nothing, understands little and proclaims many things uselessly. Who would not laugh at those sophisms with which those learned men weary themselves and others, and in which they waste their entire life, and which are indeed useless to others and harmful to their own lives? Theirs are the sophisms that were frequently ridiculed by Cicero and Seneca. And we may see them in that story about Diogenes who was attacked by an abusive dialectician who said: "What I am, you are not." When Diogenes agreed, the dialectician confirmed, "I am a man." When Diogenes did

1. Alexander the Great.

not deny that, the clown added, "therefore you are not a man." Then Diogenes answered, "your conclusion is in fact false, and if you wish to make it true you must begin your syllogism with me." There are many such kinds of ridiculous activities in which they indulge. They perhaps know what they are seeking—whether fame or amusement or a plan for a good and blessed life. I certainly do not. By noble minds, gain ought scarcely to be considered a worthy wage for studies. Such gain is proper for technicians; the goal of the honored arts is more noble. But when these dialecticians hear these things they become angry. This is because the talkativeness of the obstinate man is most like wrath. "So," they say, "you condemn dialectic?" Certainly not! In point of fact I know how much the Stoics respected it, that powerful and manly school of philosophers which our Cicero recalls often in other works of his as well as in his *De finibus*. I know that it is one of the liberal arts and a step forward for those who are striving for the heights and not a useless armor for those stepping into the thorny way of the philosophers. It rouses the intellect, marks a way of truth, teaches the deceits to be shunned. In short, if nothing else it makes men resolute and very keen. I do not deny that all this is true. But a place we pass through once and enjoy is not a place where we can justifiably linger; just as indeed it is insane for a pilgrim to forget the goal of his journey because of the pleasantness of the road. It is to the credit of the pilgrim to find quickly the proper limit, and never linger beyond it. And who among us is not a pilgrim? We all are on a long and difficult journey in a period of time as brief and difficult as a rainy winter's day. Dialectic can be a part of the journey; but it is certainly not its goal. And it can be a daytime rather than an evening part of it. We once did many things honestly that we would now do shamefully. If as old people we are unable to abandon the school of dialectic because we had fun with it as youngsters, we should not be ashamed by that same token either to play the game of odds and evens or ride on a trembling reed or be rocked in the cradle of children. Wonderful indeed are the variety of things and the changes of seasons which nature gladly planned to combat our boredom.

Do not think that you find these things only in the compass of a year. You will find them even more over a long lifetime. Springtime abounds with flowers and leafy trees; summer is wealthy with its fruit, autumn with its apples; winter abounds with its snows. If these things, which are not only bearable but actually pleasing, are distorted when the laws of nature are shaken then they become unbearable. Just as no one will endure calmly the frost of winter throughout the summer, or the heat of the sun raging in strange months; in the same way no one will be found who will not dislike or laugh at an old man playing with children, or be astonished at a gray-haired boy with gout. I ask, what is more useful to all disciplines than the early learning of the letters of the alphabet in which the foundations of all studies are found, indeed what is more necessary? But on the other hand what is more laughable than an old man busy with such things. You therefore rouse up the supporters of your old man with my words. Do not hinder them in any way, but exhort them, not indeed that they hasten to dialectic but that they hasten through it to better things. And tell your old friend that I am not condemning the liberal arts but only infantile old men. For just as there is nothing more unsightly than an old man dealing with elementary things, as Seneca says, there is nothing more deformed than an old dialectician. If he begins to spout syllogisms, my advice is to flee and order him to go and hold a disputation with Enceladus.[2] Farewell.

Avignon, 12 March.

2. One of the hundred armed giants who waged war against the gods.

Fam. I, 8.

To Tommaso da Messina, on inventiveness and talent.

You have asked me what to do finding yourself in that condition usual to almost all the host of writers who, although they either feel unsure of themselves or are ashamed to borrow, yet cannot stop writing because of the pleasure they take in it or because of the desire for glory natural to mortal souls. In such a perplexed and hesitant state you returned to me. First of all you would have done better to have sought a more skillful advisor, one who would have given you either a great many suggestions or the single one, the very best and the most carefully selected. Instead, you are now knocking on the door of a poor man, from whom, however, you will not depart with your hands completely empty. What I have received from others by begging I shall gladly give to you. I must confess, however, that in this matter I cannot give you much more than a single piece of advice. If after a trial you discover that it is ineffectual, you must blame Seneca. But if you find it effective you must render thanks to him and not to me. In short I want you to realize that he is the source of this advice. His loftiest advice about invention is to imitate the bees which through an astonishing process produce wax and honey from the flowers they leave behind. Macrobius in his *Saturnalia* reported not only the sense but the very words of Seneca so that to me at the very time he seemed to be following this advice in his reading and writing, he seemed to be disapproving of it by what he did. For he did not try to produce honey from the flowers culled from Seneca but instead produced them whole and in the very form in which he had found them on the stems. Although how can I say that something another wrote is not mine, when Epicurus' opinion, as recorded by Seneca himself, is that anything said well by anyone is our own? Macrobius must therefore not be blamed because he not only reported but actually transcribed a large part of one letter in the proem of his work. The same thing has sometimes happened to me and to many other greater writers as well. This much however I affirm, that it is a sign of greater elegance and skill for us, in imitation of the bees, to produce in our own words thoughts borrowed from others. To repeat, let us write neither in the style of one or another writer, but in a style uniquely ours although gathered from a variety of sources. That writer is happier who does not, like the bees, collect a number of scattered things, but instead, after the example of certain not much larger worms from whose bodies silk is produced, prefers to produce his own thoughts and speech—provided that the sense is serious and true and that his style is ornate. But in truth, this talent is given to none or to very few, so that we should patiently bear the lot of our personal talents, and not envy those above us, disdain those below us, or annoy our equals. I indeed know what you are saying to yourself silently: "this man is pulling me away from my studies and is discouraging me from being industrious while he teaches me to bear my ignorance patiently." Believe me I think nothing is more to be avoided than to allow laziness to age one's talents. When Cicero writes that men seem to him to be lowlier and weaker than the animals, outdoing them only in that they can speak, I believe we must either be indulgent to the famous orator for the praise he bestows upon his art, or we must take him to assume that speech itself could not exist without intelligence. In general, men seem to me to excel in the ability to understand, to distinguish, and to remember, traits which nature did not allot to animals, although some of them seem able to distinguish and in certain ways to remember. So where are we now? I urge and beseech us all to drive away vigilantly and most vigorously the ignorance in the shadows of our mind and make every effort to learn as much as possible while on this earth where the road may lead us to heaven. But let us remember in our striving that we are not all born under one star, so that because of our natural slowness our road may not extend to the very top. We must therefore be content with the limits of the talents that God and nature granted us. If we do not do this we shall never be able to live without anxiety. And as long as we pursue the knowledge of things, a road we must travel without interruption until our very last breath, new areas of darkness will appear daily into which our ignorance cannot reach. This is the source of our sorrow and indignation and disdain. Since the unlearned multitude will not see these dark areas, they live more gaily and calmly. And this is the reason why knowledge which ought to be the source of sacred pleasure becomes a source of very troublesome anxiety and extinguishes that very life which it promised to serve as guide. Therefore let moderation be present in all affairs. It will induce us to be truly grateful to the Eternal Dispenser not only for what pertains to fortune or to material things, but also for what is good for our soul, however little it may be, for He sees clearly what is good for us, and liberally grants us not what He knows to be more pleasurable but what is more useful. Just as that old man who owned a few acres was justifiably praised for equating the wealth of his mind to the wealth of kings, so will that man be praised who though ugly, dull or stammering, compares himself to Alcibiades for his beauty, to Plato for his genius or to Cicero for his eloquence. Therefore let not the man who lacks talent be lacking in equanimity; as for the man who possesses it, let discretion act as a moderator of all things so that he can judge his true strength with a clear judgment, lest perchance by flattering himself he should weigh himself down with an unbearable weight. This would be against what is written in the *Art of Poetry:* "Select your subject according to your talents, you who write; and consider well what your shoulders can bear and what they cannot." To be sure talent should be assisted by study and should be supported by contemplation, but it should not be compelled to ascend to heights that it cannot reach. Otherwise, aside from the fact that all attempts to do so would be useless, it often happens that while we long for the impossible, we neglect the possible. Now let me introduce a brief and, unless I am mistaken, useful thought, and a memorable one which I read in Quintilian, a very keen man. Since he wrote it briefly and clearly I prefer not to change his actual words: "It frequently happens even to gifted youths that they are worn out by labor and through the desire of speaking excellently they descend into the depths of silence. Concerning this matter I remember the Julius Secundus, my contemporary, and, as is well-known, truly loved by me, a man of wonderful eloquence but nevertheless of boundless diligence, told me what had been told him by his uncle. This was Julius Florus, a prince of eloquence, who practiced in Gaul with a fluency possessed by few men and worthy of his relationship to Secundus. When he happened to see Secundus who was still going to school, he asked him why his wrinkled brow. The young man openly admitted that although it was already the third day, and in spite of all his labor, he could not find a good beginning for his theme topic. As a result not only was he overcome with grief in the present but also felt despair for the future. Florus smilingly said, 'Do you really wish to speak better than you can?' " This is what Florus said to his nephew. And Quintilian in turn says to us, indeed to all of us, "That is the way it is. We should try to speak as well as possible, but we must nevertheless do so according to our ability. In order to improve, study is necessary and not impatience." This advice about eloquence can be extended variously to the other activities of men. But since the subject of this letter has to do with talent and eloquence, we must, as with everything else, learn to bear calmly either an excess or a lack of these qualities. If there be anyone upon whom the stars look with such benign light that he suffices unto himself without outside assistance and can by himself express great ideas, he owes much gratitude to the grace of heaven. Let him avoid arrogance and enjoy the gifts of the Lord with great humility and let him be unconcerned about the ways of the bees. For us, however, to whom such fortunate things do not befall, let us not be ashamed to imitate the bees, remembering what our Virgil has to say about them, "mindful of the coming winter they work in the summer, and, in between seasons, they store what they need." Let us also try to do so while there is time and while life glows and our talents are vigorous. Let us not wait until the cold of old age steals upon us and the winter clouds replace the brightness of the summer. We read in the work of the same poet that the bees also "at the return of summer keep busy among the rural flowers under the sun." And in another place he again says: "During the bright summer they settle upon the various flowers in the meadows and buzz around the white leaves while all the fields echo their murmur." Thus if we wish to apply with advantage the advice handed on by this illustrious teacher of conduct, let us adapt whatever is written about the bees to the activity of human inventiveness. What is our summer if not the flaming period of life? Similarly what is more like the cold winter than old age? What benefit do we expect to derive from this period of our lives and from this leisure, what harvest of talent, if now we stop frightened in the face of toil? What will posterity carry away from our granaries if we stand still in a sluggish idleness? "Naked does the farmer plough and naked does he sow; winter is a lazy time for him." But lest my subject slip from bees to farmers, now in the meadows and through the countryside let us settle on the various flowers of many others. Let us examine the books of learned men and from them let us alight on their very rich and very sweet lessons as though we were lighting upon the white lilies. But we must do so tirelessly as well as modestly and gently. Let us establish an honorable goal for our studies and not the vainglory of the multitude that derives from the witticisms of a windy argument. Let that goal be achieved through the effect of truth and virtue. Believe me it is possible to know something without noisy quarrels. It is not noise that makes the learned man, but contemplation. Therefore, unless we are determined to appear rather tan to be, we will enjoy not the applause of the foolish multitude but rather truth and silence. And we shall be happy at the soft sound brought to us sometimes by words of genuine writers. Thus the fields will resound not with sharp noise but with a soft murmur. Since as you can see I have gone much further than the resolution of your doubts required, I shall add something else to what I have said thus far. Flee every place where one lives in a shameful or pompous way and shun the judgment of popular favor. You must know also that that place would be injurious no less to the bees than to you which "either emits a heavy odor of filth or resounds with the blows from a cut-out stone and an offended echo resounds." Do not think that this advice is directed to you alone but to all who are involved in the creation of praiseworthy things. It is primarily by two things that the creative genius of many is choked, namely, the habits of passionate appetite and the distortions of popular opinion. While the former sit inwardly the latter are located outwardly, and the mind becomes weakened and is kept far from the recognition of the truth. These are the things I thought I should say about imitating the bees. From their example, select and conceal the better ones in the beehive of your heart and hold on to them with the greatest diligence and preserve them steadfastly, lest anything should possibly perish. And be careful not to let any of those things that you have plucked remain with you too long, for the bees would enjoy no glory if they did not transform those things they found into something else which was better. You also, if you find anything of value in your desire for reading and meditating, I urge you to convert into honey combs through your own style. From them will flow forth what the present and future ages will ascribe to you with the best justification. Finally, that we may pluck no flowers today if not from the trees of Virgil, let me add the following, "From here you will squeeze sweet honey at certain times of the year, and it will not be so sweet as it will be clear, and will overcome the bitter taste of Bacchus." Farewell.

11 April.

Fam. I, 9.

To the same Tommaso da Messina, on the study of eloquence.

The care of the mind calls for a philosopher, while the proper use of language requires an orator. We must neglect neither one, if, as they say, we are to return to the earth and be led about on the mouths of men. But I shall speak of the care of the mind elsewhere; for it is a great undertaking and an enormous labor, though very rich in harvest. At this time in order to avoid slipping into a subject other than the one that I set out to treat, I urge and admonish that we correct not only our life and conduct, which is the primary concern of virtue, but our language usage as well. This we will do by the cultivation of eloquence. Our speech is not a small indicator of our mind, nor is our mind a small controller of our speech. Each depends upon the other but while one remains in one's breast, the other emerges into the open. The one ornaments it as it is about to emerge and shapes it as it wants to; the other announces how it is as it emerges. People obey the judgment of one, and believe the opinion of the other. Therefore both must be consulted so that one will be reasonably strict with the other, and the other will be truthfully magnificent toward the first. The fact remains that where the mind has been cultivated, speech cannot be disregarded, just as, on the other hand, there can be no merit to speech unless a certain dignity is present in the mind. What good will it do if you immerse yourself wholly in the Ciceronian springs and know well the writings either of the Greeks or of the Romans? You will indeed be able to speak ornately, charmingly, sweetly and sublimely; you certainly will not be able to speak seriously, austerely, judiciously and, most importantly, uniformly. The reason for this is that unless our desires first order themselves (and you must know that no one can achieve this except a wise man) it is inevitable that such disorder will be reflected in our conduct and in our words. The well-ordered mind is the image of an undisturbed serenity and is always quiet and peaceful. It knows what it wants, and does not cease wanting what it desires. Therefore, even lacking the ornaments of oratorical skill, it is able to call forth most magnificent and serious words harmonious with itself. Moreover, undeniably the most un-usual often emerges when the movements of the mind are composed. But when these are in agitation little of any significance can be produced. The study of eloquence requires much time. If we did not need it, and if through its own power our mind could silently display its good traits without the support of words, great toil would yet be necessary for the sake of those with whom we live. For without doubt, our conversations would be of great assistance to their minds.

However, stepping forward, you say, "How much safer for us and more effective for them it would be to exhort them to let us provide for their eyes examples of our virtue. Delighted by the beauty of such examples they would be seized by the urge to imitate. For we are aroused perfectly naturally in much better fashion and much more easily through the stimulus of deeds rather than of words. Through this pass let us advance more readily to the highest reaches of virtue." In truth I am not opposed to this. How I felt about this you were already able to understand just now when I warned that among the first things that must be done is the ordering of the mind. Nor do I think that without good reason the Satirist said: "You owe me first of all the riches of the mind." These would certainly not be first if anything came before them. Furthermore, how much help eloquence can be to the progress of human life can be learned both in the works of many writers and from the example of daily experiences. How many people have we known in our time who were not affected at all by past examples of proper speech, but then, as if awakened, suddenly turned from a most wicked way of life to the greatest modesty through the spoken words of others! I shall not report here what Marcus Cicero said about this matter at considerable length in his books *On Invention*, for what he said there is very familiar, nor would I cite the fable of Orpheus or of Amphion, the former of whom lured huge beasts with his song and the latter plants and stones which he is said to have moved at will, except as one understands that because of their outstanding eloquence both were able to inculcate gentleness and patience in all things, the one into lustful and savage men whose customs make them very like beasts, the other into rustic and rough men who were as unmanageable as stones. Add to this that such study permits us to be useful to those living in distant regions with whom we will never be permitted to socialize but to whom our words may perhaps come. And indeed how much good we will do to our posterity can very well be judged when we consider how much our greater predecessors have left to us.

But once again you remark: "What need is there to work hard if everything advantageous to men has already been written during the past thousand years in so many volumes of a marvelous perfection by god-like talents?" Lay aside this anxiety, I say, and don't ever let it drive you into laziness. This fear was already removed by certain of our great ancients, and I shall remove it from the minds of those who come after me. Let thousands of years flow by, and let centuries follow upon centuries, virtue will never be sufficiently praised, and never will teachings for the greater love of God and the hatred of sin suffice; never will the road to the investigation of new ideas be blocked to keen minds. Let us therefore be of good heart; let us not labor uselessly, and those who will be born after many ages and before the end of an aging world will not labor in vain. What is rather to be feared is that men may cease to exist before our pursuit of humanistic studies breaks through the intimate mysteries of truth. Finally, if no sense of charity toward our fellow men drives us, I would still consider the study of eloquence of the greatest aid to ourselves rather than something to be held in the lowest esteem. Let others hold their own views. I cannot tell you of what worth are to me in solitude certain familiar and famous words not only grasped in the mind but actually spoken orally, words with which I am accustomed to rouse my sleepy thoughts. Furthermore, how much delight I get from repeating the written words either of others or sometimes even my own! How much I feel myself freed from very serious and bitter burdens by such readings! Meantime I feel my own writings assisted me even more since they are more suited to my ailments, just as the sensitive hand of a doctor who is himself ill is placed more readily where he feels the pain to be. Such cure I shall certainly never accomplish unless the salutary words themselves fall tenderly upon my ears. When through the power of an unusual sweet temptation I am moved to read them again, they gradually take effect and transfigure my insides with hidden powers. Farewell.

Calends of May

Fam. I, 10.

To the same Tommaso da Messina, a description of an avaricious old man.

You know that your little old man is very well in health. Conduct helps not only the mind but also the body; thriftiness is the sister of good health. Rest assured that this man will become immortal unless he is destroyed by hunger. So thin and emaciated is his little body that neither fever nor gout can find any place in it. His very appearance attests to the nourishment of the man, the pallor of his face, the leanness and cavity of his eyes, the sorrowful eyebrows, and his unpolished austerity. His shoe pulled up in the manner of a cothurnus and his small mantle frazzled with old age must be added to the picture. If he only knew some literature you would call him a philosopher or a poet, for his bare back smacks of the philosophical and his ill-shod feet of the tragic. Whatever might be added to this would be superfluous. So that I might explain in a few words, he is not very unlike the old man whose conduct and mentality are sprinkled with salt by his servant in the *Aulularia* when he says: "The pumice stone is not as hard and parched as this old man. If ever he sees smoke emerging from his kindling wood he cries out quickly for support from men and gods because all his belongings have perished and he himself has been destroyed. Indeed when he goes to sleep he ties a bellows around his throat lest by sleeping he should lose some breath. He even stops up his lower mouth lest by chance he lose any breath through that opening; he laments over the water that he pours forth when bathing, and by Hercules if you ask him for the use of his hunger he would never give it to you. Once indeed a barber cut his nails and he collected all of them and carried off the clippings . . . then a kite snatched some victuals from him and the man came to the praetor crying, and began to demand as he wept and wailed that the kite be bound over to him by bail. There are six hundred other stories that I would remember if there were free time."

Thus did the servant in the play of Plautus speak, but concerning our old man the inquisitive story teller would find six times six hundred such stories. Whoever would see this man or would hear him only once governing the management of a household by rules of economy known to no philosopher would call in contrast prodigal the guest of Apuleus Milo. But we are lingering excessively over the defects of others; let us return to our own. All of us mortals, or almost all, suffer from a certain disease; we are pulled by opposites, and what Flaccus says is indeed true, "when fools try to shun a vice they fall into the opposite one." What do we believe to be the difference between the cakes of Rufillus and the goat of Gorgonius, or between the loss of Aristippus and the epigrams of Staberius? One need not travel on distant byways to seek what makes one happy. Vice dwells in extremes; virtue in the center. Farewell.

Fam. I, 11.

To the same Tommaso, a description of a famished parasite.

I gather that your first request I handled successfully so that you are making a second one. I think you wish to test my capabilities in handling the demonstrative genre. I wish you were testing me in writings of praise rather than the contrary! But since that is what you want and the matter can be handled without names—although the exactness of the circumlocution takes the place of a proper name—I shall comply with this second request of yours. The man you inquire about is a "wandering buffoon" as Horace described him: "one who certainly has no stall and when hungry one who cannot distinguish a fellow-citizen from his enemy." In short he is the most insolent of all who ever devoted themselves to the art of the parasite. Nevertheless he is not at all happier than if he were the laziest of all. The sailor is not as fearful of reefs, nor the farmer of hail, nor the merchant of thieves, as everyone is of him. Everyone avoids him, everyone yields to his passage as if he came loaded down with thorns. Everywhere he finds empty roads, abandoned dwellings, bolted doors. One flees at his approach as if he bore war in his lap. However all these things never befall him more inconveniently than at this time of the year. Summer, however it may be, is the haven of the poor. A single tree suffices as garment, as meal, as roof and as bed.

But now what happens? There is a conspiracy of winter, old age and want. No one offers any aid and what is worst of all his wretchedness finds no compassion. I saw him today being buffeted by a strong north wind. He had his robes tucked up high and he permitted his hair to be blown about by the wind like Maro's Venus. If he had a yellow hat made of wolf skins, he would appear, among other things, to be going to war like a Hernian in his uniform adopted by the Pelasgians; for his left foot was naked. He was driven by such fury that he could admit about himself what that dangerous parasite proclaimed about himself in Plautus: "my fist is a military machine, my elbow is a catapult, my shoulder a battering ram." That is the way he appeared, but in such a manner that among the threats, the traces of a long hunger could be perceived. In short, as Plautus himself says, "I saw neither a more hungry man nor one more overcome by hunger nor one who accomplished less in whatever he began doing." Finally when I had turned aside from his sight into an alley, as though I were evading a pirate's galley in the shadows, I saw him *en passant* exhaling balls of smoke through the mist and it was as though I were passing by the cave of Cacus or one of the Aeolian islands. I heard I know not what quivering and confused sound issuing forth from his throat. I do not know what he wished to say, so broken into pieces were his words. I believe that he would find comfort for his feet and for his shoulders in that utterance of the Satirist: "Be patient and await the crickets." You have what you wanted and you have made me scurrilous. Farewell.

Fam. I, 12.

To the same Tommaso da Messina, the rest of the dispute with the garrulous aged dialectician cited above.

Here we are tempted again. Your dialectician, as you write, cannot be silent. Are you surprised? I would be surprised if he were silent since his fame depends on noise and insults. But it is a good thing that he knows not how to write and that I cannot hear him from here. In this way both my ears and my eyes (because of the intervening sea and land) are safe from his ignorance. So the entire weight of the unfit interlocutor falls upon your head, and deservedly, since you showed my letters to the dialecticians. Admittedly, from all the things that you say you had learned from his coarse barking, the foremost and greatest was that he says that of all the arts ours is the least necessary. Here finally he spews out the venom that was so threatening in the other letters. But is this what he warned that he would use in his assault upon our studies? Very clearly. He said, "Your art is the least necessary of all." First, let us examine this art; although I do not know what art he attributes to us, except perhaps the poetic art. He claims this to be the least necessary. This I do not deny. It seemed so even to our predecessors. "Poetry was born and invented for the benefit of souls." And Horace himself testifies that poetry itself shows it to be for pleasure and ornament and not for necessity. Therefore hurrah for your dialectician. May he abound always with sharp horned syllogisms since he feels as we do and is not ignorant of all things as I thought. But that burning and fiery talent is not restrained within these boundaries. What then? He twists together a swift enthymeme saying: "If it is less necessary it is also less noble." Oh how badly his madness is covered! Now he shows himself not only a dialectician but also a madman. If necessity ennobles the arts, the most noble of all would therefore be the shoemaker's, the baker's and the other lowest of mechanical trades. But philosophy and all the others, the ones that make life blessed and cultivated and decorated, if they do not contribute to the needs of the multitude, are the ignoble ones. Oh new and exotic doctrine unknown to Aristotle himself whose name such arts would disgrace! He indeed says: "All are indeed more necessary but none are more worthy." Let him read the first book of the *Metaphysics* and he will find these words. But I am ordering the old man to proceed in an unknown region of truths and to go along an exacting path, not a light labor indeed! Farewell.

11 December, at the source of the Sorgue.

Fam. II, 1.

To Philip, Bishop of Cavaillon,[1] that he must bear the death of his dear ones with composure.

Your virtue removes from me the enormous difficulty of having to write to you now. For just as the cure of a bodily affliction is more difficult the more serious it is, so it is with the mind. For both, a healthy condition requires no cure or a very light one. And just as with the former there is little or no need for a doctor, with the latter there is little or no need for a consoler. With you, therefore, excellent sir, I should be more careful if misfortune had either crushed or battered you. Since you have borne the blows of fortune with a strong heart, you have snatched from me the role of consoler and have imposed the duty of a praiser and admirer. In this manner, as I was saying, you have cut off from me the need for a more worked-out style. For in order to have consolation pierce the mind of a sorrowing listener, it needs great majesty of words, as well as weighty and bold sentences. For virtue a simple and unpolished witness suffices, nor is it necessary to color the truth of things with fancy colors since virtue applauds itself, and content with its own proclamation, does not need the sounds of a theater audience. I had recently come to you shocked by the bitter report of the premature death of your beloved brother. I measured the extent to which your mind must have been stricken by the anguish of my own heart. Nor did I consider that certain blows which might be fatal to fresh recruits are scorned by strong and proven soldiers, and that certain ones terrified by the flowing of the blood of others would cry out, groan and grow pale and would often collapse in terror, while the ones from whose breast the blood flowed would remain silent, and undaunted, with dry eyes, view their bleeding wounds. Thus I had come a sad and sick doctor approaching a healthy patient. I found your face displaying signs of your having been caught between the affection of a proper piety and the dignity of your own character, between brotherly sympathy

1. One of Petrarch's earliest and dearest friends whose diocese included Vancluse of which he was the feudal lord.

and manly courage. Both attitudes pleased me; one is fitting to your gentleness the other to your wisdom. It is human at the death of one's dear ones to shed tears as evidence of one's devotion; it is manly to place a limit upon them and to control them after they have flowed for some time. The condition of your face indicated that you had fulfilled both these conditions as was fitting. Added to this were words filled with so much depth of feeling that I who had come with the intention of consoling you recognized that you did not need my help, and that I was myself deriving comfort for my sorrows. I shall, therefore, say nothing in the way of trying to console you. I praise, I approve and admire, and I am amazed at the magnanimity of your mind.

You lost a very fine brother. Indeed you did not lose him, but you sent him ahead to the fatherland to which you also must go. Let us speak like the multitude; let us not feel like the multitude. You lost a brother; you would not have lost him unless he were mortal. The complaint therefore is not about the death of one man, but about the mortality of nature which introduced us into this life subject to the rule that we must exit at the command of the one who calls us back. "But he was recalled before his time which seemed the painful result of a too hasty edict." There is no fixed time in this life. We are debtors without limits. If we were bound to a specific day, we could at least delay, evade, and blame the avarice of the overseer. Now we cannot complain about swiftness as we could repayment of what we owe as soon as we accept it. "But he could have lived longer." And he could have died sooner, and he could have died differently, and although no dishonorable death could befall a distinguished man, he could nevertheless have died a more difficult death. He indeed died just as he lived, so that you owe thanks to God because of the kind of brother He gave to you and because of the way He took him away from you. If you consider the destiny and variability of human affairs, not only will you not mourn, but perhaps you may even rejoice that he is dead. For death often intercepts the labors of our present life and often preempts them. Who could enumerate the anxieties and distresses of this world, the afflictions, the tribulations and all the insults of fortune; who could enumerate the dangers of the soul and body and the throng of diseases that vie for both? Although we are not overcome by all of these, we nevertheless remain subject to them until we are removed from their power on the last day. And so your brother is now immune from all of these through the kindness of a timely death. We are wrong, oh kindest sire, and we err too vulgarly when we say that in dying we are snatched from an agreeable life. If we were to consider more deeply, we would realize that we avoid countless evils through death. I could easily show this with the help of authority and rationalization and examples, except that the brevity of a letter does not permit a long discourse. Now the happy youth does not fear those things, for he has escaped from this place and departed from us for a short time, leaving behind him such a reputation that the feelings and heart of those who remember him are charmed by the sweet recollection. Someone might say, "But this is what we are grieving about, that death has snatched from us a good and distinguished man, because the praise of the dead together with the recollection of the harm done to us prompts the tears of the living, and the irreparable loss creates an inconsolable bereavement." This, I am aware, is often said by many. But I, as I recall telling you personally, view it quite differently. Socrates was condemned to punishment by the highly unjust sentences of his judges, and he went to his death in the same state of mind he had always maintained in life. His was a great spirit and firm, and he was not given to yielding to the yoke of fortune. He was happy to leave behind by dying the threats of tyrants whom he had disdained during his lifetime. He serenely brought to his lips the cup of poison which had been given to him by the executioner, but was distracted by the grief of his wife who was influenced by other feelings which made her grieve because her husband was dying a just and innocent man. Upon hearing his wife, Socrates turned to her from his drink for a short while and said: "What then? Did you think that I should die a guilty wrongdoer?" This he said with his usual eloquence. To return to where I had left off, therefore, I disagree with the opinions of most and believe as follows: the death of evil ones must be mourned since it kills the soul and body; but the departure of good people should be accompanied by joy because, mercifully snatching them from this valley of affliction, God has transferred them to more joyful things. Unless perhaps the death of your brother has seemed so much more bitter because it overcame him far from the boundaries of his homeland. But we know better, being acquainted with those highly truthful words of the poet, "Every soil is homeland for the brave," and we also know the even more true saying of the apostle: "Here we have no abiding city, but we seek another." These words seem contradictory but they are not. Each of the writers expressed briefly what he felt but because of the diversity of their speech each spoke in a different way, yet each nevertheless spoke the truth. If you accept the words of the poet, your brother could not die outside his homeland. But if you believe the apostle, everyone dies outside his homeland in order to return at length to it. And indeed if you accept the words of both, you will find nothing to complain about because of the distant place in which a man dies. Perhaps we must grant to the living that, induced by certain either honest or base feelings, they feel one place should be preferred to another. But certainly for the dead there can be no interest in where the best place to die would be. And if someone does not find it so, he should know that he is still wallowing in the errors of his wet nurse or of gossipy women. When the philosopher was asked where he would prefer to be buried, he answered that it really didn't matter, saying: "After all, the nether world is equidistant from any given point." We to whom Christ by ascending to heaven left the hope of ascending with him, maintain otherwise, saying: "What does it matter whether we lie in Italy or in France or in Spain or on the shores of the Red Sea? From everywhere there is an equal distance for ascending to heaven." We must travel that road though it be narrow and difficult. But we have a guide. If we follow him we cannot lose our way. If we consider that road what difference does it make where we rest this burdensome body? Unless, of course, there is reason for believing that on Judgment Day it would be more difficult to reassume a body buried in distant places. But that most pious and truly worthy mother of such a son [2] did not fear such things when at the moment of death, she made arrangements for her burial saying: "Place this body anywhere. Do not let it concern you." And when she was asked whether she feared a death far from her native land, note what she answered: "Nothing is far from God nor is there any reason for fearing that He would not know whence to resurrect me at the end of time." This is what that Catholic woman said. We, who are Catholic and profess to be men, shall we indulge in any more woman-ish feelings?

But I know what it is that survivors lament so bitterly at the death of friends. They mourn because clearly they will never see again those they loved with the highest affection. Let such credulity be for the pagans, and not even for all of them, but only for those who believe that souls die with bodies. Certainly Marcus Tullius, whose being a pagan is both well-known and lamentable, was not of this opinion believing that the soul was immortal and that famous spirits would find a heavenly dwelling place after this life. Other-wise he would never have introduced Marcus Cato the elder in his book which he calls *Cato the Elder* with the following words so full of hope: "Oh blessed day, when I shall depart for that assembly and meeting of divine souls, and when I shall depart from this tumultuous crowd! I shall be depart-ing not only to join those men about whom I have previously spoken, but to join my Cato, than whom no better man has ever been born, and no one is more distinguished in dutiful-ness." And later in that same book he says: "I am indeed carried away by a desire to see your predecessors whom I cherished and esteemed; nor will I meet only those whom I knew personally, but also those about whom I heard and read and about whom I myself wrote." These things and similar things which Cato says in Cicero's works testify suf-ficiently to what both believed. However, whatever they believed, whose hopes had been largely vain and deceptive, a sure hope is offered to us by One who cannot be deceived and does not know how to deceive. This hope is that at

2. Monica, mother of St. Augustine

length we too will go where we trust your brother went. Someone might say, "What shall I do in the meantime? I am torn by a desire, I am overcome by love, and I am tortured by an eagerness to see my brother again." What more should you do than those do who have been torn away by misfortune from very dear ones? They preserve their memory and keep the image of the absent ones deep in their minds; they love them, they speak of them, and they wish them a good journey. You must do the same and I am sure that you have. Keep your brother in that part of your heart which is free of oblivion; and love him dead as much as you did alive, or even much more strongly; compel him to return to you more often through pious and frequent commemoration; pray that his journey be favorable and that he return swiftly to his homeland after having overcome the ambushes of his perfidious enemy. This world was never his nor our homeland. We are but pilgrims here where we awaited him with useless prayers as he hastened to higher goals. This is a place of exile; he has set forth for his homeland. Let us pray that he arrives safely and without hardship. What could be of benefit to him, that let us do. To pray for the dead is a devout kind of service. But tears are for women and do not befit men unless perhaps they are very few and fully controlled. Otherwise they are harmful to those who weep, and they are of no help to those for whose love they are shed. If you still feel the torments of desire, remember that it cannot last long, for the life of man is brief, so that if the lost one cannot return to us, we must soon enough quickly set out for him. As Cicero says, "All short things must be borne even though they may be burdensome." Your brother has been freed from countless labors and has hopefully reached eternal rest or is about to do so. We abide in the battleground of a flowing century. For that reason, if anyone deplores the fact that he has been left behind, let him understand that he may deserve to hear the reproach of Cicero, "To be greatly distressed by one's own misfortunes bespeaks a person who is rather a self-lover than a friend." If indeed he laments because of another's departure, he should be fearful lest, as Cicero also said, "he be guilty of envy rather than friendship." I have said all these things not so much for your information as for your glory, because, as I said at the start, you do not stand in need of any external consolation, thanks to the eternal consoler. Furthermore, what needs could these short letters satisfy coming as they do from the wellsprings of a withered talent?

It is superfluous to add a number of examples of those who are remembered as having borne manfully the death of their dear ones. Nevertheless, that you may understand among whom I number you, and that even in such great company you may confidently hold to your original stance, I shall here enumerate the most noble examples from all of antiquity as my memory permits, for very few of my books have followed me into this solitude. Emilius Paulus, a most magnificent man and the highest honor of his age and of his homeland, from four sons of a most remarkable talent, gave two for adoption outside the family, depriving himself of them, and death seized the other two within the space of seven days. He himself, however, endured his bereavement with such lofty courage that he appeared in public. His misfortune seemed to offer such consolation that when the Roman people heard him speak he seemed to fear that his grief have an ill effect on someone else rather than upon himself. In my judgment he earned no smaller glory from this than from the splendid triumph that he scored at that very time, for he indeed appeared victor over Macedonia as a result of the triumph but over death and fate as a result of his loss. Pericles, an Athenian general, lost two sons in four days and not only failed to lament but showed no change in his regular behavior. The Cato the elder whom I mentioned previously is known by anyone having any acquaintance with history to have been extolled by all who knew him. What is more important, without any historical accounts his fame grew so great among all peoples that once anyone heard him it seemed that hardly anything could be added to the sum of wisdom. This is so true that he is venerated as much in the judgment of the ancients as in the agreement of the moderns as Cato the most wise. And yet among the many outstanding qualities of that man, we admire nothing more especially than the restraint with which he is said to have borne the death of a son, a fine person. Xenophon, upon hearing of the death of his son, did not stop performing the sacrifice that he had begun. Then he removed from his head the crown that he was wearing, laid it aside, and somewhat later began carefully asking questions about his son's death. Hearing that he had fallen in the heat of battle, he replaced the crown on his head in order to show that one should not grieve over the death of anyone unless he has died in a shameful and cowardly fashion which may be the reason why this very wise and indeed Socratic man had laid aside his crown at first hearing the announcement. Anaxagoras at the announcement of the death of his son said, "I hear nothing new or unexpected; for I, being mortal, knew that I had begotten a mortal." Indeed an answer worthy of the man! How many there are, even from the ranks of philosophers, who while pretending to grasp the concept of mortality, nevertheless could not have borne silently the blows of an unexpected death! Nothing unexpected was truly able to affect Anaxagoras for he constantly bore in mind those words we find in Seneca: "All things are mortal and mortal according to an uncertain law"; as well as what Seneca wrote in another place, that he knew all things were in store for him and therefore he would say to whatever befell: "I knew it." Many other examples of similar steadfastness have occurred to me, but the limits of a letter do not permit further inclusion. As I now approach the end, if it seems to anyone that perhaps your resignation is different from these highly commendable examples, inasmuch as you did not lose a son but a brother, I shall calmly allow him to believe as he pleases. Indeed because I myself have undergone the experience not of having suffered the loss of a son but of having felt the hurt of losing a brother, I am more competent to address myself to such a case. I am therefore making no affirmations nor am I trying to compare types of mourning. However I do know this, that often it is easier to replace a lost son than a brother. Farewell.

From the source of the Sorgue, 25 February.

*A letter of consolation on the misfortune of a dead and un-
buried friend and some thoughts concerning the rites of
burial.*

I grieve that you have lost a good friend but I am more
upset that you seem to have lost your sense of judgment. You
are consoling yourself neither in a manly nor in a philosophical fashion nor are you mourning one who deserves to be
mourned, for the departure of a courageous man must appear
enviable rather than sad. If I might summarize briefly the
sense of your letter, you do not seem to me so much to be
deploring your loss or the unexpected death of your friend
(something I could perhaps forgive popular prejudice), but
rather the kind of death and the injustice done to his unburied body when it was thrown into the Egyptian Sea. I
cannot accept these complaints more typical of old women
rather than of the rabble. Indeed I wonder whether against
this scrupulous concern about kinds of burial one could not
oppose that saying that being cast into a grave is a simple
matter? Have you forgotten the short verses of Virgil de-
claring the same thing, verses that have become so familiar
even to young children that they have become proverbial?
But if you consider death, you deceive yourself if you believe that it makes one happy or wretched. This verse of
another poet is sufficiently well-known: "One is not made
wretched by death." It is life that makes people wretched
or blessed, and he who has conducted it well until the flight
of his last breath stands in need of nothing more, for he is
happy, secure, and in port. What sort of person, therefore,
do you suppose succeeds in reaching this summit of happiness
regardless of whether the earth presses him down or the sea
twists him 'round or flames consume him? But since I understand you are particularly disturbed about his burial and
are distressed about this more than any other problem, how
much happier do you believe is one who is plunged into this
earth than another who may be drowned by waves? I believe that you feel as you do because of the horror created
in a poem of Virgil where he said, "The waves will bear

you, and the hungry fish will lick your wounds." But what if raging dogs tore his wounds, or if a pack of famished wolves tore to pieces his members after having dug up the grave? I believe you will answer, "These too would be unfortunate." Thus the most fortunate of all will be those who enjoy the unshaken, undisturbed quiet of the grave. There is nothing more childish than this idea, for when you have made provisions for all contingencies, those organs that were spared destruction by beasts you cannot deny to the hostile worms. So now please note that what you feared from perhaps the most beautiful of animals will happen necessarily from the foulest of animals. In truth the first kind are not to be feared so much since they are a daily occurrence. You see, therefore (and here I shall repeat something which I have said often and not myself only, having shared the opinion with the most illustrious philosophers), that whatever we suffer in this life that is burdensome is not so much a natural thing but the result of feebleness of our mind, or, to use the words of the philosophers, the result of the perversity of opinions. We fear new things, and take lightly customary things. Why should this be except that in the one case the unsuspecting mind is upset by the unexpected appearance of things, and in the other a shield is provided by repeated meditation or reasoning, a shield which opposes all misfortunes. Note the custom of sailors which allows that the bodies of their mates be buried at sea without concern. I cannot avoid mentioning one illustrious example out of many. Lamba Doria, a very rough and strong man, is said to have been the leader of the Genoese in that naval battle in which they first battled the Venetians and which is the most memorable ever fought in the days of our forefathers. Having sighted the enemy fleet he was aware that the hour of battle would be at hand, and although his forces were smaller, when the time came he exhorted his men with magnificent brevity, and joined battle with the enemy. When in that encounter his only son, a most handsome young man, who was stationed on the prow of the ship was the very first to be struck by an arrow and loudly mourning bystanders had encircled the fallen youth, the father rushed forth and said, "This is not the time for mourning but for fighting." Having turned subsequently to his son, he perceived no life remaining in him and said, "Dear son, never would you have enjoyed a more beautiful burial had you died in your homeland." Having said this, and though armed, he picked him up still armed and warm, and threw him into the deep. In my opinion, at least, he was most fortunate in that very calamity since he was capable of sustaining such a misfortune so manfully. And in truth that act as well as his words so enkindled the spirits of the fleet with courage that they won an outstanding victory that day. Nor was he held less compassionate than if falling upon the body and mourning effeminately he had become incapable of action, especially in that state of affairs when the country was in such a crisis. You would tear your cheeks with your nails seeing something similar happen to your dear ones; not so much because of the sorrow of death but because of the shameful burial. Sailors, like all other men, also grieve at the loss of friends, but they bear it bravely when they are buried at sea; and this happens because they have learned to endure such things over many years. Why then do I not become indignant with Cicero because custom is stronger than reason? Could an uncultivated sailor have borne such things without tears because he had become accustomed to them while you, a learned man trained in the fine arts and supported by so great a number of examples, could not do so though relying on reason?

It would appear appropriate to observe how numerous in history are the rites used by men in conducting burial services and how thoroughly opposed to our customs they have been. Among these, certain ones used to keep the body in the home after having preserved it with the greatest care. In others, people were accustomed to cast the bodies to their dogs for the sole reason that, having bought them and reared them for a long time, according to the means of each family, they considered the stomach of a well-bred dog the best kind of burial. We also read of certain others indeed who ate the bodies themselves. Artemisia, Queen of Caria, perhaps the most famous example of conjugal love, considered nothing more appropriate for her beloved husband than upon his death to bury him in a live grave. Having cremated him and having saved his ashes with great care, she carefully sprinkled them on her drink, thereby providing the beloved with the hospitality of her own body. There is little reason for questioning whether she acted properly. What is important is that you understand that all things that distress do so not because of themselves but because of human judgment by which they are produced and reared, and that custom counts very much in the process. The Queen fed upon the man she loved. If you were to see any of our ladies doing the same, you would be horrified and would turn your eyes from the frightening spectacle. But the same done by custom would not be called inhuman or an example of outstanding love but an ordinary act of respect. Nor is it necessary to seek only foreign examples. It was a custom of our ancestors in this very Italy to burn the dead, a custom to which the accounts of history testify as well as the discoveries that have occurred up to our own day of urns buried underground containing human ashes. Nor indeed is that a very old custom. Previously, as now, everyone was buried, until cremation was devised as a kind of remedy against the implacable hatred of the civil wars which raged even in the burial places. In that manner one was spared enemy insult through the power of fire. Thus the Scipios as statesmen who knew that they were truly valued by the state lie buried all together, nor was there anyone of the Cornelian line ever burned prior to the dictatorship of Lucius Sulla. He was the very first who, against the custom of his family and aware that he was widely hated, wished his body to be cremated fearing, as it is reported, that the followers of Marius would venture to do against him what he had done against Marius. The example had served its purpose, and others followed it who had no reason at all for doing so. Subsequently the custom of cremating prevailed and the practice began to assume authority. Eventually what had started as a form of remedy became honorable and it became a serious shame not to abide by the custom of cremating. Hence was praised the patriotism of the man who gathered small pieces of wood on the shore of the Nile in order voluntarily to cremate the body of the great Pompey who had been shamefully beheaded. From this action he acquired a great reputation, for who would know anything about Codrus except that he had burned the body of Pompey? That other Codrus from Athens is, of course, known for another kind of patriotism and a peculiar death. To burn the dead today is considered an act of extreme injustice or vengeance. Whence comes this variety in one and the same people? Of course with the passage of time and the changing of customs we find changes in the opinions of men. Nor am I going to examine again what I have heard great men sometimes discuss, namely, which type of burial is more noble. There is the custom which I recall being our ancestors' and which is known to be practiced by many people even now, but with an added law that restricts burial within the city to only a few who were entirely exempt because of their unusual excellence which absolved them from such laws, and these Cicero recalls in the third book of *Laws*. Then there is this custom of ours which taken up from our ancestors continued as a custom of the Christian religion. To compare these two is not what I wish to do at this time. I would rather complete what I started to say, that many things seem horrible to us because through long habit we conceive many errors which are of no concern to others having different customs. If, indeed, casting aside all else, you ask me, as is appropriate to your profession, for the truth of things not according to the rumors of the rabble but according to careful reasoning, you will find my opinion to be that the wise man turns away from error and that the swarms of fools are either to be pitied or to be laughed at. Farewell.

Fam. II, 3.

To Severo Apenninicola,[1] a consolatory letter on his exile.

Although I believe that "exile" comes from *exilio* or, as Servius prefers, from the idea of one who goes *extra solum*, I believe that it is really not an exile unless it happens unwillingly. Kings often exile themselves from their kingdom, doing so especially at the time when the boundaries of a state must either be preserved or defended, or when they devote themselves to the propagation of their glory. No one would ever dare call them exiles unless it were someone whose very reason had been exiled, since indeed they were never more worthy of being called kings. Therefore it is necessary that force and pain of some kind intervene in order to have a real exile. If you accept this, you will then understand that whether you are an exile or a traveler resides in you. If you depart sad and dejected you will know without doubt that you are an exile; but if indeed not forgetful at all of your own dignity nor under constraint, but willingly and with the same appearance and state of mind that you had at home, you obeyed the order to depart, then you are a traveler and not an exile. For you will find in various kinds of things to be feared that no one is wretched except one who makes himself wretched. Thus what makes a poor man is not the scarcity of belongings but cupidity. Similarly in death, which is very similar to exile, it is not so much the harshness of the thing itself as the anxiety and distortion of opinion that is painful. When these are removed you will see many men dying not only bravely but even joyfully and happily. Whence it is certainly understood that the evil of death is not compulsory but willed and is not located in the thing itself but completely in the weak thinking of mortals. Unless this were so, there would never be so great a difference of opinion regarding such a danger. I see the same reasoning applied to exile as I see in all other things. What overcomes us is not in the thing but in us. This is the power of judgment which once deflected slightly from truth soon wallows in countless errors so that it has a very difficult time returning to the truth and, unless greatly assisted, is incapable of

1. An as yet unidentified correspondent of Petrarch.

raising itself to a consideration of the majesty of its own origin. So then, I shall return to the beginning and ask: what is exile? Is it the very nature of the situation, the absence of a dear one, the indignation or rather the impatient desire of a languishing mind that is irritating? But if you firmly believe that whoever is absent from his native land is without question an exile, where are those who are not exiles? For what man, unless he were lazy and soft, has not departed from his home and his native land several times either because he was desirous of seeing new things, or of learning, or of enlightening his mind, or was concerned about his health, or was desirous of increasing his wealth, or because of the demands of wars, or at the command of his state, of his master, of his parents? Why then are such travelers not all wretched except that they resist, and do not allow themselves to be miserable? They too were without their spouses, their children, their kin, their parents, the concourse of friends, and the sight of their beloved city. Nevertheless for all of these the desire was mitigated by moderation and they found some kind of consolation for their absence.

"But their hope of returning was a great help; they would never have gone so bravely had they not believed that they would return to their native land." So be it. But in your case, who took away this hope? Especially since because of its very nature it cannot be taken from one unwillingly? A good man, despoiled of all his goods at the will of a tyrant, can be sent to prison, beheaded, mangled, slain, and remain unburied. While so many threats and blows of fortune may compel us to do many things, no one compels us to despair. We have seen men sent into exile who, before they had arrived at their destination, were called back to the homeland because of the unbearable grief of the citizens. Others, after a long time, returned with so much honor and regrets of the citizens that to me they appear fortunate for having endured such an exile. Others suddenly advanced from extreme poverty to great riches; still others attained thrones after being released from jail, and not a few managed to save their neck from the sharp blade and seemed destined for extraordinary prosperity. No one was committed to such a horrible place that he was not allowed to raise his eyes; no one viewed the loss of his belongings as so deplorable that he was unable to hope for better things. Rome recalled Cicero from exile; she could scarcely be without the presence of such an outstanding citizen for more than a few days. She recalled Metellus also who, having received the most prized letters from the senate of the Roman people while at a theater in Tralles, showing no sign of delight, assumed the same expression with which he had departed from the walls of the city; a man neither too crushed at his departure nor haughty in his return. He yielded to the madness of his homeland in his departure; he fulfilled her desire with his return; modest in the first instant, solemn in the second; but in both truly memorable. Rome tempted Rutilius with a similar recall but he remained more unyielding and considered his homeland unworthy of his return. Marcellus suffered a similar fate, but one which was far different. When he was called back by Caesar, as he returned amidst the joy of all good men, he fell into the hands of the enemy with the result that instead of the pleasant expectations of the public there was deep mourning. I believe that death was no more difficult for him than his exile, for there is only one virtue that arms and teaches men's hearts to bear misfortunes. And indeed such was his spirit during his exile that he offered clear proof of how he would have behaved in the face of death. About this I shall not withhold what Brutus says about Cicero in the book *On Virtue*, namely that he had personally seen him as an exile in Mytilene with such an unbroken spirit and so desirous of good studies, and indeed so happy and blessed, that he did not appear to him so much an exile, although he had been away a long time, as he himself felt himself to be an exile when he departed from him. He also adds that Gaius Julius Caesar, who had been the author of his exile and later of his return, while passing through those places, was so moved by shame over the exile of such a great man that he took care to bypass the city where he was located. Oh glorious exile, whose banishment one of the most powerful citizens of Rome esteemed, and over which the other felt shame! Thus was Caesar frightening to the world and Brutus to Caesar; but both felt respect for the exiled Marcellus. Who would not wish such an exile, indeed who would call it an exile when it is envied by the very fathers of one's country? I have called to mind those whom a repentant citizenry called back; but how many were recalled by fortune! No one called Camillus back to Rome: his way back was prepared by fate and the overthrow of the city and (who would believe it?) by the mad fury of the Transalpine people that spread throughout Italy. As a result he became the one man to be remembered by all exiles as well as an outstanding example of good faith and of an esteemed patriotism toward an ungrateful homeland. To turn finally to examples from our own day, how long did Matteo Visconti remain alone and a fugitive, lacking all things, bewailed by his loved ones, and ridiculed by his enemy after having been expelled from Milan, his native land, by the troops of his powerful enemy! They say that one day while he was wandering on the banks of Lake Garda in deep thought, he came across a messenger of his haughty enemy who asked him, at the request of his master, what he was doing there unattended. His only answer was that he was spreading a net. This answer, perhaps at that time considered contemptuous, soon made clear what mystery it contained. That old man, alone and inactive, caught in the nets of his foresight all his opponents as if they were so many fish deceived by the bait of an empty hope. At still another time when the messenger had returned to him again and had jokingly inquired by what roads or when he would return to his homeland, he answered with a calm look: "Now you go and tell your master that I shall return by the same roads by which I left, but not before his misdeeds begin to outweigh mine." The prediction did not prove wrong since not much later when the misdeeds of the enemy had increased to vast proportions, nourished as they were by an unaccustomed prosperity, he entered Milan as a victor after the enemy had been cast out; and in that city, as you have seen, his grandchildren and sons have ruled down to our day.

I do not want what I have been saying to appear either in your eyes or in the eyes of any good man as though I am in favor of an armed coup against one's native land regardless of how bad it may be (I consider it preferable to die a pauper in exile than to rule unwilling citizens once freedom has been lost), but I wanted simply to show in all the new examples that hope cannot be forcibly taken from exiles. If the recollection of brave men helps minds besieged with difficulties to achieve resignation, here is another outstanding and recent example. Stefano Colonna, a truly outstanding military man, was just as admirable and outstanding in his exile as he was famous in good fortune. His condition was far different from that of other exiles. To certain men it is permitted to live safely anywhere they please outside of the homeland; others when they have left their native land are able to enjoy an even greater freedom. Others are bound by stricter rules that restrict them to a particular place, where, however, they endure no harsh treatment as long as they remain there. But to this particular man his native land was forbidden and no place in the world was safe. There was no port nor refuge anywhere in his stormy existence. And he faced an enemy who was as persistent as he was powerful, Boniface VIII, the Roman Pontiff, who refused to be influenced by humility or flattery; in short the type whom nothing overcomes except death. His rage was inhuman as he sought the head of the undeserving exile in every possible way, with promises, threats, influence, deceit, authority, and money. He promised huge rewards to his persecutors and decreed punishments for supporters inasmuch as Stefano, crossing over the various bodies of water that separated with enormous distance the islands of Sicily and of Britain, often traveled alone around the frontiers of France, in great need of many things, but very strong of mind. Thus when by chance he fell into the hands of explorers near Arles and was asked who he was, he gave his name, which he could have disguised, to the group, and with unshaken voice declared himself a Roman citizen. Good God, how much dignity must have shone in his face to keep the hateful and armed bands of his questioners from angry reprisals! All kings had been urged by public edict not to offer him hospitality. When because of the edict he was ordered to leave Sicily he obeyed with the same spirit he had displayed as an exile in that province, so that it appeared as though a king were departing. Thus did he treat that king and others during the entire period of his persecution, as if indeed he were king himself. With a steadfast courage which feared no hostilities, and standing above the fluctuations of fortune, he held firm so that that poetic saying seemed to apply perfectly to him: "Behold ye the kings fearlessly, without a supplicating countenance." How often was his death announced in Rome and throughout Italy, how often was the reputation of the Colonnas declared undone and how often was it alleged that the distinguished family had collapsed with that man! Nowhere did any hope remain for him, except as it was located in his heart. Moreover, never did he depart from anywhere without bravely spending his days and nights thinking up fearless plans and being engaged in all kinds of toil. Furthermore in the midst of his search for a solution, he sometimes participated in the battles of friends (without either side recognizing him) and by general agreement victory was achieved by the mere presence of this single man. These things are certainly well-known but I believe are most familiar to you yourself and to me. Who therefore would call this exile wretched who was attended by such a retinue of virtues and who after a ten-year trial was able to return to his former state through real magnanimity rather than by chance?

But what is the purpose of collecting so many examples? So that no one, stunned by present misfortune, would be excessively preoccupied with conjecture of things to come, thereby adding to a moderately serious evil, exile, the most serious of all evils, despair. Especially since many things may bring an end to exile: an active virtue, such as the one which brought Stefano himself back to his homeland; often also the changed customs of peoples; the disappearance of feuds; a long lapse of time, something which tames even wild minds; the compassion for a victim of circumstances; the very admiration for silent courage; the services rendered to fellow citizens; the needs of the public or a stroke of good fortune. Furthermore because one has been driven out let him not reject the honor of retaining his virtues, remembering to bring this most precious of possessions into exile since he is not allowed to retain his lesser ones. Nor is it unusual in case of fire to carry off the jewelry and the gold, and to leave behind our home and all the useless or heavy belongings. But if men could be persuaded that gold must be reckoned among precious things, what can they be made to think about courage and virtue? "Silver is cheaper than gold, gold is cheaper than virtue." But anyhow, since we are not permitted always to bring silver and gold into exile, we are permitted to bring the virtues and the riches of the mind wherever we may go. We saw this done by those whom I proposed as examples for you so that you might long passionately to imitate them and so that you might not despair that what had been done so often could not be done again. I say that it is permitted to take your virtue into exile or into prison or even unto death. I said "it is permitted," but indeed it is useful, necessary, and proper. In truth the real exiles are those who depart leaving this quality behind, truly helpless, unfortunate and wretched. Indeed it is not sufficient to take with you as much of this as you may possess; somewhat more is necessary. Note how carefully he who sets forth for foreign lands prepares his provisions; he wishes that they were more the further he travels. Your splendid provisions for this journey will consist of your virtues. By having an abundance of these you will not be poor even if you lack food for the body. Therefore gather these, let these support you everywhere. I know that you have made a remarkable collection of many virtues, which is neither an inconvenient or difficult, but instead a light and pleasant, burden. I realize that your preparation requires much labor; however, once the provisions are ready, they are carried around without toil. You sought them since your youth, and you collected them in your youth, and you collected them in your home. Do not lose them now that you are older and a wanderer. Carry with you as much as you had or more, depending on what need presents itself, although I do know that though you may not want them they will come to you automatically. Indeed these provisions are never consumed by use, but rather increase, for virtue begets further virtues which increase in the midst of difficulties until they have led their possessor to the highest summit of happiness. I shall say nothing about the consolations of your exile, but they ought not to be scorned. If you had been ordered to retire to an inhospitable side of the world in the ice and eternal night of Scythia or under the burning sun, or had been sent somewhat closer but outside of Italy, you would have good cause for complaining about your ill fortune. Instead, consider how unjustified your complaints are! You have been ordered to go to Florence to remain there until the people call you back. Do you not see how much gratitude you owe to the officials who have roused you still half asleep from excessive leisure, and have led you away still clinging to your maternal apron strings out of long force of habit? And finally haven't they decided to send you out of a homeland which, if I may dare say so, is very inferior to a very flourishing city? All this, as I said, I am going to leave out since we are all naturally disposed to feel that the uncultivated and deserted lands where we were born and educated can be considered superior to all others. If that misconception would cease for a while, you would surely pardon fortune and indeed seek forgiveness because you were not previously aware of her kindness. Consider also that you took with you two sons of outstanding character, one a young man and the other really a child, with a fortunate difference in age so that you could share the burdens of your cares with the one and you could forget them with the other; you could find help in the one and consolation for your wandering in the other. These boys made your homeland delightful and you have them with you. What else do you desire? Do you expect your most virtuous wife or your wonderful parents or the flattering of your daughter to return again? It was not exile that took them away from you but death which you overcame so often despite its abuses and despite its overcoming some of your dearest possessions. Therefore, you should not now be overcome by exile, because exile cannot take away from you all the comforts of your former life and especially your boys, remnants of so many happy moments. But as I said, I shall pass over such consolations and all those things that are subject to the blows of fortune for I know that what can take away one's fatherland has power to take away one's children. I shall instead return to the more stable assistance of the virtues which neither the decrees of your citizens nor the power of tyrants nor the violence of plunderers nor nocturnal thefts can snatch away from you. If you did bring these along with you, no one could call you an exile without lying. If however you left them behind, each day will bring something new that you can bewail, every new place will not only be annoying but hostile, and would be not a place of exile for you but a prison. Farewell.

To the same Severo, on the same subject.

I see that you have lost all hope. Whether you suffer right-fully I have already questioned in my preceding letter. I regret that it afforded you no remedy nor am I certain whether the blame lies with the doctor or with the patient, who must, if he wishes to regain his health, confidently place his trust in the advice of doctors and be most obedient to their precepts. What I tried to do in my letter was to help you save some hope after you had lost your fatherland, since hope has so much power that it does not feel any present troubles and in its promise of happier things projects one's thinking into the future. So what was there that kept you from hoping? Was it the harshness of your homeland because it sent you away? What cruelty? To be perfectly honest about it, aside from exile, what was taken from you or imposed upon you about which you can complain? Were examples of outstanding men lacking? But I paraded many before your eyes, and I would cite more except that they seem to be in vain even though from them you could learn that staunch hope begets happy conse-quences. Or do you fear that your homeland will be forever angry because it has withheld a little of its usual kindness? But don't you know that fathers have been kinder to those chil-dren who had treated them badly; and that no one has burned with greater love than the one who misbehaved toward a truly loyal spouse? Or is your fear the greater because of the edict of your homeland which forbids under threat of punishment any public statement about the recall of exiles? But you must know how the wishes of the people are as loud and varied at the outset as they are uncertain and flexible with the passage of time. But there is a certain something in the minds of mor-tals that I discern only vaguely and cannot put into words: a sad and destructive perversity, which shuts ears blocked against the salutary voices of advisers, and causes them constantly to do things that make them more miserable and to avoid any-thing that might lessen their grief. There is nothing that can be imagined that I would call more foolish. Since I now find you disposed to accept the hopelessness of your return with what I might call a kind of pleasure, I shall cease trying to treat a wound which is beyond medical treatment. However, what prevents me from following the practice of those who, having lost one or another limb, in order to prevent the infection from extending through the rest of the body, annoint the surrounding areas of the wound? In imitation I too can go around the boundaries of your wound and quickly prevent with appropriate ointments the grief from extending to the whole mind. But do not be upset, for I shall not touch any sensitive spot with my fingers. I am about to say nothing against your present opinion. Rather, in order to avoid having you turn against your possessions because of one misfortune, or see the tranquillity of your whole life perish, I shall make every effort, provided you are in accord, not to lose any chance of restoring some hope to you. You imagine then that you are living in exile and must die in exile. I believe you now have what you want; that is, my admission that there is no hope of your returning to your homeland. In order to temper your illness even more, I shall concede even more to you. Not only will you die in this exile, but "separated by a whole world you must die far from your homeland and that a barbarous soil will weigh upon you." I have conceded more to your grief than you did, for while you conceded no possibility of happiness, I have proposed things that are even more gloomy. Nor do I really see anything so wretched in this that it could compel a strong man to shed tears. Certainly, if I thought you were burning with the fire of a mod love or of ambition, which seem to blaze more intensely far from one's homeland, or if too few companions followed you when you left, I would have to gather many arguments to soothe either such a flattering possibility or the inconstant evil of ambition, or to offer you comfort in your poverty. Although such arguments ought to have been easy for me to put in words and for you to accept, it is not easy to articulate the remedies for the disease under these limiting conditions. What a sorrowful and mournful thing love is! What wretchedness ambitions leads to, under what a colorful and deceiving light it hides itself, and how little it delivers of what it promises! How poverty may be tolerated with greatness of mind cannot be briefly explained by anyone. But for the present, since the seriousness of your character has not fanned the flame of love, and even if you had felt it once, your age has now quenched it, and since the manner in which you fled honors throughout your life does not allow any suspicion for ambition, and since the devotion of your homeland has helped you avoid poverty, the great labor needed for providing additional consolation is diminished for me. Your homeland afflicted you with no other discomfort than to be without her embraces. All your possessions are either yours or are with you or are under your control. I speak not only of those which could not be snatched from you, such as your modest magnanimity and your other virtues, which either that wise man, Bias, according to Cicero, Valerius and others, or as Seneca would have it, Stilbon, bragged about carrying with him when he fled from his burning fatherland. I refer also to your possessions which, to use a popular expression, you received from the hands of fortune. You departed master of your ancient patrimony as a wealthy exile and as the citizen you had been at home. And I wonder whether you might not be more wealthy than you were because you can be frugal with the riches that now remain. I must add that the greater part of men suppose that they cannot fall before all their possessions have been destroyed. You in truth did not fall but were driven out. Therefore, I believe, you are now feeling in a direct and upright fashion the wavering of fortune; and you understand on what shaky ground you stand when you appear to be great. Furthermore you do not doubt that the ill fortune that drove you out can be overthrown. And so, unlike the great majority of others, you can live on as a wealthy and cautious exile and be comforted by two great and good things against this single and indeed petty evil, if indeed in this life anything can be called good except virtue, or evil except insofar as it is the opposite of virtue. So go forth secure. Your homeland will not call you back, fortune will not return you. Instead the exile that you lament so much and the obstinate injustice involved will make your burden light. Misfortune made many men great, it singled out many others. On the contrary, adversity did not make men wretched but instead it exposed such men and did not allow them to be concealed for very long. Why do you turn pale as if fortune has a great hold on you? It does not play the part of the judge but instead of the witness. Whatever you may be is in your power. It is not in its power to decide what image it would project of you. It can do some of it through talk but it cannot lie. But who is there, unless he be guilty, who fears a witness who speaks only the truth? Fortune does not compel you into cowardice but it does count your steps, exercise your patience, suspect or disdain the cowardice of your heart, and then makes public whatever it finds out about you. Take courage and disperse the shadows of popular error and don't pay heed to the words of gossipy women. You will never be happy nor safe if you surrender yourself to the whim of the people. Whatever the great majority of men admire or fear is ridiculous; whatever they proclaim is false. Entrust yourself rather to the advice of the few. Those things among which one includes exile are not as terrible as they seem. If prolonged reading did not help, perhaps experience will assist you. Do not always look down. Sometimes raise your eyes; truth will be immediately manifest, and you will confess that exile is nothing worse than that a good man must live some distance from his homeland. And in truth he who considers the entire world his homeland cannot live outside it. For what does it matter how different are the lands in which one stops? He may see other valleys and lakes and rivers, but heaven is only one. That is where he projects himself; there is where from all parts of the world he raises his heart and transmits his thoughts believing that he is under a single roof and is crossing from room to room. You also, unless you disappoint the high hopes that I and many others have had for you, would not want to be restricted to a single corner of this huge edifice. In this manner you may call whatever land you walk upon and whatever heavens you see above and wherever you may breathe the sweet air, your fatherland. Therefore, the condition of your exile should not only be easy but pleasant. There are two things which chiefly induce the will of men to kindness: virtue, than which, as Cicero says, nothing is more lovable, and misfortune which is also inflicted on undeserving men. The first of these causes us to love and to admire outstanding men; the second to commiserate with the unfortunate. The first seems to be present in you at this time, the second seems to be approaching. All will judge you a strong man and will call you an exile. And surely if we believe Tullius, among all the virtues, the most brilliant is fortitude. So once again among the tribulations of man exile is not listed last. Unless I am deceived it would be desirable not to have the wrath of your fellow citizens slacken. It is also to be hoped that you do not accidentally lose the name of exile since you can see that in it there is nothing wretched and a great deal that is favorable to your fame. You say, "but my heart dreads toil and dishonor." First of all, I deny that either of these are at stake since I know that the event earned great praise for you since it resulted from your magnanimous opposition to the arrogance of tyrants. Furthermore, in it you found rest and the cessation of your labors as you had always desired. What is more, whoever fears dishonor which is produced by virtue is a friend of fame and not of virtue. In truth whoever flees toil ceases to desire glory to which, unless I am deceived, a difficult but well-known and delightful path leads. As I said, enormous fame awaits you alone through special privilege and without obstacles except perhaps as you may fashion them yourself. What I fear is that you behold the wound that has been inflicted upon you with the eyes of others rather than with your own, and that you measure your situation with another's judgment. This is such a daily curse that at the clamor of others large numbers of men stagger and fall much sooner than they have to, although that man has also fallen whom thousands of men are constantly advising with the worst opinions. But as you may call him very feeble who is cast down by a light breeze, you must consider truly insane one whom you may see judging his own affairs by the rumors of others and especialy of ignorant people. The more numerous these are, the more must the contagious disease which usurps the hearts of so many men be carefully avoided. If you wish to listen to others there is no lack of those who decry your situation with endless complaints and who lament your misfortune although you are safe and sound, and who half-dead sit around the bier of the living. You will hear the mournful voices, and you will see perhaps the tears which are either simulated or almost mad. You will then begin to become wretched because you will become accustomed to listening to these miserable voices. There is almost nothing which a continuous concourse with others cannot accomplish in the hearts of men. But if you choose to consult yourself and to speak with yourself rather than with others, I would never stop expecting great things from you and would call you most happy since you serve as your own judge, and I would consider you worthy of envy rather than of pity. But if you are inclined rather to believe others, then why do you not believe me as I bring to your attention truer and more pleasing things? Believe me, you were never overthrown nor will you be unless you wish it; you will suffer no dishonor, but you have a choice, as you stand on the threshold of eternal glory; you will either progress gloriously or you will retrogress ingloriously. There awaits you not toil but rest; not exile but liberty. What you once sought as it fled from you with astonishing speed you should now embrace as it hastens to meet you spontaneously. "And what was your great desire for seeing Rome? Liberty, which, though late, nevertheless looked upon me despite my indolence." This speaker in pastoral discourse boasts of having left his homeland in order to find liberty. You, a philosopher, complain. You have lived for others a long time. Begin right now to live for yourself. No one will maintain that you hastened too fast since you started off no sooner than that shepherd of Virgil whose "beard fell whiter while shaving." You have always condoned the actions of your fellow citizens since your earliest years. They blushed over your priceless largesse and they decreed that you retain at least the remaining years of a long life. Recognize the spirit of your city and consider your generosity against hers which was so great that despite its real need it permitted you to slip through its hands. Enjoy happily the immunity which is now granted to you and think of the walls of your native land as the unquiet prison of your freedom. You escaped and what is more it happened at the request of your guards who ordered you to go. It would be madness to undertake to return. You should rather turn to those studies to which you had dedicated your youth and which would have made your advanced years certainly tranquil except that your homeland which you now desire had forbidden them. However, they will certainly make your old age peaceful and venerable if it remains a despiser not only of your exile but of all casual things. I speak of liberal studies and especially of that part of philosophy which is the teacher of life. You had never removed these entirely from your mind although for a little while involvement in civic matters kept you from them. Now devote yourself to them completely since nothing prevents it, and give yourself over to the better auspices of a new life by keeping your mind busy with such activities. Read again the history of antiquity. There you will find how many imitators there were of Roman leaders and indeed of illustrious men who wished either to be sent away from their homeland as soon as possible or to be called back after a great amount of time had passed. Why was this so, I ask, if not because it was pleasant to miss the sweetness of the native soil while finding elsewhere greater occasions for the exercise of virtue? Consuls were accustomed to cast lots for provinces after festive celebrations, and the more noble ones would prefer that province in which they saw the greatest dangers, not because they chose the dangers and difficulties for themselves (unless they were mad) but because the splendor of virtue seemed most likely to be present there. Therefore either this exile of yours is a trifling matter and your complaints are out of place among the flattering voices; or it is difficult and burdensome (this the multitude asserts, but I disagree). But if any of the old character has remained in any one man, exile cannot be so bad and his complaints cannot be worthy ones if he laments over something that is desired by others. This place which the magistrates ordained as your place of exile is your province. Not everyone can cross over into Africa with a huge army and having expelled Hannibal from Italy attack beleaguered Carthage. Not everyone can go from victory to victory, at times attacking rebellious Spain and at times freeing the seas beset by pirates, or penerate Armenio or Judea and the kingdoms of all of the Orient. It is not given to everyone, following the slaughter of Numidian troops and the extension of the empire, to transport arms from the South to the North and in a very short time immerse a sword dyed with Libyan blood into the blood of Teutonic and Cimbrian peoples or after thoroughly subduing the Gauls and bringing their leaders to a violent acknowledgment of Roman virtue, pass beyond the borders of the Rhine on the one side and of the ocean on the other and then trample upon Germany and Britain in a single attack. Nor can everyone enjoy the experience of leading captive kings before his chariot. These things are reserved for the Scipios, the Pompeys, the Marii, the Caesars and the Aemilii. Such battles with distant enemies were reserved for men such as these and their likes. Your battle must be with exile whose attack you not only bear but repel and destroy if you wish to achieve whatever is necessary and if you can persuade yourself that the only protection against adversity is patience, and if you will impress deeply in your heart that very wholesome utterance of Cleanthe translated by Annaeus Seneca into Latin poetry: "the fates lead willing men and drag along unwilling ones." Farewell.

To the devout Giovanni Colonna,[1] *that minds suffer greatly from their association with the body.*

I received most eagerly your letter which was written during your journey, for I desired even more than usual to hear that things were well with you. For those companions of love, zeal and fear grow with absence. I was distressed and my heart was restless because I had learned that you were disturbed when you departed, and also because I was seeing those who had caused your disturbance, gratified in achieving their abominable desire, parading triumphantly before me the fact that they had you exiled, depriving me of your presence and of your prudent, delightful company. And my visions and dreams had also terrified me as they filled my sleepy mind in extraordinary and troublesome ways. I certainly know that one must not be afraid of questioning dreams, but this is how it is. I have set out on this road, the journey of our life leading to death, on which one must suffer heat and cold, hunger and thirst, and sleep restlessly agitated by threats and ambiguities of dreams. In short, one must suffer many things until that day awaited by the devout and feared by the wicked when this mortal garment and the fetters of this gloomy dwelling are cast off from those minds striving for heaven. Meanwhile I confess that since the road is not long, whatever the philosophers discuss and whatever others feel within themselves about the stilling or acceptance of the blows of passion, I myself have been thus far strongly subject to them. A law was imposed on me together with my body when I was born, that from its association with me I must suffer many things which I would not suffer otherwise. The poet, aware of the secrets of nature, when he ascribed to human souls a certain burning force which he called of heavenly origin, added the following by way of exception: "Insofar as mortal bodies don't slow them down and earthly organs and mortal members do not weaken them. This is why

1. Not to be confused with Cardinal Giovanni Colonna who was a nephew of this Giovanni.

they fear and desire and suffer and rejoice but cannot recognize the heavens since they are enclosed in the darkness of a blind prison."

I was wondering, therefore, why no news of you had reached me since your departure when unexpectedly your letter was delivered to me. I recognized the seal and so I read without serious care. However, because the messenger was in an extraordinarry hurry and the affair would seem to need many words for a proper answer, I delayed my response until the next day. Now I perceive that my reply must be in three parts because your various complaints fall into three divisions. One, however, which could be put briefly and which kept me from postponing my resolution was that I, being entangled in the web of my sins, have not yet been able to take refuge in a port, but am being cast about by that same storm in which you left me still battered by the waves. In vain will I try to hoist my sail as I hold on firmly, hoping that a propitious wind will rise up from the West. I am pleased only at your news and am grateful to God because I see that you have at least avoided a great number of labors, since your little ship, emerging from the same perils, "either has reached port or is heading for shore with full sail." Consequently, I can more freely cope with my problems since the desire for succeeding drives me on and I am half free of a double anxiety. Farewell.

To the same correspondent, that absence is not harmful to friendship.

I was hoping to hear some fine news from you, since your wisdom seemed to me long ago to have overcome the complaints that the stupid and ungrateful multiude loves to mouth loudly. I can see that I was indeed really wrong and I wish I could think that the complaints in your letter were someone else's; instead the writing gave evidence that they were written by your own fingers. In them you bemoan a slight matter with a great number of words more like a woman's than a man's. The gist of your lamentation is that you have suffered harshly and inconsolably because you can no longer enjoy our wonderful presence, either mine or that of our friends. I do not doubt that you have been shaken and disturbed by your sudden departure, for I know the mildness of your mind and the pleasantness of your customs which would never permit any form of sternness or a harsh turn of mind. This is why I do not understand your excessive sorrow. Countless causes might separate friends, but none separates true friendship. When this is present no friend can truly be absent. The more the distance between places separates us from the conversations of friends, by that much do we overcome the woe of absence through continuous recollection. If the power of such recollections were so great that even after death we can honor our dead friends as though they were alive, a lesson we learn from that wisest of all Romans and one of the most famous in matters of friendship, Lelius, following the death of the young Africanus; would it not be just as great if by similarly overcoming absence we can view the faces of friends located in distant places as though they were present? The poet writes "Faces and words cling fixedly in the heart." And in another place he says, "The absent see and hear those absent." Can therefore mad and obscene love accomplish what godly and moderate love cannot? It should indeed be able to do much more, for the same poet says: "First the swift stag will feed in the heavens, and straits will abandon defenseless fish upon the shores; and first, having wandered through the territories of both, the Parthian exile shall drink from the Saône or the German from the Tigris, before his face will slip from our heart." Note the following words that even Lelius, speaking about his very close friend, used: "I loved the virtue of that man which has not been destroyed." Why do you not say: "I love his virtue or their virtue, which is neinther absent nor distant but is always present before my eyes, and will always be honored by me?"

"But it is most pleasant to have friends present and to regard their faces and their eyes, to speak to them, to hear personally their answering words." And since it is helpful in this matter to refer to the testimony of poets, it is with a certain delight of the mind that we read that Anchises, happy at the meeting with his son, said with his palms extended heavenward and with a profusion of tears: "Oh son, it has been granted me to behold your face and to hear and return the familiar words." Now I am not against the idea that the presence of friends is indeed very sweet. Who indeed would deny this unless he is inhuman and even savage? But you will surely not deny that even absence itself has its pleasures unless perhaps we restrict all the beauty of friendship (which is indeed great) to the eyes alone and if we separate it from its abode which is in the mind. But if we did this, a very narrow area would indeed remain where the affection of friends can find delight. I shall remain silent concerning the role of death or prison or illness or trips whether necessary or voluntary; and who can enumerate such daily necessities of nature as sleep, hunger, thirst, heat, cold, weariness, or the innumerable occupations of studies and other responsibilities which prevent us in our very homes, not to say in our cities, from seeing the faces or hearing the voices of our friends? If governed thus, friendship would be found to be of very short duration, whereas it ought to be not only as long-lasting as the longest life but, as I said above, it ought actually to survive beyond. What role because he was blind could Appius not play in the realm of friendship? I won't mention the many others in the same category. He comes to mind first because it is not entirely believable that one who could be such a devotee of a universal state could not have friends because he had no sight. Why is it then that you bewail absence so greatly as if it could take away friendship from you when such absence really has no power in this matter nor in your other affairs except insofar as you permit it to have such power? I ask you to remember not how far you may be from someone (although how can anything be distant in this terribly tight space of which we men scarcely inhabit a tiny part?), but rather how far it is in your power through reflection to be present with absent ones. Here, therefore, is one way in which you can continually see us together: show yourself repeatedly by the frequent interchange of letters. Farewell.

Fam. II, 7.

To the same correspondent, that anxious expectations must be eliminated to live a tranquil life.

You describe in an angry manner the irksome delay that kept you in Nice for an entire month awaiting a ship to sail for Italy. But at that time you were in Italy and yet you were sighing for Italy. I say this because poets and cosmographers like to say that the boundary of Italy lies on the Varus, while the city of Nice sits on this side of it, on the shore of Italy. But of course what you meant was clear. You had in mind inner Italy and really wished to say Rome rather than Italy. I can myself perceive the cause of this illness, for youth is ordinarily full of such expectations which at that age may be forgiven. In old age, however, when all hopes should be regarded as being in the past, every lengthy and anxious expectation dealing with this life is detestable. You, therefore, who are older, probably had your reasons. I, a young man, speak about myself as a person who, although his adolescence is passed, sees your age still in the distant future, if anything can be considered long in this life. However, the more rarely I experience the annoyance of this sort of sensation, the more frequently do I complain of the remains of former ills and the more surely do I understand that a real man does not permit himself to be crushed by present things nor be tormented by future ones, but instead disdains both periods heartily and takes lightly whatever time has yielded or promised. I'll say nothing of the present since I started a discussion of the future which keeps the minds of men in suspense with great expectations through which occur, unless I am wrong, many ridiculous mistakes. Anyone awaiting the arrival of a foreign ship stares onto the sea every day and, as Lucan would have it, "is always seeing the sails of the arriving ship off at a distance." Another, on the verge of leaving the shore, invokes the clear quietness of the heavens through constant prayer. This one, without concern for appropriate measures, is always doing what the pilot of the Trojan fleet once did. He rises energetically and, according to Virgil, "he examaines all the winds and uses his hearing to judge the air currents taking

note of all the stars that are declining in the silent heavens."
Another man, trusting to the legacy of a fortunate old man,
inveighs against the slowness of death. Still another awaiting
his marriage, or the childbirth of his dear wife, or the
friendly night, counts the days, the hours and the minutes.
What more is there to say. You will remember in my *Philology*, which I wrote only to drive out your cares through
entertainment, what my Tranquillinus says: "The greater part
of man dies waiting for something." And so it is. You will
find very few who are not on tenterhooks because of uncertainty. How many plans were being made by Alexander
the Macedonian, by Julius Caesar and by many others of our
own foreign leaders when they were removed from this life!
And the death that overtook them in the middle of their undertakings was, it seems to me, the more difficult because it
was so unexpected. This is why Julius Caesar himself, overtaken by a dangerous storm in a fragile ship, when he had
begun to fear death, seemed to complain about this alone, that
"the hastening day of destiny cuts short great undertakings."
The poet knew what had been especially troublesome to such
a man or what ought to have been, when he introduced that
remark as the strongest of his complaints. There was really
only one medicine for this disease, one which is perhaps at
first taste rather bitter but in the drinking pleasant and gentle, and that is if possible to lead the mind away from earthly
things; if not, to tear it away and dig it up by the roots. For
though this may cause grief and displeasure for many people,
once the health of the body is lost, as you know, it is difficult
to restore. How much truer this is about the health of the
soul in which more violent and more frequent illnesses befall!
Therefore, do as follows: be happy with the present and you
will not feel yourself being pulled by any expectations for
the future. You say, "I wish to go to Italy and I await a ship
and a quiet sea." You should say this if your heart continued
to adhere to earthly matters and to the snares of unusual delights. But if you tried to rise above this you would say: "I
want to go to Italy indeed. But what is more useful for us
God knows and men ignore. I am awaiting a ship, but I
would not be surprised to see someone who would announce

that the ship would not arrive. And I shall receive both reports with equal calmness." You might also say, "But I have something very important to do in Italy." Now, if the study of philosophy did you any good, you would see, I believe, that what cannot be done outside of Italy cannot be very important. No matter how often you may confine me to one place, any undertaking which is restricted by a narrow space ceases to be a great undertaking. "But I wish at least to die in Italy and to be buried in my native land." Whoever says this may be an Italian but not yet a high-minded man. For what is there more childish than to be concerned about where the clippings of hair and fingernails, or where a small container of unnecessary blood may rest, and yet not care where you yourself must rest? Certainly if you consider the body, it does not really make any difference to you where by your permission you abandoned something which formerly belonged to you or when it was carried away against your opposition. But if, on the other hand, you consider the mind, no narrow place can restrict it, nor can any venerable place ennoble it; and whether it's a matter of ascending to the heavens or descending to hell, regardless of where it starts from, the labor and toil required is the same. "But it is sweet to be buried by the hands of one's dear ones." Several things are made sweet not by their own taste but by the corrupt appetite of gluttons. What can you call sweet for either the man who lacks feelings or the man who despises all such formalities? But to return to my main point, the condition of all those who live in the future is always the same: while they look into the future they do not see what is before their eyes, thereby risking certain harm as a result of flimsy hope. The present does indeed pass away while the future rarely comes as hoped for. Furthermore these things that we desire are either almost useless or they are harmful, so that as indignation often follows upon unfulfilled hope, so does disgust or unexpected ill fortune follow upon those hopes which had been agreeably fostered. Therefore, remove all hope, turn away all desire from these deceitful attractions; and begin to desire only one true and greatest good if you have indeed delayed until this age something that is so necessary.

Then will your appetite for running about cease as will your aversion toward long delays. Then, indeed, not only in Nice but, if destiny allows, in the Libyan desert will you remain without annoyance, content with your affairs and demanding nothing more. Some ask: "Can at least that one good you mentioned be hoped for so that it may satisfy the desirous soul with its presence?" Certainly not, for if you desire it fully and sacredly and reasonably (otherwise such a great thing cannot be desired), you will find that what you seek is already with you. Seek and you will find Him whom you desire deep in your soul. You need not wander outside of yourself in order to enjoy Him. If anything perchance still remains that you desire or hope for increasingly, this sense of expectation will be pleasant and agreeable. Whoever fashions himself according to this rule will often and alone among mortals enter into his bed chamber at dusk and say with assurance concerning the past what Seneca said after Virgil: "I have lived and I have accomplished whatever the course of fortune allotted me"; and he can say about the future what Horace said: "Let the heavenly Father tomorrow fill the heavens either with dark clouds or with the pure sun." Nor will he ever in his eagerness for the future be forgetful of the present or live a useless life either for himself or for others. Farewell.

Fam. II, 8.

To the same correspondent, that all things that happen natu-
rally should be borne courageously and that useless complaints
should be avoided.

I am tired of your constant complaints; I am beginning to
feel a disgust for them, and I can no longer bear your weak
character. Indeed your terror before the approach of any
particular event is like that of the newly arrived infant. You
ought to be ashamed of growing old among laments and indeed of lamenting childishly even though you are an old
man. It is childish to become astonished at anything one sees;
indeed for children all things are new and astonishing. For
old persons and especially for learned ones, there is nothing
new or unexpected that happens, nothing to be amazed at,
nothing to deplore. Therefore, why so many complaints
about things that happen regularly and according to natural
law? Prodigies do move minds sometimes. If you see a two-
headed boy, or a four-handed one, you react in astonishment.
We read in histories of showers of stones, speaking oxen, or
a mule giving birth. And yet we disdain daily occurrences.
What did you see that has caused you now to display so
much astonishment and lamentation? Your astonishment indeed compels me to be astonished; and to pass on to others
without too much seriousness this excessive amazement of
yours. You who have crossed so many seas and extricated
yourself from so many dangers and were saved from the
clutches of death so often are now describing, in astonishment and bitter against fate, how you suffered on the sea a
great and (to use the words of the Satirist) "poetic storm";
and you relate how being driven by an opposing breeze you
were brought back to the shore whence you departed. What
you consider an injustice of the sea is instead a natural thing.
You would offer a more worthy cause for complaint if what
once Caesar's fleet had to suffer between Italy and Greece
had happened to you. Because of the frozen Adriatic he was
not able to hasten his journey which was stalled because of
the numbing cold. Likewise you would have cause for complaint if you had undergone what Pompey's army underwent in Libya when the land shook under their feet, and "no

soldier could stand erect because of the trembling sands on which they stood." Now indeed, if you endured sharp stones by land, or even steep hills, and if you bore likewise the fickleness of the sea, you cannot lament as if the elements had been inimical to you, for they were simply obeying the will of nature, not yours. The other portion of your letter relates no less effeminately and weakly how you were struck by illness shortly after landing in Pisa. This you recount as if after so long a life you did not know what illness was. How can any mind prepare itself against death amidst so many daily complaints? We are too quick to accuse nature; no one deplores the fact that he is born or that he lives; yet one complains because he endures poverty, or because he experiences hardship, or because he gets old or ill or dies, as if these things are less natural than those. To be born, to live, eat, be hungry, sleep, be awake, toil, grow old, be ill, and die are all natural, and no mortal avoids them except for those in whom the headlong inevitability of death replaces the inevitability of growing old and the annoyance of hardship. Why then do we pour forth useless complaints? Could it be that since they affect only us, we are permitted to lament? Or is it because we transfer all lamentation from everyone to ourselves, and as if we were bailiffs of human kind we accuse undeserving nature? This is indeed a hateful and unfortunate business, for nature is very gentle and we betray her benefits through impatience, ungrateful to our mother and wicked against ourselves. I plead, therefore, beloved father, and, if it is not unseemly to this young age of mine, I advise you, that whatever may happen let us resolve to bear it manfully, with restraint, without wailing and without any unmanly weeping. For we have the time for deliberating, and thanks to Christ, the time for pursuing our deliberations. Let the rabble go mad. We have a considerable number of reasonable advisors whose warnings we should obey. Don't let my life influence you, however often you may read my letters. And do not let that life persuade you to look up to me personally, for sometimes you have seen a sickly doctor who, unable to cure his own sickness, is able to do so for others. I wish you well.

Fam. II, 9.

A reply to a certain humorous letter of Giacomo Colonna, Bishop of Lombez.

I was aroused from my drowsiness by your chatty letter which I read joyfully and laughingly, crammed as it was with jokes. To deflect your first barb directed at me I ask you, dear father, to note that although you direct many things at me, your very words disagree with your intention. You say that you marvel that at my tender age I can deceive the world so skillfully, that this art seems to derive not so much from experience as from natural abilities. You could have eulogized me in many more, but certainly not more magnificent, words. Whoever travels this journey of life with open eyes knows how often the world, deceiver of humankind, entangles life in its fetters and with what a bitter sprinkling of sweetness it blesses human life. We continue to look with favor upon the deceits scattered along this journey and eagerly, against the advice of Apollo, we toil against knowing ourselves. Pride inflates one man under the covering of a great and lofty mind; malice and deceit make a fool of another man under the garment of prudence or whatever false virtue seems closest. Another man considers himself strong and is instead timid and weak. There is also the man motivated by avarice under the guise of frugality, and the man whom prodigality overcomes under the appearance of liberality. The vices are disguised and the huge monsters hide under attractive coverings. Add to these a crowd of delightful but transitory and indeed passing and fleeing things. Ambition overwhelms us with honors, applause and popular flattery; dissipation unfurls before us enticing and varied pleasures; money does the same with an abundance of many things. There is no hook without bait, no branch without some trap, no snare without hope. Add to this human cupidity, rash and bereft of council, as well as quick in deceit and opportune in its insidiousness. If, therefore, in this dangerous and fleeting and insidious journey anyone whom nature or effort had made so wary that after eluding the deceits of the world he himself managed to deceive the world by showing

himself outwardly like the multitude but inwardly being unlike them, what would you say about such a man? Where are
we to search for him? In him must be a most excellent nature,
a mature and reasonable age, and a solicitous consideration of
the misfortunes of others. Yet you grant such qualities to
me; very flattering indeed, if you are not joking. But if what
you say does not apply to me today, I pray God, who has
power to free one from the infernal regions, that I deserve
your praise before I die. But where is it that you lead jokingly? You maintain that many people have held magnificent
opinions about me because of my inventiveness! I know that
the art of which you speak gave to certain illustrious men
the kind of talent through which they displayed genuine virtues to their beholders. This is the basis for the divine dis-
courses delivered by Numa Pompilius and this the way in
which the fame of the divine ancestry of Publius Africanus
was established. Such an art does not appeal to me. I know
nothing that I would like to boast of, despite the vain favor
of fate that has pursued me since my birth. I am better known
than I wish to be, and I know that however insignificant I
may be, much is directed against me by both sides for which
I feel neither depressed nor uplifted, for I know that just as
many falsehoods emerge from the multitude as do words.
This is how things have gone thus far, and I am aware that
one need not toil very much to incur the displeasure of the
multitude.

Nor does your politeness cease here. You say that I have
been fooling not only the stupid multitude with my fictions
but heaven itself. You maintain, then, that I have embraced
Augustine and his books with a certain amount of feigned
good will, but in truth have not torn myself away from the
poets and philosophers. Why should I tear asunder what I
know Augustine himself clung to? If this were not so, he
would never have based his *City of God*, not to mention
other books of his, on so large a foundation of philosophers
and poets, nor would he have adorned them with so many
colors of orators and historians. And indeed my Augustine
was never dragged to the tribunal of the eternal judge in his
sleep, as happened to your Jerome; he was never accused of

being a Ciceronian, a name, which was leveled against Jerome and caused him to swear that he would no longer touch any pagan book, and you know how diligently he avoided all of them and especially those of Cicero. But Augustine who had received no interdiction in his sleep not only was unashamed to make ready use of them but openly confessed that he had found in the books of the Platonists a great part of our faith, and that from the book of Cicero entitled *Hortensius* through a wonderful internal change had felt himself turned away from deceitful hopes and from the useless strife of quarreling sects and toward the study of the one truth. And inflamed by his reading of that book he began to soar higher as a result of his change in feelings and abandonment of passions. Oh worthy man and beyond mention great, whom Cicero himself would have praised from the rostrum, and publicly thanked, you are indeed fortunate because among so many ingrates one at least wanted to be most grateful! Oh magnificently humble and humbly lofty man, you do not abuse writers through the use of the pens of others, but rather steering the floating ship of the Christian religion among the reefs of heretics, and conscious of your present greatness without arrogance recall the truths of your origin and the early beginnings of your youth. And so great a Doctor of the Church does not blush at having first followed the man from Arpino who held a different view! And why should he blush? No leader should be scorned who shows the world the way to salvation. What obstacle does either Plato or Cicero place in the way of the study of truth if the school of the former not only does not contradict the true faith but teaches it and proclaims it, while the solid books of the latter deal with the road leading to it? The same could be said about other writers, but it is redundant to bring together superfluous witnesses for something that is so well-known. However, I do not wish to deny that many things in them ought to be avoided since even among our own writers certain things may be dangerous for the unsuspecting. Augustine himself, in a certain voluminous work of his, plucked off with his own fingers the weeds of interfering error from the extremely copious crop of his studies. And so? Rare is the reading free from danger, unless the light of divine truth shines upon the reader teaching him what is to be pursued and what is to be avoided. So long as such a light leads the way all things are secure and those things that could harm are better known than even Scylla and Charybdis or than the most famous cliffs that are found on the sea. And to put an end to this insolent calumny that I am falsely fond of Augustine, Augustine himself knows the truth. For he is in a place where no one wishes to deceive, nor can be deceived. Whence I believe that he, viewing the byways and the errors of my life, is moved to compassion especially if he recalls his own youth which the merciful Almighty brought back to the straight path from its wanderings and deviations. And now He has permitted him to become an eternal citizen of Jerusalem instead of the sandy shores of Africa where for some time enjoyable passion was leading him to death. From up yonder he views me with favor, from there he bestows his esteem upon me. How can I have doubt when I hear him, in that book which he wrote entitled *Concerning True Religion,* saying in the strongest hope: "Any angel who loves God I am certain also loves me?" Therefore if he, through the contemplation of a common God, was not afraid to assign angelic love to himself, I too, since I am a man, should dare to hope for the human love of that most holy soul which is now enjoying the delights of heaven.

But I am leaving myself open for further criticism. You say that to someone like me who even now continues to wallow in things philosophic the words of Augustine must appear almost like a dream. It would have been better had you said that as I reread all those things, my entire life should have seemed nothing more than a dream and a fleeting apparition. Sometimes while reading them I am aroused as if from a very heavy sleep, but because of the oppressive burden of mortality my eyes close again and again, and I arouse myself and continue falling asleep over and over again. My wishes fluctuate and my desires are discordant and, being so, they tear me to pieces. Thus does the external part of man battle against the internal, "now leading with a right and now with a left; without delay or rest." And unless the eternal

Father interrupting the battle with His voice saves the weary Dares from the hands of furious Entellus, the exterior part will win. How much more can I say? Hitherto I have been uncertain of my death and I have lived in anxious hope, often crying out to the conqueror of death: "Oh Unconquered One, save me from these evils; . . . offer your right hand to a wretched man and lead me with you over the waves so that I may find rest at least in the quiet abode of death."

But there is nothing more lingering than jests and nothing more flexible; wherever you direct them they follow. What in the world do you say? That I invented the splendid name of Laura so that it might be not only something for me to speak about but occasion to have others speak of me; that indeed there was no Laura on my mind except perhaps the poetic one for which I have aspired as is attested by my long and untiring studies. And finally you say that the truly live Laura by whose beauty I seem to be captured was completely invented, my poems fictitious and my sighs feigned. I wish indeed that you were joking about this particular subject, and that she indeed had been a fiction and not a madness! But believe me no one can pretend at great length without great toil, and to toil for nothing so that others consider you mad is the greatest of madnesses. Furthermore, while we may be able to imitate illness in our actions, we cannot simulate true pallor. My pallor and my toil are known to you. Therefore, I rather fear that you are abusing my illness with that Socratic playfulness which they call irony in which you yield not even to Socrates. This wound will heal in time and that Ciceronian saying will apply to me: "Time wounds, and time heals," and against this fictitious Laura as you call it, that other fiction of mine, Augustine, will perhaps be of help. For by reading widely and seriously, and by meditating on many of his things I shall become an old man before I will have grown old.

What will be the goal of your jesting? When will it stop? What are you saying? That you were also tempted by my fictions and almost deceived; indeed having been truly deceived, that you had waited some time for me in Rome so that I might simulate a great desire of coming to see you.

Finally, as expert spectators are wont to do with the trickery of mountebanks, opening your own eyes and gaining greater insight into my skill, you discovered the theatricality of my achievement. Good God, what is this all about? By directing such accusations against me you indeed make me out to be a great magician. I begin to feel like Zoroaster, the inventor of magic, or, at least, one of his followers. This would be understandable were I Dardanus or Damigeron or Apollo or anyone else whom such skill made famous. Is it not enough of a trick to be able to become a magician with mere words? But I am afraid we have lingered on this jest too long. I would like you to answer me seriously. Let us set aside my desire for seeing you in person which has occupied me heavily for four years now, during which I thought "he will arrive here tomorrow, you will probably leave the following day"; let us lay aside the sizeable number of any of the concerns which I would share with confidence with no other mortal except yourself; let me overcome my desire to see a very famous father, your worthy brothers, your distinguished sisters, and the strongly desired faces of friends; could you not guess how greatly I would want to see the walls of the City and the hills and as Virgil says, "the Etruscan Tiber and the Roman Palatine?" One could not believe how much I desire to see that city though deserted and but a reflection of ancient Rome, a city that I have never seen, for which I accuse my laziness if it were indeed laziness and not necessity that was the true cause. Seneca seems to me to be rejoicing as he writes to Lucilius from the very villa of Scipio Africanus, nor did he take it lightly to have seen the place where such a great man was in exile and where the bones lay which he had denied to his homeland. If this affected so worldly a Spaniard what would you think that an Italian like myself would feel not only about the villa at Literno or the tomb of Scipio, but even about the city of Rome where Scipio was born, educated and where he triumphed in glory both as a conqueror and as an accused; where lived not he alone but innumerable others about whom fame will never be silent. I speak of that city that has never been equaled nor ever will be; a city which is called the city of kings even by its enemies and about whose people we find written: "Great is the destiny of the Roman people, great and terrible is their name"; whose unequaled greatness of incomparable monarchy both present and future divine poets will sing. Nor will I now continue to enumerate the praises of Rome: it is too great a matter to deal with in haste. But I have touched upon these things hurriedly so that you might perceive that I do not esteem lightly the sight of the queen of cities about which I read infinite things and have written many and shall perhaps write even more unless an unexpected day of death cut short my undertaking. But assume that these things do not affect me whatsoever. How sweet it would still be to see a city with a Christian spirit as an image of heaven on earth united by the flesh and bones of the martyrs and indeed sprinkled with the precious blood of the witnesses of Truth: to see the venerable image of the Saviour of people and in the hard stone the footsteps that shall eternally be worshipped by nations and where may be perceived that saying of Isaiah which was fulfilled clearly and literally: "And the sons of those who humiliated you will come to you bowed, and all those who disparaged you will worship your footprints!" How sweet it will be to wander around the tombs of saints and through the temples of the Apostles pursuing more useful concerns and abandoning the restless anxieties of this life on the shores of Marseilles! Since this is the situation, why do you call me lazy when you know that my journey depends on the will of others? I had offered myself to you as a small but certainly continuous gift. You wished that I should obey another, if indeed a brother such as yours and so compatible with you can be called another. I am aware of no guilt. If there is any blame you must share it with yourself or with your brother.

At the very end of your letter, feeling perhaps that I might be offended by your biting jests (for sometimes the mere flattering touch of a lion of whatever size can crush small animals) you apply a bit of sweet and fragrant ointment where you seemed to have penetrated, urging me to love you and indeed charmingly exhorting me to return your love. What can I say? We impede the saying of many things not only with grief but with joy. This one thing you certainly know without my saying so; I am not so insensitive that I must have someone incite me to so generous and so worthy a love. Would that in loving I had more need of a spur than of the bridle! My adolescence would have been far more peaceful and my youth would have followed far more tranquil. Only this do I ask of you, that you do not feign that I have feigned. Farewell.

Avignon, 21 December.

Fam. II, 10.

To Agapito Colonna.[1]

I am not astonished to see in you what astounds me and all others, and what in myself I lament and bewail. It is a universal evil: those things that could without any danger be disregarded we seek eagerly; what should be sought above all things is openly neglected. We are all concerned about how fertile a field may be, how attractive a house, how obedient a servant, how solicitous a house-staff, how distinguished our clothing, how sleek our horse, how fair our wife, and how decorated the surface of our body. No one worries how beautiful and decorated is our heart. No one pledges or hopes to do anything about it. Instead what ought to be first we defer to last. "Oh people, dear people, money is to be sought first; virtue will follow the coins." Thus it is today, thus was it in the century of Horace, thus will it be in the days of our great grandsons, unless we can perhaps predict something better for our successors. Would that we could really hope for that! As things are presently going I can only predict worse things in the future although worse than they are now I can scarcely fear or imagine. Certainly to live as we do is but a taste of crime and madness so that we could not go beyond without a full collapse of society. Now! now is the time to realize what the Satirist said: "All vice stands on the edge of a precipice." Yet we exert our powers so that something mad is always happening, nor will we ever be satisfied by the older limits of traditional licence; we never attempt to make Horace appear wrong when he said: "Our fathers, who were worse than our forefathers, created us still more worthless, and so we shall create descendants who are even more corrupt." And so that we can put off this serious complaint to another time, I hold that as we continue along this path we shall make ever more true what Marcus Varro, that very learned man, thought, for if we expended upon ourselves a twelfth part of the care we expend in making certain that

1. Grand-nephew of Stefano Colonna the elder who had studied under Petrarch in his youth, and had later been named Bishop of Ascoli.

our baker makes us good bread, we would have been good indeed a long time ago. I say nothing of what we expend on jewelry, footwear, and ornaments. That's the way it will be. The useless will always be sought, the useful will be neglected. However, in your letter, illustrious friend, there was a single token of good hope. You seem to me to be suffering strongly and to recognize the state of your mind which is the first step toward well being. You seem to me to be about to escape from these fetters with magnificent indignation as soon as your body permits. Farewell.

At the source of the Sorgue. the calends of May.

Fam. II, 11.

To the same correspondent, an invitation to a poetic dinner.

Having been invited to dinner with me you will hopefully come; but remember this is not a gathering place for gourmets. What will be offered you is a poetic meal and not as found in Juvenal or Flaccus but as described in Virgil's eclogue: "Ripe fruit, tender chestnuts and an abundance of fresh milk." The rest will be a little rougher: bread which is hard and ordinary, a chance hare or an imported crane (a very uncommon sight hereabouts) and perhaps the thick skin of a somewhat rank wild boar. What else is there to say? You are familiar with the primitiveness of the places and the food here; wherefore I warn you to come not only with fortified feet but as Plautus' parasite says, with well-fortified teeth. Farewell.

At the source of the Sorgue, on the ides of January.

To Cardinal Giovanni Colonna, a description of another journey.

I have found in a region near Rome a place which is most convenient for my cares if my mind would not hasten elsewhere. It was formerly called the Mount of She-goats because, I imagine, of its being covered by thick brushwood and is considered more inhabitable by goats than men. As the location gradually became better known and its fertile lands became respected, it attracted a number of dwellers who built a kind of fortress on a rather prominent hill. Yet, as greater numbers of houses occupied the narrow confines of the hill it did not lose its ancient name of She-goat. Though an undistinguished place, it is surrounded by places that have a very celebrated reputation. On one side is Mount Soracte, famous for having had Silvester as a resident though it was celebrated even before Silvester in the famous works of poets. There is a Mount and Lake Ciminus, both recalled in Virgil. On this other side is Sutri which is not even two thousand paces away, a very dear abode for Ceres and, as is asserted, an ancient colony of Saturn. One points to a field which is not far from the walls where they say that the first field of grain in Italy was sown by a foreign king and where was yielded the first harvest to be cut by sickle. Having captivated the inhabitants with this miraculous accomplishment, and assuming the office of king, he lived out his life with the public reputation of a god and he is now worshipped through the good favor of men as an old king and a sickle-bearing god. The climate here, as much as I can tell from my brief visit, is very healthy. Everywhere there are countless hills neither too high nor of difficult access and they do not impede one's view. Among these there are shady and sloping hillsides and all around dark caves. Everywhere wooded groves arise keeping out the sun except on one hill facing north which opens its sunny breast to become a flowery dwelling for honey bees. Springs of sweet water resound in the deepest valleys; while stags and deer and doe and other wild forest bears rove over the open hills. Every kind of bird can be heard on the waters or on the trees. I skip over the oxen and the many flocks of tame sheep, the sweetness of Bacchus and the abundance of Ceres which are the fruits of human labor, and the many gifts of nature, the neighboring lakes and rivers and the sea which is not far off. Peace alone (and I know not by what crime of the people or by what laws of heaven or by what destiny or power of the stars) is lacking in these lands. Would you believe it? The armed shepherd watches over the woods fearing not so much the wolves as robbers; the breast-plated plowman turning his spear into an instrument for goading pricks the backs of obstinate oxen; the bird hunter covers his net with a shield; and the fisherman hangs his deceptive hooks and his sticky bait on his hard sword and, what is even more ridiculous, in drawing water from the well he fastens a rusty war helmet on a filthy rope. In short nothing is done here without weapons. The all-night shouting of guards on the walls, and voices calling to arms, have taken the place of those sweet notes I used to play on the lute. You will see that the inhabitants consider nothing safe, and you will not hear them uttering anything peacefully or with humaneness. Instead you will only hear of war and hatred and of things which resemble closely the works of the devil. In these places, dear father, uncertain as to what to do, I have now spent sixteen days and (alas, the power of habit!) you will see me often wandering over these hills amidst the din of soldiers and the sound of the trumpet while others take battle stations, and I constantly meditate on things which might be acceptable to posterity. Although everyone looks upon me with admiration as I go about calmly, undaunted, and unarmed, I am astonished in turn at all those around me who go about fearful, agitated and armed. Here one can see the diversity of human actions. But if I should be asked whether I would depart from here I could not give an easy answer. My departure would be desirable but my sojourn is delightful. I am more inclined to depart, not because anything is bothering me but because I had set out to see Rome. It is perfectly natural that the heart does not rest until it has reached the end of its desires. Because of this I consider that view especially attractive which held that the souls of the dead were kept from the beatific vision of God (in which the greatest happiness of men consists) until the bodies were finally gathered, something which souls could not refuse—although the opinion was refuted by the more rational judgment of many and has long been buried with its author (whom I must say you esteemed very highly, though not his errors). Farewell.

Fam. II, 13.

To the same correspondent, on his lengthy stay at Capranica and on the arrival of Giacomo and his brother Stefano.

On this mount of she-goats, which is indeed a mount of lions and tigers, that Ursus of yours, the Count of Anguillaria, lives more gently than a lamb. He is a lover of peace without fear of wars, fearless in battle but not without a desire for peace, second to no one in hospitality, vigorous in resolution, stern in flattery and unbendingly good toward his own people, a very close friend of the Muses and a tasteful admirer and praiser of distinguished talents. With him, and having a name not contrary to her character as is the case with him, is his wife, Agnes, your very beautiful sister. About her, as Sallust said about Carthage, "I think it is better to be silent than to say too little." For there are certain people who are properly praised in no better way than through admiration and silence, and your sister is one of these. This marriage seems harmonious and gentle like roses or lilies among the thorns and the sharp hedges of animosities. By the pleasantness of these two the harshness of all the rest is tempered. There has now come that wonderful and unique man, Giacomo Colonna, Bishop of Lombez, your brother. When I wrote him to tell him of my arrival, and to find out what he wanted me to do, since all approaches to your home were besieged by enemies, and I did not consider it safe to set out for Rome, he wrote to congratulate me on my arrival and ordered me to wait for him. After a few days, on the 26th of January he arrived with Stefano, his older brother, whose excellence is also worthy of a poet's pen. Both were attended by no more than one hundred horsemen and each advanced amidst the general terror of the onlookers knowing that there were five hundred and more troops bearing the enemy's banners. But their path was strewn with what makes for success in battle, their reputations as great generals. I am now living among these noble spirits with so great a sweetness that often I seem to be elsewhere than on earth and do not greatly miss Rome. We shall go there anyhow although the enemy is once again reported to have blocked more securely the roads to the city. Farewell.

Fam. II, 14.

To the same correspondent, from the city of Rome.

What news can one expect from the city of Rome when one has received so much news from the mountains? You thought that I would be writing something truly great once I had arrived in Rome. Perhaps what I shall be writing later will be great. For the present I know not where to start, overwhelmed as I am by the wonder of so many things and by the greatness of my astonishment. There is one thing that I do want to tell you, however, which happened contrary to what you expected. As I recall, you used to dissuade me from coming for a particular reason, which was that if the ruins of the city did not correspond to its fame and to the impressions I had received from books, my love for it would diminish. I, too, although burning with desire, willingly used to postpone my visit, fearing that what I had imagined in my mind my eyes would belittle at the moment of reality which is always injurious to a reputation. Such reality I am happy to say diminished nothing and instead increased everything. In truth Rome was greater, and greater are its ruins than I imagined. I no longer wonder that the whole world was conquered by this city but that I was conquered so late. Farewell.

Rome, ides of March on the Capitoline.

Fam. II, 15.

To the same correspondent, on the highly justifiable praises of his sisters, Giovanna and Agnes.

There are those who exalt unique Roman matrons of old with unique praises, and indeed ascribe to Lucretia chastity, to Martia seriousness, a holy inspiration to Veturia, the ardor of conjugal love to Portia, a sober joyousness to Claudia, wit and feminine eloquence to Julia, refinement to Cecilia, dignity to Livia, a noble firmness of mind to one of the Cornelias, an attractiveness of conduct and language to the other. Then there are those who have honored other foreign women with their praises, admiring honesty in Penelope, undying love in Artemisia, tolerance in Ipsicratia, fortitude in Thamyras, judgment in Thetis, modesty in Argia, devotion in Antigone, and constancy in Dido. I should like to have these admirers of ancient women see your sisters Giovanna and Agnes. They would indeed find in one home ample matter for praise, nor would they have to wander through all the lands and through so many centuries in their search for feminine honors. Whatever they seek anywhere in scattered form they will find in these two women. You live most happily not only because of your own virtue, but because of the glory of your father, the harmony of your brothers, and the devotion of such sisters. Farewell.

23 March.

To Tommaso da Messina, the opinions of various people concerning the very famous but doubtful Island of Thule.

The person who loves to wander on the borders of antiquity, which are rough to approach but delightful when you get there, must often tread on paths that may appear highly suspicious. This matter, indeed, that you say you have recently got yourself into, I have been pursuing for a long time, and have likewise been seeking in what part of the world the Island of Thule may be. I seek, but to tell the truth, neither with any certain idea nor with any guesses that would lead me either to a conclusion or to any hope of coming upon one. And so I am writing to you from the very shores of the British ocean and thus close (as rumor would have it) to the very island we are investigating. From here, either with the help of my long study of literature or of my new and careful search of places, I should certainly have been able to write you something reasonably definitive. There is no doubt that Thule was indeed the most remote of lands. Virgil sings of this, Seneca does also, and so does Boethius following both of them, and so do many other writers. There is also general agreement that it is located in the Occident, very far from both the Orient and the South. For us, however, who are located in the West, its very nearness produces curiosity. If it had been situated in the Orient, we should not have been more concerned about Thule than about Thoprobanen. But since we get information about Great Britain and Ireland and all the Orkneys to the north of the western ocean, and about the Fortunate Islands to the south of the same ocean either through actual visitation or through constant testimony of travelers, almost as much as we do of Italy itself or of France, we begin to take notice and to wonder and to inquire somewhat more carefully whether this island celebrated in the letters of all such travelers, emerged anywhere from the waters. The ancients and now even the Orientals and other peoples of the world confirm the opinion that it is situated in our ocean. What more can be said? We see happening to this island what often happens to outstanding men, namely that they are better known everywhere else than in their own homeland. Ask the westerners about the island; the ignorant don't even know its name, while to the learned ones who at least know of its fame, the island itself is no less unknown than to the multitude. I held an interesting conversation about this with Richard, former Chancellor of the English king, a man with a sharp mind and considerable knowledge of letters. Born and educated in Great Britain and incredibly inquisitive from his youth about unknown things, he seemed most capable of solving such obscure problems. However, either because he hoped to do what he said, or because he was ashamed to confess it (a custom which is very common today among those who do not understand how praiseworthy it is for a man who is not born to know all things to be modest and to confess honestly that he does not know what he does not know) or perhaps, as I doubt, because he preferred to keep from me information about this secret matter, he answered that he would certainly satisfy my doubt but not before he had returned to his native land and to his books of which he possessed an extraordinary number. For when I was his friend he was abroad dealing with matters concerning the Holy See for his master; at the very time when the first seeds of the lengthy war between his master and the French king were sprouting, seeds which were subsequently to produce a bloody harvest. The sickles had not yet been put aside nor had the granaries been closed down. But though he left with a promise on his lips, either because he found nothing or because of the serious duties of his pontifical office which he had newly assumed, he satisfied my expectation with nothing but obstinate silence notwithstanding the many reminders I sent him. Thus I learned nothing more of Thule from this British friend.

Several years later there came into my hands a little book on the wonders of Ireland by a certain Geraldus, a courtier of Henry II, king of the English, containing some rather thin matter, but written in a not unrefined style. In considering it for inclusion into my library, I found a small portion that made it deserving to be there. This was the portion which laboriously expressed about the same island the same questions as ours. A similar bent of mind, therefore, made me feel attracted to the author of the work. In his book he touches upon the opinions of several writers who maintain that of the islands in the ocean that are situated near Great Britain and that are between the North and West, the furthest is Thule where in the summer solstice there is no night and in the winter no day; beyond which the sea lies inactive and frozen. He cites the works of Solinus and Isidore in support of this. Nevertheless, he states that that island is not known at all to the West and he confirms that there is none like it or of that name located there. Consequently following conjecture he considers it either a famous but mythical island or separated from the others by an infinite space and thus to be sought only in the very furthest reaches of the North Ocean. He makes Orosius a corroborator of this opinion. He could also have included Claudian when he wrote, "Thule is condemned to the Hyperborean skies." Omitting this fact, he deals with the matter and argues along his own lines. You should consider the witnesses that he uses to see the extent to which they support him, and you will understand how much faith must be placed in his words. I, myself, am very far from all my books and I find this alone the only burden of this trip. Having left home I hear no sound of the Latin tongue, and when I return home I do not have the books which are my companions and with which I am accustomed to speak. All my conversations are through recollection. Therefore I am writing this to you extemporaneously and by memory so that when I see my memory wavering over certain matters I prefer silence than to commit any opinion on paper. Of course there are many things that I remember no differently than if I had books readily available since repeated reflection on such things impresses them upon me deeply and strongly. That author of whom we speak had not perhaps read Pliny the Elder who expressed himself on the matter more strongly than anyone else. I do not dare indicate how truthful his testimony is since I keep wondering, "How can an island so close and so famous be so unknown to everyone?" But I shall report what Pliny the Elder himself thinks about the matter in the second book of his natural history. He feels that Thule is an island distant six sailing days north of Great Britain where he conjectures the daytime lasts six months in the summer and the night an equal amount of time in winter according to a strong argument based on reason, as he sees it, and he furthermore uses as his source a certain Phocea or Pythia of Marseilles. If this is true, how close am I to that very Thule that we seek, whose fame, as I surmise, is great among the Indians and almost unknown among us! Servius himself, although a better grammarian than a cosmographer or poet, following his predecessors in his interpretation of Virgil's statement, "May the farthest Thule be subject to you," remarks as follows: "The Island of Thule is between the northern and western shore of the Ocean, beyond Great Britain, Ireland, and the Orkneys." You will note that almost all writers focus on one point, and seem to agree in various ways that the island lies between the North and the West and not far from Great Britain where, if they had assembled in person, they might perhaps have changed their opinion as the matter demanded. Two of them depart considerably from the opinions of the others, but whether they approach more closely to the truth or whether because of the distance their error cannot be verified directly is uncertain. Of these, one is Orosius who was mentioned above, another is Pomponius Mela, a renowned cosmographer whom Pliny is accustomed to follow in many matters, but here seemed to overlook him. He spoke of only one sunrise during the whole year, at the vernal equinox, and one setting of the sun in the autumnal equinox, and consequently only one day and one night as distinctive times of the year did he grant the Hyperborean peoples, the first inhabitants on the shores of Asia beyond the north wind and the Riphean Mountains. And if we are to believe him they are the most innocent and happy of all mortals. He maintains, however, that Thule is located among the islands of the Ocean opposite the shores of Belgium. He says that the nights are short there, dark in winter, full of light in summer, and none during the solstice. Alas, how much disagreement! Indeed to me the island seems no less hidden than truth itself. But let it be that way because what we seek with hard labor we may safely ignore. But let Thule lie hidden to the North, let the source of the Nile lie hidden to the South, provided that virtue, which is centrally placed, does not lie hidden, and likewise the path of this short life over which a great portion of men proceeds trembling and staggering, hurrying to an uncertain end over an obscure trail. Therefore let us not expend too great a labor in the search for a place which if we found, we would perhaps gladly leave. The time has now come to bring this letter to a close and to expend our time on more useful matters. This is the information that I have been able to unearth as an actual field worker, so to speak, concerning this obscure problem; seek other information from others who are more learned. If it is denied me to search out these hiding places of nature and to know their secrets, I shall be satisfied with knowing myself. It is here that I shall be open-eyed and fix my gaze. I shall pray to Him who created me that He show himself to me as well as myself to me and, as the Wise Man prays, that He make me aware of my end. Farewell.

Fam. III, 2.

To the same correspondent, against the expectations and useless labors of a short life.

How shall I answer your letters? I fear that the swift torrent of human errors has snatched our friend along with everything else and has plunged him into the bottom of the pit. He is growing old, as you can see, amidst the games and illusions of fortune, promising himself many things which, believe me, will never come. However, there is one excuse. He indeed has the same disease that strikes practically everybody. Do you know anyone who does not trouble the peace of today with the hope of tomorrow? This is mortal happiness; this is mortal life. An incredible madness, not any less so because it is universal, is this gaping at fantasies and following doubtful things after having laid aside certain good things. Men do not know how profitable it is to lose empty and false hopes. They are a heavy load, and yet they are laid aside sadly. To that extent do we delight in our own ills. That friend of ours toils and sighs and pants uselessly, and, against the opinion of Flaccus, "seeking lands warmed by another sun, bravely strives after many things during a short life." I do not accuse others of what I excuse in ourselves. The desire of seeing many things also drives us over lands and seas, and especially lately when that passion of mine drove me to the furthest of lands, forced by tedium and repelled by local customs. Hard necessity brought me back. I landed the day before yesterday, and though I had written you things during my trip, I cleaned my dusty pen again with your name first. Our friend, however, that he may return not more learned but richer, avoids no unknown shore of the world and revolves like a flying leaf with each wind current. None of his sighs, as I hope, will ever have an end except with his life. Tell him this for me. It is rare indeed that expectations are realized; but assuming that they are, misery increases with happiness. This is not difficult to understand for the man of experience, except that bad habit closes the ears to admonishing words. But he will see for himself. You stand firm and take care not to be distracted from your goal by the mob of wavering spirits. The advice of Seneca, and indeed of nature herself, is, "There is no need for much, nor for long." Farewell.

Avignon, 18 August.

Fam. III, 3.

To Stefano Colonna the younger,[1] *that to have won is point-less for one who does not know how to use his victory.*

You were able to conquer, oh most powerful man. Know how to use your victory, oh wisest of men, nor let anyone accuse you of the reproach which Maharbal once cast in the teeth of Hannibal on the day of the battle of Cannae. If he had followed advice and had turned his banners dripping with our blood from the battlefield toward Rome, you know what in the opinion of the historians was indicated. But the Lord who was favorable to Italy obstructed his wicked daring. That same God, aiding your pious efforts, accompanies you in battle, directs your steps, and His leadership will not desert your banners. He (that same God who once saved the pious though small forces of Prince Theodosius from the barbarian legions) now promises you continuous victories and the final expulsion of your enemies. You certainly uphold a most just cause, and as Christ was witness to the justice of Theodosius, so is He now to yours and calls upon you day and night to bring to a completion what he began. He is not distant from you but near you, with you, and believe me was with you while you were victorious. Otherwise how could you have routed such an army with so few troops and alone, unaware and almost half equipped for an unexpected battle, have crushed so quickly two very haughty enemies though they had been forewarned and prepared? Without doubt celestial assistance was present and will be present, your cause remaining a just one as often as you request it piously and reverently. Go, therefore, secure in such a leader and rest assured that the boy who is born again from the blood of the victims and is adorned with the spoils of the church will be rather a prey than an antagonist. To be sure, your former victory was glorious but hollow; this one may be as rich as it is easy. Go, therefore, to certain

1. One of the Colonna brothers who were very close to Petrarch, he was a Roman senator and military commander deeply involved in the battle between the Colonnas and the Orsinis and in the struggle against Cola di Rienzo which resulted in his death in 1347.

victory rather than to an uncertain struggle, and go relying
not so much upon your own power as upon divine assistance.
The very elements will fight in your behalf as they fought
for Theodosius, and, as Claudian says, Aeolus will send you
from the stars your armed winter winds; heaven will serve
you, and the conspiring winds will descend upon your fleets.
For you too will be waging war with the enemies of the
cross although they be usurpers of the name of Christ. That
this is so and that the new Eugenius has turned from a lamb
to a wolf, and from a priest to a tyrant, the oppressed and
plundered churches of Italy bear witness. The offended God-
head seeks you as an avenger not only of the offenses committed against you but those committed against Him. Do
not fail in this twin vengeance, and do not place so much
confidence in deeds already accomplished that you fail to
see what remains to be done. Whether a little, a great deal,
or an enormous amount has been done, it adds up to nothing
if the beginning has no end. And I beg you not to prefer
enjoying a victory to using it properly; something in which
the great master of military science is declared to have erred
to our very good fortune but to his very bad misfortune.
Although that one example ought to furnish sufficient caution and proof to all the generals who have existed and will
exist in the future, I shall refer to others from among our
own as well as foreigners so that you will not be influenced in
such a great matter by the recalling of only one example.
Pompey the Great, victor at Dyrrhachium, let Julius Caesar
get away when he almost captured him and could have held
onto him. Whether it was his ignorance of warfare, or the
clear superiority of the antagonist, or fortune assisting her
follower in an extreme moment, or whether (which is the
general view) it was an utterly astonishing example of humanity (would that it had turned out well!), it was soon
followed by a public calamity in Thessaly and the miserable
death of the commander himself in Egypt. And in Africa
at the same time the destruction of Cato and of freedom, in
Spain the sad destruction of the relics, in Rome the plundered
treasury, the suppression of the laws, and the Senate ready
with concealed sword, and the conqueror killed on the Cap-

itoline which he had honored with four triumphs. Then there was the harsh siege of Perugia and of Modena, and the cruel slaughter of the residents of Parma which Cicero recalls in his *Philippics,* and Pharsalia once again flowing with our blood, and those huge naval battles fought under the summits of Leuca and Aetna. Finally from that time down to our own century a series of so many misfortunes has flowed from those actions that their enumeration is impossible and their recollection unpleasant and there seems to be no end to the afflictions. What should I say about Cyrus, the king of the Persians, who, to speak the truth, was a victor in battle and a loser in victory. What should I say about Alexander, the Macedonian, who, having lived safely through war, perished at a banquet? Agamemnon destroyed that famous and proud Troy; Africanus the younger (our Policertes, so to speak) completely destroyed Carthage and Numantia; and both were safer in war than after the victory, and happier in military service than at home. Knowing that they are distant no less in character than in time and place, I have joined them in this portion of my brief letter because their fate and end seemed to be almost the same: conquerors of the enemy, each having subdued and overcome the foreigner, they perished amidst the caresses of their most abominable wives. I confess that this has nothing to do with our subject, so that I shall lead the entire matter to a single end in order to show that there is much to fear even for victors. Deeds accomplished should never satisfy, and one should persist long and continually in the fashion of Caesar pressing on energetically to success and pursuing the favor of the gods, and believing that nothing has been accomplished as long as anything remains to be accomplished. Otherwise many people will consider victory more suspect than war, and seriously wonder whether it were better not to have begun than once begun to have deserted beckoning destiny in the middle of the road. Farewell and take care.

Fam. III, 4.

To the same correspondent, that there is nothing new under the sun.

How I felt concerning the general state of your activities I had written to you, oh most courageous man, some time ago in the vernacular so that it could be understood even by your soldiers who will in part avail themselves of your trials and of your glory. Soon afterwards, however, with my inventive impulse always providing me with something new, I composed a poem for you containing matter from my own work and from others. I followed that rule whereby the first verse was mine, and the second was taken from some talented poet, so that not only the ingenious connecting of ideas but the harmony of the words would also delight a reader. In doing so I gloried in the thought that I had invented a new poetic form, until after having sent my poem I discovered that others had handled this type of poetry before me and that what the wise men of the Hebrews had said was indeed true: "There is nothing new under the sun"; and also what the comic poet had written: "There is nothing to be said that has not been said before." Recently through the messenger of your magnanimous father, Stefano the elder, I wrote in a free style prose something with which I thought I could strike several chords of your valor. If you have received it, there is nothing that I would change, nothing that I would add. Although many things offer themselves, it is sufficient to have alerted a wise man. Farewell.

Fam. III, 5.

To an unknown correspondent, that the solitary life cannot be fully commended except by an expert.

You request that I explain briefly the state of the solitary life which I seem to be living at this time, as you say, beyond the custom of our station. Whether you ask this because you are eager to imitate or to ridicule, you alone know. Perhaps you do not realize how great a matter you wish to be expressed briefly and compressed into a very narrow framework. Eloquent writers have written books on this very matter, but none in my opinion has hitherto praised such a life sufficiently. I confess that I was driven often to write about the subject, and would have done so except that I did not yet trust sufficiently either my talent or my style or my information about the matter. As for your request, I feel strongly that I would never listen seriously to someone praising the solitary life unless he had enjoyed first its sweetness in some form, for it abounds in new and countless advantages that are learned not by listening or by reading but only through experiencing. Thus I believe that one cannot learn about this except through experience. And what good is it to deal with the matter with great eloquence when those who listen either will not understand or will believe minimally. You, therefore, if, as you declare, the admiration for my solitude and the desire for imitating it attract you, you should not weary me, busy as I am with other cares, you should not implore an exposition which would be inadequate to the task. But if you (to repeat something that I say often because I believe it so strongly) make your request with a pure mind and with a desire for learning and not for testing my mind, come and see, and you will not be indebted to others for something you can do by yourself. Stop scratching the itch on your ears with the nails of another's words. Nothing prohibits you from accomplishing the same thing with fewer words. That will be more respectable than if you wrenched from me a treatise on so important a matter. This will benefit neither the giver nor the seeker except to render suspect the intention of the reader and contemptible the work of the writer. Farewell.

At the source of the Sorgue, 4 May.

Fam. III, 6.

To a friend eager for a questionable undertaking, that not all profit is useful.

Think what you will concerning the question that you have proposed. You lack neither age, nor the knowledge of books, nor the experience of life. As for me, the very consideration of dishonest matters is shameful. I do not find the highest good or any kind of good in riches or in pleasure (an opinion of the Stoics, not of the Peripatetics, with my preference being Stoic rather than Epicurean in all things). Riches and pleasure are comfortable and helpful in a mortal life; wherefore the former are called Fortune's good, the latter the good of the body. But the good that we seek lies in the mind and serves neither the body nor fortune. Though I admit that the others are called goods, I contend that they are not. Nor should you think that perhaps I have inadvertently slipped into an error by saying this. I am not ignorant of what Aristotle has to say about it, or what Epicurus felt, but the authority of philosophers does not prevent freedom of judgment. For me that opinion of philosophers seems more inspired and true which says that those who divide goods into three parts cannot be happy. The good is one, and one is that which makes us happy. Yours is far too empty and forced a happiness which involves, or rather requires, not only the beauty of the body and its total health but even riches. It is too exposed to the snares of thieves, and ultimately to excessive worry and agitation, qualities that certainly do not lead to true happiness. The happiness of Epicurus which consists in pleasure is not happiness but extreme misery. For what is more wretched for a man than to surrender the human good, reason, to an animal good, the senses? But do I seem to have lost my mind when among such great judges I should take on the controversy unasked? Well, then, let everyone believe as he pleases; it is difficult to give up inveterate beliefs. Philosophers whose names can scarcely be enclosed in the narrow confines of a letter have written a great many treatises on these beliefs. There is an entire book of Cicero which discusses the limits of good and evil. When you read it I doubt that there will be much more that your hearing or your intelligence would have to know. But since you asked from me not the truth of the matter (for that perhaps is hidden) but how it appeared to me, I shall bring the entire matter to a conclusion briefly. Do not listen to unjust advisors; they care neither about your name nor your welfare and offer you only what they themselves believe in or what they think would please you. You must consider nothing but noble things as worthy of being counted among good things. "But profit is useful." True, if joined with honesty. Otherwise you must know that there can be nothing more harmful. What Cicero himself says on this matter in his book *On Offices* is generally known. However, a large part of his readers, indifferent to the contents, examine only the words and embrace the precepts of life on hearsay as if they were tales. Remember that those books treat matters relating not to the tongue but to the mind, and contain not rhetorical but philosophical lessons. And keep in mind constantly what was once well-known to the Attics in Athens; namely, the advice of Themistocles, the explanation of Aristides and the judgment of the assembly. In like manner, despite the multitude's ridicule, I do not disdain profit, but with this proviso, that it involve nothing that appears dishonest; otherwise I shall avoid gold no less than a cliff. For gold, as Plautus says, "often advocates wrongly many things for many people." Finally, so that I may end with that same author, "I do not believe that all profit is generally useful to man." Farewell.

Fam. III, 7.

To Paganino da Milano,[1] *that the appetite for power must be controlled, and on the optimum condition of the state.*

Although I am not ignorant of how much more the Roman state increased under the rule of the many than under the rule of one man, I know that it has appeared to many and even to great men, that the happiest condition of the state is under a single and just ruler. Thus authority and experience seem to be a odds. But the question is greater than can be discussed in such a short letter. Certainly, as the present state of things is for us, amidst such implacable discord of minds, there is hardly any room left for doubt that monarchy is the best for regrouping and restoring the power of Italy which the madness of civil wars for a long time has diminished. I knew these things, and I confess that a royal hand is necessary for our ills. Similarly, I have no doubt you believe that I prefer no king more than this king of ours under whose power we live so agreeably and quietly that we do not need the kindness of Pyrrhus, the fortune of Alexander, the justice of Zaleucus, or to use instead examples from the Romans, the ardor of Romulus, the religion of Numa, the military prowess of Tullius, the grandeur of Ancus, the comportment of Tarquinius, or the prudence of Servius. Certainly if justice alone distinguishes a king from a tyrant, our king is a true king, however much the most genuine tyrants of all call him tyrant while they wish to be called fathers of their country. With these no Phalaris, no Agathocles, no Dionysius, in short no Gaius or Nero and no Heliogabalus, most loathesome of all, can contend in lewdness and roughness. Therefore, since it is part of the prudent man to preceive not so much what delights as what sets free, and in this very process to consider carefully not the beginnings of things but the results, I would

1. A close friend of Petrarch and firm supporter of the expansionist policies of the Visconti, Lords of Milan, during the decade 1339–1349. Served as governor of various cities for Luchino Visconti, and probably met Petrarch while serving as governor of Parma in 1348. The "king" referred to in the letter is Luchino.

like to ask you whose excellent advice he accepts, and whose prudence and trust you let no one doubt; I would, I say, like to ask you, dear friend, who know my mind, to give him this perhaps homely but sincere piece of advice; persuade him that he has extended his borders sufficiently with regard both to his wealth and his fame. Nothing ever satisfies cupidity and I hope that she will not deceive him with her enormous promises. Moderation in all kinds of fortune is like gold; and human happiness without setting a limit to itself is eager to advance, and extending into infinity brings with it not only a great deal of anxiety, but nothing enduring, nothing certain, nothing peaceful. Therefore, I have always liked the modesty of the younger Africanus, who, as Censor, ordered that the lustral song be changed because it sought from the gods an increase in the happiness of Rome and thus seemed too full of cupidity and unfit for the gods themselves, and that thereafter the Romans would implore nothing more than the present state of things and stability. This was certainly wise and prudent if mortal affairs were consistent and if what they sought from their false gods could have been sought from our omnipotent God. I see that many more things could be said here but what need is there of words? You know my mind; you know what I desire and what I fear. I hear that he is undertaking new enterprises. I wish him well if he continues but would prefer that he cease, for that path would be safer. Declare your opposition, I beg you, to his ambitions. Remind him of the saying of that most temperate commander: "That the Romans wished not so much to possess gold as to rule over those who possessed gold." If this is said correctly about gold, which can be hidden, what could be said about lands and cities? Likewise, if this can be said rightfully concerning enemies, what would you say about friends whom you control not by compulsion but by spontaneous agreement and of whom you may possess with full justice not only the lands or the gold but their bodies and minds? It is both more noble and safer to have friends than the possessions of friends; and where you may control those who are willing, it is foolhardy to wish to control those who are not. It is the advice of philosophers, and indeed of nature which says: "Nothing achieved by violence is long lasting." It is easy to defend the borders of a modest kingdom; the huge kingdom is difficult to achieve and very difficult to watch over. Farewell.

To a friend, an exhortation against putting faith in the answers of soothsayers or any kind of diviner.

I beg you, let us lay aside, if we can, both the sad memory of past events and the anxious uneasiness about future ones. They torment us over nothing, and like double stings disturb the peace of our life on both sides. What are we striving for, over what are we tormented? What's been done cannot be undone, nor can the future be foreseen. What need is there for astrologers against whom the authority of the saints, of philosophers and poets, and of all those who perceive the truth clamors? To skip over the words of many philosophers, who does not know the famous testimony of Virgil that the minds of soothsayers are ignorant? What Attius said is also known: "I believe nothing said by the fortune tellers who enrich the ears of others with words so that they can enrich their homes with gold." No less interesting is that saying of Pacuvius, that very ancient poet: "If they were to foresee what lies in the future they would be similar to Jupiter." Nor should you believe that the poet is much different than the soothsayer in this regard. As Isaiah says: "Proclaim what will come about in the future and we shall understand that you are gods." I therefore believe that that advice of the very learned Favorinus, mostly taken from Cicero, with which both dissuaded us from all these illusions and deceits, should not only be accepted but amplified. For either these who promise news of the future foretell adversities falsely and fill us in vain with empty fear, or, if what they foretell be true, they make us wretched beforehand. Or again, they may deal with things that do turn out, thereby doubling our suffering with the weariness that comes of waiting than which I know no greater, and with the removal of joy when achieved, or its "deflowering," as Favorinus called it. And indeed, before such joy appears, it will already have been destroyed by the preoccupied mind full of hope. If the prediction is false it is certain that the empty and absurd joy ceases in the grief and shame of a lost hope. Therefore they are not to be taken seriously who promise impossible things even for themselves and useless things for us. And so? Let everyone believe that Christ said for him what Jupiter says to Amphitryon in Plautus: "Be of good heart; I am present, oh Amphitryon, with help for you and yours. Let there be nothing you fear; send away all sooth-sayers and diviners; I can speak of future and present things much better than they," adding not "because I am Jupiter," as he says, but because I am God. He doubtless speaks many things to us constantly through the ears of our heart. If we were willing to listen to Him, we could easily disdain the promises of these mountebanks. Death is certain; the hour of death is uncertain, so that we await each hour as though it were the last; it is sufficiently beneficial to know these things. Therefore what ignorance in these men, what madness is ours, that we should be tortured by predictions that are cov-ered by thick darkness and can be seen in the future only by God? I confess that there is only one extraordinary thing in all of this vain activity, and that is that anyone who is right in most other things will be called a liar if he makes only one unusual mistake, whereas soothsayers, however false they may be, acquire the fame of prophesying truly in making a single accidental guess. Cicero marveled at this, although with different words, in that book in which briefly he builds up the art of divination in order to destroy it. Augustine in a variety of places, and especially in the book *On Various Matters*, speaking against those "who now," as he says, "are called astrologers, wanting to subject our acts to celestial bodies and to sell us to the stars and there receive the price for such sale from us," reasons as follows: "When it is said that they have predicted many true things, it happens be-cause men do not keep in their mind their errors and false-hoods, but instead, paying attention only to those things which happened according to their predictions, they forget those that did not happen. And those things are remembered which happen not because of knowledge, which they do not possess, but by some obscure combination of circumstances. But if they wish to yield to their skill, let them say that any of the dead and written parchments which many believe con-tain prophesies also foretell things skillfully. And if a verse foretelling future things often emerges from manuscripts without skill, what is so extraordinary if even from the mind of a speaker there emerges some prediction of future things not through skill but through chance?" These last words are Augustine's which apply here because of his authority and because of his faith. What else do you think opened the road to all of these deceitful doings except the ignorance of the multitude and their infinite cupidity, not to say their madness, wanting so badly to know those things which cannot be known and which it is not useful to know? You, therefore, avoid these kinds of rash and impudent men who oppose the peaceful life so that, as much as possible, you may spend this very brief time without unnecessary and inane cares. In short, be sure of this: Until you throw aside the burden of superstitions, you can desire but not pursue the blessed life. Opposites repel; fear and happiness will never live happily together. Farewell.

Fam. III, 9.

To Matteo da Padova,[1] against drunkenness.

I shall not mention what can be said at great length against drunkenness; how detestable, how dangerous, how sad an illness it is, and how much madness there is in skillfully drowning and killing off in a foaming glass one's reasoning powers with which nature has endowed man uniquely and specially. Through drink, one has no control over his feet, tongue, and mind; his head trembles as do his hands, his eyes tear, his body smells and the lingering traces of the previous day are offensive on the following day. I will not mention the way in which the passions rule, the loss of control, the stories and laughter of the people, the hatred and contempt of good friends. I also pass over the sudden alteration in mood and the ignorance of even learned men and the childishness of the man of any age, a childishness exposed to the joking and deceit and mockery of everyone. Nor shall I mention cracks in the mind crushed and weak because of a heavy burden, letting out secrets often harmful to one's self or to others and the cause of actual death to many and of utmost misery. Furthermore there are the lamentations and the inane joy and struggles and quarrels and rifts and the heedless encounter of armed men with unarmed ones. All these things I pass over since they are known and common. There is a book of Apuleius of Madaura entitled *Florida*. In it he discusses humorously what the first glass and second and following ones do to a drunkard. I shall not enlarge upon his opinion. For I know not why or how one drinks more today than formerly. Indeed, would that this were the manner in which dissipation worked. In any event, wherever we turn, we seem to have become weaker toward virtue and stronger toward vices. In my opinion, therefore, the first glass pertains to thirst, the second to pleasure, the third to passion, the fourth to drunkenness, the fifth to wrath, the sixth to quarreling, the seventh to madness, the eighth to sleep, the ninth to illness. Tell all this to that Marcus Bibulus, not the associate of Julius Caesar but yours, with whose vices

1. Unknown correspondent.

and wantonness you constantly quarrel, if you believe that it may be useful. If by chance he appears irreproachable to himself because he has not yet reached the extremes of drunkenness, tell him that it is better to have descended even slightly from the heights of moderation and restraint than to hit bottom once you have started to slide. Both virtue and vice approach slowly; no one is made excellent or evil overnight. Farewell.

Fam. III, 10.

To a Transalpine friend, a man of great repute, that cowardice does not delay death and that he should do nothing base in order to attempt to live longer.

Faith breaks my silence and charity compels me to speak. Christ is my witness that I feel compelled to write things which, if you read them in the same spirit in which they were written, would increase your good will toward me and your glory among the people. How could I pretend, if I wish not to be a false friend, that you, surrounded by great dangers, need not be roused if asleep or forewarned to be vigilant? You see what serious warfare has arisen between the kings of France and Britain. Without doubt there has been no graver situation since the days of our forefathers, not indeed in Europe since antiquity, nor was such a great opportunity ever offered to strong men to achieve glory. All the kings and all the people, uncertain about the outcome of such a struggle, and especially those who inhabit that territory from the Italian Alps to the ocean, whom the frightful din of approaching battle terrifies, have taken up arms. You alone, in such a whirlwind of happenings, sleep. The Virgilian rebuke should press upon you and like a messenger sent from heaven should exclaim: "Can you indulge in sleep under the present circumstances and be blind to the dangers that surround you?" Indeed even if nothing more than shame could bother you, you ought to have roused yourself more quickly. With what nerve and with what spirit, while others spend their time under the helmet and bear the shield in the hot sun, do you, far from the battle lines of men, and attended by retinues of women, nourished with rare dishes and covered with soft garments, remain inert in the shade and in leisure, you whom I formerly considered a man eager for honor and glory, a powerful and noble man, a youthful and strong man? I ask you, what is keeping you? Do you like elegance? Are you fleeing from labor? But listen to the words of a very strong man offered by Sallust: "Arrogance is becoming to women, toil to men." Do you fear thirst and sandy paths and terrible serpents during the dog days? But listen to the words of another man who, though less warlike, was no less strong: "The serpent, thirst, heat, battlefields are sweet things to virtue; patience enjoys hardships." But perhaps you fear death and the sword? But even here the words of another brave man come to mind: "Death is a final punishment and ought not to be feared by men." I say it ought not to be feared any more than sleep or rest. What is there of real consequence between the day of birth and death? Basically a great deal. Our birth envelopes us in the labors of human life, death sets us free. Whence that custom, taken from the innermost heart of philosophy, of grieving at the birth of one's dear ones and rejoicing at their death. But not to stray from the opinions of the multitude (from which we should indeed be retreating as much as possible if we desire salvation), let it be granted that death is to be feared, and let that notorious saying of Aristotle be produced, that death is the ultimate dread (note that he took pains not to say "the greatest" but "the ultimate"); leaving it, however, as "the greatest," do you think that by keeping away from war or seas you can really avoid death? Well known are the words of still another poet: "In vain do we avoid bloody Mars, and the crashing waves of hoarse Hadria; in vain do we fear the south breezes which are considered harmful to bodies in the autumn." Even with the greatest care given by a human to his body, he must die. "But the desire to postpone death is a drive of mortals." I confess this and I recognize the excuse of public foolishness. But first I ask you, how small indeed is such postponement! Then to how many misfortunes is it exposed! For how many people who managed to live longer did a postponed death do harm and indeed diminish the glory of their life! We abound in daily examples, but I call to mind ancient ones with greater reverence, and our own more willingly than foreign ones. If Tullius Hostilius had lived a little less long, he would not have suffered the blow of the thunderbolt. Remove a few years from Tarquinius and he will have died a king and not an exile. A longer life produced blindness for Appius Claudius, imprisonment for Marius and shameful flight and a slimy hiding place in marshes. Who more illustrious than Pompey the Great, except that the prolongation of his life obscured the splendor of so great a name? What followed such splendor but the indignity of death? What shall I say about the two Africans? How much better do you think it would have been if one had perished before the walls of Carthage and the other before the gates of Numantia? The first one would not have condemned his homeland in a famous epigram for an unworthy exile, and the second would have avoided the injustice of an unavenged death. Caesar Augustus himself, whom you would judge the happiest of all, how much more happily would he have died prior to the adultery of his already aging daughter and before he began counting her "tumors" as he used to call them with bitterness. I bypass Regulus and Cato and the others whom a noble death illumined, although I am compelled to feel differently about them than about our own (I refer to Cicero and Seneca). I would not want to have had Cato die before the Civil War lest the highly trustworthy witnesses of his steadfastness as well as his renowned toil and distinction might never have been known. I admire him with undaunted spirit, I admire him struggling with the serpents, I admire him wandering over the Libyan sands; I praise the firmness of his mind, I praise his stubbornness, I praise his freedom; I do not praise his willed death and his despair. And so that you may not think that I am perhaps neglecting foreign examples, Pyrrhus and Hannibal would have died with greater fame if they could have had their burial in Italy. For both, their return to their fatherland was unfortunate. Cyrus could also have been more famous had he died before touching the Scythian shores. Your Brennus would have been more famous if he had died before touching the threshold of Delphi. What should I say about the poisoning of Mithridates, the vicissitudes of Alcibiades, the exile of Themistocles, the chains of Aristides, the fire of Croesus? Rarely does a long life enjoy an equally long happiness. When happiness ceases it is not just a matter of being unhappy (unless a present disaster becomes even worse by the memory of past happiness); were nothing to happen to us while alive, we are nevertheless compelled to behold many things happening to our dear ones which do not permit us to call ourselves happy. Happily would Priam have departed this world, or Peleus, or Nestor, if they had preceded their children. To include a different type of example, the poisonous cup would not have killed Socrates, nor dogs Euripides, nor swords Demothenes and Cicero, nor forgetfulness Messalla, nor would leprosy have overcome Plotinus if an opportune death had preceded their overwhelming afflictions.

But enough of such examples, and especially in a matter which is clear. You see, therefore, that the desire for a longer life is blind, that a good death is to be preferred in which one can readily see that no one can be deceived, and no one can be displeased. But since custom has continued to desire harmful things indiscriminately as well as those which constantly overcome us, one may prefer to opt for the majority. Or do you hope to achieve the desired goal through sloth? You are indeed terribly wrong. How many did an excessive laziness crush whom toil and vigilance might have preserved; how many did either hangovers kill or drunkenness strangle who would have been saved by fasting! It is generally known that more are killed by food than by the sword. Whatever food people eat, in whatever corner of the earth they may try to hide, death finds them and demands, requires, and extorts its tribute. In vain do we try to evade; if we do not proceed toward death, it will follow us. Consider, therefore, what is more noble, what is more worthy for a man, either to hide and flee what one cannot avoid, or to oppose whatever comes and do what one should and follow one's fortune voluntarily lest, if one were to linger, one would be drawn forward by force. Oh pitiful sweetness of very brief delays! Who is so anxious to live that he would not prefer to die forthwith than to prolong his life the space of a single year with dishonor, destroying the dignity of all his past years? How more obscene will it be to do something unbecoming for fear of death when all that is promised is the uncertainty not of a year but of a day? You say to yourself: "I would go if only I did not fear the danger of death's approach," something that could be said anytime you are able to remain without danger. However, is it not true that either a sudden fever or some other illness (for the fate of humans may take many forms and an astonishing variety) could perhaps snatch from you the life that you denied your king? If this is so, I urge and implore you to take heed right now and raise your eyes. You will see a vast array of kings and of people tottering under overwhelming preparations, and about to collapse under the pressing power of fortune. This is no time for pretending. Your enemies are vigilant and they surround their king with a yoke of submissiveness. If he were to enjoy victory, and were to see how inactive you are now in his moment of need (and you should know that he has been hostile to you for some time), how do you think he would react? But if it were to happen otherwise, since fortune disposes of all things as it pleases, do you perhaps hope that the security you enjoy in your present repose would continue in that ardor of conquest? You will indeed appear to have held back not because you wanted to but out of fear! And the general collapse will envelope you equally with everyone else. Believe me, both sides will call you a spectator of the struggle, prepared to change directions at the nod of fortune and the will of the victor. Therefore good will appears nowhere and danger everywhere. It will be useful to recall Metius, a leader of the Albans, who was quartered with a team of four horses pulling in different directions at the order of Hostilius, king of the Romans, because he had remained neutral in the middle of two armies. Hurry, and wake up, I beg you; return rapidly, while there is still time, to your duty which has been so long neglected. To sleep in a quaking world resembles death much more than sleep. I wish you well.

Fam. III, 11.

To Guido Gonzaga,[1] *lord of Mantua, that love equates unequals.*

Truly great and wonderful is the power of love which so powerfully and tenaciously and with invisible, although by no means imperceptible, ties binds the smallest things to the greatest, and despite their inequality controls them with equal power. And why should it not have this dominion over the minds of men vigorous in their feelings and in their rational powers, if it can bind insensitive and contrary things with strong ties? The air would not cling to fire nor earth to water, nor would rivers recognize their banks nor the sea its shores nor the stars their paths, were it not that the almighty or, as people call it, sacred love of the world binds all things together in the world. Therefore He who regulates heaven and earth with equal justice did not discriminate between my humble status and your lofty one. He observes this principle: He knows how to make unequals equal, and does not allow a faithful lover not to be loved. In times past through your sensibility, and through no particular doings of mine, but only through the perception of the mind, as one says (for minds have their eyes with which, once the veil of the body is overcome, they see one another), through your sensibility, as I started to say, oh outstanding friend, you felt the extent of my devotion toward you. Love compelled you to love in return; something which a number of indications but especially two recent letters of yours which Giovanni d'Arezzo, your chancellor, showed me, made me recognize very plainly. In these letters, amazing as it may seem, while you may have sent your messenger here on many matters of high importance, you inquire not about the state of the Roman Curia (than which there is nothing more base or incredible in this day and age), not about the condition of your closer friends, not even about the transactions of your affairs,

1. Son of Luigi I, initiator of the greatness of the Gonzaga family. Following his father's struggles against the Estes, the Scaligers, and the Visconti, he recognized the authority of the latter, and was made Lord of Mantua from 1360–1369.

in fact about nothing except about me and my doings. And you berate Giovanni because, although you were curious about other things, he was silent about that particular one which alone and above all others you wished to know about. And furthermore to be certain that no one might think that you had spoken casually, you asked the same favor in two letters. I omit other things you say that would perhaps provoke marvel in those who do not know on what friendly terms Caesar Augustus held above all others Virgil, your fellow townsman, of peasant origin but hardly a man of peasant genius; and also Horace, a freedman by birth but free-born in literary skill; and in those unacquainted with the letters often filled with pleasant flattery that this ruler sent to those humble friends as if to equals. The recollection of these things, while they may diminish the wonder, increase my joy so much the more because I feel myself becoming associated with such examples, and because the road to such glory is being opened to me. As another of these friends of Caesar says, "To have pleased princely men is not the least of praises." And here indeed a new miracle emerges; namely, that while there was much to be pleasing in them I must confess there is nothing pleasing in me. For how can I hope to be pleasing to others since I am not pleasing to myself? We call a woman fortunate who is not beautiful but appears to be so to her husband; we call a slave fortunate not because his work is superior but because the love of his master is deep. Thus with me, whoever I may truly be, if I seem worthy of your esteem, I would call myself happy in your opinion, and if I possess nothing that makes me likeable, nevertheless, if I do please, that is sufficient. I would render thanks to you except that I distrust my ability to use words worthy of your kindness; and it is wiser to be silent about those things that exceed one's ability to speak.

On the bank of the Rhone, the ides of January.

Fam. III, 12.

To Marco Genovese,[1] that even those who serve the state can love piously and honestly and can also aspire to the silence of a loftier life above the din of the active life.

You have, most excellent man, made your mind perfectly clear in your letter; for no one can speak in such a manner unless he feels strongly. I feel the strength of your style (your great love dictated your words), and I gladly and eagerly hasten to open the doorway of my friendship. Why do I say "open" when more than four years ago I offered it to you at your own most welcome request? I recognize my Marco, and I embrace him with delight in these letters of yours as after a long silence he rightfully returns to me. I now perceive the extremely rich and pleasing benefits of your blossoming character. Indeed, I always hoped that from the young man you were you would become a great man. But I confess that I did not believe that it could happen so soon. Your virtue, being premature and for that reason more pleasing, surpassed my hope. I also recall that most glowing proposal of yours which in those early days of our friendship in extended discourse you trustingly revealed to me. I do not regret that now that proposal is either modified or, hopefully, merely postponed, provided you tell me, as you had promised at that splendid beginning, that you would love God in all circumstances, that you would adhere to Him, worship Him, and long for Him with your entire mind. I am not imposing an impossible rule upon you. Where I am bidding you to go is a much trodden road. How many outstanding men arrived gloriously from the storms of public life to the silence of cloistered gates; how many also, having dropped anchor far from such gates, have completed the voyage of this life most happily! The Divine Potter knows our true image. He knows what is good for us and for our soul. Often He indicates in indescribable ways the paths on which He wishes to be approached. Do not despair, therefore, that you seem to be entering a byway, or as the Pythagoreans call it, the sinister path; or that your concern for your citizens,

1. Unknown correspondent.

which requires so much of your time, appears opposed to that divine grace which you seek. Persevere, proceed, do not hesitate, do not abide nor fail in your own salvation. He is present who foresees all your time infallibly and eternally (regardless of how you arrange it). Nor is there any reason why you should meanwhile think that you were born in vain if you were to assist your fatherland with your labor and with your counsel, especially in these times when it needs you so badly and, as Plato indicates, rightfully demands a part of your birthright for itself. Heavenly is that saying of my Africanus in Cicero's work: . "For all those who have preserved, assisted, and supported their fatherland, there is certainly a definite place in heaven where the blessed experience joy eternally." Well known also is what follows: "There is nothing that may be done on this earth that is more acceptable to that supreme God who rules over all this world than the assemblies and meetings of men united by law and forming what is known as states." The time will doubtless come, my friend, which you long for, when you can raise yourself from the ground not so much as did Maro or Ennius but like Ambrose or Arsenius with wings powerful enough for flight. You will at length do what you have long done in your mind, and with the same Helper who was your inspiration; and you will accomplish it, as I hope, in the security of a more perfect age and of a more mature judgment rather than in the attempt of a youthful indiscretion and impetuousness. For just as the road is safer for the pilgrim over land free of highwaymen and over plains and solid roads under a calm sky, so when the passions are quiet, the judgment secure, and the ferment of youthful pride restrained, through the more moderate and serene years of life, one proceeds in greater safety to salvation. No age is rejected, however, as I have said, no one who participates in honorable activity may be excluded from this path. It has also been established, according to the opinion of Plotinus, that one becomes blessed and is cleansed not only through the penitential virtues but also through the political ones. To speak of a Christian example, Martha's active solicitude is not to be scorned even though Mary's contemplation may be superior.

There you have within our narrow limits of time, dear friend, as much as can be said about one of your requests, that I write you some useful information about life. What I send you came from a brief period of time before dawn and is indeed very short, but is in itself, I believe, complete if I were to add the following: a shortened path to virtue has been seen by philosophers as undertaking to become what we wish to appear. And nothing is more effective, I believe, than another saying since it pleased the same philosophers: the entire life of learned men is nothing more than a preparation for death. So far I have tried not to instruct you but merely to advise and exercise your memory. Still remaining is your request that I keep you always in mind. I find it helpful here to use your own words. Be assured that I have been doing so a long time. From when I first saw you I fixed your image indelibly deep in my heart like a faultless diamond which no time can remove, nor any place. Finally, I would like to congratulate you for the virtue and good fortune by which you deserved the friendship and kindness of so great a prince. And for the esteem granted to this little old man I express my gratitude. Farewell.

At the source of the Sorgue, the calends of January.

Fam. III, 13.

To Friar Giovanni Colonna, that the gout is common among the wealthy.

I am going to babble an old maid's tale to you but one that is apropos. A spider once on a journey met the gout and said, "Where are you heading so sadly?" The gout answered, "I met a rural and shaggy guest who tortured me with perpetual hunger and labor, and who after having kept me roaming until night among clods and stones, would scarcely allow us both in our wretched state to go back to his dusty and empty home. He would never wear shoes without holes nor be without a very heavy bundle on his back. The evening that followed would be no better than the miserable day. He would comfort me with a dinner that was dismal indeed, with old pieces of moldy and hard bread and with garlic and very strong herbs, and he would pour vinegar into his murky drinking water. It was indeed a feast day whenever some Sardinian cheese was available. Having welcomed me in this manner he would have me rest on a couch whose hardness exceeded that of his little field. Arising then at dawn he forced me back into the hated work of the fields; and thus one day followed another with no respite and no hope of repose. On Sunday he would wash the sheep of his master or repair the bed of the stream or stretch out the hedge around the meadows. I therefore am fleeing this unending evil and the home which is so unfavorable to my way of living." Having heard these things the spider said, "Goodness, how different my condition is! I had a host who was effeminate and soft and for whom pleasure was not only the greatest but the only enjoyment. Rarely did he lead his feet outside the house; and he prolonged his dinner until dawn and his lunch until evening. Sleep, which possessed his remaining activities, was sought under fancy coverings, and to sleep was devoted whatever time remained beyond banqueting and dissipation. There were costly festive dishes, all kinds of foreign perfumes, fancy wines, golden utensils, jeweled drinking cups, walls covered with silk tapestries and floors with purple carpeting, and together with all this a host of servants always in movement, running to and fro and yet present everywhere. While this throng sweeps with brooms, and while it shakes out the dust from the paneled beams, I can scarcely spin my skillful webs, and, even when I started sadly to do so, at the very beginning of my work I would see my hopes dashed and my labors useless. When I was most unfortunately driven out headlong, I sought the shelves, but without success. The solid walls of snow-white marble left no lodging for miserable me. Therefore, I fled from the presence of these pursuers preferring a peaceful exile anywhere to the endless domestic labors." When the spider had finished speaking, the other answered: "My, how many are the good things which are lost either through ignorance or through neglect! Ignorance is the blindness of the mind, negligence is the sluggishness of the soul. One must keep his eyes open and must not put off those salutary things that offer themselves. It is clear from what I have said and heard that those things which may have appeared most unfavorable to us would have been most favorable if we exchanged quarters. My host would have been most suitable to you and yours to me." This plan appealed to both and they exchanged homes. As a result it came about that the gout lived among delights in the palaces of the rich and the spider in squalor and poverty in the hut of the peasant.

I understand, my friend, that the gout has sneaked into your home, and I am astonished. I did not think that there would be room for it in such a frugal home, and I fear lest it found there something appealing. But if it is true, I shudder no more at the evil than at the cause of it. I would prefer that you would have the spider as your guest. You must resist such beginnings. There is nothing more useful for resistance than vigilance, toil and fasting. As a boy I saw a young man with the gout, and I saw the same one as an old man free of the gout. I asked him how it happened, and he answered simply that he had done nothing other than to renounce wine altogether. Cicero recounts, and after Cicero others, that certain wealthy men having become hopeless with the gout returned to health when they became poor. I dare not order you to become poor, although if you understand, it would not be necessary to command. As I hear, you profess, among other things, to be a voluntarily poor man. Do I lie? Certainly within the dwelling of the religious and especially in the hut of the beggar there is no place for wealth. Wealth and indigence do not dwell together. Poverty being excluded I fear not so much that you store gold than, as the apostle says, that you store wrath on the day of wrath. Meditate on this since you have an understanding with Christ which you should recall very well. If you have forgotten, reread the text of the agreement and you will find what you promised Him and what He promised you. As I said, I am not forcing you to become poor, not because it would not behoove you to accept and me to give friendly advice, but because it displeases me to pour forth words and to speak in vain. For I see that the very name of poverty is horrifying and shameful to you and you cannot voluntarily lay aside what you have voluntarily embraced. This was a voluntary poverty which is called thriftiness by philosophers. This I urge you to adopt. This is the one road that I hold out to you for the health of your body. As another Hippocrates I offer you this perhaps bitter but healthy drug. If you wish to be healthy, live like a poor man. Gold which is hidden in a strongbox harms only the mind, the more delightful food harms both the mind and the body. Therefore, if you wish to eliminate the gout, eliminate pleasures; if you wish to eliminate all bad things, eliminate wealth. Farewell.

At the source of the Sorgue, 22 June.

Fam. III, 14.

To an unknown correspondent, an explanation for the turning down of a loan sought in the correspondence of a certain important friend.

I disdain with unrestrained indignation the yoke of money which weighs down kings. I shall not allow, God willing, that the soul become a servant of metals when it is disposed to greater things. However, although I forbid money to dominate, it refuses to submit and the one it cannot add as a slave it scorns as a master. I shall say even less: money is more proud than I have said and wishes to have me neither as master nor as a companion. It refuses my control, and does not admit my friendship. It breaks the crowbars, it unties all knots, it scorns the lock of my strongbox. When I seem to have locked it up, it seems to slide away through invisible cracks. As often as I consider that matter irksome, I also look upon it with favor when I look around me and observe those whom it has usually made its slaves or given hospitality to.

Since this is so, you will forgive me if I do not relieve your present financial plight, something that is more painful to me than to you. But so that you do not think that by writing you gained nothing, know that there is an abundance of excellent pledges that I have ready for you. However, I was not able through any expedient to persuade your servant to bring them to you. Order him to return to me, but with less stubbornness. Otherwise my own servant will come to you, although I would like our wound to be known to no one except the doctor. Furthermore, I should like to add that from your letter things appeared for both of us more humorous than pleasant. I received comfort for my condition, not because I delight in having your company in my poverty, but because it is not right for me to be indignant since so great a man has so much in common with me, and because you no longer have to seek an excuse. And so that you may not become too concerned, I already had my pen in hand, and in order to keep any information from reaching the ears of the greedy usurer concerning my affairs, I had determined to ask whether you could offer assistance to my needs. What should I say? I am not unaware of the fertile areas of philosophy and the very plentiful matter with which minds can be armed against the webs of fortune, among which poverty is not the last. And while such things are not permitted to dwell with us, because as Flaccus said so elegantly, "Something is always lacking to a meager patrimony," there are also many things that can be said to be healthy not only for us but generally. Although I could speak about them, I shall not do so in order to avoid following that public custom of exchanging words for things. It is an easy friendship to offer advice in place of help. In such cases which are common in my house (and they could have been very rare except that I am careless about my patrimony because of my more noble cares) when I have found many kinds of remedies either concocted by myself or by more learned men, then I try that most effective solution of all which says that all fortune has its annoyances; or that other one which may be very true if one were to undertake some serious investigation, that every life even though it may appear very happy on the surface, is tormented; or finally that the most troublesome and demanding, and if you want to look more deeply, actually the most miserable state of all is that of wealth. On the other hand, though difficult, poverty is extremely safe and unimpeding, while the intermediate condition is best of all, and I rejoice that among the rarest gifts of God this has befallen to us. If sometime we lack anything, heavenly generosity compensates us with great numbers of gifts for what we lack and causes our good fortune to be sweeter for us because of the brief taste of bitterness. But if we lack many things, indeed all things, I nevertheless feel that I am happier being needy in a praiseworthy fashion than abounding with riches in a base fashion, and that those who place dishonest wealth before honorable need do not enjoy true wealth. Farewell.

31 December.

*to a quarrelsome friend, that just as the friendship of good
people is to be sought, so is the enmity of evil people to be
shunned.*

Try to be liked by all good men, and do not fear that you
may have too many friends or that I am suggesting too
much of a task for you. Wherefore I say that if you were
to make none but good friends, they would be few. "Good
men are indeed rare; they are rarely as many as the gates
of Thebes or as the sources of the wealthy Nile." You ask,
"Who says so?" What does it matter? If you approve the
saying, why do you seek the answer? As Augustine says,
"All truth partakes of the truth." I agree. Would you perhaps deny it? Experience speaks, which is not accustomed
to lie; the truth speaks, which cannot lie. But if you want
to know the human author, it was Juvenal who said it, most
skillful in such matters and acquainted most deeply with
the ways of men. If you do not believe him, listen to another
one, through whose mouth speaks One who not only knows
but created men. And what did he say? "There is no one
who does good, not a single one." The poet said few, the
prophet said no one; and according to each one's perspec-
tive, they are both right. Since one must not despair that
good men can be found, and since when we begin to despair
of all we must necessarily also begin to despair of ourselves,
consider that some men are not only good but excellent. For
the sake of harmonizing these differing opinions, listen to
Flaccus who speaks out arbitrarily: "No one is born without
defects; best is he who is marked by fewest." And indeed
it is so. The stoics certainly clamor in their pledge to remove all disease that is rooted in souls. They would become
the most outstanding of doctors if they could only deliver
on their promises. But in this life of men, from among whom
we must choose our friends, experience shows that there is
no mind, regardless of its serenity and tranquillity, which is
not sometimes moved by light concerns and shaken by upsetting human affairs. Just as an armed ship blown about
the high seas is not overcome, so also for the mind the best

praise is that it does not succumb. So that, though the Stoics disagree, it happens that in this life in which we know nothing to be perfect, we consider a healthy state any light and curable disease. Therefore, to return to the main subject of this letter, with this kind of man try to make friends by whatever means possible, not with those having no defects at all, but with those whose defects are inferior to their virtues (a group that you will learn is in itself very small). However, you will accomplish this in no better way than through the imitation and practice of their conduct and zeal. On the other hand, however, be neither friend nor foe nor acquaintance to the evil ones whose number is countless. They focus on your looks and ignore your mind. Pay heed to the advice of that man who warned: "Let all things be different within, but let our looks adapt to the people." Let them believe that you do what the people do. But you should do the tasks that are yours and something always a little greater in your own eyes. In such a way you will most likely avoid safely the hazards of the world, being dear to the few, unknown to the many, and hateful to no one. And do not think that today I have been philosophizing without basis. I hear that you have undertaken a huge war and a severe feud against wicked opponents and are wavering as to whether to reform them or destroy them. To do both things is of course impossible, and I consider it somewhat easier to destroy them than to correct them. I praise the stings of a generous indignation, but I do not praise an indecisive contest and vain zeal. If, in fact, it is wise to shun useless toil, what do you think about that toil whose only fruit is hatred? Therefore sound a retreat, I beseech you; otherwise be certain that you will be needing many legions. Farewell.

Fam. III, 16.

To Paganino da Milano, that patience is the only remedy in adversity.

My, how many things can be said now in answer to your letters! But neither have I the free time nor do you need the help of words. I am considering another kind of remedy. The power of fortune is great, as is its speed. Without doubt, of all those things which happen either in books or in the midst of the life of men, and they are indeed many and varied, this is the most important. I confess that there are some difficult and serious and unpleasant things that you are undergoing. There is only one consolation in adversity: patience. And especially if you disdain earthly things, if you keep in mind that you descended into this arena of life not for pleasure but for toil, if you endure adversity with great effort, and recall that a soldier's courage is tested in war, the sailor's in the storm, and a good man's in adversities. Farewell.

Fam. III, 17.

To the same correspondent, the time to think is before acting.

Far be it for me to dissuade anyone from complying with a reasonable request; but I remind you to observe foresight just as I thus far have observed hindsight. There is nothing more pleasant or more sweet than to be a partaker in helping someone who is deserving and needy. On the other hand, there is nothing sadder than unexpected ingratitude. It is indeed a sign not only of great knowledge but of great fortune to discern among so many hiding places of the heart the pure minds from the false ones, and to recognize before becoming acquainted whose prayers are sincere and whose tears are wretched, whose need is fictitious and whose flattery is feigned. It is common for most men to be mindful of those things that they wish to come to pass, and forgetful and slow when it is time to express gratitude. Men's minds are subject to so great and so sudden change that someone you may see entreating you in the morning you would not recognize in the evening after his request has been granted. About these *Ecclesiasticus* says: "As long as they may receive, they kiss the hand of the giver and they lower their voice in promises; and at the time of restitution they will request time and will speak words of weariness and complaint." You know the rest. But since we live among ingrates, we should not stop for that reason, otherwise virtue will seem to have been overcome by vice. I believe we should go a little more cautiously.

Farewell, and for whatever you are to do, think carefully while there is time for changing your mind; for subsequent deliberation is too late.

To Giovanni dell' Incisa,[1] *to whom he has entrusted the search for books.*

What formerly forgetfulness or laziness often kept me from doing, I want now to deal with, dear brother. And if I may be allowed to brag I shall do so in the name of Him in Whom alone it is safe to brag. Divine mercy has now almost freed me from the throes of human cupidity, if not perhaps altogether, for the most part at least. It was from heaven, therefore, that this was granted to me either through the goodness of nature or through age. Having indeed seen so many things and considered so much, I have finally begun to understand how many are these desires with which the human species burns. Lest you consider me immune to all the sins of men, there is one implacable passion that holds me which so far I have been neither able nor willing to check, for I flatter myself that the desire for noble things is not dishonorable. Do you wish to hear the nature of this disease? I am unable to satisfy my thirst for books. And I perhaps own more of them than I ought; but just as in certain other things, so does it happen with books: success in searching for them is a stimulus to greed. There is indeed something peculiar about books. Gold, silver, precious stones, beautiful clothing, marbled homes, cultivated fields, painted canvases, decorated horses, and other similar things, possess silent pleasure. Books please inwardly; they speak with us, advise us and join us together with a certain living and penetrating intimacy, nor does this instill only itself into its readers, but it conveys the names and desire for others. To cite some examples, Cicero's *Academicus* made Marcus Varro dear and attractive to me; and the name of Ennius I heard in his books on *Offices;* from a reading of the *Tusculan Disputations* I first felt my love for Terence; from the book *On Old Age* I became acquainted with the *Origins* of Cato and the *Economics* of Xenophon and I learned that the same book was translated by Cicero in his same *Offices.* In the same way

1. Theologian and Prior of the monastery of St. Marco in Florence. A relative as well as a close and trusted friend of Petrarch.

the *Timaeus* of Plato made me aware of the talent of Solon; the death of Cato made me know the *Phaedo* of Plato, while the interdict of Ptolemy made me know Hegesia of Cyrenaicus; and I believed Seneca even before I ever saw the letters of Cicero. Augustine prompted me to start looking for Seneca's book, *Against Superstitions*. Servius revealed the *Argonautica* of Apollonius; Lactantius as well as others made me long for the books on the *Republic;* Tranquillus the Roman history of Pliny; Agellius the eloquence of Favorinus, and likewise the budding brevity of Annaeus Florus prompted me to seek the remains of Titus Livy. To pass over the most famous and widespread works which do not need witnesses, the fact remains that when a more famous witness testifies, such works sink more deeply into the mind. For example, it is in the *Declamations* of Seneca that the eloquence of Cicero is praised and that an unusual announcement of his genius is made; while Virgil's prolific eloquence was shown by Eusebius in the *Saturnalia*. It was the respectful and humble testimonial by the poet Statius Pampinius to the *Aeneid* of Virgil, whose footsteps deserved so much to be followed and worshipped, that informed his *Thebaid* as it was about to be published; while the judgment, universally unquestioned, proclaiming Homer the prince of poets, was given by Horace Flaccus. I am citing more writers than is necessary, for it would indeed be much too long to recall everything I learned in my youth in reading Priscian, the grammarian, as, for example, how many foreign names of books he compiled, and how many later ones by Pliny the Younger, or how many contemporary ones I found in Nonius Marcellus, and how often they truly excited me. Therefore, to return where I left off, no one will be astonished that minds were inflamed and deeply shaken by those books, each of which openly displays its sparks and its stings and also bears hidden within it other qualities which reinforce themselves in turn. Therefore—while it shames me, I must openly confess it and yield to a truth—the passion of the Athenian tyrant (Pisistratus) and of the king of Egypt (Ptolemy) always seemed to me more excusable, not to say noble, than that of our leaders, because the zeal of

Pisistratus and that of Ptolemy Philadelphus seemed more noble than Crassus' lust for gold although he had more imitators. But in order not to have Alexandria or Athens downgrade Rome, and Greece or Egypt downgrade Italy, outstanding thinkers are part of our heritage as well, and they are so numerous that it is too difficult even to name them. And they were so dedicated to these things that there may be found among them those who held the name of philosopher more dear than that of empire, and I might add that they were eager not so much for the books themselves as for the contents. There are those who accumulate books like other things with no intention of using them, but with the sole pleasure of possession, and not so much to aid their thought as to ornament their rooms. To mention but a few examples, the Roman library was the care of the divine Emperors Julius Caesar and Caesar Augustus. In choosing an overseer for such an enterprise the former appointed a man who was not inferior to, and perhaps (without intending any slight) superior to Demetrius Phalerius who had been famous in Greece for this activity, that is to say, Marcus Varro; while the latter emperor appointed Pompeius Macer, a most learned man. Asinius Pollio, the very famous orator, also displayed the greatest enthusiasm for the Greek-Latin public library and is said to have been the first of Rome to make it public. Of private concern, on the other hand, was Cato's insatiable desire for books, to which Cicero testifies, and Cicero's own passion for acquiring books about which ample testimony may be found in his letters to Atticus of whom he makes the same request with great urgings and prayers as I do now to you. If it is permitted to a very great talent to beg for the services of books, what do you think should be permitted to a poor one? I have not achieved what I had considered most important in this portion of the letter and what seems scarcely credible without citing the zeal of a very learned man and the friendship of princes which calls one back to reality. Amonicus Serenus is remembered as having a library containing 62,000 books all of which he left to Gordian the Younger who was then emperor and a disciple of his, a matter that made him no less famous than the empire. I say all these things as an excuse for my vice and as a comfort to such renowned colleagues. As for you, if you care for me, make this request of some trustworthy and lettered men: let them search throughout Tuscany, let them roll out the closets and chests of their church people and other men of letters in case something might emerge that might be suitable to soothe or irritate my thirst. On the other hand, although you know in what lakes I am accustomed to fish or in what thickets I am accustomed to go bird hunting, to avoid having you be deceived I insert as a separate enclosure those things which I especially desire. And so that you might be more vigilant, know that I sent the same requests to other friends in Great Britain, France and Spain. Make an effort not to let anyone surpass you in faith and industry. Farewell.

Fam. III, 19.

To his Lelius,[1] *concerning the stubbornness of human expectation.*

Hope in men is so obstinate and determined even against proven misfortunes that none is deterred from his undertaking: not the farmer facing bad crops, not the sailor facing the storm, not the architect facing the destruction of buildings, not the father facing the tragic destruction of his children. Because all these have the same things in common we see the famished sowing, the shipwrecked sailors sailing, those barely saved from ruins undertaking to rebuild upon the same foundations, and childless adults undertaking further procreation among the very graves of their children. I have before my eyes here some fishermen exhausted from cold and hunger. It is extraordinary and utterly unbelievable that though hungry and naked all day, they yet spend their nights awake until dawn with the same lack of success whether they use hooks or nets. They accomplish nothing, they suffer uselessly and in vain, and they lose time which could perhaps more usefully be spent differently. Nor, obstinate from the beginning, are they minded to turn away from the dangerous eddies. Thus a long-lasting habit of undertaking bitter activities becomes pleasant. Sweeping the unproductive sands in the deepest stream beds, they discover the poverty which they flee amidst the waves and the reefs, never finding perhaps what they so obstinately seek. Indeed I'm not sure whether still other examples which may be simpler to relate are not more worthy of admiration. I speak of the striving of beasts, which, though they leave their lairs very often, are never still. The tiger never ceases to produce new offspring and, if they are lost, to feed older offspring; doves deprived of the comfort of their young lose none of their drive in their remaining activities; Philomena, after the theft by the shepherd, follows her lost young

1. Lello di Pietro Stefano dei Tosetti was a very strong Roman supporter of the Colonnas. Petrarch first met him during his journey to Rome with Giacomo Colonna in 1330, and he became, with Socrates, one of Petrarch's most intimate friends. Petrarch classicized his name in memory of Scipio's closest friend, Laelius.

with a long sigh and very sweet plaints, and suspends the nest from the very same branch, tempting fortune with subsequent births. I shall now tell you something which is unknown to you but widely known by all the inhabitants of this valley. For some time an eagle has been living in these mountains. A foreign swineherd, not less shaggy than the swine he feeds but even rougher than the wild boars, secretly lay in wait at the eagle's nest considering his soul worth no more than it perhaps really was. Having let himself down with a rope (I remember all this with horror) from the very high cliff which from the clouds overhangs the source of the Sorgue, he approached the lofty home like a rash hunter and removed from the concerned mother her featherless young which were her hope. He tried it once, twice, and other times, and finally forced the eagle to move, for having seen her nest emptied so often, she after a while carried away her nest and all its holdings to another portion of the cliff. There she revived again the hope of replacing her lost offspring, but I'm afraid with no better luck than before. For that persistent enemy of hers, desirous of petty gain, extravagant of his life, is already preparing more rope and knots with which hanging in the void he may capture the usual spoils from the unusual perch.

In our discourse we have now slowly descended to the smallest of subject matters. Neither does the wrong done to the bees when their honey has been stolen remove the sweetness of making honey, nor does the flooding of the underground stores of the ants lessen their industry and their pleasure in constant going to and fro, nor do they despair of being able more happily to undertake what had already been undertaken unhappily. Otherwise, if the heart's hope perishes with the succession of events, human motivation which we perceive on all sides will become inert as fortune interferes regularly in all human actions. A life which is already withering can lead only to an inglorious end. And perhaps so that this would not happen to any living being, and especially to man, tough and determined hearts were given to humans. To climb back again in one easy step from lowest matters to the loftiest, the elders rebuilt the city of Rome which had been burned by the Gallic Senones, a matter in which the authority of Camillus with the help of omens prevailed against the resisting tribunes. Similarly those elders of ours returned to the battle lines after the defeat of Allia, and after the defeat of the Ticino, and after Trebbia, and after Lake Trasimeno. And following the disgrace of the Caudine peace they won a most glorious victory. And after Cannae, a most serious and almost fatal wound to the republic, in order to avoid having Italy abandoned by its cowardly citizens, the flashing sword of Africanus won the day despite the advice of Cecilius Metellus. And if the unbending hope of one man, and indeed of a very young man, had not supported the wavering minds of many old men, the empire would have been finished, and there would have remained no memory of the Roman name and no trace of Roman power. For Hannibal, to use the words of the historian, Florus, would have made an Africa of Italy, and indeed not Latin but African colonists would possess Italy. And if anyone of Italian blood would have survived after so many disasters he would have been nothing more than a small stream of water mixed with the open sea among the foreign customs and victorious foreigners. Therefore what we are not and what we are, I confess openly, we owe so far to the positive hope of a single man. So much for now about our own. What should I recall about the Spartans or about the Carthaginians who never ceased hoping as long as they existed? What about the Saguntini who, while hoping until the very end for help from us, accepted incredible afflictions from a very cruel enemy? It would be tedious to discuss all such examples. Therefore, so that my discussion may cease where it started, hope is the last anchor of a threatened ship. If this anchor tears away from those who are struggling in the stormy sea, there is no way left in life, no port for rest, no return to safety. You may now wonder what such a long disquisition wished to show. Only one thing: that you count your friend among that number whose hopes are few and perhaps vain, but always strong. For me these things needed to be explained more carefully so that you might be aware of the affection of the writer. Other things you understand without mention. Farewell.

Fam. III, 20.

To the same correspondent, a complaint about his silence and
what a relief it might be to be freed from useless expectation.

I have often labored with my letters to entice you to write,
but I have thus far failed. I shall continue to interrupt your
silence hoping that you will be ashamed to listen to so many
noises of your friend in silence. I shall force open your lips
either in indignation or perhaps in a smile or in a flow of
words. I will not care too much about what you will reply; by
your simply beginning to speak I shall be the victor. If old
concerns hold you, I shall add new ones; if you have lost the
pen of laziness, I shall give you back the pen of assiduity. But
if perchance you are puffed up with pride and, to confess
something which I cannot possibly suspect, you consider it
unworthy of you to correspond with your friends, I feel that
I must drag you from that extremity of mind and bring you
back into the even fold of friendship. Therefore be assured
of this: I shall not stop directing complaints and laments to
you until you return to your former level of interchange of
correspondence with me—at least as long as we continue to be
so close that neither can claim a lack of messengers and the
exchange of letters amounts almost to handing them to each
other—or until such time as you make clear the cause of such
a great change. The footsteps of one messenger will be followed by those of another; heaps of my letters shall appear
before your eyes; you know the writing and the seal of your
friend, and your love and respect will not permit you to
throw them away untouched. You will open them despite
yourself, and they will flatter you to read them thoroughly.
Thus, you who are avoiding the labor of writing a brief letter
will not avoid the trouble of a lengthy reading. Therefore,
believe me, free your eyes with the aid of your fingers and
teach the more ignoble parts of your body to serve the more
noble ones. Take your pen; what I ask you is not unusual.
The pen has been your sword since your childhood. Your
adulthood and the condition of your homeland later forced
you to bear other arms. Finally you returned to the more
peaceful halls of the Roman pontiff and to your former

studies, as your destiny wished. What am I therefore asking? Do what you do daily, write something, and do what you likewise never do, write to me. Soon, of course, I shall take a stand and either myself write more seldom or more briefly. I shall be happy with having triumphed and with having cast you down from that stronghold of your silence. At this point, however—and I know with whom I speak—you find cover under that old and common shield: "Oh brother, what do you expect? I have nothing to write." But I, although I could never believe that in such an abundance of possibilities and for such a talent and eloquence there could ever be lacking any subject matter to write about, I am much more prone to believe that some other cause, whether true or fictitious, has imposed such silence upon you rather than a cloak of forgetfulness. Therefore, I ask of you at least this which many have asked of their friends, but among those whom I have read Cicero comes to mind first: write that you have nothing to write; write this very fact but somehow in other words, otherwise I shall have indicated to you a path which was much too short and open to escape, which was not my intention. You will escape, if I know you, with a single leap and redeem yourself with a single word of which I was author. And I, as it happens to many, shall have fooled myself with my own advice.

But now enough of excessive complaining lest in trying to achieve revenge I punish your silence with loquacity. And to be certain to include in this letter something about my domestic problems, I ask you to intercede with our common lord for a successful conclusion of my affairs and I would consider any of them successful provided that at least one is brought to conclusion. It is a great thing, dear brother, to be freed from a vain expectation. Men do not know what an advantage it is to abandon superfluous and infinite desires. Once lost they satisfy and once possessed they torture the minds of wretched men busy with more vain things than with firm ones. And such is this madness, that they fear to be freed from their errors to make place for the truth while they promise themselves a successful conclusion to huge undertakings. Indeed, being self-indulgent, haughty, and bad judges of their affairs, they imagine themselves worthy of having all things happen at their command. Thus as Ovid said concerning affairs of love, "While each of us is pleased with himself, we are nothing but a credulous mob." Already we have lived half of our lives amidst widespread madness. As Cicero has elegantly stated: "Everyone wishes for himself the good fortune of Metellus." How many, however, are deceived by this empty hope, indeed how very few are not so deceived! Hence we must point out that if we accept the testimony of ancient writers Metellus who was forever happy had only one friend, and that friend is said not to have been at home but far off and outside the boundaries of Italy. The reference does not describe the extent to which these two actually usurped the vain name of happiness. Perhaps there will be another time to speak about this. For now, so that I might complete what I began, if no one achieves what everyone hopes, consider how many there are who deceived by the dreams of life and waiting for their fulfillment were overtaken by death, and how many will ultimately be overtaken. Terrified by this I became determined to pursue the following rule for myself: that I would not seek things that were loftier than I, that I would indeed modestly seek a few things equal to my powers, and that I would enjoy them and should I lose them that I would bear it bravely and would not be torn by sorrow. I fashioned myself according to this rule, that in order not ever to dread any coming event I had to eliminate the brother of anticipation. Wherefore I beg you, dear brother, in the name of the Heavenly Host to free me as soon as possible from this perplexity. Free me from my strong anticipation. Whatever will happen I shall bear patiently. I shall come to a close by citing that writer whose following words I particularly like: "It is a part of kindness to deny quickly what is being sought." Farewell.

To the same correspondent.

There clearly came to pass between us what is written about your Pompey and his Cornelia: "As they departed, neither found the strength to say farewell." But there was no need for too many words to be exchanged between us since they are mere conveyers of the spirit and feelings that they symbolize, and as such they are known to us, since our hearts are mutually accessible in silence. There is one thing which I would like you to do if the possibility presents itself. A certain young man knew a young maiden with whom he was madly in love and who did not discourage him when he proposed marriage to her. And all this (and please note this in particular) happened either *in thoro* or *in Thor*. The lord of the place—should I call him noble or uncouth?—called for the death of the young man whom he had persecuted with a grievous and ancient hatred. The young lady publicly forgave the young man saying that nothing had happened between them contrary to her wishes, and asked that her promise of marriage be carried out. He agreed if this were possible, but being presently confined in a prison he knows that he will be tried before a prejudiced judge. However, were the fetters to be removed and both parties exonerated, being of the same age and attitudes and wealth, they would be able to celebrate the highly desired marriage. When all these things were reported to me first through the outcry of indignant people and then through the entreaties and complaints of friends, you came to my mind first of all as someone who should be sought out to render assistance in such a distressful situation. We too, dear brother, were victims of love at some time, and it behooves us to render assistance to others in love. Although such things do not affect our master or his lofty spirit, I do not believe that he is so hard or inhuman that he would not commiserate with such human weaknesses. Nor should we suppose that rural types undergo passions with less suffering. That bow-bearing Cupid has equal power over all kinds of men. I know that Virgil writes that "a sudden madness overcomes the incautious lover," and adds "indeed pardonable," but then finally adds something frightening, "if the Manes knew how to pardon." For I fear lest that more cruel Bellerophon possessing no human traits and furthermore inflamed by anger might not be more thirsty for blood than is proper. However it turns out, let us fulfill our duty, I by appealing to you, you by appealing to our master that he seek through his letters from the previously mentioned lord of Thor the liberation of his prisoner as a voluntary gift. My steward whom I have sent to you for this one purpose will inform you of the man's name and of all the particulars. You will find him no more urbane than the lover for whose madness we are asking indulgence.

At the source of the Sorgue, 26 April.

To the same correspondent, on the notable effects of eloquence and of music and the fact that the most savage beasts are soothed by flattery and sweetness.

What do you wish me to say to you? It is as I have heard and read. No nature is so rough that it is not soothed by the sweetness of customs and words. So did that elder Africanus of mine pacify with speech Syphax, the king of the barbarians unaccustomed, as Livy says, to Roman ways; and even more surprisingly pacified Hasdrubal, the Carthaginian leader, a barbarous and savage enemy to Rome, during the progress of a banquet and a pleasant and friendly meeting. Thus did Julius Caesar begin speaking so mildly and caught in the nets of his Caesarian eloquence Amycla still covered with seaweed and foam, a mere naked and helpless fisherman. As a result, attracted by the unusual sound of Caesar's words and because of his admiration for his unknown host, Amycla, at Caesar's command, untied his fragile and unseaworthy boat from its safe mooring, and wanting to appear eager to obey, hastened to certain destruction. But the Africani and the Caesars aside, that prince of philosophers, Plato, was able to win over Dionysius, the tryant of Syracuse; as the poet, Euripides, did Archelaus, the king of Macedonia; the unbending, tyrannical spirit of the first and the barbaric excess of the latter could not resist, and the hardness of both was softened by talent and eloquence. The orator, Antonius, offers another example of this kind, one which surpasses all wonders, for he held in check with a flattering speech the cruel executioners sent to kill him when they had already drawn their swords. His eloquence conquered their cruelty except that one of them, not having heard him speak and arriving after the others had left, like an asp not hearing the voice of the enchanter, struck him with the venom of his wicked deed. But why do we search for examples from among men? We see bears, leopards, lions and other fierce, powerful beasts, softened by flattery, patiently obeying the command of a weak master and accepting chains, prison, threats and blows. And we see birds who roved the skies, against the primeval law of their nature, preferring human companionship to their own liberty, and we see them spending their life in fetters with a covering over their heads, with no further hope of seeing their native land, controlling their hunger, following the will of their feeder, taking food from his hand, recognizing the voice of their captors, obeying their calls, going and returning according to the order of their owner, and bringing back excellent catches not for themselves but for their master. Concerning fish I do not remember reading anything similar except that dolphins have an affinity for humans by some strange kind of attraction. And there is a historical or rather a fabulous story about a certain Arion who seated on the back of this fish rides about the crashing waves of the sea. And it is said that this unusual passenger sings to the lyre, the instrument making the voyage easier, the music charming the ears and lifting the unusual vessel over the surface of the water. Such a story, it appears, could not be accepted except as fable, for instead of rudder, mast, sail, and oars there was only the sweetness of music.

But you will ask to what purpose all these strange allusions. So that you may understand that I consider your talent among the greatest since, having freed your bait from the rocks, you have succeeded in capturing with your words and presence the friendship not of men, beasts, or birds, but of this aquatic animal which was brought up among fountains and rivers. He did indeed return to me unmindful of himself and mindful only of you. When I asked him questions about his master and his friends, his answers concerned Lelius alone; how he had admired his handsomeness, his conduct, his speech, his dwelling, his clothing, and as if he were one unknown to me he praised him in his rude and atrocious speech. When he wove very long stories about him to me which I often interrupted with Terence's question, "Alas, do you praise him to me?," he would start all over again from the beginning. What more can I say? I understand that you have taken away from me with your skill my farm hand. I confess that I did not grieve nor was I envious; I was astounded that you in one hour were able to do more than I in all of ten years. It is truly astonishing unless you blend in your conversations some form of magic art. Now, therefore, captured by love for you he is returning to you once more with this letter. At the same time he is counting on you for some kind of assistance through the intervention of our master in order to set free his friend about whom I wrote you the day before yesterday and who now is threatened with a desperate situation. However, the mind of the judge which I have feared from the very beginning, obstinate in wanting the young man to be punished, may not be open to entreaty. Rumor has it that he is going mad with grief and envy, according to what they say, over the plucking of the maiden's flower to which he himself greedily aspired; furthermore, that he is most indignant because in this love affair the flattery of a nobody accomplished more than his own useless riches. But though words may, perchance, be wasted on deaf ears, the merit of compassion nevertheless will remain unblemished with our lord, and the fruit of goodness with you. The young man, with my help, will also pay off the debt of his gratitude. As for that unfortunate lover, if it cannot be otherwise, he will repay the sweetness of his love as many have done with the bitterness of death. Meanwhile you will reckon this messenger among your humble friends, for he considers you among his foremost masters. Indeed he seems to me to be more desirious of your favor than of the life of his former friend. Therefore in order to impress you deeply and to indicate with a symbolic little gift that his soul is most delightfully devoted to you, he brings you a small bottle of the softest of all liquids, oil, which flowed from the fruit of our trees covering these hillsides perfectly naturally and, as they say, virginally because not subject to force. Here I would say that the inventor of the olive, Minerva, dwells after having deserted Athens, except that sometime ago in my *Africa* I had already placed her on the shore of Genoa in Porto Venere and in Lerici. Farewell.

At the source of the Sorgue, 29 April.

Fam. IV, 1.

To Dionigi da Borgo San Sepolcro [1] *of the Augustinian Order and Professor of Sacred Scripture, concerning some personal problems.*

Today, led solely by a desire to view the great height of it, I climbed the highest mountain of this region which is appropriately called Windy Mountain. The idea for this trip had been in my mind for many years. As you know, my destiny has been to live here since childhood. This mountain visible from any direction has always been in my sight. The drive to do what I did today finally overcame me, especially after having re-read some days ago in Livy's history of Rome how Philip, King of Macedonia—the one who waged the war against the Roman people—ascended Mount Hemo in Thessaly from the summit of which he believed two seas were visible, the Adriatic and the Black. Whether his belief is true or false I have been unable to ascertain, both because the mountain is far removed from our land and because the disagreement among the authorities makes it a doubtful matter. To mention but a few, Pomponius Mela, the cosmographer, asserts without hesitation that it is true; Titus Livy considers it false; as for me, if I could climb that mountain as readily as I can this, I would quickly clear up the uncertainty. But putting this matter aside, I shall return to my mountain, and tell you that it appeared excusable for an ordinary young man to do something considered appropriate for an old king. Yet in thinking about a companion to accompany me, I found no one, alas, who seemed to qualify for the undertaking, so rare even among dearest friends is that perfect harmony of inclination and of custom. One seemed too slow, another too careful; one too deliberate, another too rash; one too gloomy, another too joyful; finally one too foolish and one, whom I wished to have come along, appeared too prudent. The silence of this one, the impudence

1. A professor at the University of Paris whom Petrarch met in Avignon probably in 1333. His extraordinary learning and abilities prompted King Robert to appoint him professor of theology at the University of Naples in 1338–39.

of that one, the size and weight of another one, and the thinness and feebleness of still another terrified me. The cool incuriosity of this one and the burning concern of another dissuaded me. Although they are serious, such faults may be endured at home—for charity supports all things and friendship rejects no burden. But on a journey the same faults become very serious. Therefore my delicate mind, seeking honorable delight, carefully considered each quality individually without detriment to any friendship, and it quietly foresaw and rejected whatever seemed to be troublesome for the proposed trip. What do you think? I finally turned to a strictly domestic assistance, and I disclosed my plan to my only brother who was younger than I and whom you know well. He was delighted at the news and rejoiced that he was considered both a brother and a friend by me.

On the determined day we left home and came to Malaucène in the evening, a place at the foot of the mountain, looking north. We lingered there for a day and finally the next day with our individual servants we climbed the mountain after considerable difficulty. It is a steep mountain with rocky and almost inaccessible cliffs. It was well said by the poet, however: "Persistent toil overcomes all things." The day was long, the air was mild, and the determination of our minds, the firmness and readiness of our bodies and other circumstances were favorable to the climbers. The only obstacle was the nature of the place. We came across an elderly shepherd on a slope of the mountain who made every effort with many words to keep us from continuing our climb, saying that fifty years earlier, driven by a like youthful motivation, he had climbed to the very top and had brought back from there nothing but repentance, weariness, and his body and clothing torn by stones and bushes, and that no one had been known before or since to dare undertake a similar climb. As he shouted all these things, we, like all young people who refuse to heed warnings, felt our desire increase as a result of the prohibition. When the old man observed that he was arguing in vain, he accompanied us a short way among the cliffs and pointed out the steep path, giving and repeating many warnings as we turned our backs to him. Leaving behind with him our extra garments and whatever else might have been a hindrance, we made ready to start the climb alone, and began to do so cheerfully, but, as usually happens, weariness swiftly followed our extraordinary effort. Not long after our start, therefore, we stopped on a cliff. From there we once again began our climb but more slowly; and I, in particular, pursued a more modestly inclined mountainous path. My brother proceeded to the heights by shortcuts over the ridges of the mountain, but I, being weaker, turned toward the lower reaches. To my brother, who would call me back and indicate the most direct path, I would answer that I hoped to find an easier passage on the other side of the mountain and that I would not be afraid of a longer road if I could advance more easily. Having offered this excuse for my laziness, I was still wandering through the valleys without finding a more gentle access anywhere by the time the others had reached the summit. The road got longer and my burden grew heavy. Meanwhile, exhausted with weariness and troubled by the confused straying I was determined to seek the heights. Finally after I had reached, tired and distressed, my industrious brother who had refreshed himself with a long rest, we climbed along for some time side by side. We had scarcely left that hill, however, when I, forgetful of my former wandering, pursued the easy length of the paths and headed down hill to end once again in the valleys. Thus as before, I encountered serious trouble. I had tried to put off the annoyance of having to climb, but the nature of things does not depend on human wishes, and it is impossible for a body to arrive at a summit by descending. What more need I say? This happened to me three or more times within a few hours, not without my annoyance or my brother's laughter. Having been thus frequently deluded, I sat in one of the valleys and there proceeding from the physical to the metaphysical in mental flights I reproached myself with these or similar words: "What you have experienced so often today in trying to climb this mountain you should know happens to you and to many others as they approach the blessed life. This is not easily realized by men, however, because although the movements of the body are visible, the movements of the mind are invisible and concealed. The life we call blessed is certainly located on high, and, as it is said, a very narrow road leads to it. Many hills also intervene and one must proceed from virtue to virtue with very deliberate steps. At the summit lies the end of all things and the limit of the path to which our traveling is directed. There everyone aspires, but, as Naso says, 'To wish is not enough; you must long for something so that you may succeed in anything.' You yourself certainly—unless as with many other matters, you are deceived in this too—not only wish but long for it. What detains you? Certainly nothing except the more level and, as it looks at first confrontation, less impeded road of earthly and base pleasures. Nevertheless, after you have wandered widely, you must ascend to the summit of that blessed life burdened by labor ill-deferred or you will sink slowly into the pitfalls of your sins. And if—God forbid—the darkness and shadows of death should find you there, you would lose the eternal light in perpetual torments." Incredibly such meditation brought new strength to my mind and to my body and made me willing to face whatever remained. How I wish that I could complete with my mind that journey for which I sigh day and night as I overcame all the difficulties of today's journey with my physical body! And I wonder why what may be done through an active and immortal mind without any physical action in the blinking of an eye should be far easier than something done over a period of time at the indulgence of a mortal and perishable body and under the cumbersome weight of heavy limbs.

The highest slope of the mountain is one which the inhabitants call "Sonny." Why I do not know, except that I suppose it is said by way of antonymy, as in some other cases, for indeed it seems to be the father of all neighboring mountains. On its summit there is a small plain. There finally we paused in a state of exhaustion. Since you have heard what thoughts ascended into my mind in the ascent, hear, father, the rest, and please grant one hour of yours to the reading of what happened to me in one day. First of all, moved by a certain unaccustomed quality of the air and by the unrestricted spectacle, I stood there as in a trance. I looked back. Clouds were beneath me. And suddenly what I had heard and read about Athos and Olympus became less incredible to me when I looked out from this mountain of lesser fame. I then directed my sight toward Italy where my heart always inclines. The Alps themselves, frozen and snow-covered, through which that wild enemy of the Roman people once crossed and, if we believe the story, broke through the rocks with vinegar, seemed very close to me although separated by a great distance. I confess that I heaved a deep sigh toward the sky of Italy which was visible to my mind rather than to my eyes, and I was overcome by an overwhelming desire to see once again my friend and my homeland. However, the way this happened led me to feel shame for my as yet unmanly desire for both these things, even though I did not lack either an excuse or the aid of scores of great examples for wanting both. My mind thus was overcome by a new thought and was transferred from those places to these times. And I began saying to myself: "To-day completes the tenth year since you departed from Bologna after completion of your youthful studies." Oh, immortal God, oh immutable wisdom, how extensive and how many changes within me during this interim! I shall skip an infinitude of them since not yet being in port I cannot recall in security the storms through which I have passed. The time will perhaps come when I shall enumerate all of these storms that beset my life in their appropriate order, prefacing it with those words of your Augustine: "I wish to recall all my past foulness and the carnal corruption of my soul not because I love them but so that I might love you, my God." As for me, there still remains indeed a great deal that is uncertain and troublesome. What I used to love I no longer love. I am wrong, I do love it but too little. There, I am wrong again. I love it but I am too ashamed of it and too sad over it. Now indeed I have said it right. For that is the way it is; I love, but something I would like not to love, and would like to hate. Nevertheless I love, but unwillingly, constrainedly, sorrowfully and mournfully. And in myself I miserably experience the meaning of that very

famous verse, "I shall hate if I can; if not I shall love unwillingly." The third year has not yet passed since that per-
verse and worthless inclination, which held sway over me
and ruled over my heart without opponent, began to be
replaced by another inclination which was rebellious and
reluctant. Between these inclinations a very insistent and
uncertain battle for control of my two selves has been going
on for a long time in my mind. Thus I pondered the decade
just past. Then I began to project my troubles into the future and asked myself the following: "If it chanced that
this transitory life would be extended another ten years
for you, and you were to approach as far toward virtue as
during the past two years—through your new inclination
doing battle with your old—you retreated from your former
obstinacy, could you not then, although not certainly but
at least hopefully, go to meet death in your fortieth year
or disregard calmly the remainder of a life which is vanishing into old age? These and similar thoughts were running
through my mind, dear father. I was rejoicing in whatever
success I had enjoyed, I was weeping for my imperfections
and I was bewailing the general mutability of human actions.
And I seemed somehow forgetful of the place to which I
had come and why, until, after laying aside my cares as
more suitable to another place, I looked around and saw
what I had come to see. Having been reminded and almost
awakened to the fact that the time for departure was at hand
because the sun was already setting and the shadow of the
mountain was growing, I turned to look behind me toward
the West. The boundary between Gaul and Spain, the Pyrenees, cannot be seen from there not because anything intervenes as far as I know, but because the human sight is
too weak. However, the mountains of the province of Lyons
could be seen very clearly to the right, and to the left the
sea at Marseilles and at the distance of several days the one
that beats upon Aigues-Mortes. The Rhone itself was beneath my eyes. While I was admiring such things, at times
thinking about earthly things and at times, following the
example of my body, raising my mind to loftier things, it
occurred to me to look into the *Book of Confessions* of St.

Augustine, a gift of your kindness, which I shall always keep on hand in memory of the author and of the donor, a handy little work very small but of infinite sweetness. I opened it and started to read at random, for what can emerge from it except pious and devout things? By chance it was the tenth book of that work to which I opened. My brother stood by attentively to hear me read something from Augustine. May God be my witness, and my very brother, that my eyes happened to light where it was written: "And they go to admire the summits of mountains and the vast billows of the sea and the broadest rivers and the expanses of the ocean and the revolutions of the stars and they overlook themselves." I confess that I was astonished, and hearing my eager brother asking for more I asked him not to annoy me and I closed the book enraged with myself because I was even then admiring earthly things after having been long taught by pagan philosophers that I ought to consider nothing wonderful except the human mind compared to whose greatness nothing is great.

Then indeed having seen enough of the mountain I turned my inner eyes within, and from that moment there was no one who heard me speak until we arrived back at the foot of the mountain. The passage had tormented my silence, nor could I believe that it happened by chance but rather thought that whatever I had read there had been directed to me and to no one else. On recalling how Augustine had supposed the same thing happening to him when in his reading of the book of the Apostle, as he himself relates, he first came across these words: "Not in banquets nor in drunkenness, in beds or in rudeness, in strife or in envy, but put on the Lord Jesus Christ and do not provide nourishment for the flesh in your lusts." Something similar had already happened earlier to Antonius when he heard these words written in the gospel: "If you wish to be perfect, go and sell whatever you own and give to the poor, and come and follow me and you will have your treasures in heaven." And believing that these words of Scripture had been read particularly for him, as his biographer Athanasius says, he gained the Lord's kingdom for himself. Just as Antonius upon hearing these words sought nothing more, and like Augustine, who having read went no further, so did I find in the few words which I have given the main point of the entire reading, and silently considered the extent to which true judgment was lacking to mortals who in overlooking the most noble part of themselves scatter their interests in various directions and become lost in vain speculations. What could be found within they go seeking without. I admired the nobility of the mind except as it had voluntarily deteriorated and wandered from its first beginnings and had converted into disgrace what the Lord had given to it for its honor. How often, do you think, upon returning home that day, when I turned back to look at the summit of the mountain, it seemed to me scarcely a cubit high in comparison with loftiness of human meditation if only it were not plunged into the mire of earthly filthiness. This thought also occurred to me at every step: if I had willingly undergone so much perspiration and toil to take my body a little closer to heaven, what cross, what prison, what torture rack should frighten the mind drawing nearer to God and willing to conquer the extremes of insolence and mortal destiny? And this thought also occurred to me: how many are there who will not divert the mind from this normal path either from fear of hardships or through desire for pleasures? Too happy man!—if there is any such person anywhere, I would think it is about him that the poet gave his verdict: "Happy is he who could know the causes of things and submitted his fears an inexorable fate and the rumblings of greedy Acheron to his scorn!" Oh with how great zeal one must toil, not to achieve a more lofty place on earth, but to trample underfoot our appetites which are exalted by earthly impulses!

Among these movements of my searching heart and without any sense of the stony pathway, I returned late at night to that little rustic inn from which I had set out before daylight, the full moon offering a welcome service to the wayfarers. And meanwhile, therefore, while the duties of preparing the meal occupy the servants, I have gone alone to a hidden portion of the inn in order to write this to you hastily and extemporaneously lest with delay my determination to write might subside with the change of place or of our feelings. See, therefore, beloved father, how I wish that nothing of me be hidden from your eyes, having carefully opened not only my entire life to you but even my simple thoughts. I beg you to pray for them so that having been rambling and unstable for so long, they may sometimes find rest, and having been tossed about hither and yon, they may be directed to the one, the good, the true, the certain and the stable. Farewell.

Malaucène, 26 April.

*To the same correspondent, congratulations on his trip to
Robert, the greatest king and philosopher, and the salutary
effect that the conversation of famous men has on one's peace
of mind.*

My ears have heard nothing sweeter since they heard you
announce that, upon summons, you visited the king. "I await
your comment," you say. Since I cannot respond briefly,
I shall respond at length. Your mother once wished for you
a long life which turned out to be exposed to countless
dangers and misfortunes. At other times she wished you
wealth, that extraordinary snare for human minds and deadly
burden upon freedom. At still other times she wished for
you beauty of the body which is very often the cause of
deformity of soul. What can I say about your comrades or
about your nurse? A single law governs all females: they
desire silly things, and they dread things of small account.
Your father, it is proper to believe, wished for loftier things.
He desired for his son what the Satirist said, "The eloquence
and fame of Demosthenes or of Cicero," things which are
often full of danger as is attested by the fate of both men.
The ears of the Lord are therefore fatigued by the many
empty prayers either your own or of others on your behalf.
I do not desire any of these things for you. Why? Because
it is foolish to seek furiously what can lead to a bad end.
I wish for you what I wish for myself, a blessed life, to
which many aspire but which few achieve. For the path
leading to it is rugged and narrow and difficult, while the
byways leading away from it are pleasant and smooth. As
with archery, in a number of human activities, to stray from
the mark is very easy. Hitting the mark is the goal, and because there is only one path to the mark but countless paths
away from it, the object is difficult to attain. Indeed what
I call the blessed life, which may perhaps have been viewed
differently by very gifted and learned men, may be perhaps
deserved and hoped for by human endeavor while enclosed
in the prison of the body, but it can never be embraced
and possessed. It is thus that one runs in this race-course:

the goal lies where all desires are appeased. This conviction is not held by us alone, for must not Cicero have been alluding to something like this when he said that this life is a passageway to heaven? Yet there are times when mortal life has some similarity to eternal life, so that while it may not be truly blessed (for that is truly blessed to which nothing more can be added), yet at times it may look upon human miseries as far beneath it, and even from the lowest depths it may gleam with the light of celestial happiness. This light certainly cannot be provided by weath nor by the applause of the maddening rabble, nor by power or pleasure, but only through the aid of virtue and peace of mind. While others may disagree with me on how best to achieve such peace, it is my considered opinion that nothing contributes more than familiarity with noble talents, and conversation with outstanding men. You perceive, I think, what I mean. Nevertheless I shall speak more clearly. "Who is more outstanding than Themistocles in Greece?" said Tullius; and I faithfully repeat: "Who in Italy and indeed who throughout Europe is more outstanding than Robert?" When thinking about him I find I admire his character more than his crown and his mind more than his kingdom. Him do I indeed call king who rules and controls not only his subjects but himself, who takes command of the passions which rebel against the mind and would crush him if he yielded. Just as there is no clearer victory than to overcome oneself, so is there no loftier king than the one who can rule himself. In what way could any man be my king who is ruled by ambition? In what way could he be invincible when misfortune overwhelms him? In what manner could he be serene whom sorrow beclouds? How could he be magnanimous whom the fear of the least things frightens? And to forego the shining names of the virtues, who can convince me that that man is free whom the multiple yoke of various desires weighs down? I shall descend and ask how we dare call someone a man who preserves only the outward aspect of a man, but is as ugly and as frightful as a raging beast because of his ferocious character? Therefore it is only by an astonishing if general folly that a man is called king who is not a ruler, not free, and often not even a man. It is a great thing to be a king; it is a very small thing to be called a king. Kings are far more rare than the multitude believe; the title is not an ordinary one. Sceptres would use up less jewels and ivory if only true kings carried them. True kings carry within themselves what makes them vulnerable. They are truly kings when their guards are gone and their trappings are removed. Only the worship of exteriors makes the others terrifying. Robert is truly illustrious and truly king, for his true might is indicated by his many examples of incredible patience and moderation about which it would perhaps be better to speak another time. How widely he rules is made evident in the multi-lingual and multi-customed people and the large range of separate regions he controls. In a certain tragedy of his, your Seneca summarized what a king ought or ought not to do: "Wealth does not make a king, nor purple vestments, nor a royal aspect, nor royal quarters of gold; he is rather king who lays aside fear and the evils of a cruel heart." A little later he adds: "A good mind possesses royal power; it has no need for horses nor for arms nor for the useless weapons which the Parthian hurls from afar when he simulates flight. Neither does it have need to overthrow cities with machines that have been moved into place in order to hurl rocks from a distance. A king is he who fears nothing." These are the words of Seneca. To this king, therefore, to bring an end to what I started to say, you proceeded upon being called. That he should send for you, and that you should obey, could only have resulted from the very great similarity of your desires. Indeed how much comfort for his great cares he has garnered I would reveal if I were speaking to anyone else. As for you, there was no manner in which you might proceed more quickly to that internal peace which you often sought and to which the troubles of Tuscany drove you. I therefore congratulate both your prudence and your good fortune, and I repeat somewhat more confidently those words which I spoke at the time. When first hearsay and then your own letters told me that you had left Florence for Naples I said to myself and to my friends: "Our Dionysius is striving for peace of mind with great steps and he has entered upon the straight path to the blessed life."

As for myself I send you only the following news: I shall be following you shortly for you must know what I think about the laurel crown and how upon balance I have determined that only the very king of whom we speak and no other will bestow it upon me. If I shall be considered sufficiently worthy to be called, all well and good. Otherwise I shall pretend to have understood differently the sense of his letter which he himself sent me with the highest and most friendly courtesy though I am unknown to him; and as if in doubt I shall play primarily the role of seeming to have been summoned. Indeed I have answered his royal style in a very common manner as if stunned by lightning, for our talents were too different, and our lutes, as they say, too unequal. Farewell.

At the source of the Sorgue, 4 January.

To the famous king, Robert of Sicily.[1]

A highly unusual brightness has blunted my eyesight. Happy is the pen capable of writing with such magnanimity. What shall I admire first? The exceptional brevity, the majesty of the ideas, or the divine charm of the eloquence? Oh illustrious king, I confess that I never believed so great a matter could be said so briefly, so seriously, so elegantly, and truly I never expect anything again like it from a human mind. So that one might know that you hold the hearts of men in your hands, a power to which the effort of all illustrious orators aspires, you move the mind of the reader with such a variety of emotions that without effort one can follow the train of your thought everywhere with a wonderful ease. At the very beginning of your sober discourse while you deplored most magnificiently the greatest of human miseries and the most bitter burdens of hardships and that most harsh inevitability of death as it gradually creeps from the roots of the tottering trees and branches, I was moved so deeply that frequently sighing as I read, and terrified by our inevitable destiny and even detesting this name of man, I found myself nearly wishing not to have been born or ever to be born. When this happened, and I thought all my peace destroyed, the hand that had inflicted the fatal wound soon began to offer a pleasing remedy. I recognized that the author of the unexpected grief and of the sudden consolation was one and the same, and I was never more certain of the power of eloquence. So powerfully through the choice of a few words and under the pretext of the immortality of the soul and of future rebirth did you uplift my sick and wavering mind that I was soon rejoicing at having been born a mortal. For what greater blessing can one conceive than, once divested of our garment of flesh and thus free from these chains, reaching the day (following the completion of certain cycles of time) when we, having overcome death, put on immortality, thereby restoring in-

1. Ruler of southern Italy from 1309 to his death in 1343, and scion of the French Anjou family.

dissolubly and reforming the rotten garment of our flesh half eaten by worms and altogether rotten? Although none of the classical philosophers ever achieved this hope, the belief in immortality is nevertheless very ancient, not only among our own thinkers but even among those who have never heard the name of Christ. Except for Epicurus and a few others from his notorious flock, there was no one who denied the immortality of the soul. I shall bypass in this matter people such as Pherecydes who was the first proclaimer of this belief among the Syrians and his disciple, Pythagoras, and all of his following, as well as Socrates and all his followers. Plato, a very great man, published a notable book which Cato of Utica used, it is said, as a comfort on his very last night so that he might more boldly approach contempt for this life and love for his decreed death. Later Marcus Cicero in his *Tusculan Disputations* and in the sixth book of his *Republic* with his divine sort of oratory proclaimed the same beliefs; and again in his dialogue, *Lelius*, on true friendship, and in that book which is called *Cato the Elder* dealing with the defense of old age, and in many other places he touched on this belief. Thus it troubles me terribly that so much revealed truth should remain unknown. But to whom am I speaking these things so foolishly? Surely not only to the king of our day but to the king of philosophers. Please forgive me if the heat of discourse has driven me not only to embracing your royal teachings to which I owe so much but to confirming them with appropriate support, because they have affected me so deeply that I now confidently and full of hope await that day of death so dreaded by the human race.

Such a day has been experienced by your granddaughter whom you celebrate and refer to at the end of your letter. It appears to me that she is rather to be envied than to be mourned for her sad fate. For although she was snatched away in the flower of her age and of her beauty, and with the lament of almost the entire world and especially of the two kingdoms where she was born and where she was transported amidst tears and weeping as a rare and select object of distinction, she herself is happy not only because she has crossed over the frightening threshold of death to the pleasures of the eternal life but because you have glorified her for all time in your highly noble praises. For who can really dare to declare dead and indeed not gloriously alive the one whom God in heaven and you on earth wish to have live? I say, oh doubly fortunate lady who, in place of one temporal life which in itself was brief and uncertain and exposed to a thousand misfortunes, has attained, as it were, two eternities of which one is owed to a celestial king and the other to an earthly king, the former to Christ and the latter to Robert! Receiving these two gifts from such generous givers, she should for that reason seem more fortunate because she has been favored by those who are most worthy of favor both in heaven and on earth, for a great deal accrues to such gifts from the character of the donor. It matters a great deal from whom you receive a kindness and to whom you may consequently be subject. I shall of course not touch upon the condition attained in the blessed immortality of heaven, nor upon the most blessed alteration of such a life, for my strength is not sufficient to pursue such ineffable matters. How great, in short, is the glory which you have acquired for her with your highest praises? There is little doubt that as long as the epigram or epitaph, however you prefer to call it, lasts (and I am confident it will be eternally) in which you honor the memory of your departed granddaughter, so long will she survive with you and with the most famous names of all the ages. There are those who might wish that a similar eulogy for an untimely and lingering death could serve as compensation for a limited life, and those who with endless sighs will repeat the words presumably spoken by Alexander the Macedonian about Achilles: "Oh fortunate one to have found such a singer for your virtue!" But I fear that the length of this letter may displease you, and besides, your highly elegant brevity warns me not to ramble any longer. I therefore stop, praying to God and all heavenly creatures, to ordain that your serenity, decorated with the twin laurel crown for military triumphs and for letters, continues to flourish most happily.

At the source of the Sorgue, 26 December.

Fam. IV, 4.

To Giovanni Colonna, Cardinal of the Roman Church, where best to receive the laurel crown.

I find myself at a difficult crossroads, and do not know the best path to take. It is an extraordinary but brief story. On this very day, almost at the third hour, a letter was delivered to me from the Senate, in which I was in a most vigorous and persuasive manner invited to receive the poetic laureate at Rome. On the same day at about the tenth hour a messenger came to me with a letter from an illustrious man, Robert, the chancellor of the University of Paris, a fellow citizen of mine and well acquainted with my activities. He, with the most delightful reasons, urges me to go to Paris. I ask you, who could ever have guessed that anything like this could possibly have happened among these cliffs? Because the affair does indeed seem almost incredible, I have sent you both letters with the seals still attached. The one letter calls me East, the other West; you will see with what powerful arguments I am pressed hither and yon. I know that in almost all human affairs there is hardly anything enduring. If I am not mistaken, in a great portion of our cares and actions we are deceived by vain shadows; nevertheless just as it is the spirit of youth to be more desirous of glory than of virtue why (since you afford me permission to brag confidentially) should I not consider this as glorious for me as did the most powerful African king, Syphax, when he was called into an alliance by two of the greatest cities of the whole world, Rome and Carthage? That was indeed a tribute to his rule and to his wealth. This is being granted to me personally. His devotees found him amidst his gold and his jewels seated on an exalted throne and attended by armed guards. My friends found me in the morning wandering in the forest, in the evening over the meadows or walking on the banks of the Sorgue. I was offered an honor, whereas aid was sought from him. But since pleasure is hostile to reason I confess that though happy about the event, I entertain grave doubts in my mind, being driven on the one side by the charm of novelty, and on the other by reverence for antiquity; on the one side by a friend, on the other by my native land. The fact that in Italy there is the king of Sicily, whom among all mortals I accept as a judge of my talents, turns the scales in one direction. So you can see the flux of my uncertainties. You who did not hesitate to extend your hand in their behalf, help my fluctuating mind with your counsel. Farewell, oh glory of ours.

At the source of the Sorgue, calends of September, at eventide.

Fam. IV, 5.

To the same correspondent, acceptance of proposed advice.

Not only do I accept your advice, I embrace it. It is magnificent and most worthy of your wisdom and humanity. I am not troubled by the fact that you are a friend of my native land, for you are a greater friend of truth. I shall go where you order. If anyone perchance should wonder about the choice I shall refer first to the reasons and then to your name, for quite often authority is accepted in place of reason. There now remains only the determination of what words I should use to excuse myself to my dear Robert of Paris who will, I know, understand my action, so that not only he but that famous university will realize, when the news becomes public, that its case was well-presented. But concerning these things I shall speak to him more at length personally; for I hear that he is himself coming to me for the express purpose of taking me to Paris. If that is the case, I shall conclude the affair at that time. To what you ask at the end of your letter, until I have had sufficient time to mull it over, I cannot respond unless I were to fabricate an answer. It is a story which is foreign to my nature, and what makes it even more so is the fact that in the meantime I have been involved in matters that are totally extraneous. It is as Sallust says: "When understanding is involved, the mind is king." Furthermore, the matter is very old and has been absent from my memory for a great number of years. Therefore, to use the words of Plautus, "A long day makes the mind uncertain." But we shall discuss that at greater length in person.

At the source of the Sorgue, 10 September.

Fam. IV, 6.

To Giacomo Colonna, Bishop of Lombez, on the same matter.

Not for the first time today do I understand the tricks of fortune. She does not so much attack us as scatter and separate us lest we offer each other consolation in happiness or adversity. She knows how many cares once troubled my heart, cares which only you could help to alleviate. Then in my frantic search for advice upon returning from the North I discovered that you, the only comfort of my heart in that pressing affair, had departed. Even though you had departed for Rome, your homeland and the homeland of everyone, always longed for by me above all other places and at that moment desired not only for itself but because of your presence there, my heart was sad and downcast because of the difficulty of joining you. I appear to be in exile wherever I am without you, and at that particular time being especially distressed and burning with love, I envied Rome for you and you for Rome. I was in such a state that with fate opposing my youthful enthusiasm the few years in which we lived apart seemed like many centuries. As you saw, I finally came to you despite the rigors of winter, of the sea, and of war. Love does indeed overcome all difficulties, and as Maro says, "devotion conquered the difficult journey." While my eyes sought their venerable and delightful object, my stomach felt no disturbance from the sea (although naturally very impatient about the uncomfortable condition), the body felt no rigor of winter or of the land, and the mind felt no threats of danger. Thus I proceeded to you completely committed, thinking only of you and not seeing other things. Once I found you, no memory of the lengthy road remained. And now that same fortune turns her sneers against me so that as I head for Rome you have gone to Gascony and the furthermost shores of the West. It appears that we are most separated when I most desire you, oh supreme token of my glory. But the very nature of human desires is such that what is longed for most is achieved with greater difficulty. But so that you may be mentally present, if not in person, know that driven by the desire for the Delphic laurel!—which once was the unique and special object of desire of outstanding rulers and of sacred seers, but now is either scorned or forgotten—I spent a great number of sleepless nights as I often revealed to you. And when I in my insignificance was eagerly implored by two of the greatest cities, Rome and Paris, one the capital of the world and queen of cities, the other the mother of the studies of our time, after careful consideration and thanks primarily to your great brother who above all others served as my advisor and counselor, I determined finally to receive it nowhere else than in Rome on the ashes of ancient poets and in their dwelling. So on this very day I have begun my journey. It will require more time than usual for I must first go to the king, visiting Naples, and only then take the road to Rome. There I shall remain a few days, and if I am right, the affair will take place on the Capitoline on Easter, April 8. You ask why so much trouble, enthusiasm and care. Will the laurel make me the more learned or better? You say I will become perhaps more famous and therefore more exposed to envy; that the mind is the seat of knowledge and of virtue which find their proper seat there and not in leafy branches like little birds. "To what purpose therefore this pomp of foliage?" What will I answer, you ask. What else except those words of that learned Hebrew: "Vanity of vanities, all is but vanity"? Thus are the ways of men. Farewell, and do let your thoughts accompany me with favor.

Avignon, 16 February.

To Robert, King of Sicily, on his laurel crown and against those who praise the ancients while always despising things of the present.

How much the study of the liberal and humane arts owe you, oh glory of kings, which you yourself preferred to pursue with considerable industry, if I am not wrong, rather than attempt to become more famous through the crown of a temporal kingdom, has been known to the world for some time. Recently you obliged the abandoned Muses with new kindness by solemnly consecrating to them this talent of mine, however small. To this end you decorated the city of Rome and the decaying palace of the Capitoline with unexpected joy and unusual foliage. "A small matter," someone will say. Nevertheless it is something very conspicuous because of its distinguished novelty and because of the applause and delight of the Roman people. This custom of the laurel crown, which has not only been interrupted for so many centuries, but here actually condemned to oblivion as the variety of cares and problems grew in the republic, has been renewed in our own age through your leadership and my involvement. I know many other outstanding talents throughout Italy and in foreign countries which nothing would have kept from this goal except for its long disuse and the ever suspect novelty of the affair. After my personal experience with it I am confident that the novelty will wear off in a short time and the Roman laurel will be vied for through competition. For who could seriously hesitate when King Robert is one of the patrons? It will be of help to have been first in this competition in which I do not consider it to be inglorious even to be the last. I myself would not have been imbued with such a desire feeling so unworthy of such an honor unless your support had provided me with strength and courage. And would that you could have adorned the joyful day with your most serene presence which in fact, as you yourself were accustomed to say, were it not for your age which did not allow it, your royalty would never have stood in the way. I actually felt through many signs that you enjoy testing for yourself certain customs of Augustus Caesar and particularly the one which caused him to show himself not only gentle but friendly and warm to Flaccus, son of a freedman who had previously been an opponent; and not to despise the plebeian origin of his Virgil in whose talents he delighted. An excellent trait indeed, for what is less becoming to a king than to expect an artificial nobility in those of outstanding virtue or talent who actually possess the kind of true nobility with which you yourself could provide them? I am not ignorant of what certain contemporary men of letters who belong to a haughty and lazy group opposed to this would answer. They would say: "Maro and Flaccus are now buried; to waste fine words on them is in vain: distinguished men have long perished and only the mediocre remain as with wine only the dregs remain at the bottom." I know what they might say and what they might think; nor can I oppose them on every count. It seems to me that those words of Plautus applied not only to his age when a taste for such things had barely begun, but even to ours. He says, "The flower of poets lived at that time, and they have departed hence for a common abode." We indeed can more worthily complain in such a way, for in those days there had not yet arrived those whose departure he laments. However, the intention of these men is most suspect, for they do not say what they do in order to lament the destruction of knowledge, which they wish to remain destroyed and buried, but in order to discourage through despair the contemporaries whom they are unable to imitate. Doubtless the despair which holds them back motivates us, and the bridle and chains which affect them, are goads and spurs to us so that we try to become what they believe no one can become except one of the ancients. Although I confess that such men are rare and few, there are some. And what forbids one to be one of the few? If this very rarity deters everyone, there would be in a short while not a few but none at all. Let us make an effort, and in keeping our hope alive perhaps we can achieve the goal. Maro himself says: "They are able because they know they are able." Likewise, believe me, we too will be able if we truly believe it. What is your opinion? Plautus deplored his age, grieving perhaps the death of Ennius or perhaps of Naevius. The age of Maro and of Flaccus was also not just to such great talents. The one, poet of divine inspiration, while he lived, was harassed by endless contentions among his rivals who slandered him as a plagiarist. The other was accused of insufficient admiration for the ancients. It has always been and always will be true that veneration is accorded the past and envy to the present. About you, however, oh greatest of kings, worthy to be numbered among philosophers and poets, one can say with even greater truth, what Suetonius says about Augustus: "He fostered the talents of his century in every possible way." And you foster the talents of your century and always favor them with your kindness and indulgence. And I speak as one who has experienced also what follows in that author: "You listen kindly and patiently to writers reciting their works, not only poems and histories but orations and dialogues. But you feel offended that anything he composed about you unless it is done seriously and by distinguished writers." In all these things you have imitated that same emperor, and you have turned away from those who are unhappy with everything unless they are attracted by the impossibility of ever achieving it. I have recently been honored by these ways of yours and by your courtesy just as many others have, by mere chance and without deserving it. Not, as I said, would your royal esteem have stopped here if either old age were more distant or Rome closer. This messenger of your majesty, who intervened in your behalf in all the functions, will tell you personally what happened to us either in Rome or after our departure, whether joyful or dangerous. As for the rest, your very last words urging me to return to you as soon as possible shall remain forever in my memory, and as God is my witness, not because I was taken by the splendor of your court as much as by your talent. I expect from you riches different from what are usually expected from kings. Meanwhile I pray that He who is the fountain of life, and the King of kings, and the Lord of lords prolong the years of your life and ultimately transfer you from this mortal throne to an eternal one.

Pisa, 30 April.

Fam. IV, 8.

To Barbato da Sulmona,[1] *royal secretary, on the same laurel crown.*

On the Ides of April, and in the 1,341st year of this age, on the Roman Capitoline, in the presence of a large multitude and with great joy, there occurred what the King of Naples had decreed for me the day before yesterday; Orso dell' Anguillara, a friend and senator, a man of lofty talents, honored me with the laurel crown as approved by the King's judgment. The King's hand was absent, though not his authority nor his majesty; his presence was felt not only by me but by all who were there. Your eyes and ears were also absent, though your mind is constantly with me. The magnanimous Giovanni was likewise not there who had been sent by the King and was hurrying with astonishing speed when he fell into a Hernician ambush beyond Anagni. I rejoice that he was able to escape, but, though he was expected, he could not arrive in time. You will be informed about the other things that happened beyond all hope and expectation. But so that I might learn from fresh experience how sad things always accompany joyful things, we had scarcely left the walls of the city when I, together with those who had followed me on land and sea, fell into the hands of an armed band of thieves. How we were freed from them and were forced to return to Rome, how upset the people were because of this, how we left on the following day supported by an escort of armed men, and the other events on our trip would make too long a story for me to attempt to relate here. You will know everything from the bearer of the present news. Farewell.

Pisa, 30 April.

1. A member of the distinguished circle of humanists in the court of King Robert, he met Petrarch during his first visit to Naples in 1341. He was appointed royal secretary the following year, and upon the death of King Robert in 1343 he became head of a "school" of Petrarchists in Southern Italy. Petrarch dedicated his *Epistole metrice* to him.

Fam. IV, 9.

To Cardinal Giovanni Colonna, on the liberation of the city of Parma.

Returning from Rome, in possession of my long-desired laurel crown, and like a victor bearing with me the title of Laureate, which I modestly wish to announce to you knowing that it will delight you, I, today (to give you further news which will also delight you), entered Parma in the company and under the auspices of your friends from Correggio. As you know, we have been excluded from the city, but on this very day they too entered the city which had been returned to them after the garrison of tyrants had been expelled. Following the sudden shift in fortune and with the incredible rejoicing of the freed people, peace, liberty and justice have returned to the city. Overcome by their entreaties with which they accompanied their hope for your approval (about which I have no doubt), I determined to spend the summer here. They maintain indeed that they really need my presence which was certainly an indication of flattery rather than necessity. For in truth, of what use could I really be in this state of affairs? I take pleasure not in the noise of cities, but in the silence of forests. I hwas born not for legal cares or military matters, but for solitude and quietness. Indeed they themselves, aware of my desire, promise me real quiet when the din and ardor of exulting joyfulness diminish from sheer exhaustion. For whatever it might have been, I simply had to surrender to their kindly requests. You will see me at the beginning of winter. I say so unless you prefer it to be sooner or fortune later. Farewell.

23 May.

Fam. IV, 10.

To Pellegrino da Messina,[1] on the sad case of the untimely death of a friend.

I feel impelled to defer my painful grief which cannot be contained within the boundaries of a letter. The blow is not one to which my mind is accustomed and cannot be lightened by ordinary remedies, it has descended very deeply into my heart. Untamed fortune watched the place and time for the blow and waited for it to have its fullest effect. In what might be called the springtime of life she snatched away my Tommaso whom I can never mention without tears, with the best flower of his rare talent still promising the richest fruit of virtues and great accomplishments. His premature death, I must confess, makes all mortal things worthless to me. I see now how great is the strength of our existence and what I can hope for now, and I am warned by the example of that very close brother of mine. Our ages were the same, as were our minds, and our desire for knowledge, not to speak of an amazing sameness of inclination. We were truly one, we progressed on one path, we sought a single goal. Our work was similar, as were our hopes and our goals. Would that our end had come at the same time! I intend to lament this most bitter blow of the fate with myself, and, if I can, to apply the necessary remedies to my very deep wound and to console myself with my letters and with an appropriate volume. This is what Marcus Cicero first did at the death of his most beloved daughter in that divine and indeed inapproachable style of his. Many centuries later Ambrose did the same thing at the death of his brother. If only my affairs allow, I too should like to attempt the same with a more humble style for the death of my friend. In the meantime please accept the epitaph which you requested, still moistened with tears, and let my brief song appear upon the tomb and my grief upon the body of my friend. Farewell.

"Behold Tommaso, fortunate in talent and in mind, whom the hastening day of destiny snatched away. The land near

1. Brother of Tommaso Caloiro.

Pelorus gave him to the world, and the same land greedily took him away, and a death hostile to wretched me suddenly cut down the flower still young with fresh vigor. Shall I therefore express my gratitude for so great a gift by celebrating through song the Sicilian shore or should I rather lament the shameful theft? I weep. There is nothing sweeter to sad people than weeping."

Fam. IV, 11.

To Giacomo da Messina,[1] *on the death of the same friend.*

After the death of my dear Tommaso, I confess that I wanted to die but could not; I hoped for it but I was denied. I know what Annaeus Seneca would have answered had he heard this: that it is useless to wish for something that is in our power to attain. But I, though I follow the ideas of such a man in many things, disagree with him in many others and especially in this hasty and rash opinion which would not be difficult to disprove through the authority not only of our own philosophers but also through the testimony of foreign ones. But now is not the time for me to do so. Therefore, to come to the matter at hand, deeply shaken by the very sad announcement that I had lost the best part of me, and detesting a solitary and uneasy life without him, I was conveniently stricken with a fever that caused me most willingly to approach the very threshold of death. But when I desired to cross over the threshold I saw written on the gates: "Not yet, not until your hour has come." I continued worrying, but when I was finally repelled I suddenly returned to this life and now live so that anyone can see that I am living most unwillingly. However I do live hoping only for what others fear, and I cultivate my grief with the idea of the brevity of life. For I know that I have a treaty with death and a business agreement with the flesh. Would that I could spend whatever time remains in my life in such a way that I will be in readiness at all times and, as they say, hold what I owe always in hand in order that the words of the Psalmist will apply to me, "My soul is always in my hands." Farewell.

1. Brother of Tommaso Caloiro.

Fam. IV, 12.

To Cardinal Giovanni Colonna, a consolatory letter on the death of his illustrious brother Giacomo.

Grief impels me and love urges me to write something. Only despair of achieving anything positive dissuades me; for I believe that you do not need such help with the most recent anguish inflicted upon you. Will grief overcome? Will love conquer? Will despair yield? Impelled by an innate devotion I return to my pen which I had hitherto rejected and cast aside, for no other reason than that thereby the sorrow which burns within and oppresses my mind will cease for a while. And would that I could become—though untimely and unfit—the consoler of your grief! I know that Tiberius jeered at the envoys of the Trojans when they came somewhat tardily to console him on the death of his son; after hearing their message, he answered that he too was grieved at the death of their most notable citizen, Hector. But your mind is not on such things, nor are these your ways. Your devotion is very well known, your kindness common knowledge, not only to your own but to everyone. I am aware of how many sighs restrained perhaps by the strength of your mind or assuaged a little by the passage of time I may be renewing with these words of mine. I shall never attempt to lessen your misfortune with mere words. I shall rather confess that no one of all whom I have seen, heard or read about has lost more in the death of a single brother. See how abundantly I surrender to my tears and how I leave wide open a path for my sighs even as I eagerly try to eradicate completely your distress. Meanwhile let the sorrows flow in whatever way they can, recalling, however, that soon they will be able to emerge by hidden exits and, as happens with mournful minds, will continue to search constantly for different outlets to your grief. I see that your loss is enormous and in many ways extraordinary because of the death of so great and so beloved a brother. But I would consider it an infinite and inestimable loss only if death had destroyed him and not merely separated him from us for a short space of time. However, while he was here how little was the part of his life he spent under your eyes? I ask you, reckon the time as do the most devoted lovers, and recall the time from the end of your infancy to the present. Far from his homeland during the most glorious exile of his father he was brought into life. He uttered his first cries in a distant land; then, a boy of respected ability, he spent much of the more tender years of his life apart from you, but even when he was with you, you were both of an age when you were incapable either of sound judgment or of founding an enduringly solid love. Thus he was either far from you or he was in effect absent from you. Then, as he approached the end of his adolescence, because of his great and unequaled love of letters, he wandered far and wide sometimes through Italy, sometimes through France. And so, while busy satisfying his noble thirst by traveling through different lands, he plunged into almost every type of study, and thereby obligated himself until his manhood to live in voluntary exile.

After this, through admiration for his virtue, which earned him dispensation without any trouble, he was early raised to the bishopric. He performed his duties in such a way that all prominent men except himself felt shame that he did not occupy a more lofty position. He was completely free of any ambition or avarice, and happy in his fate he notably occupied the rank of bishop. Not only did he not desire a loftier position but rather indeed detested and hated such elevation and feared the heights of supreme good fortune as if they were a precipice. Witness to all of this is not only the tenor of his entire life and his language which he did not change even in the most intimate moments, a sign of his lofty and tranquil mind, but the letter which he wrote you with his own hand and which testifies fully to his seriousness, modesty, and contempt for earthly things. As I reread it I do so always with many tears of happiness, for that letter is with me since you considered me worthy of being its custodian and capable of replying to it. Now I even seem to behold him as if he were present and seem to hear his living voice; indeed because he so completely covered in the letter with very few words those things that pertain to sobriety of the mind and to the blessed life, there remains little need for the special learning of philosophers. Among other things, amazing as it sounds, while we were trying so hard to have him occupy a loftier position, he affirms with a religious oath that he is far happier with his state than one might believe, that he did not wish under any condition to rise higher, and that he not only hoped but desired to die in the very state he found himself. Yet, however unwilling, he would have risen to the height to which his renown and the merit of his blood entitled him, had envy, which rules courtly minds, not intervened; and after such envy had yielded to his glory and to his virtue, had an ever ready death not outstripped the course of his most vigorous youth at midpoint. But I shall return to my main line of thought. Having been made a bishop, and feeling the very demanding care of the office which had been entrusted to him, he forthwith departed from you and hastened to his own see, not at all alarmed by so great a change of affairs and of place. He who had been nourished amidst Roman wealth and charms, very serenely and calmly crossed to the heights of the Pyrenees. His arrival brought changes not as much to his features as to those of the region, nor did it seem that he himself had crossed over into Gascony, as that all of Gascony seemed to have passed over into Italy. Having journeyed with him, I find the very recollection of that trip makes me happy as I recall his gentleness in his good fortune, his humility over his many natural endowments, the respectability which is so much to be admired in that kind of person, finally his constant thoroughness in his observance of all his rites, and his seriousness which is more to be desired than hoped for, not so much in a young prelate as in an older one. Interrupt me, whenever you find me in error; but in all that time, you did not see your most beloved brother. On returning he perhaps stopped to enjoy for a while the highly desired company of his brother. I truly believe that he hoped to do so, for I am certain that he desired it. But that lady who controls the actions of men, Lady Fortune, prohibited it. Being summoned by the troubles and cries of his home and of his homeland, he felt obliged to go to Rome where I too after a long period of absence followed him, as you know, having been charmingly invited and having finally received your permission. I believe that God brought all this about so that as an admirer and witness of his twin virtue in peace and law I would take an active interest in the deliberations of that most prudent soul. After seven years in his homeland where he observed that steadfastness of patriotism and of mind which makes Rome recognize that he alone preserved what remains of her, and even while confessing that she owes her preservation to his ashes, he came back to you but remained no longer than to direct to you his very last salutation and farewell. He departed at once feeling distress because of the vacancy left in his deserted see and being desirous of a solitude which he felt would compensate for the long time he had spent in the press of a great many people. And so, having decided to live for himself as he had lived for his homeland and for his friends, he once again returned to his bishopric. There, living with great honor and becoming a victor over himself as formerly he had conquered others, he entrusted his life most exemplarily to God and to man. At length having spent one year there, and still a young man, he was transported from the storms of this life to a port of rest and to a happier kingdom.

Review with me each one of these moments, dearest father, and do not be displeased to talk about your brother with one who mourns in him the loss of his own honor. And as nurses are accustomed to do with infants who have fallen let me try after such a grievous misfortune to find whatever comfort there is in words. Examine with me therefore the total time of your brother's life. You will admit that he spent a very small portion of his life with you and that you tasted his sweet brotherly company always in haste and, as they say, barely skimming its surface. And if you did not thus far grieve his absence, cease to do so now. However, what your wounded and torn mind will now answer me in silence I understand and know, for through frequent injuries by death I have become highly experienced. Your mind will say, "Are you not trying to convince me that the condition of death is the same as being absent? When he was absent

I hoped longingly to see him again, I knew where he lived and through constant reports I was comforted over his absence. But now that comfort and all hope has perished." I confess, indeed, that death and absence do not appear to me the same, but I do find a certain greater comfort in death. Both conditions do indeed remove the body; neither one removes the soul. Yet absence constantly holds distressed minds in suspense whereas death removes all needless anxiety from them. For who can withstand the absence especially of brothers or friends and feel secure unless he is completely unaware of human misfortunes and has no regard for the power and fickleness of fortune? Others can see for themselves, but from the time I have been here I have never received a letter from a loved one without trembling and fear. Even when I learn that all is well I am not free of concern. For who assures me that while the letters were reaching me across the Alps and over the sea some misfortune might not have befallen since it usually occurs in the blinking of an eye? Nor does it shame me to boast to you in friendship that I have devoted a great deal of time and study to this so that I would have my mind armed and prepared for sudden onslaughts of misfortune, and so that I might attain, if possible, what Seneca says: "The wise man knows that everything remains to be seen; whatever happens, he says: 'I knew it'." In truth, not feeling myself wise in countless other things, I feel the same way about this particular distress which to this day no matter how hard I try I have been utterly unable to overcome. Death must have freed you from such anxiety, and, unless I am wrong about the greatness of your mind, it truly did so. You know where your brother is and how he is, and you need not be fearful, as usual, of change in his fortune. If justice, if faith, if devotion, if charity clear the path that leads above; if the mind set free from earthly fetters is borne upward in freer flight; if heaven is the ultimate and eternal abode of good and well born spirits, we can be sure that your brother has ascended there. And unless some contamination of our mortality should be impeding him, which I certainly do not believe, he is on his way and now hastens freely and cheerfully to his fatherland. Moreover, wherever he is, he often turns his eyes to you and beseeches you not to impede his most happy departure with your mourning. Nor should the desire to see your brother upset you. You will see him in good time much more honored than before and much more joyful. Why not, since I myself do not despair of seeing him? Otherwise, I must confess, I would be inconsolably distressed. For who would deny me, a Catholic although a sinner, that hope which I find the Gentiles possessed? You understand to what I refer. I speak of Cato and Socrates whose opinions on this matter it is not necessary to recall since I believe they are better known to you than to me. Death, therefore, cannot forever take away from you the sight of your brother's presence, but has simply postponed your seeing him. Even if she had carried him off forever, there would still be no proper occasion for unbridled mourning; you mourn him either because he has been freed from toils and dangers, in which case your tears, I ask you to consider, are rather those of envy than of compassion, or because you have been deprived in the middle of this journey of pilgrimage of an important escort and have been abandoned by a most pleasant and delightful companion. It is a valid, but by no means sufficient, reason that distinguished minds are overwhelmed through such losses by the affliction of their own misfortune. Moreover, it is most fitting that as often as the memory of your loss returns before the eyes of your mind, so often should it also recall divine grace; for he is an ingrate who mindful of losses is foregtful of benefits. Therefore, while that bitter reflection which says, "Alas, what a brother I have lost!," stings the mind, let that other thought soothe it: "Oh what a brother I had, indeed what a brother I have and shall have eternally! Although he did not enjoy a stay here only as brief as was necessary for him, for me, for the fatherland, and for the world, it became of greater advantage to him alone to be separated from evil; thus God took him considering clearly his welfare and not ours." Indeed He might well have considered our welfare also, for who is capable of contemplating the hidden and inscrutable causes or effects of divine providence, when the Apostle himself, if I am not mistaken, said: "Who knows the judgment of the Lord, or who was his advisor?" What man dares to judge whether it is possible to answer anyone who is lamenting the death of another what was once answered in 3 verses on a tablet to a father concerning the death of his son: "Men wander through life with ignorant minds. Etynous enjoys the happy consent of the Fates. Death was good for both you and him."

Human rashness resists all goading and with the horns of its pride vainly opposes attacking fate only to be finally vanquished. What can I now say about the empty vows, the joy or the complaints of men? Concealed truth lies hidden on high; we are surrounded by a dark cloud; we are ruled by chance; blind we are led by the blind, nor do we know what is to be wished or feared by us, perceiving only through the shadow of the flesh. We groan at what is good for us; we rejoice at our wretchedness; we weep and we laugh without reason. Let each one follow his own opinion, to me the greatest of errors appears to be that we do not freely commit ourselves and our goods to God, that we put any trust in our own counsel having so often been deceived by it; that we are taken by so great a love for this mortal body of ours that we are hardly ever able calmly to depart from here or see our beloved ones depart, as if we were born for no other reason than to cling to the thick filth and to the dregs of our flesh, wallowing in the eternal whirling of the world's vicissitudes and the mockery of fortune. This would certainly not happen to those who meditate upon the many dangers of our desires. First of all, life is brief and the time of life is most fleeting. The sea of human affairs is made rough and stormy by adverse blows. Ports are rare and hardly accessible to men. Reefs are countless on all sides among which navigation is difficult and utterly uncertain. Hardly one in a thousand can swim his way to safety. Thus does Fortune rule us, lying in wait for every level of man. Thus does the fragile boat of our mortality strike against each obstacle. And can we among these obstacles wish for ourselves or for our loved ones a little longer life, when indeed, to tell the truth, this means but a longer exposure to peril?

Let whoever wishes to pretend that having once entered upon the journey of this life under favorable stars and with favorable fortune and finally with God on his side, he can have nothing harsh and troublesome happen to him. I declare that it is an impossibility, certainly unheard of through the centuries. Besides, even though danger may not be present, fear does not vanish. Therefore it would perhaps be more fortunate and less ill-advised, if it were up to us, to act like sailors who in a suspicious body of water are accustomed to turn their helms cautiously and lower their sails long before sunset, and thus seek the port of life and die while still in a budding age and in strength of mind and body and before reaching the point where longer life leads to the last difficulties of old age. Oppressed by such difficulties people complain about living and fear dying and thus often accuse the very time for which they had wished. Finally, they do not know what they do and do not wish to, so great is their uncertainty. Meditating on these and like things we have reason to abstain from blaming the decrees of heaven or the hastiness of death; otherwise our anguish and complaints will appear to be entirely selfish. Indeed I do not doubt that your brother, so dearly recollected, neither lived more than was necessary for himself nor was called when the time was least opportune, although for many, among whom I count my wretched self, he departed long before we wished or suspected.

I refuse to believe that you would find any consolation in those very unmanly expressions of feeling appropriate to inferior minds, such as: "Why did death overtake him so far away? Why is he not buried in his fatherland? Why could we not see him die?" Things such as these even that strong man who was nevertheless prone to tears seemed to lament in the works of our poet when he said: "I was unable to see you, oh friend, or to offer you, before my departure, a resting place in your native land." I shall not allude to popular sayings or try to show how truly small this earth is through geometric demonstrations, or that from whatever place one departs, the path to heaven is one; or that all our lands are not only a homeland for the strong but the birthplace of man. Who does not know such things? I shall rather refer to two things, both determined by divine providence. First of all, of course, that two cities although very dissimilar but extraordinarily honored by him while he lived should both courageously share the deceased, with Rome retaining the perpetual and eternal reputation of his citizenship, and the venerable church of Lombez the remains of its lord, a church which unless I am wrong in my prediction will never possess a more renowned inscription in all the centuries to come if of course you permit his remains to be in its possession in perpetuity. I hear in fact that you are considering having the remains transported to Rome, a matter concerning which I do not intend to influence you in so as not to seem unfair either to the city of which I am a citizen or to the church in which I am a clergyman. A second providential touch seems to be that only one of us was present to receive his departing embraces and words, thereby sparing the other such a sad experience. As everyone knows, wounds are less disturbing to the ears than the eyes.

I have prolonged this letter more than is proper, and I hope that, furnished with far stronger weapons against all misfortunes, you will find nothing in him to praise more highly than his faith. So let the matter come to an end; let the weeping cease; let the tears dry and lamentation be silenced. Do not consider your brother dead, for he lives. We instead die daily without being aware of it, and, oh human blindness, we fear death, beginning of the true life. Let him, therefore, be present not in your mourning but in your thoughts and in your conversations as though he were alive. Outlaw in your halls that silence of the pusillanimous which so many observe in homes which are in mourning where they avoid even the name of the deceased as though it were something sorrowful. Indeed, let his name resound gloriously and let it sink its roots in your home and stretch out its branches widely, especially because tombs need not fear the cloud of envy which eagerly settles on men of great reputation. If death made many who were hated and unknown at home and in the forum famous and popular, imagine how much more we can expect for this man whose life was always most delightful and remarkable, and if there is anything loftier than a superlative, whose death was even more remarkable? I urge you also to keep far from your door that other abuse of the rabble which I notice many following, especially Romans, that abuse which I have sometimes reproved, of never mentioning the name of the deceased without prefixing it with some expression of affliction like, "That poor man, that victim of misfortune!" They then drag out the unfinished name whose very first syllables can hardly be understood. Your brother unquestionably lived happily in this world and departed even more happly and now lives elsewhere most happily and should, therefore, be mentioned without hesitation. Lucan reports the words of the dying Pompey: "Let one not become wretched because of death." Well said, otherwise all men who have been born as well as all those who will be born in future centuries are miserable. Finally, I wish to stress one point again and again, and that is that certain distinguished men to whose names I need not refer, were not more praised for anything than because they bore the death of their beloved manfully. To this you ought to apply yourself more diligently since if you look around you, you will see that your actions are regarded as examples, that you are, as it were, among the loftiest mirrors, and the eyes of all are fixed on you. This your industrious dignity and the majesty of your very large family and the temperance of your past life acquired for you.

On the nones of January.

To Lelius, not a consolation but a lament over the same death.

We have lived too long, dearest Lelius. We should have died before God snatched away our most kind and considerate father, comfort of his sisters, joy of his brothers, hope of his friends and terror of his enemies; a model of conduct, a temple of virtue, an image of respectability, patron of literature, lover of studies, herald of talent and infallible judge of merit; envious of no one, envied by all men of note; pious, gentle, modest, moderate, courteous, stable, strong, just, liberal, generous, high-minded, foresighted . . . alas, I fail in my praises and cannot find what I may say worthy of so many virtues. I am either beguiled by love or the sudden veil of death has been drawn over the most radiant and visible light of the clergy in this age. When I received the announcement my heart alone knows in how great an eclipse I was plunged in my wretchedness, but my eyes are witnesses thereof. However, except for the tears of the parents and of the brothers, I think none can flow more copiously than yours. This is suggested to me by the gentleness of your mind and your deep devotion which you inherited but in which not satisfied to equal your father, you excelled. Alas, how often and with what joy do I think of that day which I hoped was approaching, when, yielding to the kind letters of the deceased, and crossing from the Apennines into the Pyrenees, I would stand unexpected before his desired presence and would reverently offer him my Roman laurel crown which, though unworthy, I wear, and which long before his simply hearing of it from a distance had afforded him occasion for great delight, expressed in a very elegant gift, a personally composed poem. Furthermore, I also hoped to offer him the new foundations of my *Africa* which would have been the second of two small but devout gifts. The Almighty forestalled my desire and I was not worthy to see such a happy and joyful day. How shall I now resolve my difficulty? How shall I make future plans for myself? What shall I do? Often I say these things to myself with tears: "Where are you preparing to go, oh unhappy one? The one you sought has departed. Where will you go? To his brother's palace which is in mourning and has been widowed of so great a splendor? Or to his tomb where your hopes are buried? Both would be places of anguish. Has not misfortune brought you enough mourning without your indulging in further tears, either by intermingling with a throng of grieving mourners or by kissing the fond hand of a haughty pope?" Such is my condition until you provide a sail for my feelings and give a definite direction to my shaky resolve. Farewell.

Fam. IV, 14.

To Sennuccio di Firenze,[1] *concerning the condition of his domestic help.*

I have in my home three pairs of servants, or, to speak more modestly, of lower class friends, or to tell the truth, of domestic enemies. Of the first pair one is far too simple and the other is far too shrewd. Of the second, one is rendered useless by his childishness and the other by his age. Of the third, one is mad and the other shamefully lazy, and as in Cicero's saying in a letter to Socrates, one is in need of a bridle, the other of a spur. Faced with such opposition I used to attempt to correct the situation, but now I sit as a simple spectator, nor can I stop wondering at the minds of those who regard mobs of servants as something glorious, and are commonly found in the company of those whom they feed, delighting, that is, in the company of their domestic underminers. It is enough for you to know my need, nor do I believe that you expect me to beg you for help. If by chance there should appear anywhere in rather humble straits a spirit whose age and conduct are moderate, you will have found a man in whom such qualities as I seek are to be found—I would not say perfectly but tolerably—and who could be not my servant but my colleague, friend, and master. Yet I fear that I seem to be committing you to a search for a Phoenix which usually is reborn only after 500 years, exists singly in all the world, and isn't known to us in the West. Farewell.

1. A popular though minor poet of Florence, friendly with both Petrarch and Dante. Born around 1276, he was exiled in 1313 for having accompanied Henry VII to the very walls of Florence. He then joined the papal court in Avignon where he met Petrarch.

Fam. IV, 15.

A controversy with a certain famous man against vaunters of knowledge which is not theirs and against excerpters of literary ornaments.

It is difficult for me to say how much my ears, weary of the rabble, were charmed by your letter which I read over and over again. Although the letter appeared to you too wordy, as I learned from its ending, I myself found nothing wrong with it except excessive brevity. Therefore, I was unhappy to read that you threatened hereafter to be more brief. I would prefer that you would be more lengthy. However, you are free to do as you please. You are the father; it is not proper for you to yield to me, but for me to yield to you. But do you believe that it will all depend on you? Do you not know that the fact is often different from the intent? You will perhaps hear things which, though you are desirous of silence, may compel you to speak. Would you like me to follow through since I seem only to be threatening? I start by saying that I hold the same opinion of you which Macrobius held of Aristotle regardless of whether it was based on love or on truth. I believe that there is hardly anything that you do not know. If anything emerged from you opposed to truth, I surmise that either you gave it too little thought or that you were joking, as Macrobius also says about Aristotle. Of course what you say about Jerome, that you prefer him among all of the doctors of the church, is not new to me at all; this opinion is quite old and widely known. Indeed, you dispute in vain when you speak of comparisons where superlatives are involved. You cannot be wrong, for whatever choice you make will be the greatest and the finest. I recall having many discussions with your dear friend from Lombez, Bishop Giacomo. He, following your footsteps, constantly preferring Jerome, and I Augustine among Catholic writers. If indeed I were not afraid of offending either you or the truth, I would say, dear father, what I feel. Just as the stars are many and varied and bright, and this one is called Jupiter, another Arcturus, and another Venus, yet is Augustine the Sun of the church. But, as I said, I hardly attach any importance to this since the choice is a safe one and judgments must be left free. But as for what follows, namely, that you prefer Valerius among the moral philosophers, who would not be astounded if it were said seriously and persistently and not for stimulation and jest? If Valerius is first, where does Plato fall, or Aristotle, or Cicero, or Annaeus Seneca whom certain great judges in such matters place before all? Unless perchance that judgment of yours excluded Plato and Tullius as I was greatly surprised to read in that part of your letter where, for some reason, you asserted that they are poets and are to be included in this group. If you can prove this, you will achieve more than you perhaps think, for with Apollo's support and the approval of the Muses, you will have added two inhabitants to the shady peaks of Parnassus. I ask, what moved you to believe that, or to say it when Tullius appears as the greatest orator in his first books and as a famous philosopher in his last ones? Just as Virgil is everywhere a poet so is Tullius never one, since, as we read in his *Declamations*, "Virgil lost all felicity of talent in his prose; Cicero in his poems." What shall I say about Plato when he has deserved the name of prince of philosophy by consensus of the greatest men, and when Cicero and Augustine and many others always except Plato in all of the works in which they declare their preference for Aristotle over other philosophers? Plato might be thought of as a poet if regard is paid to Tullius' account of Panetius' calling him the Homer of philosophers, but this was intended to mean no more than the prince of philosophers, making him among them what Homer is among poets. What are we to reply to Tullius himself who somewhere in his letters to Atticus calls Plato his god? In a variety of ways all of them attribute to Plato divinity of talent, at times using the name of Homer, and, what is even more distinctive, the name of god.

Therefore, availing yourself of this opportunity, and considering the extraordinary pleasure derived from speaking about unknown things, you should plunge deeply into an examination of the great poets. You should discover of each poet who he was, in what period he was born, his particular poetic style, and the status of his reputation. It would take too long to pursue other individual details in your letter, many of which have never been heard of and others which you could have taught all of us in our desire to learn from your eloquent letter. But, if it is permitted to my profession to interject a thought, I marvel at why you are so unfamiliar with the name of Naevius and of Plautus that you thought I was saying something quite strange because I cited them in my letter to you, and you imply, although with concealed admiration, that, as Horace says, I dared "to form a new person." So thoroughly do you dwell on this matter that the only possible answer appears to be that I be condemned for my boldness in introducing upon the stage new and foreign names. You halted your attack, however, and finally felt it best to blame your own lack of knowledge. This you did most modestly and politely. Yet although your words suggest one meaning, your true meaning, unless I am mistaken, seems to be different, once again most surprisingly since you seem to be so familiar with Terence. For he almost at the very beginning of his proem to the *Andria*, recalls Naevius and Plautus together with Ennius in the same verse. And again in his *Eunuch* he mentions Naevius and Plautus, while in his *Adelphis* he makes mention only of Plautus. Both of them were recalled by Cicero in his *On Old Age*, and by Gellius in his *Attic Nights* where he transcribes the epigrams of both in a very ancient language. But what am I doing? Who, may I ask, ever hears the name of poetry without the names of these men? That is why, dear father, I marvel with good grace at your astonishment. I beseech you not to let this fall into strange hands, for where your fame is most acclaimed, there is where it must be guarded most zealously. With me of course you can speak as if to yourself, and, as the learned do among themselves, change and retract what you may have said. But after your words have reached the public, that possibility is gone and you must undergo the judgments of the many. Thus I am returning your letter to you by a trustworthy messenger, and this one along with it, a copy of which I shall be keeping for no other reason than to refresh my memory by consulting it should you decide to answer. You introduce one further unusual and unknown opinion

(I speak quite freely since I cannot do otherwise having started this way), when you state that Ennius and Statius Papinius were contemporaries. I ask you, dear father, how you ever arrived at such a chronology? Who ever sought such information from you? Anyhow, check this more carefully. You will find that Ennius flourished under Africanus the Elder, and that Statius, after several centuries, flourished under Prince Domitian. Unless I am mistaken, you now have reasons for wanting to answer and will not be able to do so as briefly as you thought.

By your leave let me add one thing in good faith. I recall having written you what I am about to say some time ago while I was spending my youth somewhere in Gascony, and I did so rather bashfully, as behooved my age, because I expressed my displeasure at the vernacular writings which during that period you had occasionally sent to Giocomo Colonna whom I mentioned before and whose love attracted me to those lands as it would have attracted me to Ethiopia. But at that time I spoke childishly as one who had scarcely been weaned. The time has now come for my words to be manly, and therefore, as I said, if you will give me leave . . . what are you saying? I believe you are laughing. Fine, you have given me such leave. Listen, therefore, dear father, and observe and take particular care that no outsider intervenes. I am speaking to you, and I desire that you be judge of your writings which, although I seem to attack, I would defend against any detractors. Nor am I unaware that this letter of censure of a son to a father appears too strong and insolent, but love forgives boldness. Just as I wish my reputation to come to me through real worth rather than through unclear popular approval, so was your reputation of particular concern to me since my young years. This is what is compelling me to speak, lest, if I remained silent, you might hear the same from others, or, what is even worse, might be torn to pieces by anonymous critics. Certain unjust judges of such matters would measure your abilities by such small things as you playfully include through the oversight of the wandering mind. I have noticed that in all of your writings you try your very best to be clear. This explains your searching through unknown works so that in borrowing some things from some writers you insert them among your own thoughts. Your disciples applaud you, astonished by the countless names of authors and call you omniscient, as if you were an expert on all those whose works you quote. Learned men, however, easily discern what belongs to you and what to others, and even what has been interchanged, what has been borrowed, what has been stolen, what has been drawn in considerable substance and what has been borrowed unconsciously. It is childish glory to show off one's memory. As Seneca says, it is shameful for a man to search for little flowers, for it becomes him to enjoy the fruit and not the flowers. You, who are so venerated in this age and so famous in your profession, and indeed (to soothe your feelings rather than to be constantly stinging) being the only prince without comparison in our time interested in scholarly matters to which you are dedicated; you, I say, for some strange and childish reason went indifferently and blindly beyond your limits into foreign areas, and with the day coming to an end, you wasted your time plucking little flowers. You like to test unknown fields where, often failing to find a path, you either wander endlessly or sink.

You like to follow in the footsteps of those who display their knowledge as though it were merchandise in the marketplace, while in the meantime their home is barren. It is certainly legitimate to strive for what may make of you more than you seem to be. But boasting is always painstaking and dangerous. Remember also that while you may wish to appear great, countless other things occur which not only reduce you to your true size but sometimes even reduce you to inferiority. To the unique mind it is sufficient to deserve the glory of one field of knowledge. Those who pride themselves in being honored in a great number of arts are either divine or impudent or insane. Who among either the Greeks or the Romans can be remembered as having presumed so much? New customs bring new rashness. Such men carry before them glorious titles so that, as Pliny says, "they may deserve recognition, but when you look underneath, dear God how little you find there of any substance." You, therefore, so that I may now end, if you believe me at all, be satisfied with your limits, do not imitate those who promise all things, who deliver nothing, and who, handling all things and, as the comedian says, perceiving all things, understand nothing. There is an old and helpful Greek proverb which says, "Let him who knows some art exercise his skill therein."

Farewell, and I beg you to forgive me if you feel offended.

17 August.

Fam. IV, 16.

To the same correspondent, additional thoughts on the same argument and concerning the University of Bologna.

It is just as I thought. Openness begets anger, truth begets hatred, advice begets scorn. So what shall I do? Words cannot turn back. I would have been more flattering if I had thought you enjoyed flattery . . . nay, I would have been even more harsh and would have freely condemned your present reaction which I consider effeminate in a strong man. Since I now realize that openness is hostile to friendship, perhaps silence is my wiser course of action. But fearing that also, since silence may also produce anger, I shall speak so as not to offend again. However, I shall do so as briefly as possible that you may realize that I speak under compulsion. First of all, I make you the judge of all that I said or shall say. You claim in a brief opinion that, "I erred in certain things, in many things, in all things." I certainly rejoice that it was I who erred rather than you since deformity is more apparent where there is more light, and error is more hopeless in an old man. Nevertheless there is something further that I must ask. You are present; therefore I appeal to your tribunal; there is no need of counsel, for you alone sit in judgment. You prefer Jerome to Augustine. This I knew, but what you offer as a reason for your preference I confess I do not understand. What, I ask, does it mean when you say that you prefer him not because he is greater, but because he is more useful to the Church? You say that you have proven this with a very long argument in a certain work of yours which I wish you would have sent with your letter. But apparently you wished either to spare your messenger or your letter. You did, however, add what you considered particularly pertinent to the proof of your demonstration, that is, that your conclusion was verified by Augustine's own authority. But are you not aware that in his conversation a person generally avoids mention of himself? "But really," you say, "Augustine openly confesses that he preferred Jerome to himself." Who cannot see the obvious answer? Here alone, I say, I cannot agree with the judgment of that most holy soul who was admittedly accustomed to speak about and judge others very favorably and himself humbly. I indeed gave to Augustine the palm for fruitful labor within the Church. I did not do so obstinately however like one who feels bound to a particular opinion, or school, or man, so that I could not change my opinion once the truth were disclosed. I had learned this from Marcus Tullius, and from father Augustine himself who does not deny that he himself had learned it from the same Tullius. For as a boy I had carefully learned from Horace not to swear on the word of any one teacher. You yourself do not hide how many such sources there are, and having abandoned this part of your defense, you soon slip into another one saying that after considering everything, there was nothing that had drawn you into this opinion except the undeserved and extraordinary ingratitude of the Italians toward Jerome. This remains the only defense of your opinion; but this is, I repeat, an argument which I cannot at all understand or grasp. What is this ingratitude you speak of? I confess that we are ungrateful not only to saints but to the Lord of all saints. Why is there special reason for complaining particularly about Jerome more than about any of the others? Or what fault is it especially of the Italians rather than of men in general since he himself was not of Italian extraction and dwelled mostly in the Orient? Turn, dear father, to whatever argument you like; your reason, in my opinion, will not suffice to prove your point unless it be perhaps the silent impulse of the mind which substitutes for reason a pious rather than a carefully weighed devoutness. But I shall avoid lingering on things which degrade and in a certain way profane such holy names in the trivial disputes of a sinner, something which I consider very close to sacrilege. Therefore it would be wiser to be silent about these things, for excessive rubbing and striking together of precious things is dangerous.

I pass on to Plato and Cicero whom you try to make poets because they wrote two fictitious stories containing lessons of conduct and, as Macrobius testifies about one of them, because these stories seem to be rounded out with a touch of the three parts of philosophy and are, without concern for the rules of metrics, inserted in the midst of books dealing with politics and the state. To no purpose Macrobius defends both of them against their attackers who maintain that fictitious stories should not be invented by a philosopher; whereas I congratulate these two, and if possible Aristotle, and Seneca, and Varro, for being included in the rolls of poets; for these latter could perhaps more properly be so included rather than Plato or Tullius. For Aristotle wrote about poetry and poets, and Varro wrote books of satires and about poets; he also composed a fairly good poem on Jason and the Golden Fleece. Seneca, however, wrote tragedies which certainly deserve the next to the highest rank if not the highest in literary merit. But why, I ask, did you not make them actors since during their lives they perhaps said or did something silly, especially Tullius who wrote so many laughable things in his *Saturnalia;* while his freedman, Tiro, wrote a book on the jokes played by his master? Why not make them fishermen or boatmen or something similar because they relaxed themselves by casting fish lines or by rowing when off on vacation? Do you wish in the dispute to make an analogy with a military custom so that just as a single duel produced the Torquati and the Corvini, one story would suffice to produce a poet? To be a great writer requires perseverance; a single sample does not suffice. Enough of this. In your last letter you make no mention of Ennius and Statius. And I believe that you recalculated the number of years on your fingers. Finally I shall say nothing about that long and drawnout portion of your argument where you attempt to argue that my advice is unjust because nothing is lacking to your judgment—except that I am happy for you that you hold this opinion of yourself. Oh happy you who are satisfied with your own personal judgment! Oh how I wish that you could teach me this art so that I would know how to flatter myself with similar judgments! I really do not know whether it might not sometimes be better to enjoy error than to grieve always over the truth.

To your argument that makes me appear almost to have violated a military oath because at the height of my powers I started to abandon the study of law and Bologna, the answer is simple; although I believe that as one who made that city and that university particularly illustrious, you would not like it. Since therefore I have disturbed you enough, I shall not make mention of the defenses I have been accustomed to use to justify myself, for this problem I have often discussed with many people and especially with Oldrado of Lodi, a very well known jurist of our day. There is only one thing that can be said without hurting any feelings. Nothing which is counter to nature can lead to any good. Nature begot me as a lover of solitude and not of the marketplace. In short be certain of this much: that I never did anything prudently (which I tend to believe), but, if I did, this is among the first things which, if not wise, has certainly been fruitful, namely, that I saw Bologna and that I did not remain there. Farewell.

31 August.

Fam. IV, 17.

That one's life style must be controlled by one's capabilities and that nothing encourages an enthusiasm for lavish entertainment like bad examples.

I do not wonder that you find delight in lavish entertainments. Once this was the bane of only a few homes, but now it seems a custom residing perpetually in all of them, except when poverty obstructs the entrance. The cause of this is not our nature which would thrive long and pleasantly on too little rather than too much: rather it is habit and even more so imitation that are the real culprits. For who possesses so much self restraint that his eyes are not sometimes attracted by the extravagance, the elegance, and the fame of a neighbor? The advice given by the old man of Plautus in his *Aulularia* is useful: "Let elegance be according to means, and glory according to desert." If men would remember this, the road to lavish extravagance and unjust profits would be closed and men would live much more peacefully. Now selfishness begets blindness, and the blows of ill will crush the control of reason. I beg you, however, to try as hard as you can to be a follower of your own inclinations rather than an imitator of the intemperance of others. Avoid destructive examples; we possess minds that are too prone to evil. One teacher of selfish pleasure suffices for a great number of people. Frugality quickly gives way to excess unless our firm reason strengthens the resistance of our thoughts, teaching them to follow the true good and to avoid false good. Why do you admire the bright garments and the glittering stones on the fingers of your neighbor? It is a masked happiness. Expose the man himself and you will not deny that he is most unhappy. Misfortune hides under the gold and he is both envious and wretched, something which I consider an extreme form of evil. I shall conclude differently than did Plautus about his Epidichus: "This," he said, "is that man who found his freedom in wickedness." As a matter of fact, this wickedness found him wealth, power, and the friendship of kings, but it destroyed him and his freedom. Let him keep

for himself without envy those many things he possesses
which are so great in the eyes of the multitude. Do live happily and contented with your possessions and especially with
what he lost, and farewell.

Fam. IV, 18.

A rebuke to a friend.

I am a friend to you and not to your ways. However, since you ask what my opinion is of you and of all your affairs, I shall let Plautus answer for me very briefly and truthfully, answering each point with almost single words. First of all, I do not like your love affair which is an unfortunate burden to the soul. You are becoming involved in an obscene fire. I ask you like the servant of Plautus in the *Asinaria*, "Is this woman whom you embrace but smoke?" If you ask me why I inquire, I answer because your eyes are always misty with tears. So much for you. As for your little woman, you can read for yourself what is said in that comedy known as *Curculio:* "two women are worse than one." As for the servant, I say what the same poet says in the *Epidichus:* "He is too expert in evil doing." I add this on my own: you are too quick to believe, too inclined to comply. If these things are false, my friend, scold me; but if true, correct them, and farewell.

Fam. IV, 19.

To the same correspondent.

You do not deny the accusation made by your friend, and you do so frankly. This modest confession of guilt affords great hope for the improvement of your life. Your being silent concerning your servant is also a sign of caution. Indeed anyone you do not wish to accuse you cannot excuse. But that you should try to excuse the little women I consider either improper politeness or blind judgment. You yourself appear to be what you think you should feel about them, when you call one of them excellent and the other bearable. I consider what Plautus says in his *Aulularia* much closer to the truth: "There is no excellent woman; one is really worse than another." Farewell.

Fam. V, 1.

To Barbato da Sulmona, on the death of King Robert of Sicily.

What I feared has happened. What I dreaded I am suffering. My fear has turned into grief and my prayers into tears. Not long before I foresaw it, our illustrious king has abandoned us; and his age, though well advanced, made his death no less hard to bear. Alas, dearest Barbato, how I fear that those other presentiments of mine may also come true, presentiments which my distressed mind, always a too certain prophet of evils, now suggests to me. I am really alarmed about the youthfulness of the young queen, and of the new king, about the age and intent of the other queen, about the talents and ways of the courtiers. I wish that I could be a lying prophet about these things, but I see two lambs entrusted to the care of a multitude of wolves, and I see a kingdom without a king. How can I call someone a king who is ruled by another and who is exposed to the greed of so many and (I sadly add) to the cruelty of so many? Therefore, if on the day when Plato departed from human affairs the sun was seen to fall from the heavens, what should be seen in the death of that man who was by nature another Plato, and in his wisdom and glory second to no other king, and whose death furthermore has opened the way to so many dangers on all sides? May almighty God assist in these matters and prove that my pious solicitude is greater than necessary. But granting that for others all things come to pass beyond all expectations and that my fear prove useless, who will console me, dear friend? Or who will alleviate my grief? For whom shall I stay awake nights henceforth? To whom shall I dedicate these talents or this zeal however small they may be? Who will raise once more my collapsed hopes, who will rouse my sluggish mind? I have had two motivators of my abilities; this year has taken both from me. Over the first I grieved with Lelius during my recent stay in Italy where I sought in either place a suitable partner in my grief—and over the second I grieve today with you, and I shall continue to grieve as long as I live. And I who sometimes console others, do not now find any argument or words to console myself. From this therefore my despair of consolation, my shame in weeping, and my distrust that the power of style is adequate to dispel either. Yet conquering all, my hope of seeing you soon bids me be quiet. I shall obey, and shortly when I am with you I shall weep freely. Meanwhile I am writing these words to you as I weep at the source of the Sorgue, a port which is known as a haven for the storms of my mind, where yesterday evening I fled alone after receiving the very sad news in the morning on the shore of the Rhone.

29 May.

Fam. V, 2.

*To Giovanni Colonna, an expression of gratitude for the
great honors rendered him.*

I express my gratitude for many other favors and for the
extremely valuable favor of your letters which always precede me whenever I come to Rome. I recognize the traps of
your love, for I was received more in the manner of an angel
than of a man. There is nothing more energetic than a lover.
Even borne on the wings of the North Wind I have never
found everything not prepared for me. I will be astonished
if I do not become accustomed to your feelings toward me,
for a habit prolonged lessens the wonder of things, alleviates
pain, and diminishes pleasures. Who can enumerate the many
honors which throughout my life you showered upon me? It
would take too long to repeat examples of how you have
treated me almost as an equal although you were my master;
extending to me the courtesy of conversing with me; granting me freedom as a man though I lived under the rule of a
master; your sharing of secrets; your according me privileges,
honors and esteem, all of which are so pleasing to recall. Out
of a thousand I shall refer only to one which will amaze you
in seeing how deeply it is rooted in my heart and blood. Remember when following some serious trouble which arose
among certain servants of yours, recourse was made to arms,
and you, angered by a just indignation, and proceeding as
though in a court of law, assembled your servants and bade all
of them to take the oath of truth, including Agapito, bishop of
Luna, your brother. I too raised my right hand, but you, though
still harboring your feelings of anger, withdrew your Bible,
and with everyone listening, said that you would be satisfied
merely with my word. And to show that you did not regret
this, nor felt your kindness to have been unwarranted, whenever similar cases arose, though having all the others take the
oath, you never allowed me to do so. What can be more
distinctive than this judgment of so great a sire? Let as many
greedy people as wish to consider gold and precious stones
highly valuable, they cannot value an honor such as this. You
have renewed in me, most esteemed father, the ancient honor

of the philosopher Xenocrates which Cicero mentions in his letters to Atticus. When he was required by the law to take an oath in order to act as witness, he was excused from having to do so by the Athenians who believed in his respected trust. I say that this is what you renewed in your dealings with me, except that what happened to him when he was in an advanced age, you did to me while still a youth, and what happened to him but once, you do for me continuously. Do you think that I could ever forget such things? The account would be terribly long if I were to adduce additional examples, and neither the time nor the place is appropriate. I hear the voice of your great father who has decided to follow me outside the walls of the city although I do not want him to do so. Today I shall be a guest at his Preneste. There I shall find waiting for me that very famous man who is his grandson and your nephew through your brother.

Rome, nones of October.

Fam. V, 3.

To the same correspondent, on his journey and the horrors of the ruling Council of Naples.

That I should break my word was almost necessary for me and certainly useful to you. I promised that I would undertake a sea journey for no other reason than the common belief that it is more expeditious and fast to go by sea than by land. I boarded a ship in Nice which is the first of the Italian cities in the West, and I arrived at the port of Monaco when the stars were high in the sky. There I became silently angry, for on the following day we unwillingly stayed on after having tried several times to depart in vain. The next day we raised anchor in a dangerous storm, and, after being tossed about for the entire day by the large waves, we arrived at the port of Moritz during the stormy night. We did not therefore enter the city. I stayed in an inn on the seashore sleeping on a kind of sailor's couch and had to take my meal as my hunger dictated and my sleep as my weariness demanded. There I became still more indignant as I perceived the tricks played by the sea. Why say more? After considering several plans throughout the night, I decided at dawn that I would prefer the rigors of a trip by land rather than subjection to the waters. Therefore, after having my servants and all my baggage placed back into the ship, accompanied by only one servant I started along the shore. Fortune intervened favorably in my decision. Among the hills of Liguria for some unknown reason some German horses were on sale which appeared lively and powerful. Having hastily purchased some, I continued my proposed journey but once again not without being bothered by sea-like troubles. A serious war is presently in progress between the Pisans and the lord of Milan, caused, as you know, rather by the arrogance of minds than by territorial problems, for the Apennines have separated the borders so that the ancient boundary of the Po no longer applied. But arrogance knows no bounds, and ambition is satisfied with no limits. So although I had started out on a straight path, the fact that near Lavenza both armies had encamped, with the lord pressing forward seriously while on the other hand the Pisans defended their Mutrone with all their might—I was compelled at Lerici to believe myself once again on a sea journey. Passing by Corvo, the huge cliff so called because of its color, and then the white cliffs and the entrance to Macra and then Luni, once famous and powerful but now carrying an empty and insignificant name, I spent the dead of night in Mutrone itself in the care of the Pisans and then managed to make the rest of my journey overland without serious obstacles. I shall not continue with an account of where I ate and slept or what I saw or heard in any particular place. I shall hasten instead to my conclusion. Through Pisa after leaving Florence on my left I came to Siena and then to Perugia. Then I arrived at Todi where I was received by your men of Clairvaux with great joy. Under their guidance I entered Rome by way of Narni on the fourth of October when the night was already well advanced. My precipitous haste thus made me at this time a night traveler. I nevertheless determined to visit your great father before I retired. Good God what human majesty, what a voice, what a presence, what a face, what clothing, what mental power for his age and what strength of body! I seemed to be looking at Julius Caesar or Africanus except that he is older than either of them. Nevertheless he seemed to have the same appearance which he had seven years previously when I left him in Rome, or as when I had seen him for the first time twelve years before in Avignon. It was amazing and almost incredible that this man alone does not grow old while Rome itself does! With fatherly affection he asked a few things about you and your situation, though I had found him half undressed and ready to go to bed. What remained to be said we postponed until the following day. I spent that day with him from morning to night, and there was hardly a single hour that was spent in silence. But I shall tell you about the other things in person. He was gladdened in an extraordinary way by my arrival, hoping, as he said, that your friends would find an end to their imprisonment and distress through my diligence, the hope of an old man which I am sorry to say proved false.

But not to keep you any longer, having departed from him

in Rome I came to Naples where I visited the queens and participated in their Council meeting. Alas, what a shame, what a monster! May God remove this kind of plague from Italian skies! I thought that Christ was despised at Memphis, Babylon, and Mecca. I feel pity for you, my noble Parthenope, for you truly resemble any one of them since you reflect no piety, no truth, no faith. I saw a terrible three footed beast, with its feet naked, with its head bare, arrogant about its poverty, dripping with pleasures. I saw a little man plucked and ruddy, with plump haunches scarcely covered by a worn mantle and with a good portion of his body purposely uncovered. In this condition he disdains most haughtily not only your words but also those of the Pope as if from the lofty tower of his purity. Nor was I astonished that he carries his arrogance rooted in gold. As is widely known, his money boxes and his robes do not agree. To be sure you know his sacred name; he is called Robert. In the place of that most serene Robert who was recently king, this other Robert has arisen who will be an eternal dishonor of our age just as the other was its only glory. I shall now consider it less unbelievable that a serpent can arise from the remains of a buried man since this insensitive asp has sprung up from the royal tomb. Oh supreme shame! See who has dared invade your royal throne, most excellent king! But this is the trust one can have in Fortune. She not only turns human affairs around but overturns them. It was not sufficient that she should remove the sun from the world, thereby superimposing dark shadows over it, but after having snatched away our unparalleled king she did not simply replace him with someone inferior in virtue, but instead with a horrible and cruel monster. Is this how you look upon us, Lord of the stars? Is this a suitable successor for such a king? After the Dionysii and Agathocles and Phalaris, was this person (who is more repulsive and underneath more monstrous) a proper legacy of destiny to the Sicilian court, this "most unmerciful oppressor," to use the words of Macrobius? With an extraordinary type of tyranny he wears not a crown, or a habit, or arms, but a filthy mantle, and, as I said, not completely wrapped in it but only half way, and curved over not so much because of old age but because of his hypocrisy. Relying not as much on eloquence as on silence and on arrogance, he wanders through the courtyards of the queens, and, supported by a staff, he pushes aside the more humble, he tramples upon justice, and he defiles whatever remains of divine or human rights. Like a new Tiphys and another Palinurus he controls the helm of the unrestrained ship of state which, in my opinion, will soon perish in a huge shipwreck. For there are many people of this stamp, indeed almost all, except for Philip, bishop of Cavaillon, who alone takes sides on behalf of foresaken justice. What can he do, a single lamb in so great a flock of wolves; what can he do except to flee forthwith, if he can, and seek out his sheepfold? This is what I believe he is thinking of doing, but out of pity for the collapsing kingdom and in memory of the last entreaties of the king, he is detained by a double set of chains. Meanwhile how clearly do you think his voice can be heard in the seductive band of courtiers, invoking the faith of God and of men, attacking the terribly unjust plans that are proposed, and checking the impudence of many with its authority, parrying Fortune with his wisdom and placing his own shoulders against the destruction of the state which he can delay but cannot change. Would that such destruction not envelop him also! The matter has now reached the point where I have no hope in human assistance, especially with respect to the surviving Robert who in his excessive treachery and because of the strangeness of his dress deserves the name and rank of the foremost monster in courtly circles. And you will have to share some of the blame if from the information that I sent at some length in other more confidential letters you do not keep the Roman Pontiff better informed. As a fitting conclusion, pass on to him this one particular thought of mine: would he believe that the Saracen centers of Susa or Damascus might receive his apostolic exhortations more reverently, as I believe they would, than Christian Naples? If my respect for his holiness did not prohibit it, I would add those words of Cicero: "We are being punished justly, for had we not permitted the crimes of many to go unpunished, the thought of so much license would never have occurred to a single man." In truth while I am trying to relieve my angry stomach with these sputtering words, I fear that I might also be moving you to anger. If this proves of no avail, and if the temerity of such people and your patience can lead to nothing more than our getting upset, of what avail is it to try to relay the insolence of the matter with our words, something which neither Cicero himself nor Demosthenes could accomplish? Even if it were possible, such damage would accrue to the person who undertakes it that he would lose his peace of mind while the perpetrators of the crimes remain unpunished. Therefore it would be wise to bring our words to a conclusion.

Perhaps three or four times I have visited the prison known as Camp Capua, where I saw your friends who have lost all hope except in you since the rightness of their cause which should have been their primary protection has thus far proven damaging to them. As everyone knows, it is most dangerous to try to uphold a just cause before an unjust judge. It might be added that there is no greater enemy for unfortunates than the man who haughtily enjoys the spoils of their belongings, since he naturally would like to remove those who may find occasion to demand the return of what is rightfully theirs. Thus, cruelty always follows upon avarice, and it might also be noted that when there is a pirating of one's inheritance there is always the potential danger of loss of life. It is certainly a difficult lot of man not to be able either to be poor in safety or to regain his riches! If ever this happened to anyone it is now happening to your friends, for as captives there is no one who has not had some portion of their personal belongings plundered. How could such grasping plunderers possibly be concerned about the liberty or safety of someone who seems to be closely connected with their own poverty? Therefore they would have been safer had they possessed nothing. But the situation is such that they made bitter enemies with serious harm to themselves. I saw them in fetters; oh shameful sight! oh unstable and onrushing wheel of Fortune! However, just as there is nothing more ugly than that kind of captivity, in the same manner there is nothing more elevated than the minds of the prisoners. As long as you are safe, they continue to have the greatest hope in the outcome. I for my part can hope for nothing unless some greater force intervenes, for if they expect the clemency of deliberations, the die is cast: they will waste in the squalor of prison. The elder queen, formerly the royal spouse, now the most wretched of widows, has compassion, as she says, affirming that she can do nothing more. Cleopatra with her Ptolemy could also show compassion if Photinus and Achilles would allow it. This is what I see. I need not tell you with what spirit I behold it all. What can I do? One must have patience. And although I am certain of the answer, I nevertheless expect an answer, having been ordered to seek one. Farewell.

29 November.

Fam. V, 4.

To the same correspondent, a description of Baia and of the female warrior from Pozzuoli.

I have known your attitudes for some time; you cannot endure not knowing about things because an implacable desire for knowledge stirs your noble spirit. I have tried to satisfy your desires whenever my fortune had me travel to the North or to the West. I have now made a different journey, but in the same frame of mind and with the same intention of obeying. You have indeed heard the account of my arrival and of the mishaps that happened to us on our journey, and then what transpired in Naples in the negotiations on behalf of your prisoners and the kind of hope that remains. But listen now to the rest which contains nothing to upset but rather something to delight you. Influenced by the useless waiting and the long weariness, I had decided to explore Mt. Gargano and the port of Brindisi and that length of sea that lies above, not so much for the sake of seeing those places as from a wish to leave this place. Through the persuasion of the elder queen I did not do so but instead changed my plans for a longer trip and decided to visit closer and certainly more wonderful places. But if when I depart from here the time of year does not prevent my seeing those other places, I shall take comfort in the effort to get to them, for although I shall have achieved nothing in those matters for which I had come here, I shall nevertheless see many things which I never expected to see. But concerning those places, upon my return to you after my lengthy journey through almost all of Italy, health permitting, I shall tell you in person. What I have seen so far I have committed to writing so that you may know about these things as speedily as possible.

I saw Baia along with the very famous Giovanni Barrili and my Barbato. I do not recall a happier day in my life, not only because of my friends' company and the variety of notable sights but because of the recent experience of many sad days. I saw in the winter months that very attractive bay which if I am not mistaken the summer sun must overwhelm.

This is nothing but an opinion, for I was never there during the summer. It is now three years since I was first brought here in the middle of the winter with the north winds raging, a time when one is particularly subject to danger in a sea journey. Therefore, I was unable to view from up close the many things I wished to see. However, I have today finally satisfied the desire which has occupied my mind as a result of that brief taste of things and of wishes that have been with me since my youth. I saw the places described by Virgil; I saw the lakes Avernus and Lucrinus as well as the stagnant waters of Acheron; the laguna of Augusta rendered unhappy by the fierceness of her son; the once proud road of Gaius Caligula now buried under the waves; and the obstacle against the sea built by Julius Caesar. I saw the native land and the home of the Sibyl and that dreadful cave from which fools do not return and which learned men do not enter. I saw Mt. Falernus distinguished for its famous vineyards and the parched soil exhaling continuously the vapors that are good for diseases. There I also saw balls of ashes and boiling water as in a boiling copper vessel spilling over with a confused rumbling. I saw the wholesome fluid which the cliffs everywhere dripped and which as a gift of mother nature was once employed for all kinds of illnesses and later, as the story goes, mixed with the regular baths because of the envy of the doctors. Now many people of all ages and of both sexes throng from neighboring cities to the waters. I saw not only what is called the Neapolitan grotto which Annaeus Seneca recalls in his letter to Lucilius, but everywhere mountains full of perforations and suspended on marble vaults gleaming with brilliant whiteness, and sculpted figures indicating with pointing hands what water is most appropriate for each part of the body. The appearance of the place and the labor devoted to its development caused me to marvel. Henceforth I shall be less astonished by the walls of Rome and her fortresses and her palaces, when such care was taken by Roman leaders so far from the homeland (although the homeland for outstanding men is everywhere). They often took winter pleasures in places more than a hundred miles from home as if they were suburbs. Their summer delights included Tivoli and the lake of Celano and the wooded valleys of the Apennines, "and Lake Cimino with its mountain," as Virgil says, and the sunny retreats of Umbria, and the shady hills of Tuscany, and the mount rightfully called Algido, and the gushing springs and clear rivers. Their winter delights included Anzio, Terracina, Formia, Gaeta, and Naples. However none was more pleasant nor more popular than Baia. This is attested to by the authority of the writers of that period and by the huge remains of the walls, although I am not ignorant of the fact that this was a place of dwelling worthy rather of human pleasures than of the gravity of the Romans. For that reason Marius, naturally a rather rough man, and Pompey and Caesar, more noble in character, are all praised for building on the mountains from where, as was fitting for such men, they were not immersed in but rather protected themselves from effeminate elegance, the obstreperousness of sailors, and disdained the pleasures of Baia from aloft. Scipio Africanus, however, an incomparable man, who did all things virtuously and nothing for pleasure not only disdained life on the hills of Baia, but determined never to see this place which he considered inimical to his ways, a resolution very much in keeping with the rest of his life. He therefore avoided even a view of the place and preferred to live in Literno rather than in Baia. I know that his small villa is not far from here, and there is nothing that I would look upon more eagerly if I could visit with some guide places renowned because of so great an occupant.

While many marvelous things have indeed been created by that God "who alone creates great wonder," He nevertheless created nothing more wonderful on earth than man. Thus of all things I saw on that day that I am describing to you in this letter the most remarkable was the strength of mind and body of a woman from Pozzuoli. Her name is Mary. Her outstanding trait is the preservation of her virginity; although she is a constant companion of men who are often men of arms, no one, as almost everyone is ready to attest, has assailed the virginity of this strict woman either seriously or in jest, more out of fear, as they relate, than out of respect. Her body resembles rather that of a soldier than a

virgin, her strength is such as to be desired by veteran soldiers, her dexterity is rare and unusual, her vigorous age, condition and enthusiasm are those of a powerful man. She prac-
tices not with cloth but with weapons, not with needles and
mirrors, but with bows and arrows. She is marked not by the
signs of kisses and the lascivious signs of the bold teeth of
lovers, but wounds and scars. Her primary concern is with
arms, and her mind disdains the sword and death. She wages
an hereditary war with her neighbors in which already a
large number have perished on both sides. Sometimes alone,
often attended by a few others, she came to grips with her
enemy, and to this day she has always emerged the victor.
She is quick to engage in war, slow to disengage, she attacks
her enemy boldly, as she weaves ambushes carefully. She endures hunger, thirst, cold, heat, wakefulness, and weariness
with incredible patience. She spends her nights under the
open sky and travels fully armed; she rests on the ground and
considers among her delights the grassy turf or her shield on
which she lies. Among such continuous hardships she has
changed considerably in a short time. Not too long ago when
my youthful desire for glory led me to Rome and Naples and
to the King of Sicily, she attracted my attention as I saw her
standing there unarmed. When she approached me today
armed and surrounded by armed men to pay her respects, I
was taken by surprise and returned her greeting as if to an
unknown man until warned by her laughter and by the ges-
tures of her companions I finally managed to recognize under
the helmet the fierce and unpolished virgin. There are many
fabulous stories told about her; I am repeating only what I
saw. Powerful men from different parts of the world had
assembled, men hardened by warfare whom chance had
caused to stop there although they were directed elsewhere.
Having heard the reputation of the woman, they were driven
by the desire to test her strength. Hearing about this, we all
agreed to ascend to the fortress of Pozzuoli. She was walking
in front of the doors of the church in deep meditation which
caused her not to notice our approach. We approached to
ask her to supply us with some kind of proof of her strength.
At first excusing herself for some time because of pain in her

arm, she finally ordered that a heavy stone and an iron beam be brought to her. After she had thrown it into the center of the group she urged them to try lifting and competing. To be brief, a long contest ensued among equals, and everyone tried his hand as if in great rivalry while she acted as observer judging the strength of each of the men. Finally, with an easy try, she showed herself much superior to all, causing stupefaction in the others and shame in myself. We eventually left, being in a condition which prompted us to give less faith to what our eyes had seen than to the belief that we had been subjected to some kind of illusion. It is said that Robert, that greatest of men and of kings, once sailing along these shores with a large fleet, stopped at Pozzuoli intrigued by the wonders of such a woman and desirous of seeing her. In my opinion this does not seem to be quite believable because living so close to her he could have summoned her. But perhaps he landed there for some other reason, being desirous of viewing something new and being naturally eager for all kinds of knowledge. But let the burden of proof for this matter, as with everything else I heard, lie with its tellers; as for me the sight of this woman has rendered more believable whatever is narrated not only about the Amazons and that once famous female kingdom, but even what is told about the virgin female warriors of Italy, under the leadership of Camilla whose name is the most renowned of all. What should keep one from believing many instances of something which I would have been perhaps slow to believe if I had not had personal experience? Indeed, just as that ancient heroine who was born not far from here, at Piperno, at the time of the Trojan downfall; this more recent Camilla, was born at Pozzuoli in our times. This is what I wanted to have attested in my short letter to you. Farewell and enjoy good health.

23 November.

Fam. V, 5.

To the same correspondent, a description of a storm without equal.

To describe a remarkable storm in a few words and much imagery the Satirist wrote that a poetic storm had arisen. What could be more brief or more expressive? For neither the angry heavens nor the sea could do anything which could not be surpassed in words and poetic style. To avoid superfluous examples of something that is obvious, I remind you of Homer's storm and of the leader who was dashed against the cliffs and of all the misfortunes caused by Mt. Caphareus. In imitation, our poets have maintained that mountains of water are raised to the stars. But nothing can be described by eloquence or can be imagined which yesterday was not equaled and even surpassed close to here. It was a disaster unique and unheard of in history. Therefore let Homer sing of his Greek storm, and Maro of his Aeolian, and Lucan of his Epirian, and others of other storms. As for me, if ever there is a sufficient block of time, the Neapolitan storm can provide me with abundant material for a poem, although it was not only Neapolitan but spread throughout the upper and lower seas and according to hearsay was almost universal. For me it was Neapolitan because it caught up with me during a painful delay in Naples. As much as the press of time before the departure of the messenger will allow, I shall try to persuade you that truly nothing more horrible or more violent has ever been seen. Amazingly, there had been preceding warning of the approaching blow, for a certain bishop from a nearby island and interested in astrology had announced the danger several days earlier. But since such people almost never get to the truth by their guesswork, he predicted that Naples would be destroyed on November 25, 1343 not by a sea storm but by an earthquake. Furthermore he surrounded everything he said with such extraordinary terrors that a large portion of the populace, under the threat of death and thus desirous of changing their manner of life, were intent on doing penance for their sins, and abandoned all other kinds of activity. Many others made fun of such idle fears especially because of the considerable number of bad storms which had occurred at that time. Therefore, they considered the prophesy wrong as to date, and gave many good reasons for having no confidence in it. I myself was neither hopeful nor fearful, and, though favoring neither side, I inclined somewhat toward fear, for the fact seems to be that things that are hoped for come less readily than those that are feared. I had also heard and seen at that time many threatening signs in the skies which for one accustomed to living in northern climes resembled the supernatural events that occur in the cold of winter, and make one prone to turn to fear and indeed to religion. What more need I say? It was the night before the predicted day. An anxious crowd of women, concerned more with the danger at hand than with modesty, ran to and fro through the alleys and streets, and holding their children to their breasts they tearfully and humbly crowded the doorways of the churches. Worried by the public alarm, I returned home in the early evening. The sky was calmer than usual which caused my comrades to go to bed with considerable confidence. I had decided to wait, wanting to observe the manner in which the moon would set. However, because it was in its seventh day, if I am not mistaken, I stood at the windows which looked toward the West until the nearby mountain hid it in a covering of clouds, and before the middle of the night it assumed a sad look. Finally I, too, in order to make up for lost sleep, went to bed.

I had scarcely fallen asleep when not only the windows but the walls themselves, though built on solid stone, were shaken from their very foundations and the night light, which I am accustomed to keep lit while I sleep, went out. We threw off our blankets, and in place of sleep the fear of imminent death overcame us. Here is what happened next. Each one of us sought out the other in the dark and encouraged one another with our voices as we recognized each other by the aid of the ominous light in the air, while the most holy Prior David, whom I here name out of respect, and the religious of the dwelling in which we were living and who regularly used to rise for the nocturnal adoration of Christ, frightened by the unexpected danger, and bearing their crosses and their relics of saints, and invoking the mercy of God in a loud voice, all marched with their torches into the bedroom I occupied. This made me feel somewhat relieved. We then all proceeded to the church, and there we spent the night prostrate with much wailing, believing that our end was imminent and that everything around us would shortly lie in ruins. It would take too long to try to describe in words every horror that surrounded that infernal night, and although my words may fall short of the truth, they will transcend any plausibility that can be placed in truth itself. What a downpour! what winds! what lightning! what deep thunder! what frightening tremors! what roaring of the sea! what shrieking of the populace! In this state which made the evening as if by magic appear twice as long, when we finally began to glimpse the dawn, the daylight appeared imminent rather through conjecture than in actual fact. The cloaked priests repeated their sacrifices at the altar and we, not daring to look at the heavens, threw ourselves prostrate on the moist and naked floors around them. When no doubt remained that it was indeed daylight (though it continued to resemble the glow of night) and the shouting of the populace suddenly became silent in the upper part of the city, although it seemed to be increasing more and more from the direction of the shore, and we could not learn what was happening by inquiring, our despair, as often happens, became boldness, and we mounted our horses and descended to the port determined to see for ourselves and to perish if necessary.

Good God! When was anything like this ever heard of? The oldest sailors asserted that what had happened was indeed without parallel. The port was filled with frightening and dismal wreckage. The unfortunate victims, who had been scattered by the water and had been trying to grasp the nearby land with their hands, were dashed against the reefs and were broken like so many tender eggs. The entire shore line was covered with torn and still living bodies: someone's brains floated by here, someone else's bowels floated there. In the midst of such sights the yelling of men and wailing of women were so loud that they overcame the sounds of the seas and the heavens. To all this was added the destruction of buildings, many of whose foundations were overturned by the violent waves against which that day respected no bounds and respected no work of man or nature. They overflowed their natural limits, the familiar shoreline, as well as that huge breakwater which had been constructed by zealous men and which, with its outstretched arms, as Maro says, constitutes the port, and all that portion of the region which borders the sea. And where there had been a path for strolling there was now something dangerous even for sailing. A thousand or more Neapolitan horsemen had gathered there as if to assist at the funeral of their homeland. Having joined this group, I had begun to feel somewhat less frightened of perishing amidst so many. But suddenly a new clamor could be heard. The very place on which we stood, weakened by the waves that had penetrated beneath, began to give way. We hurried to a higher elevation. No one raised his eyes to the heavens, for the band of men could not bear to look at the angry faces of Jove and of Neptune. Thousands of mountainous waves flowed between Capri and Naples. The channel appeared not dark or, as is usual in great storms, black, but greyish with the frightening whiteness of sea foam. Meanwhile the younger queen, barefooted and uncombed, and accompanied by a large group of women, departed from the royal palace unconcerned about modesty in the face of great danger, and they all hastened to the Church of the Virgin Queen praying for her grace amidst such dangers. Unless I am mistaken, I imagine that you now fearfully await the outcome of such a calamity. On land we could scarcely find an escape and neither on the deep nor in port could a ship be found to equal those waves. Three long ships from Marseilles, called galleys, which had returned from Cyprus after crossing wide expanses of the sea and were anchored there ready to depart in the morning, we saw overcome by the waves with a universal outcry and without anyone being able to offer assistance and without a single sailor or passenger saved. In the same manner other even larger ships of all kinds which had taken refuge in the port as if in a fortress were destroyed. Only one of so many survived. It was loaded with robbers who had been spared their rightful punishment so that they could be sent on an expedition to Sicily, and who, having been spared the sword of the executioner, were to be exposed to the sword of battle. This huge and powerful ship, armed with the hides of bulls, although it had suffered the blows of the sea until sundown, also began to be overpowered. The exhausted prisoners hastened from all sides to the keel because of the threatening dangers. It is said that they were four hundred in number, a group large enough for a fleet, let alone a single ship. Furthermore they were powerful persons who, freed from death, feared nothing more than death which they resisted even more obstinately and boldly. In postponing the outcome by slowing down the sinking of the ship, they prolonged the disaster well into the following night. When they were finally overcome, they abandoned their tools and dashed to the upper portions of the ship. Suddenly beyond all hope the skies began to clear and the exhausted sea began to slacken its roughness. Thus, so many having perished, only the worst seemed to escape, whether because "Fortune saves many guilty ones," as Lucan says, or because "the gods thought otherwise" as Virgil says; or, as may be the case, those are most free from the dangers of death who consider life worth little. This is a digest of yesterday's happenings, but in order not to take up any more of your time and of my energy—although the account does offer ample matter regarding human behavior in times of crisis about which much has often been said but very little by wise men in view of the subject's importance—there is one thing I want to be certain does emerge: that is, I beseech you not ever again to order me to place my trust in winds and seas. This is something in which I would obey neither you, the Pope, or my own father if he were to return to life. I shall leave the air to the birds and the sea to the fish; as a terrestrial animal I shall prefer land trips. Send me where you will, even to the Indies, as long as my foot tramples the soil. I shall not refuse to approach either the Sarmatian with his bow and arrows, or the perfidious Moor. Otherwise (and pardon me for confessing it) I shall be free not only during the Saturnalia of December but throughout the year. How else could you persuade me, I pray, or with what words would you ever solicit me to sail again? "Choose a stout ship and skilled sailors." But both were available to these men. "Search for a port while the sun is out, cast your anchor at night, beware meeting with enemy, hug the shoreline"? But these people, in the full light of day, with their anchors cast into the clinging sands of a port, and being able almost to touch the shore itself with their oars, perished among thousands of grieving friends. I did not read about this, nor hear about it, but saw it with my own eyes. Therefore do stop now and let your decency at least on this occasion forgive my fear. I know what arguments are used against my position by learned men: danger is the same everywhere although it may appear more likely on the sea. So be it. Do you however behave generously and permit me to die on land since I was born on land. There is scarcely any sea between us in which I have not been often shipwrecked, although among the sayings attributed to Publius is the one which says: "He who undergoes a second shipwreck accuses Neptune wrongfully." Farewell.

Naples, 26 November.

Fam. V, 6.

To the same correspondent, a complaint about the nocturnal prowlers in Naples and about the disgustingly bloody gladiatorial games that are permitted there.

I was hoping to be free of the heavy fetters of business, and I believe would have been if the poisonous serpent had not overcome the minds of the judges who had been restrained by pity. One of the Psylli would not have been more capable of recognizing poison with his mouth than I was in recognizing it with my ear. I continue my opposition, but now I fear that the damage is fatal. However, I shall continue trying as long as any shred of hope remains. Perhaps last night I might have obtained the courtesy even of rejection had the Council not adjourned because of the approaching darkness, and had not the incurable disease of the city compelled everyone to return home early. Though very famous for many reasons, the city possesses one particularly dark, repulsive, and inveterate evil: to travel in it by night, as in a jungle, is dangerous and full of hazards because the streets are beset by armed young nobles whose dissoluteness cannot be controlled by the discipline of their parents, by the authority of their teachers, or by the majesty and command of kings. But is it any wonder that they act brazenly under the cover of darkness without witnesses, when in this Italian city in broad daylight with royalty and the populace as spectators infamous gladiatorial games are permitted of a wildness that is greater than we associate with barbarians? Here human blood flows like the blood of cattle, and often amidst the applause of the insane spectators unfortunate sons are killed under the very eyes of their wretched parents. It is indeed the ultimate infamy to hesitate having one's throat pierced by the sword as if one were battling for the republic or for the rewards of eternal life. I was taken unknowingly the day before yesterday to such a place not far from the city which is called appropriately "The Furnace" where indeed a workshop full of soot and of inhuman fierceness darkens the bloody blacksmiths at the anvil of death. The Queen was present as was Prince Andrew, a boy of lofty mind, if ever he were to assume the long-deferred crown. All the militia of Naples was also present in all their elegance and propriety. All the rabble had eagerly flocked to that place. And so I, curious about so great a crowd and about the passionate interest of well known people, thinking that I was about to view something great, focused my attention on the spectacle. Suddenly, as if something very delightful had occurred, thunderous applause resounded. I looked around and to my surprise I saw a most handsome young man lying at my feet transfixed by a sharp pointed sword which emerged from his body. I stood there astounded, and my whole body shuddering. I spurred my horse and fled from the infernal spectacle, angry at my friends' deceit, at the cruelty of the spectators and the continued madness of the participants. This twin plague, dear father, as if inherited from our ancestors has reached subsequent generations in an ever increasing tempo, and the reason for it is that the license for committing crime has now acquired the name of dignity and freedom. Let this suffice, for it is a tragic matter and I have already wasted many words speaking of it with the obstinate citizens. Indeed we should hardly be astonished that your friends, offering as they do such a prize for greed, should be prisoners in that city where killing men is considered a game, a city which Virgil indeed does call the most delightful of all, but as it stands now would not be considered unequal to Thrace in infamy: "Alas flee the cruel lands, flee the greedy shore." I certainly accept those words as relating to this city; and unless you hear otherwise, expect me to leave within three days to flee, even if my business remains unfinished, first to Cisalpine Gaul, and then to Transalpine Gaul and to you who always cause all my trips to be delightful unless they are by sea. Farewell.

Naples, calends of December.

Fam. V, 7.

To Giovanni Andrea,[1] professor of Canon law at Bologna, how much faith one should have in dreams.

You write me that you have been so deeply disturbed by a dream so real that you almost believed having seen it while awake. You were now seeing it a second time, except that what you dreamed was of something that could not happen more than once. However, even while thinking that the dream event could not be repeated, you became aware that the dream was of something you had seen before. Now you ask whether anything like it had ever happened to me, what I believe about such matters, and what learned men have said about them. The subject is indeed as vast as are the sources of disagreement, especially because this problem has not only been tackled by men of letters, but popularly, with everyone giving evidence of his own experiences of dreams. As a result it is difficult in the debate to separate the truth from the chatter. Not only do the people disagree, but learned men also, yet their opinions which you know very well you nevertheless deliberately tempt me to discuss. You know the commentary of Chalcidius on the *Timaeus* and the commentary of Macrobius on the sixth book of the *Republic* where he presents a clear and brief distinction between types of dreams. You have Aristotle's book on these and related matters. Finally you have Cicero's book on prophesy, in which you will find how he himself, as well as others, viewed the matter. Why do you want me to repeat what is very well known? It is indeed curious that anyone knowing the authority of the ancients should want to hear my opinion, but I suppose friendship does curious things. If you really place any importance in my judgment and believe that my opinion is valid for the matter at hand, I agree in this with my Cicero as I do in so many other things. However I do so without

1. A learned and famous law professor at the University of Bologna and considered one of the outstanding specialists in canon law. He held the chair in canon law at Bologna for forty-five years, and was a teacher of Petrarch. As an admirer of St. Jerome he wrote a carefully researched biography of the saint.

obstinacy and am ready to alter my agreement with him if anything more certain should appear, refusing to assume the arrogance and rashness of asserting anything with finality, something he himself advises in his book *Academic Questions*. There you have it. If you should wish to hear me dealing with this matter in a more elaborate fashion, I have in hand a book entitled *Liber memorandarum rerum* which if it is ever published will deal in a first part more fully with these matters. However, to the many examples of the experiences of others which I have collected in that book, I shall add as you request two personal experiences of dreams, one pleasing, the other sad, but both about a verified event. To both of them there are witnesses whom I told of my dreams after I had them and before they came true. My recollecting both will thus give satisfaction to you and be pleasant to me.

I had a friend in my early years than whom at that time neither nature nor fortune had given me any dearer. Being suddenly stricken by a serious illness he was given up as lost by his doctors and I despaired for my own life. There was only one kind of consolation I could find, and that was to weep. I wept constantly day and night. Then one night, having been awake until dawn, I finally submitted my weary eyes to a sad dream. I suddenly saw him before me and the sight made me emit terrible groans which awoke my colleagues. As I later learned from them, when they saw me asleep, though they perceived I was having some kind of troubled dream, feeling sorry for my many hours of sleeplessness, they preferred to let me have a disturbed rest rather than none at all. However, my sick friend seemed to approach me and to gently wipe my tears pleading that I put an end to a grief which had no basis in fact. And when I set about refuting his words and complaining about my fate, I seemed to hear him interrupting my complaints saying: "Be silent; whatever you are about to say I know; but here is someone approaching who will put an end to our conversation; I beg you to renew your hope for my health through him, and rest assured that I shall not perish at all from this disease unless I am forsaken." As he was saying these things there was a loud knock on the door of my bedroom which caused both sleep and the vision to vanish. I looked around, and in the light of daybreak I saw standing at my bed one of the doctors who had been very friendly to both of us, and who, despairing of my friend's health, had turned all his attention to comforting and consoling me. I approached this very dear and courteous man with many prayers, urging him to return to my friend and not abandon hope (especially in the case of a man who was so young), so long as any sign of breathing remained with him. However, as he pointed out very sadly, he admired my grief and useless anxiety, but could profess only the art of curing and not reviving, being a doctor and not God. I, in turn, with my eyes still wet with tears shed during the night, with sound mind though somewhat upset, explained to him what I had seen and I warmly sought his assistance in this misfortune. What else can I say? I convinced him even though he was highly reluctant. He went and soon returned bringing news of somewhat better hope. All the others who had deserted the sick man likewise eagerly returned, and in this fashion my friend was returned to me from the hands of death herself. Even though I am attracted by the sweetness of such recollection, and may linger too long on personal matters, I shall not refrain from relating the following.

Giacomo Colonna, the younger, a man in our time of the greatest note and endowed with a nature that would easily have been truly superior in any century, was a person who valued my friendship and with whom I lived on friendly terms. Only in one matter have I felt that fortune had not been as unfair as she might have been with me; very rarely has she permitted me to be involved directly in my griefs, but rather caused me to be hurt from a distance and preferred to have my ears feel the blows, thus sparing my eyes. Many things can be said about that man which I shall pass over, since they have no bearing on present matters and there is nothing indeed that you could hear about his ways that would be new to you inasmuch as, of all the bishops, it was this one that you preferred cultivating and honoring for yourself. You cultivated the outstanding talent of a truly noble youth during his adolescence, like a skillful cultivator of talents capable of extracting the fruit from the flower. You soon came to love the excellence of his virile mind which was best known to you; then you bestowed upon him honors worthy of his merit and priesthood which he so truly deserved; finally you accompanied him with compassionate tears and deep human affection even though in his exit from so many concerns and from the midst of the labors of life he proceeded to better things, and you did so like a father insofar as dignity was concerned, like a son insofar as age was concerned, and like a brother insofar as intimacy was concerned. But I shall return to the matter at hand. He, then, hating the hubbub of worldly life, fled his venerable father, brothers, and native land and like a distinguished patron he once again sought his see and withdrew to the retreats of Gascony. As he had everywhere lived the rest of his life magnificently, he there now lived the last portion, in an utterly episcopal and dedicated manner as if aware of his approaching end. However, being in Cisalpine Gaul divided from him by a considerable expanse of land, I was at that time enjoying some rest in this very garden from which I am writing to you. Rumors brought me gossip about his illness, but it was such that fluctuating between hope and fear with great anticipation I used to await more certain announcements. I shudder even as I recall those moments, for the very place where I saw him clearly in the quiet of the night lies here before my eyes. He was unattended, and was crossing this very brook in my garden. I went to meet him in a state of astonishment asking him many things: where he came from, where he was going, why in such haste, and why he was traveling alone. He answered none of my requests but as he was most pleasant in his conversation, he said smilingly: "Do you remember when you lived with me on the other side of the Garonne how annoying the storms of the Pyrenees were to you? Weary of them and determined to depart for good, I am on my way to Rome." Saying these things he had already hastened to the outskirts of my residence, as I was urging him to take me with him. Having gently denied my request time and again with his hand raised, he finally said with a change of voice and in another tone: "Stop, I do not wish to have you as a companion at this time." I fixed my eyes upon him and I recognized from his paleness that he was dead. Overcome by fear and sadness I cried out so loudly that awakening at that very moment I heard the very last sounds of my cry. I marked down the day and recounted the whole story to my local friends and wrote about it to absent ones. After twenty-five days the news of his death was brought to me. When I check the dates, I note that he had come to me on the very day on which he had passed away. Finally after three years his remains were brought back to Rome (which I did not know and did not even suspect), his soul, as I hope and desire, having returned triumphantly to heaven.

But enough about dreams; let us rouse ourselves. This much I point out. I have faith in dreams not because Caesar Augustus, that very great man both as a ruler and as a learned person, may be said to have been of contrary opinion, and there are many today who agree with him; nor because a dream made either my master or my friend appear before me in my anxiety, nor because one died and the other lived, for in both cases I saw either what I wished for or what I feared, and fate happens to coincide with my visions. My faith in dreams is no more than Cicero's who considered that the accidental truth of one of his dreams did not undo the ambiguities of many others. Farewell.

27 December.

Fam. V, 8.

To the same correspondent, on the condition of a lustful young man.

You would like to know what I think of and what I hope for this man of yours? A prisoner of a harmful and, what is worse, a shameful passion, he is completely entangled in a net of evil. Meantime he may appear angry, and indeed oftentimes is forced to be. Such is the nature of love, such the life of lovers. They become angry and they quarrel, and conclude their many battles in repeated truces, hardly ever keeping even for a moment to a single purpose. Of life's difficulties there is nothing worse than this fickleness and fluctuation. In consequence you will rarely find them happy, but often sad; you will always find them changeable, but never consistent. You write that this young man of yours has now become revolted by his pleasures. I believe it, since I am certain it could not be otherwise. For who is so obstinate that he may not sometimes open his eyes and, seeing his wretchedness, hate it? However, I do not agree with what you add, for you express the greatest hope that such signs indicate he can loosen himself from his chains. I myself believe that considering the age and mental bent of the man, he will become more embroiled unless God's help is very close. Since it is the custom of a snared bird to become more entangled by trying to shake itself loose, I would be more optimistic if his love seemed to be ending in oblivion and silence rather than in animosity and quarreling; the former is a sign of a restored mind, the latter of offended love. I fear what Terence says in his *Andria*: "The anger of lovers is but a renewal of love"; I fear what Seneca said to his Lucilius: "Nothing revives more easily than love"; I fear those words of Virgil: "Oh wicked love, what do you not compel mortal hearts to do?"; I fear everything Cicero has to say about this matter in the forth day of his *Tusculan Orations*; finally I fear the general agreement on this matter of all the philosophers, and the opinions of poets. But above all things I am frightened by the abominable skill and inextricable snares of the panders and the harlots; I shudder at the flattery of the sirens and the

clinging snare of passion; I tremble at this harborless Charybdis, notorious for the shipwreck of so many, in which he is
now navigating. In short there is nothing, as matters now
stand, which I do not fear. For what he now threatens cruelly,
or angrily imagines as he blurts: "Am I going to let her. . . .
Why she! that fellow! and me, too! she doesn't!" and those
other things that follow, the ending will be as Terence ex-
presses it: "All she has to do is rub her eyes hard and squeeze
out one little make-believe tear, and that will be the end of
(his) talk. She'll blame it all on (him), and (he'll) be the one
who pays." * Let him rage with loud clamor and let him
noisily declare himself free, but if I were to be the judge, I
would agree with the judgment of the old woman who mur-
murs that he has fallen into slavery. Why? Because I know
in what way her murmur is more potent than his clamor, and
to what extent some skills surpass others. Between them there
is neither equality nor similarity. One is made of iron, the
other of clay; one is like fire, the other is like stubble; one
reflects swiftness of feigning, the other ease of believing;
one is composed of countless hooks, the other of as many
hook-eyes. You know everything, and although your age ex-
cludes you from these concerns, I speak of nothing which is
really unknown to you. Doesn't the old woman in the *Asinaria* of Plautus appear to you rightly confident in these matters? You will recall that she speaks thus to the angry and
menacing young man: "Your mind here at home is held fast
by the nails of passion; hurry as much as you can with oars
and with sails, and flee, for the more you attempt to gain the
open sea, the more the waves carry you back to port." The
witch was certainly sure of herself since she had learned of
such youthful adventures through the experience of a full
life. To these things I shall add only this one: that you give
thought to the fact that by the passage of time cities are destroyed, kingdoms transferred, customs changed, and laws
altered; yet those things that pertain to minds of men and the
diseases of the mind are almost all the same as they were
when Plautus imagined his stories. What you say is pro-

* Trans. of F. O. Copley, *The Comedies of Terence* (New York,
1967).

claimed quite frequently by this man, if he does indeed proclaim it everywhere, namely that he did burn with passion once but no longer was its victim, is indeed a fatal sign of this disease. The short verse of Naso is well known: "He who says too often 'I do not love,' does indeed love." I do not believe in words but in deeds, and not quickly in these unless an opposite way of life is tenaciously pursued in order to wash away the stains of the previous life. A quick remedy does not help a lingering illness. What we learn through long practice must be unlearned through long disuse. You now have this prediction of mine concerning your young man, and would that events will prove it false, for certainly the right hand of the Almighty is powerful, and as with the conversion of David He could in His forgiveness and in less time than it takes to say it raise one from the lowest depths of misery.

But you know that holds very rarely and for very few men. Farewell.

13 May.

Fam. V, 9.

To the same correspondent, on the condition of a dissolute old man.

You have brought up a subject unlike the one in your first letter, that of a dissolute and lustful old man, yet more appropriate for satire, for, according to the rhetorician, "A lustful young man sins, a lustful old man is mad," and in confirmation Plautus: "We sometimes rave as old men,"—not only sometimes but in fact very often. This was true in ages past; now however we crawl as infants, we play as children, we go mad as youths, we do battle as men, we rave as old men. Thus missing no portion of life, we bring some form of folly into each age through a graded series of errors. I know not what to say except that were it not for some ray of light shining among so many shadows I would certainly agree with the ancients who believed that next to dying the best thing is not to be born. There is one excuse, however, that this kind of old man seems to have: their need for consolation in their feeble age; and now indeed such liberty is openly accepted. Thus in his *Asinaria* even Plautus excused his lascivious old man saying: "If unknown to his wife, this old man enjoyed some pleasure, he did nothing new or astonishing, or different from what others have been accustomed to do; there is no one of such an unyielding temper or firmness of mind who would not, should the occasion arise, indulge himself." This is what Plautus said, and this is what we all say either as young men for whom lust is an honor, or as grown men for whom lust is a habit, or as old men for whom lust appears as a venial sin. How often will you find an old man who, when an opportunity presents itself and there are no witnesses present, would not immediately forget his lack of virility and rush into an affair like a young person, flattering himself with the thought that delight and pleasure are both beneficial and proper, and that the only comfort of old age is lust, which is, in truth, the disgrace and destruction of old age? You must speak to our old man and make him pay attention to what he is doing, where he is going, and how contrary to his age, how unbecoming and how dangerous and inconvenient his lust really is. Perhaps modesty and fear may be effective in accomplishing what reason and satisfaction ought to have done long ago. But if he continues, convey to him only these words of mine: that he must stop soon because as the lust of youth leads to old age, the lust of old people leads to the grave. Farewell.

Fam. V, 10.

To Barbato da Sulmona.

As is our custom I am moved to share with you my circumstances and my hardships. As you know, warfare has ceased in Parma; we are surrounded by the great rebellions not only of Liguria but of almost all of Italy, and we are confined within the borders of a single city not because of a lack of courage in our men (which they have often proved in bold sallies), but because the cunning of the enemy is such that it reveals neither the road to peace nor the road to battle, but is confident that it will conquer by weakening our spirits through patiently subjecting us to the slow weariness of a siege. Therefore, under the often varying hand of fate, the besieger himself becomes besieged and the outcome is not yet certain. In any event, the issue is being fiercely fought by both sides, and, unless I am wrong in my prediction, the ultimate day of reckoning approaches ever closer. I waver in my mind and do not lean completely toward either side, striving not to fall prey either to empty hope or to useless fear. In this condition we have been experiencing the siege not for a few days only but for many months, certainly not the least of military misfortunes. In this predicament I have recently felt a desire for freedom, which I pray for and seek to embrace enthusiastically and, as it flees from me, pursue through the world. For some time a desire for my Transalpine Helicon has gripped me because my Italian Helicon is aflame with war. And so I have been driven on the one side by hatred, on the other by longing. But what could I do? The road leading West had become completely inaccessible. I turned to the East, and although all the roads there seemed full of enemy, yet a short trip in that direction seemed safer than the longer route through Etruria. What more need I say? Departing with a few men through the enemy positions, I undertook a journey at sundown on 23 February. When in the middle of the night I arrived at Reggio, a hostile city, a group of bandits suddenly emerged from ambush with loud shouting threatening death. Deliberation was not possible, with time, place, and the surrounding enemy threatening.

What could a few men unarmed and unprepared do against a great number who were armed and experienced in violence? Our only hope lay in flight and darkness. "His friends flee and are covered by the darkness of the night." I confess that I too removed myself from the danger of death and the resounding weapons. Just when I thought I had evaded every danger (I ask you, how can any man consider himself safe?), whether because of a ditch or perhaps a tree trunk or a rock barrier (for the darkness of that cloudy and blinding night made it impossible to see anything), my most faithful horse fell headlong to the ground with such a blow that I was stunned and felt broken into pieces. Nevertheless I managed finally to collect my courage and rose to my feet, and I, who despite the many days that have elapsed cannot yet bring my hand to my mouth, at that moment supported by my fear sprang once again upon my horse. Some of my companions returned home, some, undaunted by their vain wanderings, did not abandon the undertaking. Our two guides having lost track of the road markers provided by heaven and earth, exhausted and disturbed, compelled us to stop in an out of the way place from which, to add to our terror, could be heard the voices of enemy guards of some close-by camp. Heavy rain, too, had begun to fall, mixed with raging hail, and amidst heavy thunder we felt a constant fear of a more dramatic death. My report would take too long if I covered every point. While we spent that night, which was truly hellish, lying under the open skies on the wet ground, the swelling and pain of my injured arm increased more and more. There was no grassy turf on which to sleep, no branches of a leafy tree or protection of a cave, only the naked earth, the agitated air and raging Jupiter, and, along with the fear of humans and of beasts, the many discomforts of an ill body. Among so many difficulties only one reason for consolation existed which perhaps you will be astonished at and pity: having placed our horses crosswise on the road, we used them as tents and as a covering against the storm. At first they snorted and were restless, but they soon became silent and quiet, as though they were not without some feeling for their wretchedness. They thus provided us with a double service on that awful night. And thus after so much hardship and anxiety dawn finally arrived. As soon as the weak light indicated a path among the bushes, we hastily left the unsafe places. Arriving at a friendly town called Scandiano, we learned that throughout that night a large band of horsemen and foot soldiers had lain in ambush around the walls to capture us, and because of the great storm had departed shortly before our arrival. Try now to deny that fortune is indeed mysterious and powerful enough to change careful plans into destruction, and errors into wise actions. I am fooling with you, dearest Barbato; you know my feelings about fortune; it is but a formidable word. However one wants to look at the matter, our mistaken path proved to be useful as was the storm; we avoided worse things by means of bad things. In that place, therefore, at the arrival of dawn I revealed what had happened amidst many tears on the part of my companions; and since a delay in that place did not seem too safe either, wrapped in tentative bandages, I arrived over mountainous paths in Modena and on the next day in Bologna. From here I am writing these things not as I usually do but with the hands of others so that you will not worry about my condition and my affairs. Regarding the care of my body, all that can be humanly done is being done. While there is much hope for my recovery it certainly will not be swift. The doctors expect help from my age; I expect assistance only from almighty God. Meanwhile my numb right hand does not obey me, but my courage becomes more resolute in adversity. Farewell.

25 February, Bologna.

Fam. V, 11.

To Andrea da Mantua,[1] *that the words of detractors should be despised, but their writings should be refuted with writings.*

Hardly ever have I been given a more just reason for complaint or richer occasion for self-defense: I am being maligned at every crossroad. What shall I do? My attacker has attained the point of injustice; disreputable people are slandering my reputation. My detractor deserves to be despised, for he is the more annoying the more he is vile. It is difficult to pretend, yet the dignity of silence is preferable to justified complaints. Let them sharpen their tongues, for I do not fear words. If they express themselves in writing, I will reply, for so long as I live I shall repel the attacks of living critics. But what if they threaten me after I die? For, as I hear, they constantly give birth to a ridiculous mouse or an Indian elephant. But when I ponder the matter, I can only say that should they wait until I am no longer present, they would be behaving in a vile fashion and would be heaping upon me accusations that could hardly be called magnanimous. What else shall I say about their opinions except what I usually say, the same as was said by Plancus against Asinius Pollio which Pliny the elder recalls at the beginning of his *Natural History:* "With the dead only ghosts can contend"? Therefore, if they have something to say, let them reveal it while there is someone who may answer. You will see the offended party become popular because of the insults. Thus Aeschines made Demosthenes more famous, Galba did the same for Cato, Sallust for Cicero, Emilianus for Apuleius. Otherwise they choose an inglorious type of battle when they speak against an absent person and battle with silent ashes; although in this age of ours that is precisely what in their impudent way they hope to do. Farewell.

1. Little is known about this admirer of Petrarch who presumably defended him against his detractors and critics.

Fam. V, 12.

To the same correspondent, on the same matter.

That Theon of ours, or if you prefer Bion, is looking for trouble; I recognize the hissing, the asp must be close by. Should I be indignant or astonished that he does not spare me who would not spare even Homer himself? I think he believes that I get the same pleasure he does from such doings. He is indeed very wrong; nothing is more pleasing to me than silence; after that, nothing is sweeter than a conversation with a friend. If he persists, I shall flee; but you ask what I would do if he does not allow me to do so? I shall remain silent. If he does not permit even silence? I shall speak. How much will I say? Nothing will be briefer. And what shall I say? I shall threaten him with a kind of insult he has never heard; he will be upset and shocked and perhaps, as may happen, disturbed by his conscience, he will be silent. And this will be the end of the dispute because there is nothing that checks the tongue of a critic more than the fear of a sharper tongue. If this does not stop him, with what other arms shall I drive out this gnat? I shall take vengeance like an old woman and shall say to him what one old woman is said to have said to another: "Oh greatest of men and more modest than all, oh cultivator of the virtues, oh ornament and hope of the fatherland; you certainly have never heard anything like this." Now what do you say? Have I not tried hard enough to keep my promise? Either I am mistaken, or though his ears have become hardened to insults, he never heard one like it before now, not from the mouth of a lover, or of a flatterer, or of a mocker, or of a devotee regardless of his impudence. I believe that that unusual style will astonish him; you will laugh, and I meanwhile shall escape. Farewell.

Fam. V, 13.

To his Socrates, the desirability of not delaying salutary advice.

If you have not yet put to rest your heart's anxieties (I being aware of my own troubled state), and if my entreaties can be of any avail for either of us, I beseech and implore us both to drive away at once all the things that torment us and to suppress finally the restlessness of our minds. And let us not be troubled because we have delayed too long or have begun too late. You will not persuade the traveler who gets up late one morning that though the sun may be high he should return to his bedroom in order to prolong his sleep until that evening even though he feels heavy from sleep, or feels distress from excessive drinking, or feels exhausted with weariness. You will rather persuade him that it will be much better to hasten, to double his speed, and to try hard to compensate with energy for what sleep had done. We too, if you reflect, are wayfarers, and an endless journey awaits us, and the hour is already late, for we have been wasting our morning in sleep. We should therefore rise much more vigilant lest perhaps the night should press upon us as we loiter. The matter invites many more considerations but time is short and what has been said certainly suffices for men of good will. Farewell.

Fam. V, 14.

To the same correspondent, on the annoying relations with servants.

Recently I was reading some charming stories by Plautus for the sake of fleeing boredom and relaxing my mind, and thereby for a short moment with the help of the ancient poet avoided the heavy cares of life. It is certainly astonishing how many pleasant stories and elegant pieces I have found therein, and what trickery of servants, what old wives' tales, what flattery of harlots, what greed of panders, what voraciousness of parasites, what anxieties of old men, and what youthful loves. I now am less astonished at Terence for having achieved such great elegance following such a leader. But we shall speak about other things in due time, for there is much to be said, and for those who have abundant free time (if by chance such a thing should ever happen to us), these are very pleasant matters. For the present I shall include only one which most appropriately happened on this very day. There is a comedy of his entitled *Casina*. In it a man and lady disagree over the marriage of their young maid. A domestic war ensues; indeed one that you might call a civil war. As a result all things seem to fall apart for the two married people who appear so united. They agree on nothing whatsoever: the father pursues his own love affairs, and the mother those of her son. Two servants, who are very obstinate rivals, eagerly aspire to marry the girl, one supported by the father and the other by the mother. The servant who is abetting the lust of the master proved unmovable when the mistress of the house begged him to desist from helping his master. When he was asked by his master, who had overheard the final words of the dispute, with whom he was quarreling, he answered, "With the one with whom you are always quarreling." "With my wife, then," answered the old man as if understanding the matter in a roundabout way. To this the servant answered in a manner which was neither servile nor impolite and which, as I read today, seemed to be directed in a certain way to myself. "How can you speak to me of your wife?" he said, "You are indeed almost a hunter since you fill your time night and day with a dog." This is what that servant replied. What can be said that would be more suitable for me? My life has certainly not included a wife and though subjected to a variety of storms it has remained immune from this Charybdis. But there is another kind of trouble for which the words of that servant could be suitable; and while I have undergone the experience for quite some time I was not aware of his words. I knew that I was living with dogs, but that I was a hunter I did not know unless reminded. Servants can be called dogs, being, as they are, biting, gluttonous and barkers. I can bear all these qualities except the last, for barking is too averse to the tranquillity I seek. But of all that bands of dogs there are two that are absolutely unbearable to me, for I have managed to bear with the others up to now. One of these is the one whom I sent to you today with many letters of friends (among which I added this letter after reading Plautus). You can therefore keep this one for yourself if you wish to become a hunter or send him into the woods or into the slaughterhouse, provided that he never returns to me. The other is that other raging old man whom you know very well. Decency prevents me from driving him out, not so much out of respect for him as for his age and long friendship. Therefore since my Plautine servant declared that I was a hunter I shall do what considerate hunters do. I shall not drive a loyal dog from the house although he has become useless because of his old age and his mange, and most troublesome because of his barking. However if I cannot send him away, I shall flee myself and leaving the empty house for him to enjoy I shall seek other regions. Since I have not yet decided where this shall be, you will read my decision in a more confidential letter. In sum, I can become a fisherman at the source of the Sorgue, as my thinking goes for now, but I certainly shall not be a hunter nor shall I spend my life with dogs such as these. Farewell.

Fam. V, 15.

To the same correspondent, an exhortation.

All of us who are born are called to the Campus Martius; some however for no other reason than to make noise and to add to the number; others to enjoy the honors and rewards of hard effort. To belong on the side of these we must make a deliberate choice and effort. The outcome He alone will see in whose hands we have placed ourselves and our affairs. The will for it rests indeed with us. Therefore it behooves us to make up our minds, to become candidates, and to implore the approval of the Supreme Commander and of His friends, for such assemblies are intended not to determine a consulship or a praetorship but, as the young man in Plautus says, our very existence. Farewell and be vigilant.

Fam. V, 16.

To Guido Sette, Archdeacon of Genoa,[1] an excuse for not writing.

I have lost a letter that I had addressed to you. This has resulted from the messenger's delay, and the brash desire of my companions who, in their constant desire for novelties and, to use the words of Solinus, in their usual wanderings through my library, driven by impatience rather than zeal, must have come across that letter, read it and taken it without my knowing. They said that they feared lest a copy of it also perish, as had happened in many other instances when my friends became upset and condemned my carelessness. When I had learned this, I urged them to return it to me, and they hurried to search for it. Why take any longer in explaining what happened? The truth is what someone once said: "Haste does all things badly," for while all desired to find it no one succeeded; and while it was handed to one of them with the consent of all in order to be transcribed, to everyone's sorrow he either lost it or pretended to have lost it—I do not know how except that I never saw it again. I shall confess one thing which I am not ashamed to do with you: it is hard to believe that I could have become so concerned over anything so small. Rarely on other occasions have I perceived my frailty so clearly. I turned everywhere and for many days and nights I sought the lost letter while I complained, at times rebuking the rash confidence of my companions, at times my own casualness, accusing them because in admiring my style more than it deserved they acted inappropriately, and myself because in my search for an untimely glory from the first fruits of my studies I was perhaps becoming too harsh with my friends. Of course even the greatest mental blows are mitigated in time. I have now stopped complaining, and modesty has expelled sorrow; I am indeed ashamed to have complained so bitterly. Since no remains of that letter survive except the loving recollection, as Augustine says, let it indeed have per-

1. One of Petrarch's earliest friends whose father had moved his family to Avignon at the same time as Petrarch's father. Reared together in the papal court their friendship lasted their entire life.

ished so long as my pen remains. Meanwhile, as I return to my usual habit of writing, I wanted to let you know the reason for the interruption lest you be upset by my unusual silence. Farewell.

Fam. V, 17.

To the same correspondent, that the works of ugly people can be beautiful.

I am not unaware of your astonishment that I should appear to bear so badly the loss of a single letter. For it is not evidence of great talent to hope for glory from one's letters. The followers of true philosophy do not doubt that true glory proceeds not from words but from deeds. For me glory is not what is acclaimed by the rabble whose praise noble minds find almost disgusting, but rather that which flourishes and is nourished by the serious and pleasant recollection of virtuous works in the heart of distinguished men, and of which God and one's conscience are witnesses without theatrical applause or the support of the multitude. This alone is real glory because its roots are deeply implanted in firm soil, and it is not subject to chance. The kind that is based on the prattle of men is, to begin with, of short duration, is very easily overthrown, and then is forever tossed about by those very blasts that raised it on high, so that it eventually falls to destruction. Furthermore, even if it could last forever, the fact that it is sought only with the most vulgar and least noble means made it unattractive to the truly noble minds, being but the cheap wages of servile labor. Mulling over these things in my mind, I confess that I was astonished at myself and reproached myself severely. On the other hand as I recalled how pleasant the reading of that letter had been for me, I softened my self criticism and I acquitted my longing for it of all fault. I am not certain whether true or false, but I persuaded myself with a number of arguments that I had deplored its loss without any reference to a desire for windy praise, but rather because I had felt that it was useful to me. And what made me so confident was not any skill or talent, but that true Teacher of the arts and Master of skills who made me dare to hope that that letter composed by the hand of so great a sinner would not only be pleasing to readers (which would be of little account) but perhaps even beneficial. In it I had said many things against fortune, against the softness of men and especially my own; and with many exhortations to virtue and not a few attacks against our century and against the vices that now seem to rule over all the world, I had provided the letter with a double spur. So true was all of this that upon rereading it I scarcely thought it was my work and I felt far more respect for it than I usually do for my writings.

Nowhere is it written that Phidias and Apelles were handsome; nevertheless the remains of the outstanding works of one survive, and the fame of the other has come down to us. Therefore, despite so many intervening centuries, the remarkable talent of both artists lives on in different forms, of course, because of the different materials used. The work of the sculptor is of course more durable than that of the painter whence we learn about Apelles in books and about Phidias in marble. I believe the same about Parrhasius and Polyclitus and Zeuxis and Praxiteles and about all the others concerning whose personal beauty nothing is said because of the outstanding beauty of their works and their distinguished reputation. To move now from the ancients to new things, and from foreign artists to our own, I know two outstanding painters who were not handsome: Giotto, a Florentine citizen whose reputation is very great among the moderns, and Simone of Siena. I also know several sculptors but of lesser fame (since our age is truly mediocre in that art form). In any event I noticed with them something about which perhaps I shall say more in another place, namely that the works of single artists differ a great deal from their creators. If anyone were to seek the cause of such difference from them, they would answer, I think, not what Mallius the painter who, having been asked by his friends at a dinner why he had produced such ugly children when he had painted such beautiful forms, answered: "because I paint in the light and I conceive in the darkness." His answer is of course facetious. More truthful would be the answer of those who would say that both the appearance of a body and the possession of talent (which is the form of the soul from which these works which we praise and admire emerge as if it were a fountain) are gifts of almighty God, not of men, and they must be received not only naturally but gratefully, whether they are bestowed liberally or sparingly, since they are free and always exceed human merit. Nor ought any man question the reason why anything is done to a greater or lesser extent by Him whose will is the highest and inaccessible cause which no human efforts may grasp; for the more "man strives to achieve the great heights," the more "God will be exalted," and mortal insights are frustrated in the depths of His council.

I enter gladly upon this argument even though I could have bypassed it so that you would not marvel if I too were to write a beautiful letter though ugly myself; and if in that letter, to use the words of Gregory, I an ugly painter depicted a handsome man. Consequently its very form in which it outdid its sisters was the reason for its loss and my grief, so that I would understand why sometimes outstanding beauty is harmful not only to bodies but to writings and why one should seek moderation in all things. Thus my letter, which I had begotten but not yet adopted, caused me to grieve over its loss as if involved in some kind of funeral rites, and in my memory I celebrate its anniversary grieving that it had been removed so swiftly from my very presence and, so to speak, had been destroyed in its very cradle. My plaint in this matter is deeper because any hope of seeing another letter arise from the bones of that one, as if it were a Phoenix rising from its ashes, is very small. None of its remains have survived, for against my custom I had entrusted all of it to writing and none to memory. Therefore when I now search for it in my memory I do not find it nor do I recognize any imprint of the departed one. All I retain of it is the recollection that it was very pleasant for me to write it, even more pleasant when I read it, but most unpleasant when I think about it, just as happens when a bit of honey taken from a tasty honeycomb is brought close to one's lips and then suddenly drawn away. With the removal of the sweet taste only the bitter remembrance of the sweetness would remain. Being upset over these things, I stopped writing for a long time. I detested my waking hours and judged everything by what had happened in that single event. I finally realized that it was not wise to act like a sailor who leaves sailing for fear of a single shipwreck or a farmer who destroys his plow because of one bad year, and so I returned to my pen. But again I ask, what shall I do? Your letter has also perished and followed its companion. As far as my memory helps me, there were two things that I especially enjoyed in it. I rejoiced, as is the custom among men, that fortune had been more kind to you than usual, although I am aware that the joy that comes from believing in the propitiousness of fortune is frivolous, since fortune was never friendly to anyone without preparing even more intimate deceits, and she exalted no one except to prepare his fall from greater heights. But this is one of those human errors which are countless and which, to use the words of Cicero, "we seem to have sucked with the milk of our nurse," and which we all wish we could lay aside in our old age. I received greater joy from the end of your letter where you seem to be acquainted with the uncertainties of fortune and to have your mind ready for any eventuality. This is what I wished, this is what I hoped, this is what I sought from God, that He would provide me and my friends with strong minds that disdain the inconstancy of things. To request that we undergo no adversity in life is to no purpose; but that we should bear patiently whatever happens is indeed a worthy prayer. Indeed, unless I am mistaken, I saw your mind in your words, and I said to myself: "Now he is a man, he stands erect on the earth and contemplates the heavens." Farewell.

Fam. V, 18.

To the same correspondent, on his present condition.

I send you briefly news of my condition about which you inquired. Although among true philosophers there is only one good for men to pursue and not three, namely the one found in a mind which is well disposed by heaven and distinguished by the possession of noble habits (since those of the body and of fate are not truly to be considered goods but merely conveniences of small utility), because I believe that you wish to hear about all three goods, I shall do what you desire. In what condition my mind is, I neither know fully, nor is it for me to declare. As Augustine says, "Those shadows in which my possibilities are hidden from me are to be regretted since my mind questioning itself about its own powers believes that it should not easily trust in itself." As far as I am able to say, however, human distress holds me thus far either sitting or lying in the mire of the flesh and in the chains of my mortality. I seem, however (unless I falsely feign to myself to appear this way), to be most willing to emerge from this condition. But I am weighed down by my burdens, and the unyielding yoke of inveterate habit prevails over me. Who will free wretched me from its slavery unless that Lord who "frees the chained slaves and enlightens the blind"? Fate has waged a continuous war against me thus far. Knowing that communing produces discord I labor not to have anything in common with her in order to live in peace. Empires, kingdoms, wealth, honors, and other such things are hers and let her keep them. None of them appeals to me. Let her leave for me those things which are good for my soul if there are any left. These are not her gifts and I require that they be free of her control. Why does she rage, why does she threaten? For too long have I been her debtor. Let us total up all our accounts and let her take back what is hers. Too long have I watched over her depository. What is she weighing? There is no reason for delay or struggle; let her take back whatever it is and let her depart and never return. She has already taken a large share, and whatever little remains is a troublesome burden for shoulders striving for loftier things. Insofar as the body is concerned, I am not the one you left behind. The guest of my body, disagreeing sharply with it, wages an implacable struggle. Anxiety over this struggle has caused a change in my appearance which is premature, so that you would scarcely recognize me at our next meeting. This sort of thing, however, does not disturb me. As long as I was healthy I had believed with Domitian: "Nothing is more pleasing or shorter than beauty." I was indeed born for greater things than to be the slave of my body. "Seneca," you say, "said this." Who denies it? And I say it as will many after me and as perhaps many did before him, and whoever will have said it, provided he did not lie, said a distinguished and splendid thing. I said not only that, but I shall say what follows and in both things I know I am not lying; would that I were not being deceived. Let it not be said that because of the love of my body or the desire of this life I fear the day of death, for I have appropriated this other saying of a very deep truth for myself, namely, that what is called this life of ours is really a death. Farewell.

Fam. V, 19.

To Clement VI, the Roman Pontiff,[1] that he must flee the mob of doctors.

The announcement of your fever, most blessed father, brought trembling and horror to my limbs; nor shall I speak to flatter you or to say the same things as that man about whom the Satirist says: "He cries if he sees the tears of his friend," or elsewhere: "If he says, 'I feel hot,' he perspires." But rather do I resemble him who, as Cicero says, was concerned about the welfare of the Roman people in which he saw his own included. My welfare indeed and the welfare of many others depends upon your health. My trembling therefore is not pretense, for I am not concerned about the danger of another but about my own. All of us who depend upon you and hope in you may perhaps appear healthy when you are ill but we are not. Since speech deserves to be brief always but especially in those things which are transferred from a human mouth into divine ears, I shall say a few things to you now with humble mind and respect. I know that your bed is besieged by doctors; this is the first reason for my fear. They all disagree purposely, each considering it shameful to suggest nothing new or to follow upon the footsteps of another. "There is no doubt," as Pliny says elegantly, "that all of them strive for a reputation with some kind of novelty and they regularly use our souls as an item of trade . . . and it happens only in this profession that whoever professes to be a doctor is immediately believed although it is impossible to imagine a more dangerous falsehood. We do not, however, reflect about this because everyone is flattered by the pleasure of his hope for himself. Furthermore, there is no law to punish this dangerous ignorance, and no example of such a wrong being punished. They learn by submitting us to dangers and they experiment unto death itself. Only for the doctor is there maximum im-

1. Pope from 1342–1352. During his serious illness in 1352 Petrarch sent him advice through an intermediary suggesting that he beware of doctors. When the Pope expressed his wish to have the message in writing, Petrarch obliged and was thenceforth mistrusted and attacked by the medical profession of the day.

punity for murder." Most merciful father, look upon their multitude as if it were a battleline of enemies. Learn by remembering the epitaph of that unfortunate man who ordered only the following words to be inscribed on his tomb: "I perished because of a mob of doctors." In our own time the prophesy of Marcus Cato the elder seems to apply to our times best of all: "Whenever the Greeks transmit their literature and especially their doctors to us, we shall be corrupt in all things." Since nowadays we do not dare live without doctors (although without them innumerable nations survive perhaps better and more soundly, the Roman people living thus for over six hundred years in a flourishing manner according to Pliny), choose for yourself, however, only one who is outstanding not because of his eloquence but because of his knowledge and trustworthiness. For now, unmindful of their profession and daring to emerge from their own thickets, they seek the groves of poets and the fields of the rhetoricians, and as if called not to heal but to persuade, they dispute with great bellowing at the beds of the sick. And while their patients are dying, they knit the Hippocratic knots with the Ciceronian warp; they take pride in any unfortunate event; and they do not boast of the results of their cases but rather of the empty elegance of words. And, lest your doctors think that I have invented any of this today which I often ascribe to Pliny because he said many things about medicine and spoke more truth than anyone else about doctors, I have indeed followed him in most parts of this letter, and let the doctors therefore listen to him. "It is obvious," he says, "that whoever succeeds in speaking among them should instantly become the arbiter of our life and of our death." Because I have gone further than I intended with fear urging on my pen, I shall stop now by saying that you ought to avoid the doctor who is powerful not in his advice but in his eloquence, just as you would avoid a personal attacker, a murderer, or a poisoner. To such a doctor one can most justifiably say what that old man in the *Aulularia* of Plautus said to his loquacious cook: "Go away, you were brought here to work in your specialty and not to make speeches." For these reasons, take good care of yourself and have high hopes and a joyful mind which help in wonderful ways the health of the body if you wish to save yourself, all of us, and the church herself who is ill together with you.

12 March.

Fam. VI, 1.

To Cardinal Annibaldo, Tusculan Bishop,[1] against the greed of the Popes.

Maro called envy an unfortunate thing, and rightly, for what is more unfortunate than to be tormented both by one's own ills and by the good fortune of others? Indeed the remark a certain Publius jokingly directed against a certain Mutius who was renowned for his envy and his maliciousness was elegantly put; for as we read, when he saw him sadder than usual, he said: "Either something disagreeable has happened to Mutius or something good has happened to someone else." That is exactly how it is; the envious person blames his own problems on the good that has occurred to someone else, and, as Flaccus says: "He grows lean because of the wonderful things that are happening to someone else." To grow lean by the abundance and prosperity of others as much as by one's own hunger or starvation is certainly a great wretchedness. But I would not fear to assert that avarice is a more unfortunate vice than envy or than all of the other vices. Although envy frequently produces dejection, it is inactive, whereas avarice is both sad and active. Although pride always thinks something great about itself, it still takes pleasure in its false opinion; avarice always feels itself famished and wanting, nor is it ever deceived. That poetic verse is indeed very true: "The miser is always needy." For if he is a miser, he desires, which the very name of the vice indicates. As Seneca says, there is no doubt that "it is not the one who has too little but one who desires more who is truly poor." And in consequence it may be concluded that the scarcity of possession does not cause need, since nature is satisfied with a little; one who properly satisfies his needs is indeed wealthy, for he lacks nothing. But an unsatisfied desire for possession feels that it lacks whatever it desires;

1. A descendent of an illustrious family and very learned in canon law, he was appointed by Pope John XXII as Archbishop of Naples and later Cardinal of Tusculum, near Rome. He was also sent as emissary to seek to expedite peace between the kings of France and England. His taste for pomp and splendor had become almost legendary by the time of this letter.

yet because it desires all things, by its wishing it makes even unnecessary things necessary. Avarice thus makes one's property, which before had been minimal and easily manageable, an incurable and immense problem. Once again that saying which is so popular with philosophers is indeed true: what misers possess they lack just as much as what they do not possess; except that in my view the miser seems to lack more what he has than what he does not have. In the former case he undergoes nothing but constant anxiety and well-grounded fear, while in the latter he sometimes enjoys a brief though false joy which delights him and makes him preempt the desired good through false hope. Wrath is sometimes overcome by a certain wild and, as they say, inhuman sweetness; avarice is never assuaged, for it burns still more with success and, as the Satirist says: "The love of money increases as the money itself increases," and whoever does not have any, desires it less. Whoever does not have it has less longing for it. In one of his letters Annaeus Seneca attributes one cause to this phenomenon for which many causes can be found. He says: "money makes no one wealthy; in point of fact there is no one in whom money has not inspired a greater desire for it"; and he continues: "You ask what may be the cause of this? He who possesses more begins to be able to have still more." This argument considers the fact that those things that cannot be possessed are neither desired indiscriminately nor hoped for because the difficulty of possessing them is so great as to render them almost impossible. Unless he is insane no one wishes wings with which to fly, and only a mad person hopes for them. But for a journey many people wish for a horse, a vehicle, or a ship, and all wish for the soundness of their legs. If such soundness should be irreparably lost, all hope and desire cease. I often add another argument to Seneca's, which goes as follows. The poor man seeks land or money only as a result of natural need which is usually very small and modest, and he seeks them only for those uses for which they are intended. Concerning these Flaccus says: "Do you not know how much money is worth? Of what use is it? It purchases bread, vegetables, a sixth of wine and whatever else human nature cannot do without." Human desires are thus restricted to such narrow limits; the rich man, however, abounding in necessities *ad nauseam*, roves through luxuries with his insatiable mind and provides it with extensive land holdings which are not intended as fields to relieve wants but as kingdoms to support pride, and is wont to view large quantities of money not as money but as mountains of gold. In these things, of course, lies the endless kingdom of avarice. Nor indeed is there any way of selecting since there is no limit to growth. Whether such limit is stretched out to the outer boundaries of a region by trading and plundering, or whether all the gold were made level with the mountains, as the other Satirist says, he would find no reason to stop. For he can go on wishing until with the boundaries of his fields he will have crossed the seas and the mountains to the ends of the lands, until the quantity of gold exceeded the Alps and he touched the stars with his head. He would be to such a degree more powerful than Caesar that he would not only bound his empire with the ocean but it would extend across the ocean, and finally he would be wealthier than Midas so that not only what he touched but also what he saw would become gold. We have seen many men who, when after their search they had arrived somewhere they had never imagined, had left all of their hopes and their original desires far behind them, become mad over again as they entertained new desires and new hopes. If you would recall to them their former condition, they would become angry and behave as if modesty might be something plebian or as if they themselves had become better because they were more greedy. Their dissoluteness having increased with money and desire, they are ashamed of humble desires. What hope can you therefore entertain for these, either of expectation or of desire, except that there may be nothing left anywhere that would be desirable? For as long as something does remain to be desired, they will hope for it and desire it, and when they have achieved their closest hopes others will constantly appear. Therefore, there will be no end except death itself. It would not happen this way if they did not always think of things to be sought, but sometimes looked closely at themselves and the things they did seek. But those things that appear precious to seekers become meaningless to those who obtain them, thus making desire infinite because it has no boundaries in which such gains may be contained, and sadly avarice is never satisfied, for as the prophet Aggeus said: "He who collects wealth puts it in a perforated sack." I come now to the other plagues. Concerning the one which we call *accidia* (sloth), the same things may be said that were said about envy. However, gluttony and lust often enjoy their own delights in which they rejoice and receive fugitive joys. Avarice enjoys nothing except the most bitter anxieties, for while it covets those things that it desires it neither possesses them nor sees them once acquired except as punishment, whence its restlessness and agitation. Since this is the case, avarice can justly be called the most fatal of all the "sisters" and is called by the Apostle the root of all evils.

I am aware that you wonder why today I wish to linger beyond custom on what some call a troublesome philosophy. However, I do not speak to you any more than I do to almost all mortals who are of your kind, and especially to those upon whom that mighty passion, as I perceive, has placed its throne and as a victor implanted its standard. I become more indignant the more unlikely appears the reason for your being a victim of cupidity. For whom do you amass these piles of gold? A legitimate posterity is denied you. A frugal and moderate existence befits you best; what remains belongs to Christ's poor whom you do not fear to cheat and plunder while their lord observes from above and threatens vengeance. And you know not for whom your crime may be useful in the future because meanwhile it has become laborious and destructive and even fatal. Many excuse their conduct in the name of their children, and they cover the vice of their mind with a curtain of devotion. So do the expectant lioness and tigres become wilder after giving birth, and love of new offspring arouses even tamed beasts. For you there is no excuse and no covering up of your vice. You stand naked before the eyes of the entire world, and you are pointed to with the biting reproach of all the peoples. They say, "Behold the heralds of virtue who speak splendidly about eternal life and at length about the liberty of the mind, and are nevertheless beyond reason pledged to earthly things and are slaves of avarice." For in truth although his reference may be general, does David not seem to be referring especially to you when he says: "Only a breath is any human existence. A phantom only, man goes his way; like vapor only are his restless pursuits"? And to signify the madness of a pontifical avarice to come after many centuries, he said more specifically, "he heaps up his stores, and knows not who will use them." * These things are certainly said of you more than of any others, oh greedy Pontiffs. We both see and read of parents who pile up treasures for their children, although fortune often prevents their parental intentions when what was due for certain ones falls to others. However, the purpose of parents is well known. I ask you what indeed are your intentions? What do you accomplish? For whom do you pile up treasures except for the devil and for his angels, who anxiously observe you, count the days, and eagerly await your inheritance in order to erect on the threshhold of hell with the booty taken from the plundered poor the highly pleasing trophies bearing your name? You inquire in astonishment: why do you bring up those things today rather than earlier? Is is possible that until now we have not been avaricious or that avarice was not a vice? Or must I believe that you are now for the first time opening my eyes to something that you yourself had not seen before? I shall reply to your wonderment. I knew that you were all greedy and that avarice was a vice, and I knew that there is no one anywhere who did not know this and that this is not the first time I open my eyes to both things. But when the day before yesterday I came to visit you, and I saw your altars, indeed the altars of the Lord of virtues, loaded with silver and gold and jewels, and I stood there in amazement stricken by the maddening brilliance, I said to myself: "Here are the new arms of avarice, a new way of perishing. It is not sufficient for us to be avaricious, but we must also make Christ so and 'we call the gods and Jove himself to a share in the booty,' " as Virgil says. Indeed you appear to justify these riches, which have been

* Douay version

badly acquired by making the poverty-stricken Christ a participant in your plundering and theft, and setting him unwillingly amidst your gold. This is not the way to soothe divinities. Have you not read in Seneca that the gods were propitious when they were of clay? And yet the gods were certainly never propitious nor even can be, for how can one be propitious to others who is wretched within himself? I therefore do not like Seneca's opinion, only his words which I would like to apply to a happier subject. Surely Christ has always been propitious to the human race; but he was far more real when he was made of clay. Now that he is made of gold and jewelry he is angry and does not hear our prayers because of his most understandable indignation. He does not dislike gold, but those who are hungry for wealth and whose desire and search has no end. The earliest men openly confessed what they really felt: they sought riches in order to abound in them. You seek in order to adorn Christ: a pious work indeed if he wished to be adorned with the spoils of the unfortunate rather than with the virtue and devotion of the faithful, and if cupidity joined to lying were not more hateful to God. I have often noticed something similar among the rulers and the masters of the earth who seek books with great zeal, and search for them, seize them, buy them, not because they love letters, of which they are ignorant, but because of avarice. They seek rather to ornament their bedroom than their minds; their concern was not for knowledge but for reputation, not for the thoughts expressed in the books but for their prices. In truth they do not lack an excuse which is somewhat colored but nevertheless false. They say that they are considering their offspring and posterity, and that huge libraries are compiled, according to what they say, for those who are not yet born and are uncertain about the kind of a life they may have to lead. In truth, however, they act because of their own greed and ignorance. What is the purpose of your attempts at collecting so much? You will answer that it is to fill the temples of Christ with gold. But what do you say to the exclamation of Persius: "Oh souls bent toward earthly things and empty of celestial things, of what benefit is it to introduce your customs into the temples?" And so that you should not believe that these words are for others, hear how he immediately afterwards calls you by name: "Explain, oh Pontiffs, what gold does in the sanctuary?" Answer, oh Pontiffs, for he is speaking to you. Answer this one young man, all you elderly ones; answer this one poet, all you theologians; answer this one pagan, all you Christians. What can you say? What is gold doing in the sanctuary? If you prefer not to answer a poet, should you not at least answer the prophet who requires of you not gold but other kinds of ornaments for the temples? You read in Malachias: "The son honors the father and the slave will fear his master; if therefore I am the father, where is the honor owed me? And if I am the master, where is the fear owed me: The Lord of hosts speaks." And to let you know that he is speaking to you, he adds: "To you, oh priests, who disdain my name, do I speak." I indicate this unless there is someone who thinks that this complaint would apply more worthily to other times than the present. As I said, I see the multitude burning with avarice, and I confess that nothing can serve as an excuse, for there is no excuse for sin; if the excuse is valid, it is certainly not a sin. But the dearness of children and the manifold needs and ignorance of the multitude mitigate the crime. Oh Pontiffs, I beg you ask yourselves: what does this madness for possession avail one who lives among so many certain riches, amidst so much knowledge of human and divine things, and in a solitary and celibate life which prohibits considering the morrow? You will probably refer me to those well known words: "The Church possesses the gold." It is good if it does possess it, but very bad if it is possessed by it. The riches of men can please; men of riches definitely do not please, those men who having completed their sleep find nothing left in their hands. Therefore the answer which Persius gives to his own question is perhaps closer to the truth. When he asked a second time: "What is gold doing in the sanctuary?" he concluded: "Indeed only this, the same thing that it has done for Venus when dolls are consecrated to her by a young girl." I beseech you, therefore, let the useless gold depart from the temples and let it be contributed to the other temples of the Lord, that is, for the use of men in want; let it become the love of Christ rather than the ostentation of the century; and let it not always serve idolatry under the pretext of devotion. Do you not know that avarice is the slave of idols? No people abound among so many idols, and to no one can it be said more fittingly: "Beware of idols." Believe me, oh Pontiffs, Christ could have had gold but refused it; he could have been rich when he lived among men, but he preferred poverty; he could have used vases from Corinth, but he preferred earthen jars. Do not, oh Pontiffs, seek frivolous excuses or increase the fodder of avarice in the name of Christ or as nourishment for your madness. Christ does not need your gold, nor does he take delight in your superstitions. He seeks rather the pious acts, the noble thoughts and the humble wishes of the pure and naked heart. What place is there for gold among such things? Do not, oh unhappy ones, be concerned about how proudly you sacrifice, how elegantly, how brilliantly, but rather how piously, how humbly, how chastely, how moderately. Sacrifice rather what the prophet king after having broken his chains sacrificed to his liberator, namely, the host of praise, and call upon the name of the Lord. Sacrifice, I say, the sacrifice of praise, the sacrifice of justice and hope not in gold but in the Lord. Hear the Psalmist, oh you who are hard of hearing, as he calls out day and night: "The contrite spirit is the sacrifice worthy of God." What need is there of gold in this? The need is for the spirit, but only if it is contrite; the need is for the heart, but contrite and humble. This is the sacrifice which is pleasing to God and achievable to man without digging under the earth. The need is for a humble and unstained mind, but there is no need for either pure or unprocessed gold. I know not what more to say and I fear wasting my words. But if, after the Prophet, you would not mind hearing Persius once again, see what that pagan said to his Pontiffs in those days: "Why do we not offer to the gods what great Messala's blear-eyed offspring could not offer even out of his great dish?" And in order not to leave any doubt as to what this offering to the gods was which those who were proud because of their birth and wealth, the blind sons of the wealthy, are not able to make, he subsequently defined it as "the ordered justice and right of the mind, and the holy recesses of the intellect, and a heart imbued with nobility and virtue." Striking words indeed and worthy to have been said about Christ himself. Farewell, and lend a fair ear to these faithful criticisms.

Fam. VI, 2.

To Giovanni Colonna of the Order of Preachers, that one must love not sects but the truth, and concerning the remarkable places in the city of Rome.

We used to walk widely by ourselves throughout Rome, and you are indeed acquainted with my peripatetic habit. I enjoy it very much and find it most appropriate to my nature and personal habits. Of the opinions of the Peripatetics certain ones please me, others hardly at all, for I do not love sects but the truth. Therefore I am at one time a Peripatetic, and at another a Stoic and sometimes an Academic. Often however I am none of these, especially at those times when something suspect appears in their writings which is opposed to our true and blessed faith. For we are permitted to love and approve philosophical schools if they are not opposed to the truth, and if they do not turn us from our primary purpose. When by chance they attempt this, whether it be Plato or Aristotle or Varro or Cicero, they are all to be disdained and trampled upon freely and steadily. Let no sharpness of disputation, no mildness of words, no authority of names affect us. They were men, and to the extent that they could accomplish this through human curiosity, they had both knowledge of things and clarity of expression and were fortunate in natural genius. But they were wretched in their lack of the knowledge of the highest and ineffable good, and like those who trust their own strength and do not desire the true light, they often stumbled over an immovable stone in the manner of the blind. Therefore let us admire their genius in such a way that we venerate the author of such genius; let us have compassion for their errors as we rejoice in our grace; and let us realize that without any merit we have been honored and have been raised above the greatest thinkers by Him who deemed worthy of revealing to children what he had hidden from the wise. In short let us philosophize in a manner which the very name of philosophy suggests, for the love of wisdom. Indeed the true wisdom of God is Christ so that in order to philosophize rightly we must first love and cherish Him. Let us be such in all things that above all things we may be Christians. Let us thus read philosophical, poetic, or historical writings so that the Gospel of Christ resounds always in the ear of our heart. With it alone are we sufficiently happy and learned; without it no matter how much we learn we become more ignorant and more wretched. To it all things must be referred as if to the loftiest stronghold of the truth; on it as if on a single immovable foundation of literary truths, human labor can safely build. And we must not restrain ourselves from diligently cultivating other teachings which are not contrary to it, for although the returns may be limited in so far as any real accomplishment is concerned, we shall appear to have added a considerable measure to the enjoyment of the mind and the cultivation of life. I have said these things at random as far as they seem to befit a letter of this type. Now I shall proceed.

We used to wander together in that great city which, though it appeared empty because of its vast size, had a huge population. And we would wander not only in the city itself but around it, and at each step there was present something which would excite our tongue and mind: here was the palace of Evander, there the shrine of Carmentis, here the cave of Cacus, there the famous she-wolf and the fig tree of Rumina with the more apt surname of Romulus, there the overpass of Remus, here the circus games and the rape of the Sabines, there the marsh of Capri and the place where Romulus vanished, here the conversations of Numa and Egeria, there the battle line of the *trigemini*. Here the conqueror of enemies who was in turn conquered by a thunderbolt, and the builder of the militia; there the architect king Ancus Martius; here the organizer of social classes, Priscus Tarquinius, lived; there the head of Servius glowed; there sitting in her carriage cruel Tullia crossed and made the street infamous because of her crime. Here however is *Via Sacra*, while over there are the Esquiline Hill, the Viminal, the Quirinal; here the Campus Celius, there the Campus Martius and the poppies cut down by the hand of the proud one. Here one can still see the wretched Lucretia lying upon her sword and the adulterer fleeing his death, as well as Brutus the defender of violated chastity. There is threatening Porcina and the Etruscan Army, and Mutius beset by his erring right hand, and the son of the tyran competing with liberty, and the Consul pursuing (to hell itself) the enemy expelled from the city; and the Sublician bridge broken behind the brave man, and Horatius swimming, and Cloelia returning on the Tiber. There may be seen the house of Publicola which was fruitlessly suspected; here Quintius used to plow until through his merit the plowman was made dictator; from here Serranus was led away to become Consul. This is the Janiculum, this is the Aventine, that is Monte Sacro, on which the angered plebians withdrew from the rulers; here the lustful tribunal of Appius stood, and Virginia was rescued from violence by the sword of her father, and there occurred a worthy end to the dissipation of the Decemvirs. From here Coriolanus, who was perhaps about to triumph with his arms, departed after having been conquered by the devotion of his supporters. This is the rock that Manlius defended and then fell from; here Camillus repelled the Gauls as they gaped at the unexpected gold and taught the despairing citizens how to recover a lost fatherland with a sword and not with gold. Here armed Curtius descended; there was found underground the head of a man with an immovable face which was viewed as a prediction of the highest and firmest form of empire. There a deceitful Virgin fell under arms after having been deceived by her own deceits; here is the Tarpeian fortress, and the wealth of the Roman people collected throughout the world; here is the silver goose; there is Janus the guardian of arms; here is the temple of Jupiter Feretrius; this was the temple of Jupiter, this was the home of all the triumphs; here Perses was brought, from here Hannibal was driven away, here Jugurtha was destroyed as some believe, others indeed believe that he was slain in prison. Here Caesar triumphed, here he perished. In this temple Augustus viewed the prostrate kings and the whole world at his feet; here is the arch of Pompey, here is the portico, here is the Cimbrian arch of Marius. There is Trajan's Column where he alone of all the emperors, according to Eusebius, is buried inside the city; here is his bridge which eventually assumed the name of St. Peter, and Hadrian's fortress, under which he also lies buried and which they call Castel Sant'Angelo. This is that massive rock surmounted by two bronze lions which was sacred to the deified emperors, and on whose summit, rumor has it, rest the bones of Julius Caesar. This is the shrine to the goddess Tellure, this is the temple of Fortune, this is the temple of Peace, which was rightly destroyed at the arrival of the King of Peace; this is the work of Agrippa taken from the false gods to be dedicated to the mother of the true God. Here is where it snowed on the fifth of August; from here a stream of oil flowed into the Tiber; from here, according to tradition, the old Augustus, following the Sibyl's advice, saw the Christ child. This is the insolence of Nero and his raging extravagance in the buildings he raised; there is the house of Augustus, on Via Flaminia, where some maintain is the tomb of the Emperor himself; this is the Column of Antoninus; this is the palace of Appius; this is the Septizonium of Severus Afrus which you call the temple of the sun but whose name I find in the form I use written in history. On these stones still survives after so many centuries the great rivalry in talent and skill between Praxiteles and Phidias; here Christ appeared to his fleeing Vicar; here Peter was crucified; there Paul was beheaded; here Lawrence was burned, who after being buried here, was succeeded by Stephan. Here John scorned the burning oil; there Agnes after her death came back to life and forbade her kin to weep; here Sylvester hid; there Constantine got rid of his leprosy; there Calixtus mounted his glorious bier. But where shall I end? Can I really describe everything in this short letter? Indeed, if I could, it would not be proper; you know all these things not because you are a Roman citizen but because since your youth you have been intensely curious especially about such information. For today who are more ignorant about Roman affairs than the Roman citizens? Sadly do I say that nowhere is Rome less known than in Rome. I do not deplore only the ignorance involved (although what is worse than ignorance?) but the disappearance and exile of many virtues. For who can doubt that Rome would rise again instantly if she began to know herself? But this is a complaint to be dealt with at another time.

We used to stop often at the baths of Diocletian after the weariness which ceaseless walking about that city had produced in us, and indeed we would often ascend to the roof of that building, once a home, because only here could we enjoy the healthy air, the unimpeded view, silence and desired solitude. There we did not discuss business, household problems or public affairs of which we had previously sufficiently unburdened ourselves. And as in our travels through the remains of a broken city, there too, as we sat, the remnants of the ruins lay before our eyes. What else may be said? Our conversation was concerned largely with history which we seemed to have divided among us, I being more expert, it seemed, in the ancient, by which we meant the time before the Roman rulers celebrated and venerated the name of Christ, and you in recent times, by which we meant the time from then to the present. We also spoke much about that part of philosophy which deals with morals, whence it gets its name; and sometimes indeed we discussed the arts and their authors and rules. Thus once when we had entered into this latter subject you asked me to explain clearly where I thought the liberal arts and the mechanical arts had their beginning because you had from time to time heard me talk on the subject. I responded quite simply because the hour, the absence of trivial cares, and the very place encouraged me to go into the subject at some length, and because your attentiveness suggested that the subject was indeed pleasing to you. I assured you, however, that I would say nothing new, nothing that was really mine, and yet nothing that was basically borrowed, for from whatever source we learn anything it is ours unless by chance forgetfulness takes it from us. You request now that what I said that day I repeat and commit to a letter. I confess that I did say many things which I can only repeat with different words. Give me back that place, that idle mood, that day, that attention of yours, that particular vein of my talent and I could do what I did then. But all things are changed: the place is not present, the day has passed, the idle mood is gone, and instead of your face I look upon silent words, my spirit is impeded by the din of the business matters I have left behind, matters which until recently roared in my ears, although I fled as soon as I could in order to answer you more freely. I shall, however, obey as best I can. I could send you to some ancient and modern writers from whom you can learn what you seek; but you made provisions for me not to do so when you asked that I say whatever I have to say on the subject in my own words because, as you observed, everything I say appears most pleasing and clear to you. I thank you for this opinion whether it is really true or whether you do it by way of stimulating my mind. Here is then what I said at that time, perhaps with the words of others but certainly the same thoughts. But really, what are we doing? The subject is clearly not a small one, this letter is already too long, and we have not yet started, though the end of this day is at hand. Would it not be a good idea for me to give some rest to my fingers and to your eyes? Let us put off what remains until another day; let us divide the labor and the letter, and let us not cover two very different matters in the same letter. But what do I have in mind? What am I promising you when I say another letter tomorrow? This is neither the work of a single day nor a task for letters, it requires a book which I shall undertake (if I am not impeded and frustrated by major cares) when fortune returns me to my solitude. Only there and not elsewhere am I myself; there lies my pen which at present rebels everywhere I go and refuses my orders because I am preoccupied with burdensome matters. Thus, while it is constantly busy when I have plenty of leisure, it prefers to have leisure when I have much to do, and almost like a wicked and insolent servant, it seems to convert the fervor of the master into its own desire for rest. However, as soon as I get back home I shall compel it to take on its duties and I shall write about what you seek in a separate book, indicating what has been written by others and what are my own ideas. Indeed just as I am accustomed to writing these friendly letters almost as amusement in the very midst of conversations and bustle, in the same way I have need of solitary quiet and pleasant leisure and great and uninterrupted silence in order to write books. Farewell.

30 November, in transit.

Fam. VI, 3.

To the same correspondent, consolation against certain diffi-culties of life.

Though we agree fully on almost everything, there is one basic disagreement between us, and that is that you are too querulous, too self indulgent in lamenting your lot, too complaining about your affairs, excessively involved in excusing yourself and accusing fortune, and finally too soft in tolerating the human condition because you are yourself a man. I must confess that the beginning of your letter moved me to tears; for why should I consider hiding my own feelings, and where I demand firmness from you why disguise my own softness? Where I order you to be happy, I cannot deny that I myself am sad. But I flatter myself in this; tears shed for the misfortunes of others are more noble than those shed for ourselves—even though all things being common to us nothing can be said about one's own situation that does not apply to another's, for what is another's is ours. This is true not only in close friendships but even in the general society of men, as the Satirist said in teaching that no evil is foreign to the good man and that cares are given to human beings for an indication of their natural compassion. This the Comic had said somewhat earlier: "I am a man; I consider nothing human alien to me." I do not deny the truth of this, yet in this public duty of sharing one's humanity there are degrees whereby from the widest concept of humanity, so to speak, we narrow down the scope to kindred and friends, and universal love of all is gradually compressed into a certain individual love and kindness toward the few. Therefore, why should I once more hide from you what follows? Just as the beginning of your letter moved me to tears, the ending of the same letter moved me to laughter. "But those are opposites," you say. I know, but sometimes both laughter and tears do emerge from a single source. No less sorrowful was Democritus, perhaps, who "used to exercise his lungs with a perpetual laughter," as he says, than Diogenes who was continuously wet with teardrops. Nor was Hannibal more happy in the misfortunes which befell his fatherland when he laughed over them, than the people who mourned. On the other hand, if we are to believe Lucan, Caesar was no sadder when he wept over the death of his son-in-law than the army which applauded him. But let us return to you. The first part of your letter pointed out how huge an accumulation of many, indeed almost all, tribulations had fallen upon you, and it did so in a style which was both wretched and distinguished. Upon reading your account I could not restrain my tears and I shed still others when I saw what you called the stains caused by your own tears. I do not know why we have greater compassion for the man who laments his misfortunes manfully than for one who does so effeminately. I continued to read attentively with my mind and eyes and felt charmed by the very sweetness of the style as I read, even though the letter was quite long. However, having read the rest of the letter with moist eyes waiting to discover what it was that you had endured about which you very greatly complained and grieved, I suddenly found your explanation of the entire matter in three or four words near the end of your letter. You were in Tivoli, you explained, an old, gouty, poor man and among the many ills you had to bear the worst was that you had lost all hope of ever seeing me again. Restrained by illness, you say, you cannot move from where you are or dare to call your friend to come to you from so great a distance caught as he is in the burdens of his infinite duties well known to you. This is the ending that you give to your tearful letter. Here, I must confess, is where I laughed. Someone might say. "But indeed do these things seem insignificant or unimportant to you?" Certainly not, but they are so ordinary and so common that it is scarcely discourteous but truly laughable that a man should be either indigant or astonished at such discomforts.

To start from the beginning, what man ever lived who did not grow old by living? We read that our earliest fathers lived for many centuries but do we not also read that they grew old? But I disregard those who lived at the beginning of time who were brought forth to the light, as it were, in the childhood of time itself as if confirming their vigor and durability which enabled them to reach almost the thousandth year of life, and yet grew old, even though more slowly. I repeat that I am disregarding these about whose age there usually is much disagreement among great thinkers and who are unrelated to our present purpose. So I turn to those whose age is both less extraordinary and more suitable to our purpose. Abraham grew old, Isaac also, and so did Jacob. Concerning the first one it is written: "And Abraham was an old man and had seen many years," and later: "failing he died in a ripe old age and advanced in age and in the fullness of days." About the second it is written: "And Isaac grew old and his sight grew weak and he could not see," and later: "He died an old man and in the fullness of his days he was gathered to his kinsmen." Concerning the third it is written: "The eyes of Israel grew weak because of his very old age and they could not see clearly." You can hear for yourself that it was not only old age but also the fading away of and failure of the eyes. Moses was perhaps stronger about whom when he died after one hundred and twenty years of life we read: "His eyes did not grow weak nor did his teeth fall out." Did he nevertheless not grow old because he happened to be a stronger old man? His successor Joshua, an outstanding soldier who killed so many kings and scattered so many people, was not able to resist old age but rather heard the Lord say to him: "You have grown old and are an old man": and he himself said to the assembled people: "I have grown old and am at an advanced age." That is the man whom, because of his incomparable faith, God obeyed and instructed the sun and the moon to be still, and they were. But was he able to hold back even a single day of his swift life or hasten it or slow down uncoming old age? What shall I say about King David? Is it not true that he also "grew old, and reached a ripe old age, and however much he covered himself with clothing he could not keep warm?" He who had been so inflamed with the love of God and men became so cool in his brief old age that he lay with a maiden for protection against the cold. And he said concerning himself: "I was a young man," and immediately added; "for I have grown old." You may find perhaps someone whose days you envy but no one enjoying perpetual youth. Everything that has risen must of necessity either set immaturely or set in maturity by growing old.

In secular histories you will find no like spans of human life and if you should by chance come across one, you may be sure it was intended to be taken humorously rather than historically. Indeed the history of distinguished deeds previous to Ninus, king of the Assyrians, who seemed to be a contemporary of Abraham, as Macrobius likes to point out, is prior to the time of the Greeks. Thus all the historians who go back in their writings to very early times begin with Ninus, and only after many ages have we begun to gather examples from our own ancestors. Some think that this should not appear too surprising while other argue, as I have pointed out, that with the aging of the world life becomes shorter and bodies become more fragile. Among foreign people indeed, to touch briefly upon the most famous example, Nestor lived a very long time, having survived, according to what is written, even unto the third age of men, although Seneca limits his age to ninety-nine years while Ovid extends it to beyond two hundred, which is more in accord with Cicero and Homer. Hiero of Syracuse also lived a long time as did Masinissa, king of the Numidians, the first seeing his ninetieth year, the other surpassing it. Highly praised was the old age of Solon and of Sophocles: the first grew old without interrupting his studies and constantly learning something more; the second being close to death wrote a very noble tragedy at an age when those who do reach it are scarcely in full possession of their mental faculties. Isocrates, the orator, after he had published his outstanding work almost at the same age, that is ninety-four, survived five more years and was able to enjoy the late pleasure of the success of his work. I have read not only about Homer's old age but about his blindness; whether old age or some other cause lay behind his blindness I do not know if you have discovered in your readings, but I have not found the answer. Nevertheless, what kind and how pleasant must we consider Homer's old age accompanied and made richer as it was by all his pleasant cares and duties? What remains of these cares after thousands of years affects and fills me with so much sweetness (and I believe the same must happen to others) that often, unmindful of my own cares and forgetting my present ills, I find complete rest in recalling that blind old man. Carneades achieved a peaceful old age at ninety, Xenophanes Calophonius at past one hundred, Democritus and Cleanthes at ninety-nine, Gorgias Leontinus at one hundred and seven. Chryssipus undertook a work of astonishing brilliance in his thirtieth year and left it behind when he died in his eightieth. At the same age Simonides recalls that he entered a poetry contest. We read that Socrates reached an advanced age and would have lived longer if the poisoned cup had not prevented it. His outstanding student, Plato, having completed his eighty-first year, died on the very same day as that of his birth, and in those studies in which he had for a long time exercised his mind he achieved the proper limit of a human and perfect life as established by himself. Indeed many illustrious philosophers achieve the same limit, among them Dionysius Heracleontes, Diogenes the Cynic, Eratosthenes, Xenocrates the Platonist and the prince of all, as we have said, Plato himself. His own student Aristotle did not go beyond his sixty-third year, a number which is dangerous and they say frightful for the human species in that it brings either death or extraordinary calamity. Why this is so, some try to rationalize, others allude only to personal observation of long experience. Which of the two arguments is the more forceful, let those decide who present them. If they relate truth, our own Cicero was not able to cross this barrier of human life not because of old age but because of the wicked command of cruel Anthony. And since we have reached our own Romans by way of Cicero, we might recall how venerable was the old age of Numa Pompilius the Roman king, but even more venerable that of Cato, of Camillus, of the Fabii, of Metellus, of Valerius Corvinus, almost all of whom achieved the same age, one hundred years, as did the blind Appius from whose blindness all the citizens of the entire republic expected leadership. Augustus grew old in a most glorious fashion, Pompey in a more unfortunate one; but we are not here talking about fortune but about age. Certainly Augustus himself, the greatest and most powerful of all monarchs, after the founding of the empire, as some like to believe, and after having governed it for a long time in the greatest peace, which no one denies, passed away peacefully in the seventy-sixth year of his life among the many tears of the Romans and in the embrace of his most chaste wife. Augustine achieved the same age so that there is a great similarity both in their names and in the period of their life. Jerome, on the other hand, having reached his ninetieth year lived longer; Origen, and also Ennius the poet, reached seventy; Bernard sixty-three; concerning Ambrose and Gregory I am not similarly informed. Without a doubt, however, they all achieved a ripe old age since God Himself who is the fountain of life watched over them to avoid letting such men whose life was to be of such benefit to the Church not live long enough. Asinius Pollio reached the eightieth year; Marcus Varro lived beyond the space of a single century leading a rich life and writing. Seneca has spoken a great deal about his old age, although an old man, and would have lived even longer were it not for his mad disciple who forbade it.

I now ask your indulgence, dear father, to permit me to interpolate here a subject which is much occupying my mind, and to add to the illustrious examples of so many glorious elders a unique example which though indeed humble and recent is truly noble and which it pleases me much to recall with veneration, something I would not dare do if I were addressing anyone but you. My paternal great grandfather was a very holy man and of considerable ability to the extent one may be so without cultivating letters, so much so that not only did his acquaintances consult him about family matters, about business affairs, about legal affairs, and about the nuptials of their children, but also officials about affairs of state (as we learn about Appius Caecus), and even men of letters both at home and abroad consulted him about matters of high, even philosophical, import. All marveled at his answers, the fairness of judgment and the sharpness of his mind. His name was Gattius and he was endowed with a character and a devotion that lacked only a strong promoter in order for his memory to be consecrated. Even after I had passed adolescence there were many who continued to speak about the wonder of that man, but I prefer to pass over these and would not even have mentioned him in order not to bother you with excessive examples. In any event, that man after having lived a harmless and happy life, as I heard our elders relate, in the one hundred and fourth year of life, also, like Plato, on his birthday, but older than Plato by twenty-three years, and furthermore in the same room in which he was born, on the hour which he had predicted long before to many friends as the hour of his passing away, amidst his sons and grandchildren, with no suffering either of body or mind, and speaking of nothing except God and goodness, simply dozed off, as it were, while he spoke. And they say that among his very last words were those of David: "As soon as I lie down, I fall peacefully asleep," and having scarcely uttered these words, he became silent and fell asleep peacefully. I thank you, dearest father, that you have allowed me to recall the memory of my great grandfather, and to include his name in this short letter to you, because I do not know any worthier place in which he deserved to be recalled than among distinguished elders.

But what am I doing? A short letter of consolation has turned into a long history. However, you will grant me your indulgence if you know with how great a pleasure I have dwelled upon these excellent and selected elders to whom I wish that you at this moment, and myself not too much later, should be added. Although we may be dissimilar to them in other qualities, we are at least similar to them in equanimity. Do not believe that I have completely strayed from my subject, for the question is whether one should complain about becoming an old man when one recalls that such outstanding men became old? Indeed, who will not share with even greater joy the fate of these most fortunate men, and accept old age in common with such men? Who indeed of all these men lived for a long time and did not grow old? Is there anyone whose long life we read about who did not end up with old age? But we, with a contrary desire and battling with ourselves, wish to live a long time, indeed always, never growing old and never dying. I know what you will answer: that you were not ignorant of all these things but that you were complaining about growing old before your time. All who are growing old have that common complaint; and Numa Pompilius, whom I mentioned above, was grey haired at a very early age, as was the poet Virgil; all who live in these times have the same complaint. I myself am wont not so much to complain as to be astonished because I had grey hair considerably before my twenty-fifth year; although I won't forget how once my father, in other respects neither healthier nor stronger than I, having looked in the mirror and having seen on his head perchance one hair becoming truly white rather than a pale grey, although being older than fifty, gave vent to his amazement and to his complaints by upsetting not only the entire family but the entire neighborhood. This is what pains our times; this is what our youth bewails: that in a short time ways of living and of growing old have changed a great deal. While I perhaps agree with the latter assertion, I deny the first: one does age more quickly than usual. It may be that that is not true generally; but I affirm without hesitation that one does indeed acquire white hair more quickly than usual, whether the cause lies in an earlier aging or in the large number of worries that one has today. There is little doubt that where our ancestors were involved in more useful cares we are involved in too many cares. And there is nothing which causes the flower of youth to wither more rapidly than the anxiety of cares and a troubled mind. Otherwise the ways of living, unless misfortune or guilt cuts them short, continue to remain almost nearly the same, as is stated in the *Psalms*. But since your religious modesty makes me certain that you do not complain about your hairs which you indeed gladly accept, though they may be untimely, I doubt not that you would enjoy them if as Claudian has his Stilican say, "White hair comes in haste making appearances venerable." I am therefore sure that you complain about other inconveniences of old age which some writers consider in great numbers, but which Tullius limits to four as follows: the diminution of strength, a weakening in the ability to apply oneself, less desire for pleasures, and approaching death. I can indeed say many things here to offer you consolation, except that it would be rash to review what Tullius has treated formally. You have his book *On Old Age* which contains a section on Cato the elder. Once you have read this you will find that nothing more need be added, I feel, to make old age less troublesome and even more pleasing to you. As for old age coming too rapidly and ahead of time, I shall say only this: abiding infirmity of the body is present there too is our old age (according to the most learned men), thus wherever an abiding infirmity of the body is present there too is our old age. For just as at the end of life is death, so a lingering weakness whenever it befalls is the end of a blooming and healthy youth. Therefore the term old age must be applied either to the end of life, or to the end of the fuller life, regardless of the stage in which it occurs, we have fulfilled the time granted us and old age is the legitimate consequence.

What, think you, should I say about poverty? Who is not poor except for someone who desires nothing? Those who seem extremely wealthy are really poorer than others because they need more things and poverty is nothing else but the need of necessary things. But those who are seemingly wealthy, driven from the truth by false opinions, create for themselves the necessities which appear merely excessive to those who are not quite so mad, and even superfluous to the sane, and in truth to the learned appear harmful even and deserving to be fled from at any cost. The wealthy are therefore the poorest of all, needing and excitably pursuing countless things, even twisting their need into desire. I am not unaware of their response to such charges: namely, that poverty is despised with more difficulty in fact than in word. I do not disagree; I confess it is a difficult thing, but, good grief, how safe, how secure, how convenient, how free and finally how pleasant it would be if we could be induced to love poverty in our mind! But let us stop praising poverty lest we be justifiably ridiculed by the people. They say (and I wish they were lying) that we praise poverty but love wealth. How common it is to find men who, having much praised poverty, flee from it with all their might? Cupidity will be overcome and eternally rejected by the minds of men, or rather completely destroyed, only when poverty has as many lovers as it has praisers. However, it would have many more lovers if the good it does along with the peace and happiness it brings were more widely known. Thus far, however, it remains as it was in the age of Lucan, a gift of God except for rare cases not yet understood by mortals. Among illustrations the exceptions are Valerius, Cincinnatus, Curius, Fabricus, Regulus, examples which touch minds blinded by avarice and cupidity only so long as the time it takes to read or hear about them, and then only superficially. But much more notable are our most holy elders who traveled around the world introducing truth into the hearts of men, very happy in hunger and nakedness, triumphant in overcoming and treading upon the necessities of life, and with whose bare feet the earth was not worthy to be tread. Venture to follow their examples yourself, "Dare, oh stranger, to condemn wealth." It was not accidentally nor without due consideration that he said: "Dare do so." More great men have disdained life and shed their blood and risked their souls than have despised riches. Dare, therefore, you too, oh stranger who do not have a permanent abode here; lay aside your burden, which is unfit for lovers of liberty, and you will arrive in your fatherland the more safely the more freely you advance. Dare, I say, to despise wealth and (to quote what follows), "Mold yourself also in the image of God." Who will hesitate to despise wealth and power when he recalls, to mention but a few examples, the sacred and humble poverty of Christ, especially if such recollection is supplemented by the awareness of how many calamities or hazards those riches which are so greatly desired and sought in every way bring with them? Certainly Solomon himself, who was considered a wise man by the Hebrews (as was Lycurgus among Spartans, Solon among the Athenians, Cato or Lelius among our Romans), sought neither wealth nor poverty from God since he considered them causes of pride and despair. What then is the answer? He said, "Grant only what is necessary for sustaining life." Our apostle followed him when he said: "Let us be satisfied with the possession of nourishment and a roof." Yet we not only seek riches, but we desire most what is harmful among them, namely extravagance and excess. I ask you, what is there in avarice that is so delightful? Certainly nothing more than the toil of seeking and the fear of preserving; nothing more, I say, than fearing catastrophies, fires, theft, robbers from within and without, and finally mice and moths; in addition, being always deeply concerned, sad, in constant state of anxiety, and burying the heart itself, though still alive, in gold, as it is written: "Your heart is where your treasure is." It is certainly true that "guarding great wealth is indeed a wretched thing!" But these things happen to us unknowingly; as Flaccus asks, "What worth does money have; what good does it serve?" To those who believe in wealth, a modest amount of it will appear like unbearable poverty. There may exist without any interference by fortune the two grades of wealth described by Seneca: "To possess what is necessary, to have what is sufficient." Let one approach the third step which is possessing in abundance, and let the fourth be added which is possession of a great deal: then one will think that nothing has been achieved until one arrives panting and raging to the possession of what is excessive. Then unless possessions begin to do harm, unless they cause unhappiness, hardship, and perhaps an early death, they are not viewed as riches. But to repeat, what am I doing in this search to help you find a defense against poverty? Whatever anyone has been able to say or to think about this matter is already known to you. There is one thing in my mind, however, besides these many well known ones, which I shall not withhold from you: namely, that just as lightening the burdens of a heavy body is necessary, so is poverty necessary for you. Indeed, though I hear that certain of your followers are turning their back upon poverty without even a quibble, you did, nonetheless, take the vow of poverty whether openly or silently. It is good that you used to flee it, that it pursued you, and that now the need of facing your vows has caught up with you, and has seized you so that you are compelled to satisfy what you owe. You are the servant of Christ; you know what pleases him. And you know what you promised him. Be silent and have patience; I cannot listen to you with objectivity. You lament about poverty to me as if you did not know that you had entered into this life naked and will leave it naked; and also as if you had professed not the poverty of Christ but the riches of Croesus. Believe me, dear father, poverty was often used to the welfare of many people, it was never useless to anyone, except to those who made it unbearable through their impatience and laments. For you, indeed, it is not useless but necessary and healthful, so that without it you will not be able either to expect salvation or to keep your agreement with your Creator. These are the points I wished to mention regarding a noble and reasonable poverty. The type which is inconvenient and lowly and is called "foul indigence" by the poet, does not affect you, thanks be to God, a type which requires the power of greater eloquence to justify.

Let us now turn to remedies for the gout. Oh, if only anyone touched by that disease were by chance to cast his eyes upon this part of this letter, what hope do you think he might have of receiving any lotion, powder, or soothing counsel? Let him cease hoping for such things from me. I wish to spare him any toil, for if he hopes for this by reading what I write let him read no further. Indeed such remedies are despaired of by most of the more learned physicians. If you consult the others, you will learn that men of wealth need not despair at all, whereas the poor ones can hope for nothing, since very often this plague inhabits the homes of the wealthy. And if you should wish to listen to these men they will enable you to yell constantly, entirely bound up in the sufferings of present pain and the hope of future recovery, and to groan constantly besmeared with the oil of sadness and soaked with ointments. I instead would prefer that you suffered while you were dry, unbound, and unrestrained, and by dieting, exercising, and work make your weak body become strong against a new enemy. In such matters one can hope for nothing beyond words from doctors. If there is any form of help against the gout, it is to be sought entirely in poverty, or if this is difficult, from temperance of the mind. Poverty is an excellent medication against the gout, whether it is created through necessity or through choice; this latter path is called thriftiness which one defines as voluntary poverty. Concerning these things, however, I seem to have said enough in a previous letter to you when news of your condition had not yet reached me except for your problems with the gout. I should add one thing however which I was not aware of at that time: believe me it was divine permission that coupled poverty with the gout so that, just as a remedy for poison is taken from poisonous animals, and just as the bees prepare the sweetest honey out of certain very bitter herbs, in the same manner you can produce remedies for your ills from no other source than those very ills. But enough about poverty and the remedies that it provides. Concerning the moderation and the patience of the mind a longer discourse is necessary in order to provide it with authoritative reasons and examples. Here Marius and Atilius and indeed all the Roman legions come to mind for there has been no people equal to them in this kind of glory. Here also come to mind, to take another type of people, Possidonius, Anaxarchus and (though a more lowly, nevertheless I believe, a more effective example) the African slave, avenger of his master, spoken of by Titus Livy, who, though mangled by tortures, not only refused to groan, but because of his joy in overcoming his pain, gave an outward appearance of almost laughing. Such examples are almost infinite and with them one would fill not only a letter but a book. Nevertheless, as I have said, modesty and restrained silence appear best when dealing with Cicero. I have heard several notable men admitting that the second book of his *Tusculan Disputations*, which I often found helpful in my sorrows, has been of similar aid to them. I would like you to become familiar with it and have it at hand whenever you feel the pain of gout approaching with its usual symptoms. Yet for a learned and religious man in dealing with all the hardships and griefs which cannot be avoided in this mortal life it is an admittedly much sweeter, more pleasant, and more worthy medicine to recall the hardships and griefs that Christ suffered for us. Likewise it is appropriate to recall the wounds with which our wounds were healed, and that we were snatched from the danger of an eternal death; to recall the nails and the spear and the most precious blood in which our filth was cleansed as in a bath and through which we were reborn and were mildly warned to spurn earthly burdens with a lofty mind and to fear nothing except the punishment of eternal damnation with its infinite sufferings. It would be useful further to recall not only Christ for whom all things were auspicious and simple because of his divinity, incomparable glory, and unapproachable power, but also the shining host of those who are called martyrs, many, like ourselves, mortal men, not only strong men, but what is still more miraculous, often even tiny women and maidens who, insipred by the divine spirit, endured those sufferings in comparison with which whatever you suffer can be called peace and comfort. But because these examples are well known and very familiar to you as part of the core of knowledge appropriate to your calling, lingering no longer, I shall hasten to less well known matters.

There is a type of remedy which perhaps you have not thought about and which occurred to me suddenly as I read your letter and caused me to laugh, as I have pointed out. However I do not want you to be angry with me because I jest at your ills as I am accustomed to do with mine. We know that strong and learned men were accustomed to jest not only about their ills but about death, witness Prince Vespasian and the philosopher Socrates. Allow me therefore to do the same regarding the pains in your feet although my jest is not facetious but touches upon the truth. Examine, dear father, your journeys since your youth and your propensity not to stay still; you will see that like the bridle for the untamed horse a gout was required for you. Perhaps it ought to be required for me too so that I might now learn to stay in one place and settle down. Without doubt, however, it was required for you more than anyone else I know. You would, if you could, have gone beyond the boundaries of the inhabited world; you would have crossed the ocean; you would have gone to the antipodes, and your reason would not have helped you seek a halt though it is powerful in other matters. What more need I say? You were able to stay still only with the help of the gout; it alone provided a halt for you and caused you to stop. What can you say? You will obey whether you want to or not. However, do not consider it an injustice: nothing more appropriate ever happened to anyone, nor anything more suitable. The master of a ship controls its movement either by a line or an anchor, and an anchor was cast for you near the land from which you first sailed for the deep. Your fate allowed you a rambling and laborious youth. Nor did you appear to let up with old age. You slowed down only with the help of the gout. The careful herdsman collects his cattle where there is a possibility of rest and grazing once all possible escapes have been closed off. Recognize the prudence of your Herdsman: he has restricted you to very pleasant and fertile pastures, not in Persia, or Arabia or Egypt, where you could wander as if in your own suburbs, but in your own homeland with the full submission of your limbs, and after countless trips which, were it up to you, would never have ended. You enjoyed the culmination of heavenly grace when He enclosed you not in Rome, a place which honors you for your own titles and for those of your family but is not propitious for your rest, but rather he located you not far from or beyond the sight of your beloved city. What more need be said? The Tiber was assigned for the leisure of your old age, and He provided against any possibility of flight. You grieve where you should rather render thanks to the Lord who, having snatched you from so many earthly and maritime dangers and so many lengthy byways, wished to locate you finally in this land, as Maro says, where there is no lack of food either for the soul or for the body; where your books, your fervor, your abilities and the very kind of air and water and the pleasantness of the beautiful landscape can charm both the harsh and the rustic mind; where the sweet sight of your fatherland is always present as well as the moderate proximity of our friends; and where boredom and disgust exist no longer, conditions which the noise of a huge city or perhaps the perpetual conversation of so many acquaintances could produce in you. Enjoy the good things you possess, therefore, joyfully, calmly, and peacefully. You are better off than you think; you would be unable to choose a more convenient place in the entire world than the one which your fate has offered you. But you will press the argument and you will say, "Why not without these illnesses of the body?" You ask me to answer what I feel: your mind needs fetters. I beg you to accept this not as something offensive but as praiseworthy; for wherever there is more fertile ground, there we find an abundance of things whose growth must be checked and rooted out so that the crop will grow more freely; and often, where you find a more noble and more powerful horse, there will you find a wilder horse which needs much stronger chains. You would now be, as I surmise, in some other corner of the world: you would be swimming at times in the Nile, at times in the Indian Ocean or the Tanais, or you would be climbing the Rhiphaean mountains or the thickets of the Hercynian passes, an eternal wanderer and fugitive on land. There came to your assistance the devotion of Him who alone knows our ills and the remedies for them which are not on that account any less useful than they are bitter. The complaint in which you most graciously express your desire for my presence and companionship seems to be more noble and worthy of your kindness. Only in them, you say, did you find real pleasure, and you lament that these were taken away from you at a time when they were affording the greatest pleasure. To tell the truth, this is not a serious matter. If you are a friend, and indeed a father (nor have you ever proven otherwise in your special devotion and constant paternal affection), no place and no time can snatch me away from you. Place me on the highest summit of Mt. Atlas which was changed to stone by the eyes of Medusa, and place yourself on the Caucasian cliff where the bound Prometheus complained about Jupiter; and we can still sit together, eat together, chat together, and deal with serious matters. Nothing will ever intervene which will restrain us from seeing and hearing each other. Love is winged, and it crosses not only lands but the heavens and the seas; it recognizes neither the gout nor chains; and even with the opposition of fortune, it can be where it wishes. Are you astonished? It does not even recognize the power of death, and whatever seems to have avoided her it embraces. That is why you will find those who had been turned into ashes once again become whole under its power. You will find Octavia with her son, Artemisia with her husband, Lelius with his friend, despite death and, as I was saying, free of their graves, alive and present. Therefore enjoy me, for I also enjoy you. No normal day of mine passes without you, no night, no journey, no meeting; I am with you everywhere. But if by chance (since I cannot deny that it is most pleasant and delightful to enjoy the actual presence of friends provided it is not denied that often their presence is sweeter in memory than in actuality which may often be uneasy—something I myself dislike), if, I say, you perchance consider my presence useful as a comfort for your life, there is a double road that leads to it: on the one hand I would not refuse to come to you, as unlikely as that may sound, and see your summer dwelling and that of Horace the poet, and to remain as long as it is necessary to satisfy your desire; on the other if you yourself prefer to come to see me (since the human mind is accustomed to enjoying with a greater sweetness those things which it seeks with greater toil) I will not hesitate to give you such directions that you will neither be slowed down because of the defect of your feet or indeed be compelled to touch the earth with them. Let your servants carry you to the Aniene, which flows along the walls of Tivoli. There have them place you on a boat and descend downstream lying in the hold of the boat until it arrives, on the right hand, at the Tiber. Then, being now on a broader stream, you will reach the sea through the walls of the city of Rome itself. From there, still keeping to the right, but now entrusted to a stronger boat, you will enter the heart of the Tyrrhenian Sea until, having left Marseilles far behind, and, having taken a river boat, and again bearing right, you are transported to the entrance of the Rhone River where you will enter into the marshes and stony plains of ancient Arles. Soon you will see on a frightening cliff dismal Avignon, formerly called Avegnon, where now the Roman Pontiff, having deserted his proper See, despite, I believe, the nature of the place, strives to make it capital of the world, unmindful of the Lateran and Silvester. From there still traveling upstream, ascending some three miles more, you will find at your right a silvery stream. Turn into it, for it is the Sorgue, the most peaceful of rivers. After ascending its waters for about fifteen miles you will see a spring second to none and the source of the extremely clear river, as well as a very high cliff overhanging the bubbling waters so that one cannot and should not try to penetrate any further. And so that all things will continue to go expeditiously and favorably, being finally carried to land at that spot, you will see me on the right shore. For where outside of Italy could I find a more peaceful place? You will see me contented with the hospitality of a modest but shady and narrow garden, and my little house, perhaps too little for the visit of so great a guest. You will see me as you wish me, in very good health, lacking in nothing, and expecting nothing in particular from the hands of fortune. You will see me from morning to night, wandering around alone, roving over the meadows and mountains and fountains, living in the woods and in the countryside, fleeing human footsteps, following the birds, loving the shadows, enjoying the mossy caves and the blooming meadows, cursing the cares of the Curia, avoiding the bustle of the cities, shunning the doors of the exalted, mocking the undertakings of the multitude, and keeping equal distance from joy and sadness; enjoying my leisure all day and night, glorying in a partnership with the Muses, amidst the sound of birds and nymphs, and accompanied by few servants but many books. At times you will see me at home, at times out, at times standing still, at times resting my tired head and weary limbs on the babbling river bank and at times on the tender grass, and, to mention something which is not the least part of my pleasure, meeting no one except rarely someone who might want to relate perhaps a thousandth part of his cares. You will see me at times taking a stand against these things or remaining silent, at times speaking at great length with myself, ultimately disdaining myself and all things mortal. So you see, dear father, that while I summon you I seem to remove the labor of the journey. If indeed you read this and have faith in me, you will be seeing enough of me. Farewell in the meantime, for while I seem to be conversing with you, I have forgotten that I am writing a letter.

At the source of the Sorgue, 30 May.

Fam. VI, 4.

To the same correspondent, what examples are worth is shown by examples.

I do use great numbers of examples but they are all illustrious, true, and, unless I am mistaken, contain both pleasure and authority. People say that I should try to use fewer. I confess I could get along without any examples. I do not deny that indeed I could remain totally silent and perhaps be better off for it. But amidst so many evils in this world and so much infamy it is difficult to remain silent. I seem to have practiced sufficient patience in that I have not yet applied myself to the writing of satire since long before these monstrous days of ours I find written: "It is difficult not to write satire." I speak a great deal, I even write a great deal not in order to be of any particular use to my times, whose wretchedness has reached the point of despair, as to unburden myself of ideas and to console my mind with writing. Nevertheless if anyone asks why I sometimes overflow with examples, and seem to linger lovingly over them, I shall answer as follows: I believe the reader is of the same mind as myself. There is nothing that moves me as much as the examples of outstanding men. They help one to rise on high and to test the mind to see whether it possesses anything solid, anything noble, anything unbending and firm against fortune, or whether it lies to itself about itself. Next to experience itself which is the best teacher of things, I would wager there is no better way to learn than by having the mind desire to emulate these greats as closely as possible. Therefore, just as I am grateful to all those authors I have read who afford me this opportunity to test myself with appropriate examples, so do I hope that those who read me will be grateful. I am perhaps wrong in hoping for this; but I am not deceiving you with these words, for in this hope rests the one true reason for my practice. There is another, however, because I also write for myself, and while I write I become eagerly engaged with our greatest writers in whatever way I can and willingly forget those among whom my unlucky star destined me to live; and to flee from these I concentrate all my strength following the ancients instead. For just as the very sight of my fellows offends me greatly, so the recollection of magnificent deeds and outstanding names gives me such incredible and unmeasurable delight that were it known to everyone many would be stupified to learn that I find greater pleasure in being with the dead than with the living. To these truth itself would answer that those men are alive who spent their days virtuously and gloriously; these, rejoicing amidst pleasures and false joys and enfeebled with luxury and sleep, heavy with drinking, although they appear to be alive, are instead nothing more than breathing and obscene and dreadful cadavers. This continues to be, in truth, a source of endless controversy among the learned and the ignorant. So I shall continue from where I began. You therefore now have my reply to your question and to the astonishment of those who surround you as to why I use an excessive number of examples of famous men of antiquity; namely, that I hope that it will profit others as I know for certain it has profited me as a reader and writer. Furthermore, since no single individual can do anything to please all men, let them wonder and disapprove if they care to. Certainly in order that I may not seem to abandon my usual habit because of the rumbling of others, I shall not desist from including even in this letter several examples and in the examples showing what examples can accomplish.

Before Marius, all those who had to undergo amputation at the hands of doctors used to be bound, for since they were persuaded that the pain of the body could not be overcome by the strength of the mind, they used cords for assistance. Marius was the first to be amputated untied, but after him there were many others. Why was this so, I ask, if not because the example of a very resolute and strong man fired minds to imitate him, and, to use the words that were used by a fellow citizen of his, because his authority prevailed? In the war in Latium the Consul Decius sacrificed himself for his legions and for the victory of the Roman people at Veseris. Voluntarily to seek death so that you may achieve victory for others is something easier to do with words than actions. The example, however, was so effective and powerful that his son Decius in the war with the Samnites and Gauls, being himself also a Consul, determined to imitate his father, and calling him by name went in behalf of his fellow citizens fearlessly to death which he had learned to disdain after the manner of his father. In the war at Taranto against Pyrrhus the grandson imitated both, and fell finally as a third victim from the same family although not wearing the same insignia, but nevertheless with similar courage and devotion to the Republic. Never would Themistocles have been the great man he was had he not been incited by the examples of Miltiades and induced to become of equal courage with him. Never would Julius Caesar have ascended to the summit of glory had he not learned to imitate and admire Marius from his youth. He was even inspired by the statue of Alexander which he saw in the temple of Hercules at Cadiz and which soon not only incited him to a desire of achieving great deeds but according to Tranquillus caused him to groan. For indeed if statues of outstanding men can kindle noble minds with desire for imitation, as Crispus relates that Quintus Fabius Maximus and Publius Cornelius Scipio were accustomed to say, how much more should virtue itself directly bring this about since it would be reflected not from shiny marble but from direct example? To be sure, the outlines of bodies are contained more distinctly in statues while descriptions of deeds and customs as well as the condition of minds are undoubtedly expressed more fully and perfectly by words than by anvils. Therefore I feel that it would not be improper to state that statues reflect images of persons while examples reflect images of virtues. What shall I say about great talents? Imitation gave us a pair of outstanding stars in the Latin language, Cicero and Virgil, and brought it about that we would no longer yield to the Greeks in any area of eloquence. While the latter followed in the footsteps of Homer, the former followed Demosthenes, and while one equaled his leader, the other left him behind. It would be possible to point out the same thing in all men but I do not wish to appear today to proceed too far in that for which your supporters criticize me. However I am unable to keep myself from including one example which is well known to you. For indeed the example of Antonius the Egyptian and of Victorinus the rhetorician and martyr really helped Augustine who had been hesitating for a long time about which path to follow, as did the sudden conversion of those two public agents near Treves, a conversion which when Pontianus an imperial soldier described it to him (and you will find the words of Augustine himself in the eighth book of his *Confessions* if my memory serves me), he cried out, "I burned to imitate them; and it was for this reason that he told the story." This therefore is the reason for my advice that must be repeated often because of my critics and admirers; for I see how examples lead many men to virtue, and I feel how they operate in me, and I hope the same for others. If I am mistaken, the matter can do no harm; those who do not like examples need not read them; I compel no one, and besides, I prefer to be read by few. Farewell.

Avignon, 25 September.

Fam. VI, 5.

To Barbato da Sulmona, on the sad and undeserved death of King Andrea.

Alas, how violent and how inevitable are the blows of fortune even when foreseen! As you know, dearest Barbato, I am accustomed to speak often about fortune and other matters in the manner of the multitude, in order not to appear too withdrawn from common language. If I were to be asked about such matters privately I would perhaps answer in a far different manner. But I pass on, for if I adhere to this subject I shall be entangled and drawn into useless and trivial disputes. However, to continue where I left off, the idea that "fortune is omnipotent and fate is inevitable" may be seen held not only among the multitude but even in the opinion of certain very great and most learned men, and among the first Virgil. The words "omnipotent" and "fate" in such context, however, would appear suspect coming from a Catholic. Well, whatever that power may be, whether it influences human affairs through the judgment of God or through his leave, it is doubtless a great force and utterly invincible and one against which the foolishness of our efforts battles in vain. For inexorable necessity smothers human counsel easily; it destroys all the defenses against evil and all mortal remedies. And it is clear that this fact, if it has ever been understood, is especially understood and grasped now. I ask, what new or unexpected things have happened? Who had not foreseen them? And of what benefit was foreseeing them? The awful slime of evil had penetrated so deeply into all the veins of the kingdom as now to be fatal, so far advanced are the boldness and the dissoluteness of the evildoers, and the despair and grief of the pious. Everywhere the signs of the approaching storms were numerous: disturbing clouds shaded serious faces; stubborn winds pressed upon disturbed hearts; glowing eyes flashed; mouths thundered and uttered menaces; it was almost as though ungodly hands were hurling lightning. The seas of the royal court at times were swollen with anger; at times a horrible glow and crashing of waves resounded and foul birds and strange portents seemed widely to encompass

your shores. With the death of its king the face of the kingdom has changed and with the soul of a single man the vigor
and resolution of everyone seems to have vanished. We witnessed all these things and were distressed no less by future
than by present evils. But who dared to speak up when
thought itself scarcely enjoyed freedom, and punishments
were meted out not only by mouth but by nods of the head?
For that reason everyone was silent on the roads; soft whispers could be heard in homes, sad forebodings and previsions
of impending evils, and all accompanied by those silent pres-
ages, fear and grief. In short, minds were benumbed by the
eyes as if struck by the dreadful light of a close thunderbolt.
Unless I am mistaken, no one feared more openly than I and
grieved more freely. No one looked more closely at those
portents of the court, and struck out more obstinately either
with his tongue or with his pen. Alas, how great and how
evident is the truth of Proverbs! "Let him who wishes to be
a truthful prophet prophesy evil." Another one says: "It is
rarely that a calamity strikes singly." It is really so: this is
what we learned from the ancients and this is what we really
see. The series of tribulations is always great; afflictions never
go unattended; he who is struck by one of them knows that
he will stumble into many. And indeed, just as in so great
an abundance of evils there must be great numbers of
wretched people, likewise in so great a scarcity of good things
there must be few happy people. Doubtless, the entire world
is filled with wretched people and with the groans and complaints of such people. On the other hand, who does not see
how rare happiness is among mortals when one considers
deeply our journey in this life and carefully shakes off the
hold of fortune? One finds no one to be ever truly happy or
fully in control of his desires, for as we learn from historians,
even that habitually happy Metellus was unable to find one
companion in the most remote hiding places of the Arcadians.

Who therefore among those who hold these views should
be surprised that just as a spear hurled within a crowd of
people cannot stray, the same holds for a prophesy released
amidst such an accumulation of evils, and that just as the
spear would strike something alive, thus would the prophesy

strike the truth? You will remember, dear friend, how when the king was alive but near his death (and I refer to that king who alone deserved such a name) I either orally when I was present or through letters when I was absent, and not long after his death, again orally, revealed not without visible disturbance what I felt and what I feared would be coming as if I were certain of the future. For I saw the foundations of the kingdom being shaken from the top, and I saw before my eyes the serious misfortunes befalling the collapsing kingdom. I confess I did not see that the head of an innocent youth would be the first victim of that collapse. I cannot imagine what concealed from me amidst so many gloomy conjectures that one possibility which perhaps was the worst of all evils; although as I now seem to recall, I did speak to you in my earliest letters about the lamb being thrown among the wolves. Would that my prediction had been less true! Of course I viewed the rage and gnashing of the wolves as things common to doomed men—contempt, envy, deceit, theft, prison, and exile. But I had never learned to conceive of nor fear such a death for such a man, and indeed could not recall in any tragedies I had read such abominable and insidious savagery. Imagine! Our age, which is so prolific in crimes, has now committed one in which antiquity would glory and posterity find consolation; and so that every age may find an excuse for its misdeeds, a crime that might be considered the *summa* in fierceness and in inhospitality was committed in these times. Oh Naples, so suddenly changed! Oh unfortunate Aversa, indeed averse, a name which you seem to have assumed from the event that was totally averse, I say, to humaneness and trust, qualities which were owed first to the man, secondly to the king and just lord! You disdained observing any reverence for both titles, and your people broke their sacred obligation to both his capacities. Within your walls your king perished at the hands of impious fraud. Would that he had been killed by a sword or through some other form of manly death so that he would appear to have been killed at the hands of men, not mangled by the teeth and claws of beasts. Oh city, founded under an evil star, inscribed by an unpropitious boundary,

320 / FAM. VI, 5.

constructed on bloody mortar, and inhabited by cultivators of snakes, master city of cruel examples! It was a grave enough irreverence and crime to violate so cruelly and so arrogantly the sacred person of a public servant made in the image of the Lord. You perpetrated that crime not against an ordinary man but instead you tore to pieces a most mild and innocent man who was your lord and concerned about you far in advance of his years, in love with you, a boy of rare talent, promising great hope. Alas, not you, but those harsh and savage—I don't know what to call them—men or beasts or some other kind of rare monster living within your walls who, defiling the Italian lands with their barbaric cruelty, destroyed your king and theirs not with a sword, not with poison, certainly the usual and difficult death of kings, but with an infamous noose as if he had been an incendiary or a bandit. They had not only delayed granting him the crown (through long and perfidious evasion) which his head deserved and hoped for, but they threw around his neck the unkindly knots of a cord. If perhaps such news might not reach posterity because of our silence, I would pass over the unworthy mockery that was made of his body which was most worthy of another kind of funeral service and of a longer life. But you, wretched city, carry within you things which are sorrowful in all lands, in all centuries, and which befoul memory. However, you are really without blame except that resignation to crimes often implies agreement, and besides, if you are unable either to resist or avenge such crime, you are more worthy of pity than hatred. But you, oh Christ, sun of justice, who see all and illuminate the universe with your eternal rays, why did you suffer this cloud of infamy to lie upon our lands when you could so easily (unless these transgressions of men are obstacles for you) have broken through the offensive vapors of hatred hardened by the misty cold of the night with the glowing brilliance of your love? You, however, dear Robert, greatest of all kings of our day who I believe behold and commiserate with our affairs from some portion of the heavens, with what eyes did you behold this abomination? And how were you able to endure this horrible injustice to your blood? Could you not have averted the wicked deed with pious prayers? Or was it that although able you were not willing? This is a somewhat difficult conjecture, for although it may be somewhat close to the truth that you are not moved by earthly grief because of the celestial joy that surrounds you, could it really be that you were not touched by love of your creatures and your essential piety? However that may be, you are fortunate indeed that you did not see this day in person! On the other hand, had you been present, that most unfortunate day would never have dawned nor would so much envy have been allowed. For indeed your regal presence would have been the salvation of the kingdom, the conciliator of minds, the fountain of justice and the expeller of treachery, and like a salutary shade over your flock you would have been as propitious to shepherds as fatal to serpents. But if human virtue was of no avail by heavenly decree, then your death was indeed propitious and deeply opportune, for it kept your eyes, indeed those eyes that by natural law were able to observe horror and suffer tears, from having to witness such a sad spectacle. Oh grief! Your chosen, dear, pious sweet trust whom you had committed to people who ought to have watched over him and honored him was instead destroyed by them not because they were overcome with sleep or cowardice, but because they were inflamed with hatred and goaded by envy! Dear justice against all crimes! Neither his innocence, nor his blood, nor his majesty availed him, no one among men or gods, nor any memory of you which was expected to be most effective afforded him any aid. The winds of rash and desperate negligence dispersed your words and unusual warnings of a pious father and excellent king with which on your deathbed you tried to protect the future of both your family and your kingdom as much as was allowed to mortal counsel. Now the oblivion of all human and divine justice has covered them over. But enough weeping, if only because where we may think we see an end, there we may find a beginning; since, as I was saying, evil usually comes in quantity, attended by more evil, and since the good is a rare and solitary thing, I sense in this particular evil that a number of other evils may follow, for which reason in order to avoid once again being more correct than I wish to be or appearing to be a prophet of doom I prefer to remain silent. Everything may turn out better than I hope, and the anger of a few may not harm the Republic, an anger which I hope will not remain unavenged on those who possess it; for although divine justice often yields to compassion, nevertheless this happens to those who are ashamed and repent their sins, and not to those who glory in disgraceful acts. I send you these words from the fountain of the Sorgue where once again I have fled from so great a storm in Italy as if to enter a safe port, grieving over the past and frightened over the future, on the calends of August, during a stormy night. Farewell, take care of yourself and remember me.

Fam. VI, 6.

To an unknown correspondent, vices that cannot be over-come ought to be forsaken.

Leave him alone and to himself; he is old enough. The roads stand open and he can go wherever he pleases. Let go the reins of that untameable man. You strive in vain. I repeat, leave him alone; let him go where his mind directs him; believe me he will not climb. You have seen horses who are too lazy for a journey and for climbing, afraid of battle, but nevertheless impatient with others and constantly snorting. It is the mark of a degenerate mind to abuse minors, not to be able to suffer associates, to hurt when one can, and to await the occasion rather than a reason. Flies annoy the leanest oxen, the dog molests the poor traveler; number our little man among these examples. His passion for harshness and hurting becomes greater where there is either mourning or bereavement, or extreme poverty, or where there is the least possibility for defense. For this reason he does not limit himself only to those things for which he has skill, for his will is never insufficient and is always the same. Why therefore do you reprove him? You are wasting time. This evil calls for something other than words. Give him an equal opponent and you will see that drive of his lessen. A wolf will always be a wolf while the sheep is present; bring in another wolf and he will be a sheep. Why, therefore, as Flaccus says, "do you pour forth prayers into closed ears?" Why not then leave him alone crushed and buried by his own vices, swollen with pride, burning with avarice, raging with wrath, wild with passions, a slave to his mouth and stomach, always consumed with very deep stupor and, as Maro says, buried in sleep and wine. What would you do for this man? What would you say to him? You will be speaking to a barrel and indeed a full one and one which can answer nothing from within, can understand, and even hear, nothing. Licinius Crassus seemed to have been speaking precisely about one like him in saying that if only he had a bronze beard he would be lacking nothing else, for he has an iron mouth and a lead heart. He certainly has hardened ears and a calloused mind; real words do not penetrate the thick covering that conceals lies. I do not know whether you are one of those who do not mind wasting words lightly; but this I know for sure, that with this man words are wasted. Perhaps such wastage would be tolerable except that in this case hatred and contempt are the result. Farewell.

Avignon, 29 April.

Fam. VI, 7.

To an unknown correspondent, on the difference between eloquence and loquaciousness.

I do not deny that in enthusiasm for domestic affairs and for amassing wealth he is a most accomplished man and the most cautious of all I have ever known, and one who, like Plautus' old woman, has eyes not only in his face but in the back of his head. However, concerning what you said about his eloquence I most certainly disagree. A great distance separates eloquence and loquaciousness: one is a matter of quality, the other of quantity; one calls for talent and skill and moderate practice, the other for rash attacks and impudence. They are indeed opposites; and yet many people fail to see the difference. If you were to apply your mind more carefully when he speaks, you will confess that just as you have heard nothing more resolute, in the same way you will confess that you have never heard anything rougher than the speech of that man, nothing more uneven, and nothing more untimely. Please understand these words as being said not so much that I might destroy the false reputation for eloquence of someone whose name I will not mention, but so that I might correct your judgment. Farewell.

Fam. VI, 8.

To a friend in need.

How poor or how wealthy you may be I do not know. I am speaking of your money box; for without doubt you are wealthy in mind, which in the fashion of Bias carries all its goods with it, not fearing destruction either by fire or shipwreck, and which, like those who fear nothing at all, does not fear the danger of plunderers, the deceit of thieves, rust, moths, disease, death, old age, or catastrophe. But concerning your money box I have some doubts, for while I esteem your mind and your conduct and your good fortune, I suspect that just as you do not need much, so you must lack something. For just as it is mad to need countless things, so is there real truth in that Socratic Xenophon's saying: "To lack nothing is appropriate for the gods, to lack very little means being close to them." Wherefore, because I recently heard certain things about your money box from someone who was aware of the situation, I determined to be of assistance according to my means. Here therefore is a little something to which I can hardly refer as remnants of my fortune since I would be speaking more arrogantly than I wish. Similarly, to call them gifts is to say something other than I feel. I shall call it therefore one of the gifts of God for which, though I do not care for such things, He deemed me worthy of accumulating beyond hope and prayer. It is a bit of this that I send you and that without doubt you will accept courteously. In this meager thing, as if in a small mirror, you will recognize the great affection of the sender and you will think rather of the wish of his mind than the smallness of the gift. I am aware that certain strong men and certain learned men possessing the same strength of mind as yourself were once tempted in vain by similar gifts. Among these are the famous names of Fabritius and Curius, Roman leaders, one of whom is praised for having disdained the gold offered by King Pyrrhus and the other the gold offered by the Samnites. Each was acclaimed because of such disdain but one was made even more famous by the splendor of his answer. For although certain scholars confuse history after their fashion, the fact remains that the noble and famous reply, "Romans do not wish gold but to rule the owners of gold," was not made by Fabritius as the multitude believe, to the king, but was given by Curius to the messenger of the Samnites. Xenocrates had a similar experience with the envoys sent to him by Alexander of Macedonia when they were sent with fifty talents for him by the king himself. He invited them to dinner in the grounds of his academy and philosophically offered them a mediocre and quickly prepared dinner, and dismissed them. On the following day when they had returned to seek whom he wished to have count the money of their king, his rebuttal was: "Did you not understand from yesterday's dinner that I do not lack money?" When he noted that they were dejected, in order to avoid the accusation that he had scorned the gift and the legation of the king, he accepted a very small part of the large amount of money, and ordered that the remainder be returned to the king. The story is also told about the contempt of Diogenes the Cynic for that same king. When Alexander, desirous of seeing him living inside his versatile barrel after having admired the man, asked whether he wished to have something given to him by the king, Diogenes answered: "Other things at other times; right now I would like to have you move out of the sun." For it was winter, and having by chance turned the bottom of the barrel toward the north, he kept his face to the south and in such a manner the little old man sunned himself half naked but with a burning mind. This was a joke compared to the much rougher and almost arrogant answer of Demetrius who so disdained the gold that had been sent to him by the Roman emperor that he laughingly said: "If he wished to tempt me he should have tested me with his entire empire." The Indian, Calanus, while he went to a voluntary death naked on the huge pile of wood that had been raised and fired according to the custom of his native land, said to Alexander of Macedonia who had come forward asking whether there were anything he wished: "There is need for nothing; I shall be seeing you in a short time." But indeed there is nothing very astonishing about this; for what would that man not scorn who scorns that very life on account of which we desire all other things? Indeed that amazing contempt was supplemented by the fulfillment of the prophesy, for within a few days Alexander was destroyed by that cup which became the avenger of the Persians and the Indians. Somewhat more sophisticated was Dindymus who, when the same Alexander came to visit him without all his regal splendor and found him naked in a remote solitude, chose from all the gifts that had been brought to him by the very wealthy king nothing but the smallest and least expensive lest his contempt might appear insolence. But as these are incomparable examples of individual men, there is that other incomparable example of a public display of greatness. Cineas, the ambassador of king Pyrrhus whom I mentioned above, a man of outstanding talents and wisdom, when he was sent to Rome with vast gifts, having tried in vain first the Senate and afterwards, in order, all the other classes, finally approached the plebians, but also in vain. Finding absolutely no one who opened either his home or his mind to the royal gifts, he returned with all the gold that he had brought, himself feeling amazed. All of these examples, however, were tested either by an enemy king or an enemy people or by some kind of haughty donor. But Ptolemy the Egyptian king did not despise the gifts of the Roman Senate, nor Masinissa the gifts of a friendly king, nor finally did the Roman people itself, while admittedly a despiser of the gifts of enemies, scorn the inheritance and testament of the king of Pergamum whom it liked. It matters much with what spirit something is given and by whom, and just as certain kinds of contempt are fine so are others discourteous and insolent. I come as a friend and not as a tempter; nor, to confess the truth, am I giving you anything, but I am sharing with you what you yourself know has been held in common by us for a long time. And to avoid exaggerating with many words a very small gift, accept whatever it is in good spirit; especially because what it is or what kind it is neither the bearer nor anyone else really knows; and even I, if you would believe me, have forgotten. Farewell.

Fam. VI, 9.

To Philip, Bishop of Cavaillon.

I shall come to you because I feel that it is your desire and I shall bring along our Socrates who is so dedicated to your name. We shall come tomorrow, nor shall we shudder at the sight of the city although we shall be dressed in an unkempt and rustic manner. The day before yesterday we fled here hastily out of the bustling and noisy city with a wild leap as if we had jumped on to a shore from a damaged ship, with the purpose of concealing ourselves and enjoying some leisure and with clothes which appear to be most suitable for the country and for the winter. You order us to enter the city as we are: we shall obey, and all the more willingly because we are attracted by your very warm wishes. Nor shall we be unduly concerned over how we appear to others since we wish and hope that our minds will appear open and naked to you. You will not deny a favor to the wishes of your supporters, dear father, if you wish to have us as guests often, and that is that no elaborate preparation or banquet greet us but instead a friendly dinner.

Happily we bid you farewell. At the source of the Sorgue,

2 January, with a rural pen.

Fam. VII, 1.

To Barbato da Sulmona, a lamentation over the desolation of his native land at the hands of the barbarians.

Among the various cares with which I am beseiged, not the least is what I imagine as I think about your situation; for what is dearer to me than my Barbato, or sweeter? Love is an uneasy affair, credulous, fearful, solicitous, noting all things and dreading both inconsequential things, and things which are certain. This is what I always feared, this is what I often wrote, and this is what I used to say daily: such a detestable deed could not remain unpunished, and this revenge is considerably more serious than I feared. So turn, oh God, your anger against the perpetrators of crimes and strike the guilty heads with a proper punishment. Spare the devoted ones, spare the faithful. What did the innocent multitude deserve, what did the sacred land of Ausonia deserve? See how now the Italian dust is flying because of the advance of the barbarians, and where we were once conquerors of peoples, we are now, alas, the prey of conquerors. Either our sins have deserved that punishment or some evil and gloomy constellation harasses us with its baleful light, or else (as I believe to be the case) with the virtuous being confused with the wicked, we are being punished for the crimes of others. But let it not be said that I fear for all of Italy from which, rather, the rebels will have something to fear as long as the tribunal power, which has recently returned to the city, flourishes, and our capital, Rome, is not ill. But a portion of Italy keeps me concerned, namely, the part formerly known as Magna Grecia, including Abruzzi, Calabria, Puglia, and the Terra di Lavoro now truly so called, and Capua once a powerful city, and Naples now the queen of cities. Into these most delightful lands an army from the roughest banks of the Danube is rushing headlong, and a storm arising from the North covers the serenity of our skies with foul clouds, a storm which I fear will have broken forth with great thunder while I await your answer. Now the entire situation is reported to have reached a critical point; by now rumor has it that Sulmona was trampled over by the first military attack and is now in the power of the enemy. Alas, with what lamentation should I mourn that noble city, homeland of Naso and of yourself, seeing it occupied today by those among whom that great man considered exile worse than death? How miserable he must have been to have lamented not so much his exile as the place of his exile, and to have composed a lengthy book on those complaints. What would he have said had he foreseen the Danubian people and such men as are represented by the Sarmatian and Dacian archers ever storming over the snowy hills to seize his native land by force of arms. Towards these he set out by order of Caesar and was so upset that he could grieve over nothing else, curse nothing else, and speak of nothing else. What should I now think that you will say, dear brother, as you see those very things which bring tears to my eyes, and which he could not without consternation have imagined occurring in the future? Oh bones of Naso, more fortunate for being at least buried in a foreign land than if, buried with the honor of a monument in their homeland, they were being kept to be made sport of in our day! Now I would call more peaceful those tombs located between the Danube and the Bog than between the Liri and Volturno; because from those places the barbarians are fleeing in large numbers while they are swarming into these. But in following the grief of my mind I have surpassed my intent; and I would have proceeded further if this messenger had not called me back to my senses as he waited for me and repeatedly interrupted. So I return to where I left off.

I am greatly fearful for your safety, but I have no advice that I can confidently offer, nor assistance. Yet, because sometimes some men can do more than they believe they can, if you need any help from me make use of it as you please. I confess that I enjoy substantial favor with the Tribune, a man of humble background but of lofty mind and purpose, and I also enjoy the favor of the Roman people. Certainly out of no merit of my own, God has repaid me by replacing the hatred of evil men with the kindness of good men, not that I have done any harm to the former or any good to the latter, not because I have ceased being bad and am all good, but because I have determined to hate evildoers and to love good men. In truth, I often wished, if it were possible, to flee from the crowd of the former to the few members of the latter, and I still would want it that way if it were possible. If therefore my intercession with the previously mentioned Tribune and people could be of any help to you in the present danger, please rest assured that my mind and pen stand ready. Also in a region of Italy far from these troubles I have a house which is indeed small, but for two people having the same mind no house is too narrow. It is free from all harmful signs of wealth, but suffers neither poverty nor avarice, and is full of countless books. It is expecting only us, me to return from the West where it complains I have been for the past two years, and you from the East if destiny compels you and if it pleases you. Whatever else I can offer you beyond this, I do not possess. But you know the location of the house to which I invite you: that healthy location is free from fears, full of delights, and favorable for studies. Whatever plan you decide upon, may God lead to a happy conclusion. Meanwhile my fervent wish is that I have been wrongly fearful and that absence, as so often happens, has been responsible for increasing the fear of the devotee! For my mind will not rest until either I see you or through letters I hear that you are safe from these storms.

From Avignon, hastily and anxiously, 11 September.

Fam. VII, 2.

To a friend, on the need for not despising true humility.

I beg you, do not scorn your friend so much because he is humble lest you sin against the beatitude which promises that humility will be exalted. There is indeed nothing less contemptible than true humility and nothing less to be honored and less worthy of respect than true pride. However, we are deceived by making minute distinctions in this matter as in many others. We call humble the worthless, the fainthearted and the cowardly while the high-minded we call proud. On the other hand we despise the truly humble because of their suspect timidity, and we worship the proud as if they were truly high minded. We should keep in mind what Sallust reports was said by Cato the Younger: "We lost the true names for things a long time ago." If, therefore, returning to the matter at hand, you maintain that your friend is as humble as he is, I urge you to beware lest you are despising that humility which is a very lofty virtue and most pleasing to Christ; and lest you appear to be what you never were, a victim of an insolent and unbecoming pride. For who, even of mediocre ability, having read both sacred and secular writings does not realize how much Christ, our master of humility, always loved humble things? To start from the beginning, what a humble birth he chose for himself whose very face is the source of the highest and greatest happiness! Could He not have been born from whatever noble line He wished, or could He not have ennobled the one He chose? But instead He despised fame and sought humility. "The twig emerged from the root of Jesse, and the flower sprang from its root." Under its shade kings now sit, peoples rest, and all of the world is refreshed with its odor. And indeed, what was this fruit of Jesse? Was it proud? Was it noble? His maternal ancestor was Ruth, a foreign woman, needy and widowed, who followed the footsteps of her childless mother-in-law beyond the boundaries of her fatherland and was the first to be admitted out of compassion into the fields of Boaz to gather the ears of corn behind the young reapers, and then as a result of nocturnal advances was promoted to the role of wife of the owner himself, whence the father of Jesse was begotten, a man of obscure name himself. Indeed who would have known Jesse himself except for his son David? And indeed who would have known anyone of them except because of Christ who was begotten from their root? How much Saul was accustomed to scorn their origin and with what anger, and how he used to call him the son of Isai and his servant, that Saul who was a haughty fellow-citizen and who admittedly was the offspring of a very obscure family from the lowest tribe of Israel, these things anyone can learn who reads the books of Kings. David himself, although possessing unusual virtues and out-standing talent, was but a very young shepherd when he was chosen by the Lord and freed from the flocks of sheep as he himself confesses. From following the ewes he was re-ceived into the kingship, and he tended Israel with the inno-cence of his heart. Was Moses perhaps more renowned when he saw that vision of the burning and unconsumed bush, or when, having become famous because of so many prodigious signs, he set forth to free the Israelites from the slavery of Egypt by the command of God? Certainly no king or prince was he who was chosen for such labor, but a humble shep-herd, and what is even more marvelous, of a foreign flock. As for father Abraham himself and his son and grandson with whose names every corner of Scripture is full, and whose glory is so great that the Almighty received His name from them and wished to be called the God of Abraham, the God of Isaac, the God of Jacob, and use that same name for Himself when speaking about Himself, do you think that they were kings or tetrarchs? Indeed they were either farm-ers or shepherds. Sitting on base donkeys, surrounded by their flocks, they changed their dwellings with their chil-dren and wives. In this humility they deserved God as leader who then had no wish either to be so friendly with the most powerful and haughty kings of the Assyrians, or even to be known by them. Note how Jacob himself, from whom in sacred Scripture one sees how that extraordinary surname became more popular and more intimately associated with God, and who was famous not because of his pride of origin but because of his humility, returns from his long and demanding service with his father-in-law. He certainly does not return with a sceptre, crown, royal robe, a golden chariot, armed forces. Instead, secretly fleeing with the long lines of sheep and goats and oxen that had been gathered, he led away with him a large number of children and servants, and two wives and just as many concubines, the seed of countless peoples from whose womb descended the Twelve Tribes of Israel, and a so great a multitude of people whose women God rendered fertile in honor of his humility. Those things occurred in a way which on the surface made them appear contemptible, but in essence they were magnificent, for if they were to be understood only as they are recounted, who would not despise what they say?

But if temporal glory were personally superior in God's eye to humility, who would doubt in what direction that great love of God would have been much more inclined? Compare with these three aged men, who were so famous, together with all their flocks and wives, the three Roman leaders who were supported by immense armies: Scipio Africanus, who destroyed the strength of Hannibal and subjected powerful Carthage to the tributary yoke; Pompey the Great, who raised thunder in the North and in Asia and who filled his homeland not with milk but with gold, and who captured flocks, not of sheep but of kings, as he proceeded from the Red Sea to the Maeotic Marshes and the Rhiphaean mountains; Julius Caesar, who drove like lightning into Gaul and into Germany, and once having subdued the enemy finally turned his victorious spear against the organs of his homeland, and in a single battle in Thessaly defeated Rome herself, who then ruled over the gentiles and who contained within her the entire world. You perceive what this great inequality represented. The son of God who was about to be born of man could have decided to be born of these or to make those from whom he was born like the others, since he had created both. He could have made the founder of his lineage not David and the narrow limits of Judea, but Augustus ruling over the entire world, or He could have made David himself as great a prince as He made Augustus. He could have been born not in that narrow district of Bethlehem, but in Rome to which Judea was subject among the others, and in a golden bed rather than in a stable. And once born. He, who has heaven as his abode and to whom the earth and all abundance belong, could have been nourished not in deepest poverty but in the greatest pleasure, except that He scorns nobility and earthly delights (and would that He did not detest them!). Finally, He could have chosen as his successors and preachers of His name among the peoples, learned disciples, powerful princes, kings and orators and philosophers, rather than needy, unlearned, and rustic fishermen, except that He Himself is God who resists the arrogant but favors the humble, and needs neither our powers to act since his mere words are acts, nor our mortal eloquence for persuading: "For the discourse of God is alive and effective and more piercing than any double edged sword, and penetrating as far as the abode of the soul and of the spirit, and even of the joints and of the marrow, discerning even the thoughts and intentions of the heart." He had armed his disciples with such discourse when He dispersed them throughout the world to persuade mankind; armed not with consular robe, imperial crown, triumphant laurel crown, not with opinions of philosophers, not with gems of orators, not with subtleties of Sophists, not, in short, with the knowledge of words, as the Apostle says, lest the cross of Christ be made void. Among them were not a Caesar who commanded, not a Plato who taught, not an Aristotle who argued, not a Cicero who exhorted; but poor little men, feeble and unpolished, who never entered a school, or studied letters. These, however, among the swords of their persecutors and the teeth of beasts, and among flames and racks and tortures persuaded the people as they desired: that Christ God, born as man, suffered, descended to hell, arose from the dead, ascended into heaven, and will return to judge, and all the other truths that He had commanded who, as it is written, preferred the fools of the world and the weak in order to confound the strong, and who, though He had come to benefit all, chose, as Augustine says, that the fisherman profit the emperor rather than the emperor the fisherman, a fact that can be applied similarly to the orator and the philosopher.

And this occurred not in an age of ignorance and of superstition, but "when the arts and sciences had become firmly rooted and when all those ancient errors had been removed from the uncultivated life of men," and when long since "men had already become more learned together with the times themselves," than they had been in the age of Romulus —writing about whose accepted divinity Cicero says in his *Republic* and Augustine repeats in his that if hardly anyone found fictions acceptable at that time, they would certainly find them less so now, "for antiquity received fictitious fables, sometimes even absurd ones, whereas this cultivated age rejects them, mocking those that could not possibly have happened." If, as I said, in order to embellish the false divinity of Romulus, in which an already cultivated age was able to believe, Cicero brought together arguments of considerable significance, saying that Rome had scarcely been founded and that one of the Seven Hills was covered not with golden roofs and marble walls but with thorny spaces, and was occupied with rustic thatched huts and smelled redolent with the odor of shepherds; what must be said of the age of Christ when Rome was already giving laws to the world and Augustus and Tiberius were ruling, under one of whom Christ was born and under the other suffered? Between this time and the age of Romulus the changes that occurred were more wonderful than one might expect from the number of years that had intervened. Not because the intervening time was short, if indeed from the period when Romulus was torn to pieces by the Roman Senate because of his insolence at the Goat marshes until Christ was crucified by the Jews because of our sins on the Mount of Olives, a little more than seven hundred years, more or less, elapsed, if I am not mistaken. Although Cicero says, "less than six hundred," he was referring not to his time but to the age of Africanus and of the others whom he has speak in that same book of the *Republic*. Furthermore, between the murder of Cicero at the time of Antonius and the Passion of Christ at the time of Pilate, as close as I can guess, there intervened about seventy years or so. I would prolong this but your messenger is looking over my shoulder and notices each stroke of the

pen and measures the delays between each, and often glanc-
ing at the doorway and the sky he sighs. I feel pity for him,
having experienced what waiting means to the mind in haste,
and I feel constrained to say before I should: love humility
and farewell.

Fam. VII, 3.

To his Socrates, a nocturnal vision, and that a calm poverty ought to be preferred to an agitated wealth.

I shall tell you about a dream I had last night. I seemed—and I am uncertain as to why since I am not accustomed either to think or to speak about such things—I seemed to have found in that small field of mine that I own at the source of the Sorgue, a treasure: it was a considerable pile of ancient golden coins. We were taking a walk alone as is our custom. I immediately called to you and pointed out the find with my finger. We both stopped short, as will happen, because of our joy and astonishment. As I stood there I remember recalling the words of Annaeus: "Avoid whatsoever pleases the masses and those things which chance offers you; remain suspicious and fearful of all good which is accidental: both beast and fish are trapped by whatever raises their hope; such gifts which you may think come to you through chance are but traps." Deliberating over this, we joyfully and worriedly hesitated for a little while. In short, it appeared to us real insanity to disdain what is usually sought over land and sea through great labors and dangers and was being offered to us so simply. Soon we eagerly burdened ourselves with gold, and silently and secretly carried it home after having hidden temporarily those portions that could not be carried in one load. We did this once, twice, and many more times, always more greedily, and always, as is the nature of such things, our anxiety and desire increased with the money. Meanwhile an invisible murmur strikes our ears and our secret, revealed to no one, suddenly erupted by itself among the multitude. Not long after this, some older lord of these parts came forth claiming the treasure as rightfully his. We stood firm. As a result there were first some lengthy and unpleasant arguments, then contention and threats with insults always added to the disputes as the lord argued bitterly in his own behalf and we became highly indignant that such a gift of favorable fortune found in our land should be snatched from us. Thereupon several solutions were attempted and as many plans made, at times proper and cautious, at others rash and bitter as we were fired to resist not so much because of our own desire as because of the proud stubbornness of our inexorable opponent. At times, dragged from the peacefulness of the country to business in the city, and at times from our studies to take up needed weapons, we were constantly agitated by new storms of cares; at times in place of night-long efforts and most enjoyable research into new ideas there came night-long hatred and anger; finally the man turned from dispute to battle. The state of our minds being thus changed, we often felt sorry for having found the gold, and in our dreams we would philosophize as follows. "Where did we leave our serene and peaceful life? Who brought upon us these clouds of cares. Who pushed us into these storms? Were we not aware that in the possession of gold tribulation appears beautiful, and wretchedness appears splendid? Needs increase with wealth, and happiness flees with frugality." Large numbers of examples occurred to us of those who had been either unhappy in wealth or most happy in poverty. The useless wealth of Croesus and the fatal gold of Midas and the booty that was removed from the temples of Dionysius and Crassus were all scorned by us; while the happy and glorious poverty of Cincinnatus, of Regulus, of Curius, of Fabritius was praised. Great numbers of our own heroes came to mind who, naked, in solitude, burned by the sun and the cold, feeding upon roots of herbs and wild berries, with the sky above as their roof and with the earth as their bed, drank from the muddy streams with pleasure, walked along the rough and narrow path and, in the hope of a better homeland, completely despised all things mortal. However, the more examples of this kind came to mind, the more we felt sorry that we had not seen them in time but instead, as they say, had eyes in our back. Finally we reached the point where what kept us from wanting to abandon the undertaking was only the shame of unyielding. Already the risks of final battle were approaching when suddenly in the middle of the night, distressed by anger and fear, I awoke. A cold sweat covered my entire body. Thus, may God be my witness, I was weary of mind and body as if a serious and difficult matter had agitated me not while dreaming but while awake. It is not easy to say how happy I was to be freed not only of the treasure but of the anxieties, and that I possessed only enough to nourish myself without excess; and only what sufficed for life and not what afflicted it; and how I became rooted through a dream in that belief, which once awake I am convinced to be true, that wealth brings more harm than good to ambitious mortals. I finally got up at the regular hour (you know my custom) and after having recited my daily praises to God, I took up my pen as is my custom and began at once exposing in my waking state what had upset me in my sleep. And so I make you a partner in this lesson since you seem to be a partner in my dream.

Farewell and rid yourself of unnecessary desires if you wish to be happy.

14 January at dawn.

Fam. VII, 4.

To Giovanni Tricastrino, bishop and professor of theology.[1]

Mindful of your request and of my promise, I leave for, or rather (to avoid getting involved in the grammatical argument which Atticus brings up in his letters to Cicero) I am going to, Italy. I also know and recall that you asked me to put in order the works of Cicero himself and that you had often requested that I make some of them clear by introducing, as you are accustomed to say, notations in the form of sparks of light. Finally, so that your prayers might become truly irresistible you requested that the Roman Pontiff—who, aware of your dedication, had given you an assignment certainly worthy of your talent by entrusting the honorific custody of his library to you, just as once our rulers Julius Caesar and Caesar Augustus did with Marcus Varro, and with Pompeius Macer, respectively, and the Egyptian king Ptolemy Philadelphus did with Demetrius Phalerius—you requested that the Roman Pontiff, as I was saying, in some modest manner would indicate his position in this matter before I departed. What could I do? As the poem of some unknown poet says: "A request from a ruler is a violent kind of ordering and as powerful as if he were asking with a drawn sword." I shall obey if I can, for it is both necessary to obey him and delightful to please you, and likewise it is difficult to reject your requests and sacrilegious to disobey his orders. It all depends on this: how much good fortune I shall have in finding those corrected manuscripts that you seek. Being an expert in the faults of our century, you know what a lack there is of such books despite the fact that useless and unnecessary and indeed truly harmful and fatal riches continue to be sought after with so much trouble and toil. I shall devote whatever energy I may have and all my care to the search; and so that you may not accuse me of delaying, you ought to know that in an attempt to restore strength to my body which illness had depleted I have been staying in my solitude at the source of the Sorgue awaiting the temperate

1. Believed to be the librarian of Clement VI and a highly respected theologian.

weather of autumn and fearful of committing my still weak body to a long journey. When my strength has increased, God willing, and the heat has diminished, I shall take up the journey. Meanwhile I wish you could realize with what great pleasure I breathe solitary and free among the mountains, among the springs and rivers, among the books and the talents of the greatest men, and how together with the Apostle I project myself into those things which are before us, and try to forget those that are past, and not to see the present. Farewell.

Fam. VII, 5.

To his Lelius, on personal matters and on the disturbing rumors connected with the doings of the Tribune of Rome.

Time forbids me to write at great length, and sleep does not permit it. This is already the third night that I am sleepless. Still not free from my former worries, I am now burdened with new ones caused by my departure which indicate that there are many problems before me and behind me needing my attention. When I shall force myself to disdain all of them equally, which I have done in great part, only then shall I begin to enjoy some restful sleep like Virgil's Aneas who "when he was certain of his departure and when all preparations had been duly completed, enjoyed his sleep." So either I am wrong, or my long and uncertain deliberation is full of annoyance and toil; only the termination of doubt is the beginning of peace. One cannot say how the distressed mind exercised by aimless deliberation finds rest from the need for choice by arriving at a choice of one final position. Therefore when that happens I shall write at greater length. Now I speak half asleep and as if in a dream. I therefore embrace your excuse although superfluous; for I know that if distances between places are hateful to lovers, they are not with true friends. Wherever we shall be, we shall be together. Concerning your affair I shall do as you write, and as if I were doing it for myself. I shall expedite it in short order, for nothing I experience is more annoying than to drag out words. Being aware of this, I have never caused so much annoyance to friends, nor indeed shall I do so. I shall please them if I can; otherwise I shall try not to displease them. I shall consider composing the verses you request once my inspiration has been awakened at our Helicon, but without knowing how your notes which I had in my hands ten times somehow got away from me as I departed, leaving them behind. Search for them there and send them to me, although even without them I seem to know what I should be saying, if only I could come across a stopping place in a thick forest.

The copy of the letter of the Tribune which was sent me I have seen, read, and been amazed by; I know not what to answer. I recognize the fate of the fatherland, for wherever I turn I find reason and occasion for grief. Once Rome is torn to pieces what will happen to Italy? Once Italy is disfigured what would my life be? In this sorrow, which is both public and private, some will contribute wealth, others bodily strength, and still others power and advice. I see nothing that I can contribute except tears.

22 November, in transit.

Fam. VII, 6.

To his Socrates, on his private affairs and his desire for moderation.

The gist of my affairs which I entrusted to your respected confidence I now repeat without removing or adding anything. In this I am not only determined but immovable in what I intend to do. If you remember my position it should be unnecessary to speak further about this affair. But so that you may know that I am not forgetful of myself, listen to what I have to say briefly. I have never been a seeker of great fortune whether because of modesty, pettiness, or, as some great men prefer to conceive it, magnanimity. I call truths to mind which even the multitude knows and for which you are my chief witness, sometimes praising me for them and sometimes censuring me, although because of the nature of the times in a very friendly way. To use your own words, I become too stubborn in whatever I undertake. This forces me to see that whenever I seek the reputation of the greatest consistency, I seem to attain the reputation and ill fame of obstinacy. However, thus far I have not been sorry for my decisions, since all kinds of heights are deeply suspect to me, and every ascent warns me of a descent. And I would much more easily and naturally incline toward associating with those who in the words of the poet, "inhabit the lowest valleys," than those who according to the same poet, "raised their city on the mountains." This being so, if my desired moderation which Horace rightly calls golden, should come to me as it was promised long ago, I accept it with gratitude and I shall admit that it was done for me in a most liberal way. But if that hateful and heavy burden of a major office is imposed upon me, I shall refuse it and push it away. I would rather be poor than upset, although with the way things are going and in my mental condition I may not be poor. These matters and others like them, and whatever else we used to discuss among ourselves along these same lines I beg you, who know me so well, to pass on to both friends and lords, and to the lord of lords when the time seems proper, even though they have never been hidden nor kept silent by me. But there are those upon whom the truth must often be forced in order to have it penetrate into their mind, and I am not surprised that it applies also to whatever you are about to say concerning me. I know I appear more distant from the customs of our age and from the opinions of the multitude, with which I disagree strongly, not only in many matters but especially in what we are discussing. But the strength of your mind and the eloquence of your speech will drive out the incredulity of your listeners. My Socrates has always been worthy of authority and of trust in whatever he discusses, but especially in speaking of the secret thoughts of his friend; and, what is more, one listens to many things more favorably coming from the mouth of a friend than from one's own mouth. Finally, so that no one should be amused at my simplicity, do not conceal the idea that true liberality is not difficult, slow, or troublesome; that it cares for nothing except the one it embraces and will be obedient only to him. It does not order but instead obeys; it satisfies wishes and does not restrict them. Therefore we know why offering vast amounts to someone who seeks only limited quantities is a kind of denial. Farewell.

25 November, in transit.

Fam. VII, 7.

To Nicholas, Tribune of the City of Rome,[1] *indignation mixed with entreaties regarding the Tribune's changed reputation.*

I confess that you have caused me recently to repeat often and with great pleasure the words that Cicero has Africanus speak: "What is this that fills my ears, so great and so sweet a sound it is?" For what is more suitable for the great splendor of your name than such joyful and frequent announcements of your accomplishments? How eagerly I participated in this is revealed in my book of exhortations dedicated to you, full as it is of my urging and my praise of you. Do not, I pray, cause me to say: "What is this great and sad sound that hurts my ears?" Do not, I beg you, disfigure with your own hands the very lovely appearance of your fame. No man has the right to demolish the foundations of your creations except you alone; you can overturn what you founded: the architect is the best demolisher of his own works. You know in what manner you climbed to glory; if you turn your steps backward you descend, the descent by nature is easier. For the path is very wide, and what the poet has to say does not apply only to those in the infernal regions: "Easy is the de-

1. Perhaps the most spectacular political figure of the fourteenth century. As a result of an uprising of the populace against the noble rulers of Rome he emerged a champion of the new democratic form of government, and was sent as emissary to Clement to request approval of the new government. His mission failed despite his eloquent pleading, but because of his enthusiasm for ancient and early Christian Rome and his desire to restore Rome's former power and glory, he and Petrarch became fast friends. Upon returning to Rome he worked for a revolutionary upheaval in government which occurred in 1347. In his haste to deprive the nobility of their powers and to display pomp and ceremony reminiscent of classical Rome, he soon began losing the support of his followers. By the end of 1347 he abdicated under pressure from papal troops. When his subsequent attempts to persuade the emperor to destroy the temporal power of the papacy failed, he was excommunicated by the Pope, brought to Avignon where he was imprisoned and charged with heresy. Eventually he regained the favor of the Pope and by 1354 re-entered Rome as a senator ruling in the name of the Pope. In the fall of the same year he was killed by a Roman mob. Of all the rulers of the time he alone stirred Petrarch's imagination to a near boiling point.

scent to Avernus." Only in the diversity of life do we differ from the desperate wretchedness of those in hell, because as long as we are here we fall but can rise, we descend but can ascend; on the other hand no one has been returned from there. What indeed is more maddening than a man who, being able to stand, falls because of his confidence in rising again? The fall from above is always more dangerous; and what, I ask you, is loftier than virtue and glory from whose inaccessible summit you contemplate our times? And you reached this summit so energetically and along such an unaccustomed path that I do not know anyone anywhere whose downfall may be more terrible. You must fix your steps more firmly so that you stand unmoved and avoid affording a spectacle at which your enemy would laugh and your friends mourn. A famous name is not sought freely, nor indeed is it preserved easily; "for it is great labor to guard a great fame." Permit me to use with you a short verse of mine, which I liked so much that I was not ashamed to extract it from my everyday letters and transfer it to my *Africa*. And also help me avoid the very troublesome necessity of being forced to terminate in satire the lyrical foundations of your praises in which I have been heavily engaged (as my pen itself can attest). And do not think that I have fallen into this subject by chance, or that I am speaking without knowledge. After I left your court, a number of letters from friends followed my departure in which the questionable turn of your affairs and stories of your reputation much different from the first accounts reached me. They say that you do not love the people as you used to but instead only the worst part of the people, that those are the ones you obey, cultivate, and admire. What more can I say except those words that Brutus wrote to Cicero: "Your condition and your fortune are shameful!" Will the world then see you move from a leader of good men to a follower of reprobates? Can the stars have so suddenly changed against us and God have become so hostile? Where now is that healthy genius of yours? Where, to employ my accustomed language, is that guiding spirit of good works with which you were believed to be in constant dialogue, since it was not considered possible for a man to achieve such great things otherwise?

Why however do I become so upset? Things will always go as eternal law decrees. I cannot change them, but I can flee from them. You have therefore freed me from a considerable task: I was hastening to you with all my heart, but I am changing direction for I certainly shall not see you as another person. For a long time farewell to you also, dear Rome; if what I hear is true I would rather visit the Indians or the Garamantes. Are these things not true? Oh how very different the end is from the beginning; oh ears of mine that are too sensitive! They had become accustomed to glorious reports and cannot suffer another kind. But perhaps what I am saying may be false. Would that it were really so; for never would I more willingly have been wrong. The credibility of the writer I do indeed consider great, but because of a number of signs I am also suspicious of a certain envy on his part, an envy which I know not whether to call noble or unfriendly. Therefore, although grief impels me to say many things, I shall nevertheless check the impulse which I certainly could not do except to console my anxiety with disbelief. May God assist me in this, and may He make it more joyful than it sounds, and rather afflict me with the falsehood of one friend than with disloyalty and shameful actions of the other. If indeed through evil customs it has come to pass that falsehood is considered a daily and common sin, the fact remains that through the centuries there has been no license, no custom, no freedom that could free from guilt the betrayer of his homeland. It is preferable therefore that he make a few days of mine sad by lying than that you make all my life sad by forsaking your homeland. If he transgressed with words, he will be cleansed with words. If yours is indeed a real crime—which I hope is not the case—with what remedies can you ever hope to abolish it? Yours will be eternal glory or eternal infamy. Wherefore, if (as I hope is not the case) you are perhaps overlooking your reputation, at least consider mine. You know what a tempest is hanging over my head and how great would be the crowd of censurers who would conspire against me if you begin to collapse. To use the words of the young man in Terence, "therefore, while there is time, weigh everything again and again." Consider with great zeal, carefully, I beg you, what you may be doing, shake yourself sharply, examine yourself without deceit to see who you are, who you have been, whence you came and where you go, where you are permitted to proceed with unobstructed liberty, what kind of person you have been, what title you have assumed, what hope of yours you have realized, and what you professed to be. You will see yourself not as the master of a state but as its servant.

From Genoa, 29 November.

Fam. VII, 8.

To Giovanni Aretino.[1]

All your wishes are coming true, dear friend. I rejoice therefore for the freedom of our homeland, for the glory of our rulers, for the quietness of your citizens, for the increase in religion, for the public joy, and particularly for your honor by whose hands an attractive serenity and a sweet peace has descended over a city which had up to now been agitated and gloomy. I also rejoice at the desired success of your family affairs. It is very rare to have large numbers of joyful things happen, for indeed fortune always spoils pleasant things with some mixture of unpleasant things. But if ever she desires to be fully propitious, she knows how to elicit in marvelous ways unhoped-for sweetness from the very bitterness of things. Often, therefore, softening and bending unyielding things, she turns into joy what seemed to be sorrow. The gifts of fortune are to be used and not relied upon. She is now certainly using her art. Therefore what do you wish me to say? I begin to rejoice not so much at the desired events but at our very misfortunes and difficulties, as, for example, the manner in which the great and manifold joyfulness of my mind was tempered by that single illness of your body, or the many and various obstacles in my way whose effects I now hope will enable both of us to return together to our homeland. Farewell.

1. Chancellor of the Gonzaga family, rulers of Mantua, whom Petrarch met in Avignon in 1350.

Fam. VII, 9.

That open enmity is to be preferred to concealed hatred.

A country proverb says: "To make a dog's bed requires great toil." If you were to ask the meaning of this proverb, it is that you do not know where to place the cushion because the dog when it is about to lie down turns this way and that. Trifling indeed was the thought of the man who first said this; nevertheless it is true, and the same may be said about many men as one says laughingly about the dog. For there are many for whom nothing is done properly; and they so repeatedly turn about that one cannot know on what side they may fall or what they desire. When you believe that you have pleased them, you discover that you have accomplished nothing; all your labor and all your indulgence is lost. If you offer them the pleasures of the city, they praise the frugality of the country; if you are drawn away from the city, they ask for the multitude and curse solitude; if you begin to talk with them, they become annoyed, and if you are silent, they become indignant. They long for those who are absent; they despise those who are present. And often they even hate friends. To stay away from such people at all times would be highly advisable. You understand what I would like, and it is useless for me to say any more. Nevertheless I shall say something more lest in my silence I offer you and your mild nature an opportunity for dissimulation. Why do you take so much trouble, dear man? You have met someone who is far different and unequal to you, so retreat from your laborious and useless attempt; in vain did you strive to win him over, you cannot be a friend against his will, but you can become a formidable opponent. The one he presently despises he will now begin to fear if you start to reveal your anger openly; and he will realize who it was that he inexplicably provoked with a spirit of ingratitude. Pursue the custom of doctors with this sick and infected man; I urge you to try the opposite of what is expected. Since gentleness has proven vain, perhaps sternness will be more effective and animosity more powerful than love. The one he spurns because of flattery, he will fear if you openly display some opposition. I have given you advice contrary to my custom, but suitable for the matter at hand. What else can you do for one who calls love a trap and thinks that kindness is fear? Farewell.

Fam. VII, 10.

To Giovanni dell' Incisa, an apology and some thoughts on perishable hope.

Your letter, full of highly pleasing and sweet censure, reached me on the banks of the Po on the evening of March 23. Compare the day of arrival with the date of the letter and see if in that same space of time it might not have arrived from Egypt. Together with it came also letters from other friends and two who are not personally known to me but certainly illustrious young men, as you say, yet old men according to their writing. Would that our city had more of them whom it would not send into exile, or rather would at least permit their departure to bring luster to other Italian cities. But I shall pass over this inexhaustible and ancient complaint and instead turn to the letters. Almost all of them contained but one idea: I am accused of having turned to Cisalpine Gaul after my promise to come to Florence, as if I were a despiser of my native land, and as if I had deceived the expectation and desires of many people who were awaiting me there. I could answer this in many ways, and what I may answer to the letters of others I do not yet know. Although very busy I shall nevertheless respond in some manner to your request that I follow my inspiration and while holding pen in hand I let it say whatever emerges naturally. Certainly with the others, in order to equal their style of writing, I shall need the protection of the Muses. With you, however, toward whom everything of mine must be open and naked without any artificiality, I would not hide even this one thing: the difficulties of the journey, the plague of this year which has trampled and destroyed the entire world, especially along the coast, my grief, and, unless I am mistaken, the evil and unjust treatment of my homeland would not have turned me from my original journey since I had already completed the most difficult part of my effort, and had arrived at Genoa. This then is the truer and sounder reason, that, persuaded by the hope that I had conceived in my mind and fatefully dreamed, I did not think it possible that I could not bring you a happier outcome of our affairs. Therefore it gave me pleasure to wait until actual fact would succeed hope. I was already considering not only a hurried journey but a flight, and I already seemed to be about to cross the Alps of Bologna (I have called the Apennines by their common name of Alps) without any sense of fatigue. Indeed it was from there that I, unexpected although not unawaited, had decided to present myself to you and to my friends. It so happened that from there I primarily expected aid for the undertaking, with any delay in such aid being most dangerous since the greatest speed would not have sufficed. But what can I say? I know that things are solid and hopes empty; I know that whoever loses hope loses nothing—I said too little, for indeed he gains a great deal. Yet I speak as an expert when I say that just as nothing smaller than hope can be lost, in the same way there is nothing which is more troublesome. The reason is that often the things we hope for become more valued than the things we possess, and we often know by attaining them how much the flattering hope of possessions has deceived us. This is why every time hope disappears before the actual event, we consider ourselves afflicted by serious inconvenience. God therefore forestalled my plan and declared unnecessary the cares which I considered proper, so that being taught in such fashion I would recognize that the opinions of men are vain. But enough of this. I shall say nothing more on the progress of my legal disputes: the matter has been turned over to the Curia. I hope that the schemes of that thief are exposed. Nevertheless I am prepared for whatever happens: I shall rejoice as victor; if I am defeated I shall console myself as being on the side of defeated justice. This is not the first time I have been harassed in the games of fortune; and I have learned with what skills the wound of mortal hope is evaded. Let matters therefore go as they please, provided I am not moved, nor by heaven do I know where I ought to be moved. Certainly I can with a clear mind either pursue what is mine or abandon what I was never able to pursue. The philosopher's road is a short cut to wealth, and teaches not that wealth should be accumulated but that desires should be diminished. I determined to follow this course lest I should happen upon that difficult and troublesome journey of complex business matters from which God and the very condition of my nature withdrew me, as it were, by the hand. Let the results of legal action, therefore, be as they will. My poverty, which is not burdensome or base but more envied by many than I should like, will suffice for me. If it really befits me, as it seemed to Seneca, I am wealthy. Farewell.

7 April in Verona.

To the same correspondent, on the reputation of an expected friend.[1]

One would not believe how my cares have diminished and how much has been added to my delight by certain recent news which I have decided to share as briefly as possible with you since time and place prevent me from being too lengthy. I hear that our Francesco, who, after undergoing many misfortunes and dangers both on land and sea, fortunately is safe, is approaching and is already in Marseilles. And he is now first hastening, as they say, on the straight road to me and is complaining, I am sure, about the great length of the journey, using with justification those words of Virgil: "We follow the fleeing Italy and we are rolling in the waves." He thought he would find me in France but I was not able to bear that rabble of the Curia. The short jump into the homeland should be simple for him. I know that he certainly burns with a desire to see you, but, believe me (I would not write this to you if you could in any fashion subvert my plan), believe me, as I was saying, it is fortune that decides the plans of men. Between planning and doing, as the multitude says, there is a high mountain of difference. When he arrives here, which I hope will be shortly, I shall take him in my arms. Love is a powerful thing, and it believes nothing is forbidden to it. I shall appear to act within my rights if I hide him in my home like a rediscovered treasure, and shall take care that he does not slip away from me again so easily. I want to give you early notice of this so that you will bear it with greater resignation when it happens; for I shall not share him with you as readily as I am sharing news of his arrival. Friendship is much more rare and precious than gold. And, if I am somewhat more greedy than usual, let the value of the thing possessed excuse the insensibility of the possessor. I do not refuse you as a partner in the event, provided that we share it when it is

1. This and the following letter refer to a pending visit of Franceschino degli Albizzi, a relative of Petrarch.

present. Therefore if you would like to enjoy your portion of it, and indeed so that you might have not one but two parts, let your love make you come here. Farewell.

From the peaceful valley of Parma, with a rustic pen, on 10 April.

To the same correspondent, a complaint over the death of an expected friend.

Alas, what has happened? What do I hear? Oh deceitful hope of mortals, oh useless cares, oh precarious human condition! There is nothing peaceful for man, nothing stable, nothing safe: here we see the power of fortune, there the traps of death, and there the flattery of the fleeing world: we wretched mortals are best on every side, and surrounded by so many pitfalls how dare we promise ourselves any happiness? Deceived so often, and so often made fools of, we know not how to divest ourselves of the habit of hope and of a credulity which has deceived us countless times. So great is the allurement of happiness though proven false! How often do I say to myself, "Alas, you madman, alas, you blind man so forgetful of your affairs, look carefully, take note, give heed, abide, reconsider, and impress this like a fixed sign which remains indelible; recall the many deceits you have suffered; do not ever hope for anything or take fortune seriously: she is a liar, she is fickle, capricious, untrustworthy; you have at one time known her flattery and gentleness, but later you have seen her bitterness. Now that you know this deadly monster, you need no longer be taught by anyone. Take counsel from your own experience and beware of engaging with her again; disdain with equal vigor whatever she promises or denies and despise with equal vigor whatever she bestows upon you or snatches from you." I had determined to do this and had made up my mind; but after such a manly decision, here I am again falling prey like a woman and a silly man. Or should I have perhaps said ridiculously or indeed tearfully? To others perhaps I may appear ridiculous; to myself I appear deeply miserable and wretched. After so many disappointments of my hopes, I had brought my mind to hope again and to believe in this fleeting and almost serene moment of a winter night and to count upon the happiness of the following day rashly, confidently, and imprudently. I dared to flatter my bothersome cares by saying: "No, my dear Francesco will arive, my brother, my friend, united to me no less by desire than by name, no less through love than through blood; he will be arriving and has perhaps already arrived." So strongly did I concentrate on him that often I seemed to see him before my eyes though he was so distant by land and sea and, alas, I was never to see him again in this foreign exile. But following a habit of mine which is common to all lovers, I used to comfort myself over the delay and absence by imagining fictitious meetings and conversations and I used to deceive myself, as it turned out, with a certain pleasure. How often whenever some of my servants to whom he had become very dear because of his charming personality came to me to make some announcement, I felt as though I was already speaking with him; how often when anyone knocked at my door did I become restless and found those pastoral verses coming to my mind: "I do not know what certainty is: and Hylas is barking at my door. Should we believe it or is it that those who love fashion their own dreams?" Wretched lover that I was I fashioned such dreams for myself, I was tormented with such cares, I burned with such anxiety, and I fed myself on such tenuous hope like a hungry person feeding himself abundantly as he dreams. The barking of dogs, the voices of servants, the creaking of a moving hinge or the trampling of the pavement by the hoof of an animal, and any kind of noise in general would disturb me. How many times I hastily threw down books that I was reading or a pen that I was holding! How often I arose, leaped up, eager to see and to embrace my dear friend and most welcomed partner in my cares, not just a brother (to use the words of Tullius which I could make my own in this instance), but equal to a brother in his charm, to a son in his obedience, and to a parent in wise counsel. I know not whether I came to know him too late or indeed too quickly! For had I not started to love the man, I would not be shedding these tears because of his death.

For almost two years I have relied on his company and friendship, a time, alas, scarcely sufficient for conversation, not to say for friendship. I find comfort for my bereavement only in this, that we both eagerly made recompense for the brevity of time by our very strong and mortal devotion and affection and that whatever is pleasant and sacred in friendship which others enjoy over a long period of time we accomplished in a brief time; thus while our delight might have been longer lasting, certainly our mutual trust could not have been more pure or genuine nor our friendship closer. Fortune envied me my taste of the pleasure of life. I received many and great tokens of his trust both when well and when sick. These I stored in the innermost recesses of my mind as if in a safe; and I hope that he felt the same toward me and perhaps more so because nature disposed him for greater gentleness and kindness. Now however the memory of those days is both bitter and sweet for me. On the one hand it charms me, on the other it grieves me, nor am I sufficiently clear about whether I would prefer to have been known by him or not. For while it is a happy and pleasant thing to have had such a friend, it is a most unhappy and bitter thing to have lost him. Almost never have I examined anything as I now have myself, and I must confess not without shame that I find more feeling in me and less strength than I thought; for I used to think (and it was proper because of my wide reading and long experience in life) that I had hardened myself against all blows and injustices of fortune. Unhappily I was wrong: there was nothing softer than I, nothing weaker. I used to think, indeed I was certain, that I loved my Francesco most tenderly; for his love and obedience to me deserved this treatment. However, how much I loved him became clear too late, and I did not learn it until I had lost him. Now my torn mind grieves the more out of control, the more it perceives that it has lost more than it had thought. For this reason nothing upset me more than the unexpectedness of that which not only could happen but could not fail to happen: I had not considered the possibility of his being about to die. Indeed if there were any order in this torrent of human affairs, he ought not to have died before me, having been born after me. Added to this was my fervent and anxious expectation of his arrival about which I have already said much; for this he had himself promised tearfully at his last departure and had repeated in his letters. My Socrates had announced not merely his future arrival but his pending one saying that he was hastening out of France on a straight path to me in Italy.

Woe is me! Now I recall: having been happy and hopeful up to then I had a premonition of his pending departure and my approaching misery and that I would soon experience the loss of the best part of myself, and was trying to extend my very brief happiness not knowing what fortune would do to me. I used to say: "He will come to me before he goes to see his aged father and his sweet brothers and sisters. I shall hold out my hand and I shall hang on to him, nor will there be need for great strength, for I shall find in him a great help rather than resistance. The love which resides in him shall become part of me." He himself would often repeat that verse from Horace, "I would like to live with you and gladly die with you." But the hand which I had thought of holding out to him death has held out; and my saying to you in my brief letter yesterday that fortune decides the plans of men is interpreted far differently than I thought. Now that my hope is gone together with my twofold desire, what shall I do? Shall I indulge in tears and sighs and in place of my lost friend shall I embrace my sorrow incessantly? Or shall I strive to appease my mind and to escape from the echoing threats of fortune into the stronghold of my reason? The latter appears preferable, the former more pleasing; virtue drives me to one; feeling bends me to the other. And I am uncertain where I should turn or what I should chiefly follow, and it is bad for me to fall too often and to rise too often.

Oh wicked and ungodly Savona who involved me in these anxieties, what can I invoke that you deserve? You have taken away half my soul, and you have inexorably cut down a young man in the bloom of his life, amidst his growing excellence, when he was just beginning, and now you lie heavily upon the breast which my Francesco inhabited. He himself has departed notwithstanding your unwillingness; you have no control over him for you cover over only his body and my hope. For this what else should I wish you? May your hills extend in a curved arch so that in the form of a straight and harborless shore you afford an unfavorable port to ships. May your walls crumble as well as your man-made garrisons which you threw in the face of the wind and the waves. May the force of Syrtis and violence of Euripus be transported there, and the fury of Scylla and the blows of Charybdis and whatever other dangers exist under the vast sea. May Aeolus set loose his restless brothers, the South Wind and the others, which are accustomed to abusing your shores, so that while the entire world is calm perpetual storms might crash upon you alone. And may whatever either in the way of death or disease this pestilential year has spread through all the lands and seas flow upon you only; and may that plague that strikes others on an annual basis be with you eternally. And may the island of Sardinia and whatever there is anywhere under the impure heavens be cleansed; may the swamps be purified together with the sulfurous lakes and the deep, slimy marshes; and may the North become warm and Ethiopia become cool, and Africa become emptied of its serpents, and Hyrcania of its tigers, and the world of all its monsters and huge beasts, and may they all assemble in you from every part of the earth. And may the gloomy mists and the deadly waters and the inclement weather and the cold and the heat rage in you; in sum, with the final salvation of mankind may you alone perish and become the place of the dead, and the region of terror and fear, and the home of mourning and affliction. And may the pilgrim, the merchant, and finally your own citizens flee you, may the weary traveler from the highest peaks of the mountains despise you, and the disturbed sailor survey you from the deep and avoiding your infamous reefs, use his oars to hasten the work of his sails. Alas, where is my grief driving me? What am I saying? Or where am I? I, a mortal, lament so strongly over mortal things and I curse the innocent land which receives what is its due, when I know not where I myself will die and where on earth I shall return my remains. Therefore, dear brother, one must abstain from wailing and sighing and must begin praying in behalf of our brother who has gone ahead while we remain behind; that is more becoming to men. As for you, oh lovely city, which preserves my buried friend, returning finally to my true self, I express my gratitude because he would now perhaps lie in a strange land if you had not received him. The shortness of his life might have been indeed fated; and it is to your merit that my friend, although young, and yet already weary with cares, at least enjoys the repose of an Italian grave, a trifling consolation but highly desired by many illustrious men of the past. While I was hitherto desirous of seeing you to view your lands and their attractiveness; hereafter I shall much more willingly see you as the preserver of remains that are so dear to me, though it is a bitter pleasure. For if the death of her Pompey and his dreadfully mutilated body once so attracted his beloved wife to the sands of the Nile that she was unwilling to depart from there, why shall I not love the Italian shore which is the eternal abode of my dear friend? Hail, oh outstanding land, most faithful guardian of the remains of my brother; you taught me to weep more readily and to hope more sparingly. You, however, dear brother, snatched from me before your time, for whom I am grieving so deeply, farewell eternally; indeed I expected from you joy and consolation in these lands where we are continually dying, where there is no place either for joy or for comfort. I expect to enjoy all these things with greater certainty, God willing, and in greater amounts hereafter in the land of the living. But alas I am now proving what I read in Statius: "Speaking is sweet to those in misery." It is certainly so; for how many things I did not feel did I painfully pour forth impetuously rather than through rational judgment! Nor am I satisfied with speaking but instead become more excited and indeed know not how to stop: I shall therefore simply break off.

To Cardinal Giovanni Colonna, condolences on the deaths of his brothers and grandsons.

I shall freely confess (for although I may not be solvent I am a trusted debtor) that I owe you everything, certainly my talent and this little body that I inhabit as a pilgrim, and whatever external goods fall to my lot. For your palace contributed no less to my mind than to my body and to my destiny. Because I was brought up by you since my youth, grew up under you and was educated by you so far as the malevolence of intervening misfortunes or the mediocrity of my talent allowed, it is only right that I must persist in directing this pen, this hand and my mind, however humble, to the consolation and solace of your mind. I remember having done so to the best of my ability in other misfortunes of ours, and I do not believe that you have forgotten. In deed in this so serious, so unmanageable and deadly wound which death, not yet satisfied with our tears, has brought to us I have not yet found what to do, what to say, or even how to open my mouth. I collapsed in my misery at the first news of the event, and I was petrified as if at an unexpected crash of a thunderbolt. Then as soon as I could I began to collect the scattered arms of my reason and to lift my prostrate and collapsed mind. I requested the letter reporting the unhappy event of which I had sadly heard through the sorrowful announcement of that excellent man, Paganino Milanese, who rules the city. When the letter was shown me I read it with much weeping. But indeed everything in it seemed confused because of the ambiguities, and nothing could be learned with any deep certainty. The report had started at Orvieto; soon it spread to Florence and across the Apennines by means of the letters of certain clerics, which reached Bologna first; then, as always, they reached us with greater bulk and variations. In such doubt, I therefore (since nature does bring it about that those things we hear that displease us we hardly ever admit or completely accept) chose to predict happier news for myself. So did my sick mind run to the pleasantness of better hope. However, it was but the vanishing and fleeing happiness of a wretched dreamer. What more can I say? Although that hope steadily diminished with the subsequent arrival of new messengers, I was able to learn nothing of any certainty before the woeful letter of our Socrates reached me. And it was thus, amazing as it appears, that the calamities of the Tiber reached me from another world at the river Rhone. Because that letter indeed shut off any refuge for my hesitant hope, the limited power of reason, which I sometimes called forth for the comfort of my own mind and others, was crushed by the weight of tears and laments. However, I did not surrender, nor did I stop. How often, having succeeded in standing, I tried to write something! How often I brought out my books, tried to wipe off the mildew from my decaying talent, and entered like a sorrowful investigator into the most intimate recesses of my memory! In short I did everything in my power, but all in vain. I came across certain letters in prose and poetry which in response to the frequent visits of misfortune I had sent you in these last years, letters in which I was unable to find anything satisfactory not only for alleviating my anguish, or yours, but even to soothe it. It shamed me to repeat commonplaces so often, and yet because my talent had been exhausted by the earlier attempts, I did not have the strength to work out new ones. I did not, however, desist from trying to do something in the hope that perhaps some beginning might succeed beyond all expectation. I could show you three or four beginnings of letters different in styles and in almost any other way called for by the variety of events which my serious state of mind gave birth to. How I felt about these efforts may be seen by the oblique lines that my pen drew across them like so many wounds inflicted by their author and chastiser. Being entangled in these difficulties I resolved to remain silent and to commit my present grief to Christ, supreme consoler, for comfort and resolution.

I have said these things as an excuse for my silence. The fact that I am writing to you after so much time results not from a change in condition, but from the unexpected joy which of late certain recent letters of the same Socrates brought to my spirits which had become so obstinate in their grief that (according to the habit of wretched people) they had begun to find joy in their very grief. In those letters I became aware of the strength, greatness, and superiority of your mind amidst so many blows of misfortune, and I, who had borne my grief in silence, could not bear the overwhelming joy, nor avoid breaking out into pious tears and words seeing that what modesty, sorrow and respect had forbidden me vainly to attempt in empty words of advice had been accomplished by that heavenly Master to whom it is proper to render thanks not only for many other things but especially for the fact that He granted you, with all your experience in life's battles, exemplary fortitude and steadfastness. Therefore, having recomposed the condition of my weary heart and having calmed the flood of my tears which obscure the serenity of the mind the more violently they attack and destroy the appearance of truth, what else could I recommend to you or request from you, my grace and almost only supporter of my hope and that of many others, except that you must persist in your present manner and withstand the abuses of threatening fortune with a steadfast mind? And you must view the violent and arrogant laws of our nature with moderation: what we are, where we are, how long we will continue to be what we are or remain here from where we set out, what port we seek, among what reefs we navigate, how much sea we have traversed, how little remains, how much danger remains before the end, and how many there have been who having safely sailed the stormy waters perished at the entrance of the port or on the shore. Finally how heavy a yoke rests upon the children of Adam, not as on the necks of oxen for alternate hours and days, but truly always. No one enjoys immunity from this, or respite, from the day one emerges from the womb of one's mother as it is written, until the day of burial and return back to the mother of all. All we mortals are weighed down by the yoke which is as heavy as it is continuous, from which neither race, nor beauty, nor wealth, nor talent, nor eloquence, nor power can free us. Nor can arms, followers, friends, even armies, fleets, or troops accomplish this, but only patience, forbearance, and steadiness. One must call to mind what power fortune had over those who, embracing those perishable and fleeting favors of hers, submitted to her power. As for the rest, she tempts them, drives them and taunts them but does not overcome them. One should recall the examples offered by all ages, either of the wealth of very powerful people which she terminated, or of the kingdoms of very famous rulers she trampled upon, or of anything that in her rage she left intact anywhere since the beginning of the world.

There is not time to recount stories here, for I did so in other consolatory letters to you, and those that I could put together with any care are already known to you. Nor shall I behave abjectly or effeminately for I address neither a woman, child, nor an ordinary member of the flighty masses, but a strong man possessing always a lofty nature, now, as I hope, stronger than usual and greater because of the very misfortunes that have befallen him, a man marked by the repeated wounds of fortune, and with the strength of virtue greater than ever, and disdainful of her threats and battles. Furthermore I shall not apply charms and flattery to so many harsh misfortunes, nor make reference to the hope of grandchildren although even such hope, thanks to God's compassion on our destiny, may not be lacking. Instead I shall reveal you to yourself. I urge you to stop counting your reasons for mourning and to stop considering your losses; and turn your eyes cleansed by your tears, turn to those things that remain. Consider the condition of your family: the home of the Colonnas may have fewer columns than usual, but what difference does it make provided that the firm and solid foundation remains. Julius Caesar was alone in not having any brother or children, and in not knowing the name of his father. Nevertheless what that one man accomplished, everyone knows. I urge you to convince yourself of something that is most true. Fortune is least to be feared where she rages most strongly. She did all she could; in a short time she carried off your brothers and grandchildren and relations, and reduced a most flourishing family stock to a few members. Regard her fearlessly and full of noble stubbornness. Except for your magnanimous father there is now almost nothing left that she can strike. And just as nothing human has been intolerable for him, thus nothing unexpected can happen to him henceforth: he has left the boundary of mortal life far behind him. Indeed what other elder can you point out to me who can count so many years of life as he can count years of happiness and of glory? Indeed he would be the most fortunate of all who have lived in this age of ours had he departed somewhat earlier. Furthermore anxiety and fear are ordinarily for those minds who expect them; those who have already received their portion are safe. With how much comfort in fact will your fortitude supply him amidst the difficulties of his old age in which ruthless fortune has entangled him toward the end of life and from which nothing could disentangle him except his own power or the power of his surviving son! Let these things and others similar to them provide you with remedies for your present misfortune. The remaining suggestions which may appear remedies are really torments: they do not relieve, but rather aggravate. Death is not redeemed with tears nor is it overcome with weeping. It cannot be avoided, it can only be scorned. This is the only victory that can be enjoyed over this insurmountable and inevitable evil. I would say more except that I know that a mind which is erect and mindful of itself does not need a talkative consoler. Words do not raise up a man who is dejected and forgetful of his own nobility. Just continue what you have begun and behave inwardly with the good faith that you have revealed externally, unless a disturbed mind hide beneath a calm exterior. This was most dangerous to many, for while they disguised their upsets and behaved in public as though they were happy, they were dejected in their private rooms and wasted away in concealed grief. Such artifice is appropriate for an insane mind and labors only for one's own destruction. It is much safer to confess one's grief and to weep openly. Finally, to repeat something which I recall saying quite often and which is worthy of being said more often, you are located in a lofty position from which you cannot flee the sight and judgments and conversations of men; wherefore concern for your dignity and reputation should be greater. Among many injustices fortune deserves credit for having done this one good thing for you: she has provided great cause for praising you. Those who live among us and those who shall be born after us will have reason to admire you, to praise you, to hold you up as an example, and to admire the strength of your mind unbroken despite misfortunes and your noble dignity worthy of the true Roman spirit. Weeping continually over these things I bid you farewell.

Fam. VII, 14.

To Bruno di Firenze,[1] *that the judgment of love is blind.*

Your letter found me alone, or rather with only my cares as company. It was loaded with my praises, and although there was no one present I nevertheless blushed as I read it. The fact that it had followed in its content the testimony not of yourself or of another lover but of that very friendly elder took away some of the embarrassment. For to all those things that were either said therein or could be said along the same lines one could easily answer: the judgment of lovers is usually blind. As we find in Horace, Balbinus takes pleasure in Agna's polyp, while among the people there is the popular love story about the man who, overcome by the love of a one-eyed woman, was sent at length by his concerned parents to foreign shores, and having overcome his love after several years he returned to his country where by chance he met the woman he had loved so strongly. Suddenly shaken by the sad sight, he asked how she had happened to lose her eye. She answered, "I have hardly lost an eye; rather you have found yours." This was indeed plainly and admirably spoken. But let us not add further examples. If ever there were a lover, our elderly friend truly loves all his friends. With respect to any other matters, therefore, if you have any confidence in me, you ought to pay careful attention to him not as if he were Jupiter in Dodona or Apollo at Delphi, but as a particularly truthful man. Whenever his sweet and flattering words pertain to me whom he loves like a father, believe him sparingly except perhaps (and I am not certain whether this could happen to a wise man) insofar as to err and to be deceived are sometimes pleasant. As for the notable poem which was inserted into your letter, it would have received no reply, being sufficiently appreciated by the silent admiration of my heart, were it not for the great merits of your talent which radiates within the great cloud of ignorance of the multitude. You will therefore take in good part a brief poem, still in rough form, which you will receive under separate cover and which I

1. Florentine rhetorician and great admirer of Petrarch.

barely managed to compose since my mind has been so overwhelmed by grief. I send it to you not so much that it should be viewed as an answer, but rather lest there be no answer. Farewell.

Fam. VII, 15.

To Luchino Visconti, lord of Milan,[1] *concerning learned princes.*

I found your letters just as I had hoped, indeed as I had not hoped. I am happy that this exchange has at last intervened between your excellence and my humbleness, and that such a stroke of luck has opened for me access to news of you. As for what the last part of your letter bids me do, I shall devote all my care to it and shall make a special effort, especially since such labor will rather be like pleasure. While the gardener devotes himself to herbs and plants, I devote myself to words and poetry by the inviting murmur of a stream which flows plaintively and divides a fruitbearing grove that branches out on the right and left. You will now taste the first fruits of such study. Perhaps such matters do not affect a mind that is involved in truly lofty cares, as is the custom these days. Nevertheless I know that those great rulers of state, Julius and Augustus Caesar, often found relaxation from the tasks of ruling and from the labors of wars in the tranquillity of our type of idleness, and their hands which were unbending in the use of the sword they directed from striking their enemy to counting syllables, and directing their voices, accustomed to thundering at opposing battle lines and usually heard among the sounds of trumpets and the din of battle, to the sweetness of poetic rhythms. I pass over Nero in order not to stain outstanding study and glorious names through the recollection of that monster. How dedicated to the Muses do we consider Hadrian whose efforts were so determined that he slackened not even when death was near? Unbelievable as it may appear he composed, at the threshold of death, some verses on the departure of the soul, verses which I would repeat here except that I trust they are known to you and to some of your friends. What shall I say about Marcus Antoninus who, when he ascended to power not through ambition but through his merits, retained his former name of philosopher and scorned his new title, believing that

1. Powerful head of the Visconti family, rulers of Milan, and a great admirer of Petrarch.

being a philosopher is considerably greater than being a ruler? The number of such examples is huge; and there is scarcely any prince who considered himself to be both a prince and a man without a background of letters. But the times have changed; kings of the earth have proclaimed war on letters; I believe they fear that they may befoul their gold and jewels with dark ink, but do not fear to possess a mind blind and shabby in its ignorance. But it is a serious and dangerous matter to offend with words a live and powerful prince; nor is there need for a long discourse to produce such offence: whoever lives badly is offended by the naked truth. The dead however are blamed with greater safety. As the Satirist says, "The fallen Achilles is dangerous to no one." Therefore it would be wise not to name the princes of our time who are enemies of letters. It is not safe to write against one who can proscribe, as Asinius Pollio, the great orator, says jestingly against Augustus Caesar; and I now follow his example completing my public indictment without revealing the names of the guilty ones. Almost all are guilty of the same error, and while none desires to follow those rulers friendly to letters whom I have cited above they imitate eagerly Licinius Caesar who (peasant type that he was) hated letters so much that he called them "poison and a public plague," words that are certainly not worthy of an emperor but of a peasant. It was not so with Marius who was likewise of peasant stock but, according to Cicero, truly a man whose involvements or the very nature of letters caused him to turn too late to studies, but he nevertheless loved learned men and especially poets whose talents he hoped some day would celebrate the glory of his deeds. And indeed what man is there, unless he is truly imbued with a rustic insensibility, who though he may not find great pleasure in letters, does not at least desire fame for himself which is never sought without virtue, and never preserved without letters? The memory of men is unstable; paintings are transitory; statues are perishable, and among the inventions of mortals nothing is more stable than letters. Whoever does not fear them, ought to esteem them, and those words of Claudian are true indeed: "Virtue enjoys having the Muses as witnesses; poetry loves whoever does things worthy of a poem." Indeed our contemporaries who do nothing except what is worthy of satire hate letters because they fear them. Therefore they all agree with Licinius and none with Marius nor with the others. Through an apathy the likes of which has never been seen, they allow themselves to be pilfered by plebeians of that very thing which they held most precious, and have slowly arrived at a point where now amidst their wealth they are feeling very serious poverty. And so those who marched into battle for a small amount of wealth or for a small corner of their kingdom abandoned the inestimable treasure left them by their ancestors and allowed foreigners to enter into the palace of the mind, and these in turn drove them away after depriving them not of their royal cloaks but of their heavenly endowment. As a result we see that royal disgrace in which the rabble is learned while kings are crowned asses, as a certain letter by a Roman emperor to the King of the Franks called them. You therefore, being a very great man of our time and lacking nothing in order to rule except the title of king, make it difficult for me to see which of the two views of rulers you adhere to, but I do hope for all the best from you. And thus, not to prolong this excessively, I have sent your excellency a brief poem, which I composed extemporaneously among those trees—a part of which you request in such a friendly manner. If I hear that it pleased you (for I seem to have some ability in that form), I shall appear much more liberal than you think and than my situation would seem to allow. Farewell.

13 March.

Fam. VII, 16.

To Jacopo Fiorentino,[1] that honest censure is to be preferred to false praise.

Your letters full of praises for me which I wish were deserved recently reached me and soothed my mind with a wonderful sweetness. I judged in them rather the affection that they reflected than the effect that they sought. If they were sent by anyone else I would judge them as jesting; but since they emerged from the purest depths of your mind I know that they do not intend to deceive. Would that they did not deceive themselves! Thus, because I am sure that everything you write appears true to you, I rejoice in your affection, and I have pity for your error. However, I would not wish you to err less, so pleased am I at seeming to you to be what I am not. I would prefer to be what I seem; but if this is denied from on high, do continue your friendly error. Indeed, although I was unable to keep myself from returning time and again to your letters, I yet felt that reading them was fraught with danger; for so seriously and elegantly and sweetly and, in short, persuasively did you write them that great care had to be taken lest anything which you expressed so easily should turn a reader into a believer. If you succeed in this you will have a companion in your belief; except that, though your error be generous and innocent, you would involve me in a ridiculous one. Therefore I determined, not without some difficulty, henceforth to turn my eyes away from those portions of your letters, and if hereafter you wish to make me a devoted and zealous reader of your letters I ask you to deal with me in a satirical fashion rather than in a typical one, for in this there is much room. If you tried to pay close attention, you will see in me many qualities that are questionable even to the eyes of a friend, qualities that cannot escape the censure even of a favorable tongue. I beg you devote yourself to this; turn your most eloquent pen this way; reveal me to myself; take

1. An ardent Florentine admirer of Petrarch in whose personal library Petrarch found many classics unknown to him, especially works of Cicero.

over the power of your tongue; seize, bind, strike, burn, cut, restrain all exaggeration, cut away all that is superfluous, and do not fear that you will cause me either to blush or to grow pale. A dismal drink drives away dismal illnesses. I am ill, who does not know it? I must be cured by more bitter remedies than yours; bitter things do not yield to sweet things but rather bitter things purge themselves in turn. If you want to be of benefit to me, write something that hurts me.

I have received together with the other things Cicero's oration in defense of Milo and thank you for it. This is not the first time that you have shown such kindness to me; I shall have it copied and shall return it. The comedy that you seek I confess I wrote at a very tender age with the title of *Philology*. It is now located at a great distance, but even if I had it with me this common friend of ours who will deliver this will make you understand what I think of it and the extent to which I consider it worthy of your ears and of other learned men. I wish you every happiness and well-being and hope that you will always remember me.

Padua, 25 March.

Fam. VII, 17.

To Giberto, grammarian of Parma,[1] *on the academic education of boys.*

Embrace with the strength of your paternal solicitude our young man who is in need of advice and who is troubled by the torments of his age. As you see, he has now arrived at the Pythagorean crossroads of his life; never will his prudence be less nor his danger greater. The left path indeed leads to hell, the right to heaven; but the former is easy, level, very wide, and worn through usage by many people, while the latter is steep, narrow, difficult, and marked with the footsteps of few men. It is not I who say this; but rather the Master and Teacher of all who say it: "Wide is the path that leads to perdition, and many are those who enter it; narrow is the road that leads to life, and few are those who find it." Indeed if our boy were to be abandoned to himself what do you think he would do? He will either follow the rumbling of the multitude in the manner of the blind, or he will take the paved road and, as is the nature of heavy bodies, will be borne downwards by his weight. I beg you, most excellent man, aid him, guide and sustain him in his heedlessness and in his wavering. Let him long to follow the right path with you as his leader; let him learn to ascend. This he will do more readily if you were to pay particular attention to him, and if the unusual medicine of your prudence were to relieve the disease of his youth. You know on what side he leans, and on what side he may be close to destruction; let him be supported on that side with a suitable protection. It is an ancient rule of doctors that opposites are cured with opposites. If he persists in joyfulness oppose it with something sad, and if he is reduced to sadness oppose it with something joyful. If his talent becomes blunted because of too much effort, like a clever farmer restore it by means of seasonal interruptions; if he becomes rusty through inaction, let exercise make him shine again. Let toil season his rest, and rest season his toil, and let his mind be refreshed at times through rest, and at times through action. Furthermore, differences of character are innumerable

1. A Florentine teacher for whom Petrarch had high regard.

and the remedies not only for the diseases of the body but also for the passions of the mind are diverse, so that what is injurious to one, is healthy for another. In this lies the central perception of the teacher. Youthful fear is soothed by friendship and flattery, haughtiness is restrained through threats and sternness; nor is there only one rule of scholastic discipline: unimportant things are to be punished with words, serious things with lashes, one person is to be encouraged with praises, another is to be restrained by shame, another is to be wearied with labor, while still another is to be tamed with the rod. To the generous mind one must give the drive of persistence, to the exhausted mind relief, to the despairing mind assistance, ardor to the lukewarm mind, a bridle to the precipitous mind, and spurs to the slow mind. I am burdening an expert with well-known things so that his memory may once again catch fire by being rubbed. A great portion of the liberal arts consists of things they hold in common, and sometimes we revisit familiar places more readily, while oftentimes we delight not so much in new songs as in well-known ones. To return to our subject, you must, against your will, give our boy a helping hand lest he fall or lest he take the wrong road. Teach him the great danger with which one advances, and then the great labor and the great expense with which one may retreat. Show him how much safer it is henceforth to follow the straight path than to turn off of it with the hope of returning, something that drove many men to destruction. Show him that falls are easy and always ready for anyone, while ascents require great strength, great effort, and much assistance. Show him that the dreams of the rabble are vain and that its opinions concerning all things and especially about passion are wrong. Show him that along the left road there is nothing except filth, darkness, brittleness, and perishable things; and that there is nothing on the right road except beauty, brightness, and immortal strength. Show him how much more appropriately what is written applies to those who follow that former road: "They foresake the right road and they wander through shadowy paths," or those other words: "Their roads are dark and slippery," and those others "The road of ungodly men is full of shadows; they know not to what depths they are sinking." These other words are indeed more appropriate for those traveling over the other road: "Their roads are beautiful and their paths peaceful," and those others: "The road of the just is without obstacles." And about both the same thing can be said: "The Lord knows the ways that are on the right; winding indeed are those that lie on the left." Nor were these words said to one people: "Behold I personally bequeath to you the way of life and the way of death." Make him reflect upon these things, make him see how reprehensible they are according to so many available examples, and how uncertain is the wandering through the tortuous windings of this brief life, whence death often overtakes those who are returning or are considering turning back. In short, as long as the affair remains wholesome and he is master of himself and has not assumed the yoke of sin, teach him how much easier it is to shun that yoke than to shake it off, and impose upon his tender ears as often as possible those poetic words: "By this path one goes to the stars"; and those other words: "This is the path we take to the Elysian Fields, but the one on the left is full of punishments for the evil and sends them to the ungodly Tartarus." In this a wise man of the Hebrews agrees with our poet when he says: "The road of sinners is composed of stones at the end of which there is but the infernal region and darkness and punishment." At his age let him become accustomed to such warnings and let him drink of these teachings. Just as fresh material readily takes on any form, it is also easy to impress upon an as yet unhardened mind whatever habit one wishes. Whenever one offers access to false notions they are more difficult to exclude. Pursue the matter therefore while an opportune time offers some chance of desired success; and be sure of this much, that by providing that boy with this kind of assistance you do more than if you were carefully to pour within him all the liberal arts at the same time. There is little question that knowledge of letters is a great thing, but the virtuous mind is greater, although a receptive student could hope to acquire both from you. You know how much talent can achieve, you know all the better for having experienced it. I know only one thing: it befalls a few to become men of letters, but it is possible for all to be good, providing they voluntarily subject themselves to good leaders. Knowledge is more fastidious indeed than virtue, since it may be more noble. The former deems worthy of itself only the talents of a few; the latter despises the mind of no one except of those who had previously despised her. Farewell.

Padua, 26 March.

Fam. VII, 18.

To Lancillotto di Piacenza,[1] man of arms, on his multiple cares in writing letters to friends, and that love is not assuaged through poetry.

Eager to write, my right hand clings to the pen but is uncertain of what to write, so overwhelmed have I been with the many and various messengers who reached me almost at the same time. From one side the Tiber seemed to interrupt me, from another the Arno, while from still another the Rhone. One informed me of the state of our unfortunate city and indeed of its destruction which I cannot hear without tears since it had such great merit in my eyes; another transmitted to me the complaints of certain gifted youths directed against me in different styles but with a single substance, that they were indignant and seriously disturbed by my having stopped off here when I was expected there, and asking why I so preferred this place to my native land, a question which has been the source of the greatest astonishment to many people. A third messenger delivered the letters of my friends in the Curia containing the substance of a mild, but nevertheless powerful censure of my silence over the distress of my distinguished friend (a silence I was hardly accustomed to keep in less important misfortunes and which I kept not by intent, but rather because of the stupor and sorrow that I felt at the fall of that very famous family). To which was I first to turn? I owed compassion to my Roman friends, explanations to my Florentine friends, and consolation to my transalpine friends. As I hesitated at this crossroads a fourth piece of news reached me. A certain person who was related to me in name and blood, but, even more important, very acceptable and dear to me in his love and in his respect for me, while hastening to France in order to visit me, was struck down by a death which has highly disturbed me since he succumbed to illness, to the rigors of the journey or the harshness of heaven which had forced him to stop off in Savona. With what words shall I console his aged father, the bereavement of his unhappy mother, or the soli-

1. A Lombard nobleman associated with the Visconti, and a strong admirer of Petrarch.

tude of his brothers and sisters when I cannot assuage my own tears? And so, caught in the rush of events, I did what I am accustomed to do in such cases, and as is the custom of my laziness: I determined to neglect all the misfortunes equally, and indeed, if possible, to forget them. While I was in such a condition your letter which arrived so unexpectedly removed my sluggishness and returned my abandoned and forsaken pen to my hand, so sweet was its seriousness and so serious its sweetness. Without question the fact that you included the title of my *Africa* among its contents forced me unwillingly to emit a sigh, for you are not alone in awaiting the conclusion of that work. For me indeed it would be simpler to count the sands of the sea and the stars of the heavens than all the obstacles envious fortune has put in the way of my labors. I myself await its end, uncertain as to whether I had spent sleepless nights utterly in vain or whether at least some joy, though late, is reserved for me for my labor. But if all goes well I shall see to it that no one will precede you in occupying the finest seats for this performance of my talents, of whatever sort it may be. I read the last portion of your letter smilingly; for it helps to know that one has such partners in one's ancient illness, and I am compelled to believe that it is not an ordinary happening when it occurs in such a subject. And indeed the comfort of vernacular poetry which, unless I am mistaken, you humorously request of me, I would say should rather be requested and expected of you if a troubled mind can be cured with words. But alas, what Horace says is all too true: "Do you hope that through these verses you can remove from your heart your heavy sorrows and passions and cares?" They rather increase and find nourishment. Therefore the cure for this illness lies elsewhere and Aesculapius, to tell the truth, was its discoverer. The herbs with which it is prepared, however, are certainly either not in your garden or are unknown to you or else you avoid using them because of their disagreeable taste. Farewell and please accept a remedy which I consider effective against all evils of our lives: examine with great care whatever tries to affect the condition of your mind. So, if you were delighted with the beginning, meditate on this ending.

Fam. VIII, 1.

To Stefano Colonna the elder,[1] *a tearful consolation on the extremely harsh blows of fortune.*

Alas, pitiable old man, alas, most enduring leader, what crime did you commit against Heaven, what did you do to be punished with so long a life? Not undeservingly were you called another Metellus; you were alike in all things, your fatherland, your family, your wealth and attractiveness, your unique and admirable qualities of body and mind, even your outstanding wife, fertile in noble offspring, your consular dignity, the highest command in the Roman army and your honors in conquests and victories, your lengthy old age and a constant good fortune up to the very end. If she has thus far dared to introduce adversity into your life, such as the many you endured in the famous persecutions, she did so in order to remove your noted harshness and to shed light on the dignity of your glory. Fortune continued being propitious to you until almost the hundredth year of your life; and you, likewise born a prince of this world and in the queen city of this world, were able to have your name listed among the very rare examples of the kind of happiness that could certainly be hoped for in this life, not as happened to Sophidius, that needy and lowly plowman who was declared happy by a lying oracle, but as would happen to the most glorious of all Roman leaders of our age in something I would certainly call most difficult and almost impossible, the very best relationship with fortune. Excluding the Arcadian foreigner, you could, as a Roman, sit more confidently with a Roman, as a prince with a prince, a Stefano with a Metellus. Aside from the superiority of your religion which admits of no comparison between pagan and Christian, he also had to yield to you at least in the number of brothers and children

1. An elder of the Colonna family and father of the various church dignitaries with whom Petrarch was friendly, he was deeply involved in Roman politics as a member of the Roman nobility. He was introduced to Petrarch in Avignon by his son Giacomo in 1330, and was highly respected by Petrarch. He eventually outlived all of his sons and reached the age of 100.

that you enjoyed. We read that he had no brother, while you had five, all outstanding men, and, to put it briefly, no less famous for their race and good fortune than for their virtues and glory. He had four sons, praetorians, consuls, censors, and triumphing generals. You had seven: one a Cardinal of the Roman church, another would have gone beyond the Cardinalship if he had arrived at a legal age, three bishops, and two generals who, to tell the truth, were almost equal in military glory to their father. He had three daughters while you had six, concerning whose conduct I would prefer to say nothing rather than to be brief. And, dear God, what a flourishing following of grandchildren and great grandchildren of either sex! What a joyful group, what a pleasant fellowship! Not to prolong this excessively, let us take your first grandson, Giovanni, born of your first son, who was indeed divine and a young man overflowing with that ancient and truly Roman nature whom you would admit to have fully deserved the surname "Colonna" which he acquired. Nor was he called 'of Colonna,' but indeed was referred to as only 'a Colonna,' a column on which most certainly the hopes of friends as well as of the vast and ancient family rested. He had already grown into another Marcellinus, being of the same age, the same strength of mind, the same power of body, as well as love of arms, fondness for horses, and skill in riding; he was also becoming daily another Marcellus and became even more famous than Marcellus. Such being the case, wherever the Roman names echoes you appeared to the multitudes even more fortunate than the most fortunate, if such a thing is possible, and more eminent than the very greatest. But wise men bid us to expect the end, as with that most fortunate king of the Lydians who was admonished by the advice of Solon; for the fact remains that death alone decides on human happiness and even more surprisingly on eternal happiness. No one therefore can be absolutely certain; happiness is a slippery matter. Do you wish that I consider you happy? Then die; the true witnesses of life are one's remains and one's tomb; prior to this, the higher your position the more serious your fall. You would have been the only true example of happiness in our day if your departure had been like the course of your life. There is no evil that is not encompassed in a long lifetime. A lifetime of many years is like a voyage of many days. One does not see only one star in heaven or only one storm on the seas; the rudder must be constantly turned and the sails must be constantly lowered, and often, and there is nothing more dangerous in sailing than having to turn them continually because of shifting winds. You can never expect to enjoy for long an undisturbed calmness either on the sea or in life; the appearance of things changes constantly, and often a very clear morning ends with a very cloudy evening. That famous sailor of Virgil says concerning the sea, "Are you asking me to ignore the appearance of a still sea and quiet waves, or to have faith in this monster?" This is what a wise man says to himself concerning life. The well-armed mind, prepared by constant meditation, fears nothing; infinite adversity casts down the unprepared mind anticipating nothing but joyful things. But I return to the changes in your fortune.

You long ago buried five of your brothers. Who is there who would not have been cast down by the fall of so many "columns?" You nevertheless remained unshaken, and as is appropriate for a great and unconquerable mind you transferred the entire burden of your household upon yourself alone. You then compensated for the irreparable damage with immortal fame, and you found consolation in the memory of its very great deeds; and a long succession of grandsons replaced your brothers. Meanwhile your beloved and dear wife was taken from you, "Fortunate in her death and not reserved for this grief." She was indeed much more fortunate in her death than the wife of Evander. It was to her that the previous citation referred; for an opportune death decreed that she should miss seeing the bitter destruction of only one son, but your wife the destruction of a great number of children. The oldest of your sons upon whom you relied heavily passed away. After you had gone through so much, the painful double blow struck you very hard but you nevertheless remained firm on the crumbling foundations. Then when the others achieved an enviable greatness and glittered in an astonishing light of success, you made your peace with fortune, and mingling the bitter with the sweet you soothed your longing for the dead with consolation over the survivors. Now the sorrow of the earlier losses had slowly been erased, and, as I said, in your new happiness you could have died happier than Metellus. Your long life makes you resemble Priam even more than Metellus, for while Metellus was buried by his loved ones, Priam buried his. A truly different state of affairs! Oh fierce fortune! It appeared as if you had not given sufficient proof of your fickleness, so you added to the ancient examples that of our beloved Stefano whom you deprived quickly and through various deaths of his children and grandchildren, and whom you have now changed from a most happy father to a spectacle of pitiable bereavement. Oh magnanimous man, oh remarkable Stefano, for a while you appeared so happy that you could not have ever again become unhappy, and you appeared so surrounded by loved ones that you could never have feared solitude, and so close to death that you could no longer fear the death of adolescent sons. You seemed to stand well beyond the danger of any weapon. But Fortune is not only an uncontrollable and cruel goddess, but rather a servant of the Lord and most energetic executrix of the divine will. She acts secretly in extraordinary and inconceivable ways, while her games are always as mysterious and varied as they are often sorrowful and tearful. There is little doubt that in this age of ours she has given no more perfect example of her fickleness. So insidious is she that I am inclined to believe she favored your glorious ascent in order to make herself known to the world, for having bestowed so much favor upon you, she felt that your defeat would be more remarkable and your fall from so high a position would be more terrible, for you could never have been so unhappy unless previously you had been extremely happy. The great number of such outstanding children makes your losses so much more remarkable. Alas, most bitter sweetness; alas, toilsome rest; alas, fatal blandishments! What is left for men to fear or desire to hold on to or avoid? It is vexatious not to have possessed anything that pleases; it is sad to have enjoyed transitory delights. You have lived too long, I admit; but it was appropriate so that you should die a wiser man. You could have considered fortune as something dependable if you had only perceived her other face. Oh you who have been cast about by many misfortunes, what do you expect me to say? Do not hope, do not despair; one is the mark of an inane spirit, the other of a weak one. And, indeed, I ask you, for what can you hope? More children? Another wife? Age is against you, for old age is as suitable for marriage as winter is for the harvests. An aged bridegroom is a ridiculous kind of joke. On the other hand, why despair? Of so many children you have none left; if you have yourself, it is sufficient. There is no greater wealth, no better position than to have one's mind under control. We can find one who had a hundred and fifteen children; Erotimus, a king of the Arabs, as astonishing as it may sound, is said to have had seven hundred. To be in possession of one's self happens to a few. Do you miss conversations with your children? Converse with yourself. To converse with others is possible for everyone, but to converse with one's self is reserved for a few. There are many things you can converse about with yourself, for you did many things in such a long life, the remembrance of which could be most pleasant. As Cato says in Cicero's works, "Not all can be Scipios or Maximi and enjoy the recollection of their assaults upon cities, or land and naval battles, or wars waged, or participation in triumphs." But you belong to that class of men whose recollections of their own accomplishments is a glorious joy. Recall what you did at home and in the service, what you suffered on land and sea, what labors and dangers you faced, what notable things happened to you. I believe that you will confess that even without ever having had children you would have been a great man and would have been happy though not with the happiness that comes from leisure. But you were not without children, and these happened to be such that it was just as difficult to lose them as it was most pleasing to have them. Add to this that nothing unforeseen has happened to you, for your wisdom was such that you foresaw not only those things that happened to you but all that could have happened; for nothing that is possible is inconceivable to the wise man, while all things unforeseen happen to fools.

I did not want to say all this; there is something greater in my mind about which I can refresh your memory with a single word, but so that you would not think that what I once heard from you does not stay with me, I shall speak at greater length. Recall then (the image of those days is always before my eyes) the time after I had worked with you in Rome ten years ago when we by chance happened to be alone one day at dusk, and were walking on that Via Lata which leads from your home to the Capitoline. We finally stopped where that road is crossed by another which descends from the hills to the Arch of Camillus and then down to the Tiber. While standing at that crossroads, we discussed many things about the state of your home and your household, since no one interrupted us, and since at that time it was being agitated by a very serious civil war despite its record of having proven more outstanding than others in confronting outside dangers. It so happened that mention was made of one of your sons with whom at that time you were angry, I believe, because of the evil tongues of troublemakers rather than because of a father's normal anger. But you favored me with your kindness, and you allowed me to do what you had never previously permitted others to do, to prevail upon you to have your son return into your graces. In any event, after you had complained about him to me in a friendly fashion, with a changed expression you finally added words more or less like these (not only do I remember the event, but my memory supplies me with the very words you used): "My son and your friend, whom you compel me to regard with fatherly affection, spewed forth many things against my old age which would much better have been left unsaid. But since I cannot deny your request, I shall, as they say, forgive and forget. After this day you will not notice a trace of anger either in my looks or in my words. There is only one thing I must mention, concerning which I wish to make you a witness for all time. Among the first accusations leveled against me was that I had become involved in more battles than I ought to, considering the dignity of my advanced age, and thereby would leave my children a legacy of hatred and of discord. I call God to witness that I have undertaken wars for no other reason than my love of peace. Both my advanced age and my spirit now growing cold in this bosom which is of the earth, and my long experience with human affairs make me eager for peace and quiet. On the other hand, I remain firm and determined not to turn my back to hardship. I would prefer a more peaceful existence, but if destiny ordains it I would prefer to go to my grave fighting than learning how to be a subservient old man. As for what they say concerning my legacy, I wish to answer only this (and I beg you to pay the closest attention to my words): Would that I could leave my children some kind of legacy, but contrary to my personal wish fate decreed otherwise; and—I say this with great sadness—the fact of the matter is that, contrary to the natural order, I shall be the heir of all my children." While you said these things you turned your tearful eyes away. Whether you said all this because of a foreboding or as a divine admonition I do not know, although the deified Vespasian is witness to the fact that rulers often do prophesy concerning their own children when he predicted the kind of death that one of his children was to suffer, and the assumption of imperial authority for both of them. I myself must confess that on that particular day I took your words lightly as if they had been spoken by chance or perhaps through anger, nor did I suspect that they could contain so much power of prophecy. When after a long period of time I saw that the prophecy was coming true, judging from the frequent deaths of your children, I spoke about the matter with my friends. Then it spread among the people. As a result Giovanni of venerable memory, of the Roman Cardinalate, and Prince of your family, with three of his brothers already dead, succeeded with his prayers in having me recount the entire matter to him. After I unwillingly did so, he said with a deep sigh, "Would that my father were not such an accurate prophet!" In that same year, because of the fatal misfortune to your first born and to your grandsons, he began ever more to fear your prophecy to the point where, I believe, overcome by his grief, he fulfilled the prediction of his father with his own recent death and with sorrowful but confident faith in its inevitability. Just as the entire matter appeared extraordinary to those who heard it, so it is dreadful and amazing to me more and more each day. I do not doubt that you remember all of it; but I recall it in such a way that I still seem to see that ancient marble tomb which stands at the corner and on which we rested with our elbows. I also see the expression on your face, and I seem to hear those words with my very ears. Such being the case, your misfortunes should not appear intolerable since you had foreseen them so much in advance; meditation arms the mind. What do you suffer that you did not know you would? No one deplores having begotten mortal children unless he is also mad and forgetful of his own mortality. We love to have children like to ourselves. But nothing belongs to us more than the innate condition of having to die which is common to all those who are born and which alone adheres inseparably to our bones and to our very marrow. Why then do men grieve for the death of their children? Certainly not because of the certain and acknowledged rights of nature but because of the unexpected arrival of death. As much as I can determine, what happened to you was neither unforeseen nor unknown. The primary cause for lamenting which involves the grief of an unexpected blow is thus removed. Consequently, either you subject your feelings to the divine power as do all learned and well-established men, and bear whatever happened to you as calmly as you foresaw it; or, since it is difficult to overcome the rights of nature, and if it was perhaps paternal love that caused you to utter a reluctant sigh, so much time has elapsed since you first began to mourn that now it is plausible to assume that your tears have dried. Grief diminishes with time, as does joy. If there is anything good in human passions, it is that none of them is perpetual. But since a great number of words do not appeal to doers of great things, I shall come to an end.

Just as the beginning of this letter, if natural feeling has so decreed, could be read by a sensitive father with moist eyes, so will it behoove a strong and indomitable man to read the end with dry eyes. I beg you, therefore, to collect your wits and with the greatest effort receive the assault of unbridled fortune. Whoever withstands the first assault will be victor. She overcomes most people with terror rather than with her power. But what am I doing? What I urge you to do I hope that you have already done. I implore and beg you to do this lest (since the mind is often more curious about things found only in the memory) you should slide into new miseries by recalling old ones, and by indulging excessively in your fatherly grief you should once again reopen the scars of your now closed wounds. Let those things slip away that one cannot bring back: whether they afflict you or delight you is in your power. The public calls you bereft of children, an old man, a wretched man. You must believe that the multitude is mad as usual, and that you are happy. You drank from both jars of fortune and know how they taste; pleasant things made you glad, but bitter things are making you cautious so that you may understand the degree to which favorable events ought to be trusted. You already knew all this, I believe; but you will not deny the fact that you never saw it more clearly. There are no more effective schools than those in which experience is teacher; what you had heard from many quarters you have now seen, and you have confirmed with your own eyes what your ears had told you. You now see that truth about which almost all mortals speak, that Fortune is nothing; you see that what the multitude calls happiness is but a myth; you lost that happiness, and you have found another which is more sound and enduring. You say, "And among so many sorrows what happiness can you be referring to?" What do you think I refer to except the kind that no one can take away from you if you do not wish? I refer to that happiness which is the opposite of the first one: to be content with what you have; to know that those things with which you seemed to be blessed were not yours; finally, having realized your error, to attain the truth though late; but before all else that the power of fortune need not be feared by humans. What more shall I say? I shall stop here. You entered this life naked, you shall exit naked; and you can scorn magnanimously what people call the mistress of human affairs; she has hurt you so much that she can hurt no more. What else can she be planning now, what else can she be threatening? She has emptied her quiver and stands disarmed; she no longer has arms to hurl at you nor do you, in what remains, have any point where you may be struck. Farewell.

8 September.

Fam. VIII, 2.

To Olimpio.[1]

There is nothing anywhere on this earth which can be called either happy or delightful as long as we live. I realize how improperly I may be speaking: I should really have said as long as we do not live; since when we do begin to live we shall know nothing except what is sweetest and most pleasant. Note that while I depart and return happily, I do not enjoy the highly desirable pleasure of seeing and conversing with you and that excellent friend of ours. I was scarcely able to contain my tears when I returned home today and learned that you both had been here at the same time and had crossed the Alps and suffered all the hardships of the roads in your desire to see me; and that having failed to find me, as though deprived of a great expectation, you had departed sadly. I learned all this from my servants and from your letters which you left among my books like pledges of undying devotion and like payment for your brief stay and assurances of your return. But since in adversity the wise man always turns to the brighter side of things, let us imagine that it was an act of heaven, and that by not having found me as you wished, your overwhelming desire to meet with your friend has not cooled, and that as a result of the irritation caused by my absence the joy we would have had perhaps for a few days will be compensated for by the delight of enjoying each other's company over a period of many years. However, she alone can accomplish this whose inflexible hardness often blunts the weak edge of human counsel. I for my part imagine it to be so, I think about it in this fashion, I hope for it, and in this hope I find rest from the many labors that besiege me. But because how I feel about this and what I would like to urge you to do require time, and in order to allow this messenger to hasten his departure, I am compelled to defer my thoughts to another time. Farewell.

5 May.

1. Mainardo Accursio of Florence, son of a famous jurist and one of Petrarch's earliest friends, to whom he also gave a classicizing name.

To the same correspondent, an exhortation to live together and to deliberate on the most appropriate place.

I waited most anxiously and still I have not found an available messenger or a day of leisure. Therefore, the ideas that I had conceived I shall now explain in part, but not indeed as I had conceived them, for I realize how much greater power an uninterrupted discourse possesses. You know how that greatest of all eastern rivers which is distinguished by its many riverbeds can become not only passable but contemptible as well. Let us therefore comply with the circumstances and let what is possible be pleasing when what is pleasing is not possible. Since my trust in the present messenger has hardly been tested, I shall, in order to allay your anxiety, pursue only that one portion of your letter in which you advise against a return to the mouth of the Sorgue. You seem to be deeply disturbed about this, and I understand why since I was unable to resist our dear Socrates who often called me there. Being finally convinced by his entreaties, I agreed to go provided the conditions involved assured a legitimate reason for settling there and no lack of the necessities of life (of the life, I might add, of my comrades and of the great numbers who are accustomed to meet with me; for my personal life is not only provided with all the necessities I need but I fear that it may be pampered by having too many such things). If this proved acceptable to him, I would gladly have gone along satisfied about all these matters. Furthermore, I knew that our great leader was located there as well as all of you whom death had spared for me, and so I was drawn by love of you as if by most powerful chains. Now everything has changed; the crowd of friends has departed as has our leader, and my Socrates is still there alone. Although by the inveterate power of habit he desires to remain there and to have all his friends and especially me there with him, he will never dare, with all hope gone forever, summon us into lands where all of us would be foreigners and strangers. Nor would it be appropriate for men who drag around mortal and perishable bodies to say what the happy souls deprived of their bodies say in Virgil: "We have no certain hope; we live in shadow and spend our time on the banks of rivers and meadows made fresh by streams." If such things sufficed, Vaucluse, where the Sorgue originates, could provide us all in abundance with clear streams, thatched homes and straw beds; but nature requires something more. The multitude considers philosophers and poets unyielding and inflexible, but it is wrong in this as in many other things, for they too are of flesh, preserve their humanity, and shun passions. There are, however, certain limits to the needs of philosophers and poets, limits which may be bypassed only with doubt and suspicion. As Aristotle says, "Nature by itself is insufficient for indulging in speculation; this requires a healthy body, food and other necessities." And as the Satirist says, "Cruel poverty cannot sing under the Pierian grotto or touch the Bacchic wand, without the support needed by the body night and day." There is great and universal agreement among learned men concerning the needs of philosophers and poets, but all are expressed in different ways. Therefore, to continue where I left off, Vaucluse would provide a pleasant lodging for some brief period of time as it did for me earlier, to help free us from the weariness of the passions of the cities. In the long run, however, it would neither assure nor provide for our needs. Without doubt we must look ahead not only at the long run but to the very end, so that we might avoid that impropriety which Seneca directs against the human species when he says: "Everyone gives thought to the parts of life, no one to the whole." Those are true words indeed and this is what precipitated our plan so that amidst such varied occupations (which are simultaneously lamentable and ridiculous), we not ignore where we are steering the ship of our fluctuating life. I know that Vaucluse would be a desirable residence especially in the summertime, and how that retreat proved ever more acceptable to me than to anyone else you may see in my ten years' stay there. But if I might boast to you (who are indeed like another me) without sounding as though I were bragging, I ask you this: aside from the peacefulness of the mountains and of the fountain and of the woods, what of any moment has happened in that place that could be considered, if not more outstanding, certainly more noteworthy than my residing there? I may even dare suggest that for many people that place is known as much for my name as for its certainly extraordinary spring. I have said all this so that no one will suspect that I am now rejecting that rustic place which I always found most suitable for my affairs, in which I often exchanged the cares of the city for rural relaxation, and which I tried to make famous, not only in the choice of the place itself, but in my rustic dwelling and, I hope, in the stronger mortar of my words and songs.

It is pleasing for me to recall that it was there that I started my *Africa* with such great energy and effort that now, as I try to apply the file to what I started, I seem to shudder at my boldness and at the great framework I laid. There also I completed a considerable portion of my letters in both prose and poetry and almost all of my *Bucolicum carmen* in such a brief period of time that you would be astounded if you knew. No other place ever offered more ease or greater incentives. That solitude gave me the courage to collect the most illustrious men of all kinds and all centuries into one work. There in separate volumes I started indicating those qualities that should be adopted and praised in the solitary life and in religious idleness. Finally, hoping to alleviate in those shady places that youthful fire which raged within me for so many years, as you well know, I often used to flee there during my youth as though to a secure fortress. But, alas, how incautious I was! Those very remedies became destructive; for my burning cares accompanied me and the fact that there was absolutely no help against the raging fire in so solitary a place made me burn even more hopelessly. Thus, the flames in my heart spread through my bones and filled those valleys and skies with a mournful, but, as some called it, pleasant tune. From all of this emerged those vernacular songs of my youthful labors which today I am ashamed of and repent, but are, as we have seen, most acceptable to those who are affected by the same disease. What else can I say? If anything I wrote anywhere else is compared with what I wrote there, that place in my judgment is superior to all others. That residence, therefore, is and will continue to be as long as I live most pleasing to me in the memory of my youthful concerns whose remnants I continue elaborating to this very day. Nevertheless, unless we deceive ourselves, a man should deal with things other than what youths deal with. At that age I saw these other things perhaps only indistinctly, and if I perceived them, the blindness of love hindered my judgment as did the foolishness of that age and the weakness of my insights. My respect for our leader was also a hindrance since I preferred remaining subject to him more than enjoying liberty, feeling indeed that without him neither liberty nor the joys of life could be realized. Now we have lost in almost a single shipwreck both him and whatever joy remains. Furthermore, and I can hardly add this without deep sighs, that laurel of mine which was once so green has been withered by the power of an unexpected storm, that laurel which made not only the Sorgue but the Durance dearer than the rushing Ticino. And the veil which covered my eyes has been lifted so that I can now see the difference between Vaucluse and Venusian territory, and the open valleys and spectacular hills of Italy with her very attractive and flourishing cities. I can also see the difference between the single river and source of the Sorgue and so many shining springs, so many rambling rivers, so many lakes full of fish, the two famous seas in the distance, which seem to fortify both shores of Italy with their curved and splendid windings, not to mention the rest of the natural beauties, and especially the talents and customs of the people which need not be mentioned here. And yet note how many first impressions cling to the mind and how much power is exerted in our affairs by force of habit. To open all the inlets of my heart to you in keeping with the laws of true friendship, I feel my emotions rebel against my reason in this matter, and I must confess that I sigh for that valley which I have just repudiated so strongly, and a strange love for that place still seems to haunt me. I have really gone on too long and have become aware of the murmurings of the waiting messenger, and so I shall simply say farewell.

18 May.

Fam. VIII, 4.

To the same correspondent, an exhortation for moderate goals, and for not deferring plans for a better life.

All love is naturally impatient and is eager for haste; and there is no speed which is not slow for a lover. I wrote many things to you yesterday, but since many things were still left and the mind burns to express them, and since no messenger was available, I turned to my servants. Weighing their sense of obedience, I turned first to my cook to show you how much I am a victim of my stomach, since I felt that I could spare him without discomfort or indeed great inconvenience. I speak about the cook who, as you know, was considered the most vile of servants among our ancestors and began to enjoy some esteem only after the conquest of Asia. Would that we had never conquered Asia so that it would never have conquered us with its pleasures! But let me get back to the main point. My cook then will become my traveler, and a farmer will act as my cook. You know that I find great delight in country food and that I agree with Epicurus only in his position regarding light nourishment, for he placed the apex of his much-praised pleasure in his gardens and in his vegetables. I often enjoy in my rustic living a pleasure which has become continuous for me while it can be only periodic for those who are delicate and refined. Is there hardly anybody so disgustingly proud who would not find it pleasant at least once a year to recline on grassy banks under the open sky or in the hut of a friendly shepherd despite the absence of overhanging gilded beams or heavy silverware to weigh down the table, or the lack of purple draperies adorning the marble walls? Is there anyone with such a vain thirst that he is repelled by any goblet not covered with precious stones or not having lions battling in a golden grove testifying to the workmanship of Polyclitus? Or indeed is there anyone with such a fancy hunger as to be unable at some time to enjoy a rustic meal despite the lack of exotic birds from Colchis, or a flatfish caught on foreign shores, or a pike traditionally considered the best of fish captured between the two bridges of the Tiber? These things, therefore, which are sometimes tried by gentle stomachs enticed by the rarity of the experience, have always been for me the bounty of nature, and if I were allowed to change I would always prefer this kind of living. I do not reject more sumptuous meals, but I prefer to have them very rarely and after long periods of time. Do not think that I have been speaking in vain since I ought to be speaking at length about something else. Please accept what I have said without concern for my inconvenience, and do not send my cook back to me before you have given serious thought to the heart of the problem we now face. I ask you to keep an open mind and not be stubborn. What I say to one I say to all and I wish that this letter if possible be disseminated by word of mouth among all our friends. If a messenger should be traveling westward from there I wish that it could be sent especially to our Socrates so that all might know the sensible things I say as well as the foolish ones. Much can indeed be said more loftily but, unless I am mistaken, not much that is more useful. But you will decide this for yourself. I shall proceed as I had planned. Avarice has this peculiar and ugly characteristic: it is insatiable, and while it promises things in the future it forbids their use in the present. This thirst for possessions is never satisfied by seeking more things but by coveting fewer things. You need not believe me but rather the philosophers who consider this the road to true riches. As for me, I have set a limit to my desires and I accept that poetic saying as though it were spoken by an oracle: the miser always lacks something. And so that I myself would not always lack something, I did what follows in that saying: I set a definite limit to my desires, a boundary that I reached long ago despite the blows of fortune. Nor shall I fear that my descendants accuse me of sloth; I live for myself and not for them and together with my friends I am master of my own affairs and not the agent of someone I do not yet know with any certainty. However, why do I toil so greatly for myself, since it pays to walk unimpeded on a rough road? Why do we now still think about useless and fatal burdens? Flaccus puts it elegantly when he says: "Do not restrict your long-range hope to a limited space." So that you would not think that he referred to a small proportion of life rather than to all of life, he says the same thing in another place: "A short life prohibits the assumption of long-range hope." It is so; he is not wrong; nothing is truer. For although we may divide in whatever way possible and with minute distinction the brief period of this life, and try to widen it into whatever subdivisions, and reduce all such subdivisions into a single group, and carefully put them together; and although you may mentally view the whole from the first to the last day of this very long life, you will often confess that the total of this very fleeting period of time is very brief. If we look behind and around us, we shall note that a good part of this period has already been taken from us. Let us therefore come together at the end of the road which without question is the roughest part; let us abandon all superfluous things and hold on to the necessary ones. Why do we procrastinate? Why do we delay? Day follows upon day and month upon month, "and the year rolls round on its own tracks," as Maro says most clearly; and in stopping, it simply begins over again without ever pausing to enjoy some rest. What therefore is the proper way for waiting or expecting the end? We have witnessed the white-haired companions of old age and we have received the messengers of death. What do we wait for? That our eyes become blind with old age, that our legs begin to tremble, that our backs begin to curve? Who is the astrologer that can be our guarantor of a long life? The fact is that whether it be Petosiris, or Neclepso, or Nigidius among others, and indeed truth itself, how mad will it nevertheless be to delay to the very last minute what could be done in a fair period of time and conveniently?

Either I know nothing at all with certainty, or it is true that unless we are men now we shall never be. Let no one flatter us, let no one beguile us with the name of young men. I grant that we are not decrepit; nor are we old men; but certainly we are not boys either. The time has come to leave behind youthful pursuits. Did I say, "the time has come?" Would that it had indeed and that it were not passing on! But believe me, it has passed on, and a great part of it is already behind us. I do not deny that there is some left: but if it too is not to slip by because of our sluggishness we must cope with it swiftly, otherwise we shall undergo what happens to almost all the multitude: namely, that by looking back at our youth and directing our minds and eyes to it we fall into the pit of old age, and lying there deluded, we lament the frailty of nature and the brevity of life and repeat too late the complaints of the writer Theophrastus which were magnificently rejected by Cicero and Sallust and Seneca. Why do we not seize whatever little remains to us and turn it to our advantage according to that opinion of Seneca which had previously been expressed by Cicero: "Let us hasten to do what is done by those who depart late and wish to compensate for the swiftness of time," so that we might attain even before the end of the road a truly happy life that has thus far escaped us? It is never too late to do what is beneficial. For although procrastination deserves censure, all attempts at improvement are worthy of praise. There is no doubt that what is good cannot be untimely: otherwise it could hardly be good if it ceases being timely, as we believe repentance to be for the dead, which would serve only to increase their misery. On the other hand, repentance is not ineffectual for old men. Let us not be ashamed of undertaking to do now what was proper to do sooner; let us rather be ashamed of the fact that we are not doing it even now. As our hair grows white it is shameful not to realize our wavering plans. Let us therefore begin right now and let us consider clearly in what state our affairs are, nor ours alone but of all mortals in general. I ask, what is the life of man except a short breath and a thin wisp of vapor? Let each man sense what a rotten, feeble, and frail body he inhabits. We pretend in the name of a long-standing common error, and though aware of our ignorance we imagine eagerly the close proximity of an eternity. That is the way it is: there is no one who considers himself as dying. Indeed there is no one who does not know that he is mortal, but each postpones the day of his death, which could be this very day, into the distant future. Thus the very thing whose presence we fear most, we confidently assume will always be absent, since there is nothing that is more ambiguously absent and nothing that can be present with greater suddenness.

Those words of Aristotle are unfamiliar to the wretched: "Those things which are at a great distance are not feared; all know that they will die but because death is not close, they do not worry." This is what that great man said in his *Rhetoric*. I, however, agree that men are not concerned about death, and I do not deny, as he says, that the cause is negligence. But I contend that his view is false, for what can be more false than to believe that death is at a great distance when the shortness of life itself shows that it is not too far away? That it is always threatening and hanging over our heads can be seen in the astonishing power of human misfortunes, in the inevitable accidents, and in their infinite variety. Therefore, men are not concerned about death not because it is remote but because they believe it to be so. If they knew how close it is (which they necessarily know otherwise they would not turn their eyes elsewhere), I believe that either they would begin to fear death or arm themselves with virtue in such a way that they would justly not fear her as the beginning of another life. Indeed nowadays whom do you find who does not grasp the hope of a long life without any concern for virtue; and though life may be very extensive for them, it is always short. At the end of their life, though their expectation is fixed and clear, it still fails them. I ask you to point out to me someone who does not expect to outlive his contemporaries? We arrange our thoughts and our actions in such a way as to believe that no one will be our heir and that we shall be the heirs of everyone, although meanwhile our heritage may have its claimers and both sides are clearly deceived. Let us free ourselves of this mockery, and if our reason does not move us, let examples do so since they are readily available and are brought to our attention despite our reluctance. Once seen, they settle deep within our hearts, and become most difficult to overlook unless we exercise an impious contempt and a fatal forgetfulness.

Do we wish to know what we are, and where we are going, and what end awaits us after our hesitations and evasions? Then let us consider others. One may not have the eyes of a lynx or the sight of that fellow who from the watch-tower in Lilybaeum saw the Punic fleet leave the port of Carthage. I ask you to look closer, at nearby Ostia, at our neighboring dwellings, and the very cities we inhabit. But I ramble too much. Let us return to our own households and dwellings; we shall see how suddenly whatever we held dearest on earth vanishes like a dream or like a shade from before our eyes. Friends who would have gladly died for us if the situation required caused our lives to become sad and too lonely with their death. They did not leave us here perpetually but preceded us as they hastened to the same end. They enjoyed their fate in time, let us enjoy ours, for as Flaccus says: "We all are forced toward the same end, and fate sooner or later empties the urn of all as she exits." As their turn came sooner, ours will come later, but with suddenness; there is no room for delay. How little it matters whether one dies old or young! If you consider the end of life which is the old age common to everyone, that saying is indeed true that no one dies who is not old. If you consider the opinions of men, no one dies who is not a child. But I shall bypass those things, for they present themselves in such large numbers that I could never cover them all. It grieves me that I am impeded by my tears from enumerating the intimate losses and the sweet promises that this sorrowful and fatal year, which has been the worst of the century, has deprived us of. I confess that there are only a few of you from all of the human race, with whom I would choose to live and die; nor would I exclude several others except for the fact that either marriage or business or age or other difficulties have separated them from us and forced us to love them from a distance. Nor indeed is it now a matter of superiors whose kindness may be considerable but whose presence can hardly be counted upon, for there stands in the way of mutual intimacy a disparity of fortune and that poison of friendship, pride, which prompts such superiors to be fearful of demeaning themselves and to expect to be worshipped rather than loved. What impedes us from completing together what remains of our life, however little that may be, through peace of mind and in the study of the arts, and, as Seneca says, "if we have lived on the waters (to) die in port?" What we

, but let him not love anyone nor let him be loved by
" When we have assembled in a single place—what is
at can prevent us from enjoying our future? If indeed
m to approve this dwelling of mine (not undeserv-
or while perhaps it is not like the one possessed by
tinus in Virgil, "august, huge, and having a hundred
" it is certainly pleasant, solitary, healthy and fully
f hospitality for a few who get along so well); if then
cause you to gather here—let us cast our anchor, and
ear as though we had found our port. And if per-
e group of friends increases, drawn by the attractive-
r life of ease, there is a more impressive house in the
the city which I keep empty for such an eventuality.
my household would fill only a very small part of
e, even though in my desire for solitude my house-
rs huge.
do not consider these words confining chains and
t you will be restricted to one place. There will be
e of us Bologna, mother of studies, in which we
early youth; and it will be pleasant, now that our
d our hair has changed, to see it again and to view
on of that city and of our own minds with more
gment and, by comparison, to note how little we
progressed in our lives. There will be near the
a, the home of your venerable Antonnio which
e, without spurning the mediocrity of the posi-
aving turned down many more lucrative ones,
 usually say, you considered my nearness highly
here you will be the host of all. If we would like
ttle further, we shall have Milan close by, as well
e former representing the glory of land-bound
 latter of maritime cities; the former having at-
and rivers, the latter having its waters resounding
d with sails. There we shall see huge Lake Lario
earby from which the river Adda emerges; we
Verbano which is called Lake Maggiore by its
d which the Ticino intersects. We shall see the
which the Lambro and the Sebino and the
nd not far from there the Benaco from which

VIII, 5.

formerly did obediently for one lord, shall we not dare do
for ourselves while we are alive, or is it that our fondness for
servitude was greater than our love of liberty? Although that
kind of servitude might appear, if you like, more pleasing
than liberty because the affection and lack of insolence on
the part of that excellent man justified it, nevertheless to be
under another, to obey another, to live with another, could
have the appearance of a more distinguished servitude but
certainly could never be the same as true liberty. Please note
that now such liberty, although unseen, is possible for us,
and we have become our own masters somewhat sooner than
expected. Unless I am mistaken I feel I know the minds of
all of us, though perhaps I do not know all the impediments
involved. Yet I do feel that nothing which concerns you is
hidden from me. We are not rulers of the land and sea, as
Aristotle says, but this is not necessary for a happy life. We
have, however, what should suffice for our modest spirits,
being willing, as they are, to adjust to nature. But if we are
individually self-sufficient, what can we suppose will happen
to all of us when we can offer one another a hand and can
satisfy whatever needs another may have? We have more
than enough, believe me: and we shall have to fear envy
rather than want. Why then are we waiting? Why are we
divided by seas and mountains and rivers? In short why does
not a single home unite us, who were once willingly united,
unless it is because we flee any new and unusual things, and we
consider it foolish to lay aside a promised hope and not to
hear fortune beckoning us to her pursuits, even though it is
much more foolish to disdain real and solid things than to
place our hopes in vain shadows? I call upon not only my
conscience but the present letter to bear witness to the fact
that all the blame must fall on you and whoever may be slow
in accepting my sound plan.

Why do you not hasten here when the chains which tied
you down have now been loosened and cut; and please do not
accuse me of pride because I seem to lead rather than follow.
My mind is ready to do either. If there is a more suitable place
anywhere for us to live I shall proceed to it immediately. I
am not one accustomed to spurn any trustworthy advice. I

believe there is no one who has greater trust or confidence in friends. But if this place is preferred in your judgment, which your letters seem to admit, what is now keeping you? Do not be tempted by ambition; it never is about to say "this is enough"; it always seems to want more. This is so especially because, as with oil and wine, so is it with time and life: the dregs lie in the bottom! To limit yourself to such dregs while neglecting what is closer to the surface is ridiculous. It is a custom of travelers to find lodging before night; I implore that we make similar plans and after many labors of the journey prepare ourselves finally for that eternal lodging. For this I offer you, oh brothers dearer to me than light, whatever resources I command or advice I can give, whatever delight or favor can be expected of me, whatever support from the things which are improperly called mine since they really belong to fortune, in short all of myself which I can do without pride, as well as my books, my gardens, and anything else I own. However, those things which are needed so badly in this human life of ours are not few, and while they might be expressly mentioned in a letter such as this, dignity forbids it. Finally, so that I might end with a vow and a prayer, may the consoling Holy Spirit inspire us to conspire at least in this, that while we desire to continue in this life, we may aspire to peace and tranquillity, and that we who have sighed all day may breathe normally at twilight. Farewell.

Fam. VIII, 5.

To the same corresponden

I had scarcely sealed n
satisfied, the potential sw
pies my mind and though
hand, and as the messen
opportunity, I decided t
speaking at greater leng
same goads that I feel. I
and there has never be
any way—although ho
problem for human c
happiness is inseparab
piness may be lost, we
we wished, nor woul
we know that happin
the comfort of frien
and why does the slo
of all? As Seneca say
we love even when
appearance and pr
pleasure." We must
For if some philoso
that they considere
of human actions,
who would be so
pleasure which vii
I ask you, what li
friends whose pe
as one, bound as
in all things; wit
but instead harr
and unstudied c
If such a life b
shall see anyw
the expense of
and I shall ind
"Let Nero po

of gold
anyone
there th
you see
ingly, f
King La
columns
capable
the fates
let us ap
chance th
ness of ou
middle of
I and all
that house
hold appe
Please
believe tha
on one sid
spent our
thinking a
the conditi
mature jud
have truly
Po, Piacenz
you manag
tion after
since, as you
desirable. T
to travel a li
as Genoa, th
cities and th
tractive lakes
and congeste
with Como
shall see the
inhabitants ar
Eupili from
Oglio issue,

formerly did obediently for one lord, shall we not dare do for ourselves while we are alive, or is it that our fondness for servitude was greater than our love of liberty? Although that kind of servitude might appear, if you like, more pleasing than liberty because the affection and lack of insolence on the part of that excellent man justified it, nevertheless to be under another, to obey another, to live with another, could have the appearance of a more distinguished servitude but certainly could never be the same as true liberty. Please note that now such liberty, although unseen, is possible for us, and we have become our own masters somewhat sooner than expected. Unless I am mistaken I feel I know the minds of all of us, though perhaps I do not know all the impediments involved. Yet I do feel that nothing which concerns you is hidden from me. We are not rulers of the land and sea, as Aristotle says, but this is not necessary for a happy life. We have, however, what should suffice for our modest spirits, being willing, as they are, to adjust to nature. But if we are individually self-sufficient, what can we suppose will happen to all of us when we can offer one another a hand and can satisfy whatever needs another may have? We have more than enough, believe me: and we shall have to fear envy rather than want. Why then are we waiting? Why are we divided by seas and mountains and rivers? In short why does not a single home unite us, who were once willingly united, unless it is because we flee any new and unusual things, and we consider it foolish to lay aside a promised hope and not to hear fortune beckoning us to her pursuits, even though it is much more foolish to disdain real and solid things than to place our hopes in vain shadows? I call upon not only my conscience but the present letter to bear witness to the fact that all the blame must fall on you and whoever may be slow in accepting my sound plan.

Why do you not hasten here when the chains which tied you down have now been loosened and cut; and please do not accuse me of pride because I seem to lead rather than follow. My mind is ready to do either. If there is a more suitable place anywhere for us to live I shall proceed to it immediately. I am not one accustomed to spurn any trustworthy advice. I believe there is no one who has greater trust or confidence in friends. But if this place is preferred in your judgment, which your letters seem to admit, what is now keeping you? Do not be tempted by ambition; it never is about to say "this is enough"; it always seems to want more. This is so especially because, as with oil and wine, so is it with time and life: the dregs lie in the bottom! To limit yourself to such dregs while neglecting what is closer to the surface is ridiculous. It is a custom of travelers to find lodging before night; I implore that we make similar plans and after many labors of the journey prepare ourselves finally for that eternal lodging. For this I offer you, oh brothers dearer to me than light, whatever resources I command or advice I can give, whatever delight or favor can be expected of me, whatever support from the things which are improperly called mine since they really belong to fortune, in short all of myself which I can do without pride, as well as my books, my gardens, and anything else I own. However, those things which are needed so badly in this human life of ours are not few, and while they might be expressly mentioned in a letter such as this, dignity forbids it. Finally, so that I might end with a vow and a prayer, may the consoling Holy Spirit inspire us to conspire at least in this, that while we desire to continue in this life, we may aspire to peace and tranquillity, and that we who have sighed all day may breathe normally at twilight. Farewell.

To the same correspondent, on the same matter.

I had scarcely sealed my earlier letter than, still not fully satisfied, the potential sweetness of our future which preoccupies my mind and thoughts caused me to take my tired pen in hand, and as the messenger lingered, in order not to lose the opportunity, I decided to push my idea even further. I enjoy speaking at greater length and trying to spur you with the same goads that I feel. If, therefore, we all seek a happy life—and there has never been any sect that disagrees with this in any way—although how to achieve such a life remains a basic problem for human curiosity; if, as I was saying, desire for happiness is inseparably joined to the soul that, though happiness may be lost, we do not really lose it nor can we lose it if we wished, nor would we want to lose it if we could; and if we know that happiness itself cannot be fulfilled here without the comfort of friends, why do we obstruct our enjoyment, and why does the slowness of particular ones hamper the good of all? As Seneca says, "Joy can indeed come to us from those we love even when absent, but it is slight and evanescent; their appearance and presence and conversation lead to enduring pleasure." We must, therefore, seize such happiness forthwith. For if some philosophers were so desirous of obscene pleasure that they considered it the greatest good, viewing it as mistress of human actions, they subordinated virtue itself to its service; who would be so inflexible as not to be attracted by honest pleasure which virtue and its companion, friendship, can offer? I ask you, what life is happier or gayer than the one spent with friends whose perfect love and mutual affection make all feel as one, bound as if with an indissoluble knot and a single mind in all things; with whom there is no disagreement, no secrets, but instead harmonious accord, serene brows, and a truthful and unstudied conversation, as well as a perfectly open mind? If such a life befalls us I shall desire nothing more; and if I shall see anywhere a usurer or a legacy hunter puffed up at the expense of another, he will provoke no envy on my part, and I shall indeed consider him very poor. As the Satirist said, "Let Nero possess all that he stole, let him keep his mountain of gold, but let him not love anyone nor let him be loved by anyone." When we have assembled in a single place—what is there that can prevent us from enjoying our future? If indeed you seem to approve this dwelling of mine (not undeservingly, for while perhaps it is not like the one possessed by King Latinus in Virgil, "august, huge, and having a hundred columns," it is certainly pleasant, solitary, healthy and fully capable of hospitality for a few who get along so well); if then the fates cause you to gather here—let us cast our anchor, and let us appear as though we had found our port. And if perchance the group of friends increases, drawn by the attractiveness of our life of ease, there is a more impressive house in the middle of the city which I keep empty for such an eventuality. I and all my household would fill only a very small part of that house, even though in my desire for solitude my household appears huge.

Please do not consider these words confining chains and believe that you will be restricted to one place. There will be on one side of us Bologna, mother of studies, in which we spent our early youth; and it will be pleasant, now that our thinking and our hair has changed, to see it again and to view the condition of that city and of our own minds with more mature judgment and, by comparison, to note how little we have truly progressed in our lives. There will be near the Po, Piacenza, the home of your venerable Antonnio which you manage, without spurning the mediocrity of the position after having turned down many more lucrative ones, since, as you usually say, you considered my nearness highly desirable. There you will be the host of all. If we would like to travel a little further, we shall have Milan close by, as well as Genoa, the former representing the glory of land-bound cities and the latter of maritime cities; the former having attractive lakes and rivers, the latter having its waters resounding and congested with sails. There we shall see huge Lake Lario with Como nearby from which the river Adda emerges; we shall see the Verbano which is called Lake Maggiore by its inhabitants and which the Ticino intersects. We shall see the Eupili from which the Lambro and the Sebino and the Oglio issue, and not far from there the Benaco from which breaks forth the Mincio, lakes that are very well-known to the public, but names that are not even known to the learned. We shall see overhanging the lakes the lofty and snowy Alps, a most pleasant spectacle in the summer, and forests which touch the stars, and resounding streams amidst the vaulted cliffs, and rivers crashing down from the mountains, and wherever you turn the singing of birds and the sound of springs. In the other region the Apennines tower, and the sea is below us. The Tritons will be present to our eyes as well as other monsters of the sea, and the din of Neptune will be in our ears, as will be the wailing of the stones and the plaints of the Nereids. We shall walk among all these things to which I am beyond belief attracted, and along the bending shores of the Tyrrhenian, free from biting and stinging cares; and that ever-desirable leisure which those noble friends, Scipio and Lelius, enjoyed in Gaieta after their military labors, we shall enjoy on the shores of Genoa after our poetic labors. If we ever have our fill of this part of the earth, Padua will offer an abode which is no less peaceful and suitable, where not the least part of our good fortune will be to enjoy the intimate friendship of that great man under whom that city, following a long series of hardships, has now recovered its breath. Here I shall name him with the deepest respect, Jacopo de Carrara, whom I would like to bring you to love and to cherish in your mind; for while virtue may be loved in every age it should be loved more in ours because it is rare. And there will be to one side of us a city, Venice, which I consider the most miraculous of all the ones I have seen—and I have seen almost all the ones of which Europe is most proud. There will also be its illustrious ruler who likewise deserves honorary mention, Andrea, a man acclaimed no less for his fondness for art and learning than for his distinguished handling of so great an office. And there will be Treviso, surrounded with fountains and rivers, the home and marketplace of delightful living. Thus, as often as monotony, the mother of tedium, overcomes us, there will be variety, the greatest medicine for boredom; and whatever annoyance steals upon us will be eliminated by an exchange of views and by traveling from place to place. I do not doubt that you see with what arms I am attacking you, with what arts I am pressing you, and how I am mixing womanly flattery with manly warnings. I shall do everything I can to persuade you: how sincerely I do so, I myself can testify. The outcome will show how effectively. I seem to have presented all that was in me; I could perhaps, had I wanted, have said this more eloquently, but excessive feeling often hinders eloquence. I have said as best I could what was in my mind, what you could understand, and I hope what you could approve. I beg you not to consider how I have said it but what I have said; a stammering friend gives better advice than an eloquent enemy. I do not know how to come to an end, and I feel I have gone further than I intended because of my zeal. This alone I shall not stop repeating, and it is something which you yourself leaned toward without my urging you: let us assemble forthwith in this place if this pleases all of us; otherwise choose a place which pleases you anywhere in the world—for I shall object to no area of the world, no foreign country. I shall put aside all my preferences and adopt yours. Whatever allows us to be together will be acceptable. Choose where we may live peacefully what remains of our life, where we may die calmly. Farewell, and do not allow any delay to interfere with sane advice.

19 May

Fam. VIII, 6.

To Friar Bartholomew of the order of Saint Augustino, Bishop of Urbino.[1]

You did what behooves your profession when you listed alphabetically in a huge volume all the sayings of Augustine; an accomplishment of great labor rather than of glory. In it I admire your intellect which, unless I am mistaken, reflects a talent that is inclined to greater things than the desire for public approval. As was fitting, the result has justified the effort. With it you have pleased the Roman Pontiff, Clement, a very learned but busy man, and thus appreciative of such compendia. As a result you were made Bishop of your native land and were made to expect even loftier rewards—although, according to the modesty of your mind and the humility of your religion, together with the attractiveness of your native land, I doubt that you could hope for anything loftier or more pleasing as honors for past accomplishments. And as you proceeded from this work to another, you were requested to do for Ambrose what you had done for Augustine. You will obey—having already started—and you will finish, I hope, with the same ease and happy outcome. Knowing you, I say you will obey not to achieve greater honor but to be of greater service. For although the desire for loftier status does not affect you since you are happy with your lot, nevertheless it befits the just man to be as grateful for unsought favors as he is for favors that are desired and sought, for nothing is of such import in the matter of rewards as the intention of a donor. But I return to your Augustine and to you. You requested that I send you some verses that can be appended at the end of that great work which you built with your sweat from the stones and mortar of that most opulent master, and which you prepared for our present Pontiff, but even more for posterity. I have prepared them since I wish to deny you nothing; and although my mind has been distracted from such work for a long time despite the

1. Bartolomeo Carusio, Augustinian friar who had taught theology at Paris and at Bologna where Petrarch had met him during his student days. His compendium of the works of St. Augustine earned him the Bishopric of Urbino from Clement VI.

anger of the Muses, and although I have been involved in many other cares, your request has called me back to them. I am herewith sending you, therefore, a few elegiac verses and a like number of hexameters, if you prefer them, all containing the same meaning. Make use of both or neither as you please; but you should know that they were dictated hastily and extemporaneously with your messenger actually assisting me in measuring the syllables so that none was so short which did not seem too long to him. Farewell.

Fam. VIII, 7.

To his Socrates, a tearful plaint concerning that unequaled plague which befell in their time.

Oh brother, brother, brother (a new kind of beginning for a letter, indeed an ancient one used by Marcus Tullius almost fourteen hundred years ago); alas dearest brother, what shall I say? Where shall I begin? Where shall I turn? Everywhere we see sorrow, on all sides we see terror. In me alone you may see what you read in Virgil concerning so great a city, for "on all sides there is cruel mourning, everywhere there is trembling and countless images of death." Dear brother, would that I had never been born or had died earlier! If I am compelled to wish this now, what do you think I would be saying if I had arrived at a truly old age? Oh would that I never reach that point. But I feel I shall, not because I shall live longer, but because I shall suffer a longer death. Indeed I know my destiny and I slowly understand what I am heading for in this troublesome and unhappy life. Alas, dear brother! I am deeply troubled from within and take pity on myself. What would anyone who hears these words say? "You who seem to offer comfort and aid to others, who had promised us things that were superior, who ought to have formed a thick skin from your constant misfortunes and to have become calloused against all the blows of fortune and hardened to something like a flintstone, see how weakly you bear your burdens, see how often you direct your frequent wailings to us. Where is that loftiness of soul which now especially should mark your profession? Where are the magnificent words, which, if intended rather to extol your genius than as advice for life, can be no more than empty sounds and curious charms for the ears? We expected from you a heroic poem, we get elegiac verses; we hoped for biographies of illustrious heroes, we are getting the story of your sorrow. What we considered letters are laments, where we sought ingenious combinations of words, new molds for language, and sweetly ordered rhetorical colors, we behold nothing but mournful exclamations and indignant tones and tear stains. And what will be the limit or the end if you want to deplore the fate of all mortals? One heart and one tongue would not suffice. Wretched man, you have undertaken a huge and troublesome task which is useless and implacable. You must seek another source for your tears; the recent and continually new causes of grief make it impossible for excessively tired, exhausted, and dried-up eyes to produce sufficient tears. Therefore, forgetful of yourself and dissatisfied with your own misery and illness which you incurred knowingly and willingly, what else are you doing but offering poison to your friends to whom you had promised a cure? Better that you should either cry alone or learn to bear mortal things with the equanimity of a mortal; and noting that not only you or your friends alone, but all living beings are being snatched away, it is time that you put an end to your useless complaining." There may be someone of quick temper who hates such gloomy recitals and will discard them or trample on them with biting scorn saying, "Go to the devil; if you are going to behave like a woman, at least do not prevent us from acting like men." I feel all of these things and none escapes me, dear brother. I realize that a man must either drive away grief or destroy it, or control it, or finally conceal it. But what can I do? I shall die if I cannot pour out my grief in tears and words. My one consolation is that whatever I shall have written, though weak and empty, will reach your hands not as if to a stranger's but as if to my own. Therefore I shall fear no greater shame while you read these things than I felt while I was writing them.

I shall not deny that I did feel some shame; for without the control of reason I felt my mind and my style pulled along with my feelings beyond what I intended, something I find most disturbing. But what I feel to be an even greater insult is that for a whole year and considerably more I have had little occasion, not, indeed, to do, but certainly to write anything worthy of a man as a result of fortune's thundering and storming on all sides. Because of this I may perhaps be excused by a benign judge if he were also to consider that I am bewailing not something inconsequential, but the 1348th year of the sixth age, which not only deprived us of our friends but the entire world of actual nations. If anyone escaped, the coming year is gathering its harvest so that whatever survived that storm is being pursued by death's sickle. How can posterity believe that there was once a time without floods, without fire either from heaven or from earth, without wars, or other visible disaster, in which not only this part or that part of the world, but almost all of it remained without a dweller? When was anything similar either seen or heard? In what chronicles did anyone ever read that dwellings were emptied, cities abandoned, countrysides filthy, fields laden with bodies, and a dreadful and vast solitude covered the earth? Consult the historians: they are silent; question the scientists: they are stupified; ask the philosophers: they shrug their shoulders, they wrinkle their brows and they order silence by holding their fingers to their lips. Will you believe such things, oh posterity, when we ourselves who see them can scarcely believe them and would consider them dreams except that we perceive them awake and with our eyes open and that after viewing a city full of funerals we return to our homes only to find them empty of our loved ones. Should we not indeed know that what we grieve over is indeed true? Oh happy generation of our great-grandsons who will not have known these miseries and perhaps will consider our testimony as fable! I do not deny that we deserve these things and even worse; but our ancestors also deserved them, and would that our descendants will not! Why is it, then, oh most blessed judge, why is it that the violence of your vengeance lies so extraordinary upon our times? Why is it that when guilt is not absent, examples of just punishment are lacking? We have sinned as much as anyone, but we alone are being punished. Alone, I say; for I dare assert that if the punishments of all the centuries, subsequent to that most famous ark that bore the remains of mortals over unformed seas, were compared to present ones, they would resemble delightful activities, games, and moments of ease. Nor is it fitting to compare these misfortunes to any wars, for in such wars there are many kinds of remedies, and ultimately the possibility of at least dying in a manly fashion. For to die well is an exceptional consolation for death. In the present case there is absolutely no remedy, and no comfort. Not knowing the cause and origin of our misfortune only adds to the extent of the disaster. For neither our ignorance nor indeed the plague itself is more troublesome than the nonsense and stories of certain men who profess to know everything, but really know nothing. Their mouths, accustomed to falsehoods, are finally silenced, and where at first they emitted their ignorance as is their custom, they finally remain closed with stupor. But let me return to my inquiry.

Is it not true that just as for wayfarers one part of the road produces a weariness that is admitted only upon reaching another part, so does it happen to us that Your mercy, oh Lord, gradually exhausted by human faults, and depressed by the continuing increase in such faults, finally can take no more, and must subside, and that You, like an ideal wayfarer unable to endure any more have cast us behind You and angrily turned away the eyes of Your mercy? But if this is so, we suffer punishment not only for our sins but for those of our fathers. I do not know whether we are worse than they, but certainly we are more wretched. Or is it perhaps true as is suspected by certain great minds that God cares not for mortal things? Let such madness not even enter our minds: if You did not care they would not be. What must be our opinion of those who attribute our welfare not to God but to nature, when we have been dedicated to the study of Your truths? Even Seneca calls most ungrateful those who through a change of name disguise a function of God, and through impious mockery deny what is owed to divine majesty. You certainly do care for us and our affairs, oh God, but the causes are concealed and unknown to us as to why we have been judged by You the most worthy of all centuries to be punished most harshly without there being any lessening of Your justice because it is hidden from us. For the depth of Your judgments is inscrutable and inaccessible to human senses. Therefore either we are really the worst of all, something which I would like to but dare not deny, or else we are being saved through these present evils by becoming more experienced and more pure for future blessings, or else there is something involved which we are simply unable to fathom. Yet, whatever the causes may be, however much you conceal them, the effects are most visible.

But to turn from public to private grief, the first part of the second year is hardly over since tearfully I left you crying at the mouth of the Sorgue as I returned to Italy. I am not asking you to consider a long period of time; consider simply these very few days and call to mind what we were and what we are. Where are our sweet friends now, where are their beloved faces, where are their soothing words, where is their mild and pleasant conversation? What thunderbolt destroyed all those things, what earthquake overturned them, what storm overcame them, what abyss absorbed them? We used to be a crowd, now we are almost alone. We must seek new friendships. But where or for what reason when the human species is almost extinct and the end, as I hope, is near? Why pretend, dear brother, for we are indeed alone. I believe that it was God's purpose to strip us of the sweet charms and impediments of this life so that we might now more freely desire the next life. See where we have arrived as a result of the sudden changes! We are now in a position to test that saying of Epicurus: "We represent a sufficiently large theater one for the other." To be truthful to each other, how long will we be able to say this? Or what soothsayer can indicate the extent to which we can have faith in the stability of such a reciprocal theater, when on the other hand we see the columns already shaking? About what can I in writing this be more certain concerning your life than you, in reading this, can be concerning mine? Man is too frail and proud an animal, he builds too securely on fragile foundations. See to what a small number we have been reduced from so large a group of comrades: and note that while we are speaking we ourselves are also fleeing and are vanishing in the fashion of shades, and in a moment of time one of us receives the news of the departure of the other and the survivor will in turn be following upon the footsteps of the other. What are we, therefore, dearest brother? What are we, indeed? Of what do we continue to be proud? Dismayed by his torments, Cicero says in one of his letters to Atticus, "What are we or how long shall we be attending to these things?" Indeed a brief but good question, if I am not mistaken. It is also a wholesome question, pregnant with useful advice in which the alert digger will discover a great deal about true humility and modesty and great contempt for fleeting things. I say, what are we? How heavy, how slow, how fragile is our body, how confused and how restless is our mind, how changeable and how uncertain and voluble is our destiny? How long shall we be concerned about these things? Very briefly. Cicero certainly meant nothing more by this than had he said: "How long shall we continue to be the very thing we are?" By heavens, certainly not long, since just as this very being of ours cannot last long, so can it actually cease as we utter these very words. Nor should it prove astonishing if this were to happen. Therefore, oh Marcus Tullius, you ask both questions well and seriously. But I ask you, where have you left the third question which is in fact more dangerous and more worthy of being asked? What shall we be after terminating our life here? An important and doubtful matter, indeed, but certainly neglected! Farewell.

Fam. VIII, 8.

To the same correspondent, on the same matter.

There remained here with me a very small number of remnants from the past year, and particularly a very famous, magnanimous and wise man, Paganino da Milano, who was most welcomed not only by me but by both of us after the many proofs of his worth. He had already begun to become for me another Socrates. He had begun to enjoy my trust and friendship almost as you did, as well as those privileges most enjoyed by friendship, the sharing in each other's misfortunes, the faithful sharing of secrets with a completely open heart. Indeed, how much he loved you, how he desired to see you whom he had indirectly gotten to know so well, how concerned he was for your life in this public disaster! I myself marveled at how an unknown man could be loved so strongly. He no sooner saw me sadder than usual than he would ask in a friendly but anxious manner: "What is the matter? What has happened? How is our friend?" When he heard that you were really well, he would lay his apprehension aside with an extraordinary joyfulness. This man (and I say this with copious tears and would be saying it with still more, except that I am protecting my eyes so exhausted from preceding misfortunes, and am reserving what remains of my tears for impending misfortunes), this man, I say, having been suddenly seized by the illness of the plague which is devastating the world, spent the evening with his friends and what remained of his ebbing life conversing with me and recalling our past friendship and relationship. He spent that night calmly amidst his excruciating pains, and was overtaken by a sudden death that morning. And in keeping with the fatal times, before three days were over, his children and all his family followed him. Go forth now, you mortals, rage, pant, toil, circle the earth and the seas to accumulate endless wealth and temporary glory. The life we live is but a sleep, and whatever occurs in it is very similar to a dream. Death alone breaks up the sleep and disperses the dreams. Oh, if only it were possible to awaken earlier! Farewell.

Fam. VIII, 9.

To the same correspondent, on the violent death of a friend.

I had not yet satisfied fortune for it had to attack me again with sharper weapons and had to add even the madness of wicked men to the wrath of God. Woe is me! I am now beginning to fail, and as with the terror that first attacks those who are about to undergo fears, I now tremble with a gloomy cold. I have reached the point where I now fear to recall and relate what must be said. I know what I am about to say but I do not dare begin, and I would most willingly be freed from these matters and from this subject, except that my grief draws my mind on as well as the need for relating what has happened, and indeed your very anxiety which perhaps causes you to laugh at my weeping since you do not know what has happened. This then is the way things have happened. Fortune had left us two friends. Although there are others, these were the ones with whom it appeared that we could complete what remained of our lives, God willing. I ask, what hindered us? Not wealth, not poverty, nor differences of inclination, nor that great enemy of friendship, business. We were four persons with a single mind. I therefore boasted that while antiquity could in very few of its periods scarcely boast of one or perhaps two such friendships, our age could shortly boast of a single household with two pairs of such friends. I said "pairs" improperly: for it was one, and not even one pair but a single mind shared by all, as I said, which believed that experience did not allow us to wander any longer. The first of these friends was of a nature that, aside from being a most pleasant colleague, he was also a sharer and partner in our studies. The other, though not participating in these studies, possessed characteristics that result from such studies—mainly, kindness, faith, generosity, and steadfastness. In short, though lacking in liberal training, he was aware of the wealth of the liberally educated mind and was an excellent man and friend. Within our group he was even more compatible than if, like all of us dedicated to the study of letters, he had elected to spurn those other things that are necessary to life, as the rest of us had done. He therefore represented the fourth member of our varied group most conveniently and almost as if willed by heaven. We appeared to be too happy. Most cruel fortune envied us and because she had not yet cast us all down as victims of the world's tragedy, she was indignant. Our friends set out together, and having left you at the Rhone river, they eagerly sought me in Padua as if I were an actual part of them. I have undertaken a truly sad and unhappy account. I seem to contradict myself in its words, nor can I restrain myself. But meanwhile, I know not how, I am seized by something I do not wish, if indeed I can wish unwillingly, and I am undergoing something miserable and deadly and yet pleasing to my mind. Weeping also has a certain kind of sweetness with which I have unhappily nourished myself in these days, and tormented myself, and in which I have taken pleasure. For unless I do find delight in it, who compels me to deal with these sorrowful things? But it is a delight more painful than any punishment, for while memory wrenches the mind, my grief diminishes. In any event, our two friends came together with excellent intention, with fate against them, with a miserable end in sight, and with one finally heading for Rome and the other for Florence. But why, dear friends, are you separated and where are you heading? Proceed more directly, go more safely. This is not the road to take: why did you seek out the Alps and the snows? "Love conquers all and you yielded to love." You were coming to see me: this was the catch, this was the chain with which almighty love was dragging you along, after having encircled and seized you, love to which heaven itself yields, and which the reluctant elements obey in turn. Thus one cannot ask you the reason for taking the longer road. You were being pulled, you were not proceeding on your own. Furthermore your destiny drove you on, as well as mine with which I had been acquainted for some time. There was no straighter road to destruction and to my perpetual grief.

Why, my dear Socrates, did fortune wickedly bring it about that I who had not moved a foot from my home in the space of a year, should have been absent at that very moment which kept us from seeing each other and drove them in constrenation and more rapidly into the trap of waiting death. They had certainly hastened up to that point, forgetful of all toil and of all other cares except for their one hope and desire, for it is natural that a greater passion absorbs a minor one. Their minds burned to see me personally and to discuss with me the plans for their future life. So they took up their journey once again and having arranged their affairs in their native land, they returned here so that, with the addition of yourself, we would live together until our death. If they had found me, their delay could perhaps have swayed the rigor of fortune. But had they perhaps changed their plan and had accomplished the business that they had in their native land through intermediaries, tempted by love, they would have settled down with me, and now (what indeed would have stopped it?) we would all be together enjoying that peace we have desired for such a long time. But we were held by the iron-like chains of fate, and mad fortune saw to it that I was absent. Therefore when they arrived here, having learned the truth from the travelers at the gate of the city, they proceeded sad and deeply dejected to my house. Why linger over details? They checked into every corner of the house and throughout the garden (for winter had begun to soften because of the approaching spring) sitting down periodically and filling the air with sighs. Although they could go elsewhere, they both slept for the night in my bed so that, in my opinion, the place which human frailty considers important for a necessary rest would become a source of trouble and groans for me. The following day they departed, leaving a letter in the house which disclosed their sadness and their intentions, a letter that as long as I live I shall hold amidst my dearest belongings as a recollection of sorrow and an dundying cause for tears.

A whole month had passed before I returned home unaware of all these things, and, having read the letter, I heard sorrowfully and with astonishment my housekeeper repeat what it said. But what was I to do? They had departed so long before that already I was expecting their return and, like a madman, was accusing them of negligence. After some time,

I sent one of my servants to Florence urging the friend who was closer to return, and adding that he send the same messenger to the other friend wherever he might be. To this one I had written a great many things during those days, but at that moment I dispatched a hortatory letter urging on his part the rather modest choice of electing either this or any other place, whichever showed itself more opportune for our affairs in addition to our love for a life of solitude and study. Since the letter concerned all of us equally, I added that it also be sent to you through him. Virgil certainly put it well, as he did so many things, when he said: "The mind of men is ignorant of destiny." The letter carrier departed, and I in the meantime imagined all kinds of pleasant things: "These would come from the East, he would come from the west; who was happier than I? Whose life could be more peaceful?" While indulging in such thoughts which were to double the bitterness of the approaching misfortune, my messenger, on the eighth day after he had departed, returned unexpectedly during a very intense storm, wet with rain and with tears. I turned to him and having shaken the pen from my hand, for he had appeared while I was writing, I cried out, "What news do you bring? Speak quickly." He interrupting his words with a sigh said, "I am a bearer of bad news. Your friends fell into the cruel hands of bandits on a summit of the Apennines."

"Alas," I said, "what happened? What are you telling me?" He continued sobbingly and this is a summary of what he said. Our Simpliciano, that most excellent and sincere man, who went first, walked into an ambush and was quickly overpowered, falling amidst the swords of his murderers. Soon Olimpio, aroused by the cries, hastened to his assistance and stood firm under the blows of the swords of ten or more would-be murderers. Having inflicted and received many wounds, he scarcely managed to escape alive by spurring on his horse. The robbers, without taking all the booty from the dead victim, fled so rapidly that weary of body and of spirit, they could easily have been captured by the farmers attracted by the uproar, except that certain so-called nobles, dashing down from the mountains, following a mild attack by their attendants, led the hard-pressed group and their bloody spoils into their hiding places. Olimpio was seen with his sword in hand wandering far off from there, but no more has been heard about him since.

The winds have brought with them a sad omen: I do not know whether I can bear lightly the news that both have been killed. I certainly know what I should do. Shutting my doors to all consolers, I ought to devote myself alone to my grief, and either lighten my mind with tears or oppress it, either lessen my desire for mourning or satisfy it, and I should show my concerns for my friends with tearful and wailing eyes because they have been seized by ungodly hands. I am now being tormented not by one but by three passions of the mind: hope, fear, and grief. And as though pierced with a like number of wounds on one side as on the other, I know not where my wounded heart inclines, and I am distracted and torn to pieces in an extraordinary and wretched manner by raging and contradictory anxieties and messengers. For I sent messengers out again, though in a different manner, and expected some kind of news concerning the one who had survived, but while there are many different reports from all sides, nothing certain has reached me. In such suspense and anxiety of mind, I keep a careful lookout on all roads and hold my breath at every loud noise. I have now gone fifteen days. If this period of time were to be weighed against the misfortunes of the many past years, I believe that it would easily outweigh them. I was tempted to go forth and not stop until I knew in what condition the survivor was, whatever it may have been, and (oh strange destiny!) to see the alpine and deserted grave of the other. Rumor has it that a great crowd not only from the surrounding towns but even from the city attended his burial with great compassion, with the farmers expressing their anger in loud voices and predicting many things which subsequently happened, such as the fact that when the road became impassable they could foresee only isolation for themselves and expensive and destructive wars in place of the handsome profits they enjoyed in lodging travelers. I believe that I too would have gone, and, driven by fate, I would have in all probability fallen into those same hands had not the time of year and my bad health restrained me. Not on that account am I any the less uncertain as to what to do, not knowing whether the mind should obey necessity or the desire for freeing myself of the chains that bind me. I say all these things so scrupulously, dear brother, so that you may understand all the details, even though without doubt you have learned about the general situation. I dislike intensely having my mind overwhelmed with countless waves tossing about the swift skiff of hope hither and yon on the changeable and swelling sea of rumors. This kind of life is for me no more pleasant than death, and I long for its end with my prayers and I detest any delay. Just recently we seemed to be young men, and now see how we have lived two years beyond our limit. This life is now approaching the maximum of tribulations because, while I begin to count the days in the manner of lovers, I am deeply astonished at your silence and feel some new suspicions arising within me. For I hear that that plague of last year which seemed to have ended, is again invading the banks of the Rhone, and I certainly hope that you are not dead! But what am I trying to do in my misfortune? Is my present misfortune insufficiently real and true, unless in my misery I also turn to fictitious and future ones? May God change all of this for the good so that as often as I am deceived by false hope I might once be deceived by a false fear.

Thus far, dearest Socrates, indulging in my grief in an undignified manner, I have unburdened my mind of its complaints as best I could. I had to do so in order not to crack under the weight of my misfortune. Forgive me, dear Socrates, and let others who may read this also forgive me. There are times when silence is noble; but others when words are necessary. Whatever death may do from now on I shall count not only my friends but myself among the dead, knowing that none of these things occur without the will of God, since He either orders them or permits them; I shall restrain my heavy and swollen soul and tongue from mourning, and I shall avoid being like those who do not consider it enough to excuse their sin without accusing the judgment of

God. And perhaps the last sun has not set for us and we may still be able to communicate either in writing or through conversation in the future. I join to this letter a copy of the letter to the Florentines concerning this great harm that has been done to their city, hoping that you might like it. Farewell, and try to preserve yourself for happier days so that we may see each other again on this earth if heaven does not forbid it.

22 June.

To the Florentines, an expression of indignation and complaint concerning the inhuman crimes perpetrated on their borders, and an exhortation to cultivate justice and guard their roads.

I have often on various occasions wanted to write you, oh distinguished citizens, concerning a variety of matters. I have in turn wanted to urge you to restrain yourselves, to spur you on, to complain about the loss of your liberty, and to congratulate you for its recovery. I have sometimes wanted to weep with you over the many and unpredictable storms that have swept over your state and faithfully to warn you of impending shipwrecks so that by doing so I might prove to you, since no other way existed, through words which at least give evidence of one's spirit, that although I was not a dweller in my homeland I was certainly devoted to it. But when I began to consider how far the humility of my studies were from your lofty concerns, I began to feel my pen slipping from my hands. Now, however, I am compelled to write, nor am I able to restrain myself, for a deep sorrow presses upon my mind and wrenches out of me words mixed with tears. Consider what has happened (something I knew nothing about until now and wish I had never known). A very pleasant and deservingly dear citizen of yours and friend of mine while returning from France to Florence, having gone through the many annoyances and dangers of such a long journey and finally approaching his beloved homeland, practically on the very threshold of his own door and of your gates, was cruelly killed, so to speak, in your very bosom. Oh unfortunate man, who bore so many tribulations in your younger years, and often traveled through unknown lands so that you might spend a peaceful and respected old age in your homeland! Where are you going? Alas, wretched friend unaware of your destiny and safer anywhere except in your homeland, where do you hasten, where are you rushing so pitiably? Those verses befit you which say, "your piety deceives heedless you," your piety about which Cicero says, "as great as it may be toward your acquaintances and neighbors, it will be even greater for your homeland." It was that piety which without doubt drew you on, being as attached as you are to your native soil. You are now returning there as an aged person having departed as a boy, and you are carrying back to that land that had frightened you as a child the remains of your weary life, desirous of burial in your place of birth and of a grave where you had crawled as a child. But, oh evil deed, oh inhuman savageness! The most ferocious of men, nay indeed, bloody and monstrous beasts, were awaiting you unsuspecting and unarmed in the middle of the road, that dreadful species of robbers unknown on Italian shores. They do not find satisfaction in gold, which is usually the supreme desire of robbers, but must skillfully draw your blood and prevent your highly desired return to your native land and reaching your place of burial. Oh unheard of thirst for blood! What more do you seek, you raging dogs? What more do you search for from a despoiled body? There certainly was no hatred of an unknown and innocent man, nor could one imagine it. If hunger for gold is the true cause of your evil deed, once your abominable desire has been fulfilled, return with your heavy booty to the caves and workshops of your crimes and go visit your hosts who eagerly await you there. Allow him to proceed barefooted. This would be sufficient. Nothing more is sought from you. He fell at the hands of robbers, but they too must have strongholds and are able to disdain without punishment heaven, Florence and justice. How could you fear a little man alone, weary and stunned, when your strong retreats were so close. Therefore, do not add fierceness to your greed: you have carried off anything that was of any value and could be turned to your use. Leave behind his soul which was so beneficial to himself and to his friends, but would be of no use to you. What do you consider savage, what are you thinking about, what are you trying to do? What is that madness of yours? What do your flashing swords seek, what do they want? Oh savage passion without hatred, without any expectation, slaughtering without fear a being who is sacred and similar to God, dip your lustful hands into his entrails and (something which even the more generous animals would not do) fall upon the mangled body and take delight in the foaming blood.

It shames me and makes me wretched, oh outstanding citizens, nor do these many laments emerge from a small spring of sorrow, nor indeed do I grieve more because such a misfortune befell such a friend than because so great a shame befell a state which was once so glorious. What will the people say? What will posterity think? That a harmless man who, as Lucan says, among the untamed people on the shores of the Rhone river, and through the desert sof the province of Arles than which there is nowhere any land more wild or desolate, and through the heart of the Alps beset not so much by snow or wandering travelers but at present by armed troops, did manage to travel along safely not only in daylight but in the dangers of the night, and yet was struck down in full daylight in Florentine territory like a sheep destined for an ungodly sacrifice. Oh eternal disgrace of our age, that there are to be found those who dared, almost in view of your city and of that formerly dreaded palace in which was the famous seat of your justice, tear to pieces one of your subjects as they pleased! Oh times, oh customs, one might exclaim with Tullius. Even as a child I used to hear my elders talk about the unusual virtues of all sorts possessed by that people, and their outstanding justice not only in civil suits but especially in these two things in which that most wise legislator, Solon, said was the basis of a true republic, namely, reward and punishment. If only one of these is missing, the state must limp along as if on the other foot, but if both are missing, it is utterly weakened and sluggish, with the virtue of good citizens becoming dull on the one hand, and, on the other, the badness of evil citizens taking fire. Your forefathers provided magnificently for both possibilities with skills truly worthy of their Roman origin which their fame had made renowned. Therefore, just as once those ancestors of ours, the Roman people, were powerful throughout the whole world, in the same manner did I conceive of the Florentines as having followed in the same footsteps to the extent it was granted by heaven. And they enjoyed an extraordinary amount of praise among all kinds of men and were able to maintain for a long time among the people of Tuscany a kind of voluntary pre-eminence although they carefully avoided even the name of empire. But what they lacked in arrogance and envy they gained in praise and glory. Their state was therefore not called a dominion but rather the aid and protector of neighbors, wherefore the flowering name of Florence was considered proper for it and given to it since in it visibly abounded the flower of all virtues and examples of glorious deeds. The fear of all the neighboring people for such a well-mannered people was mixed with love and respect. Not only in its own vicinity but in the furthest areas of Tuscany was this state feared as a mistress of justice. For how else could one explain that among the rocky and harsh hills, and on the parched soil, and without the assistance either of a maritime port or of a navigable river, its size increased in such a brief period of time (since of almost all cities of Italy, yours is the youngest) that it almost unbelievably surpassed all the largest neighboring ones, not only in reputation or in precious merchandise (which also was a kind of miracle), but in its most fortunate production of manly offspring? Being insufficiently large for all its offspring, did it not, again like a mother fill with its subjects almost every corner of the world? What, I ask, was the cause of this so great and sudden a growth especially because it had so many adversaries? There are some who say that the atmosphere which was most suitable for producing such offspring was the cause, thereby attributing to nature or to fate what really belongs to virtue. Others count among the causes the industry of your energetic people, their versatile minds, and a temper most suitable for all the arts. This may indeed not be wrong provided one recalls that it overlooks the first and greatest cause of all by saying nothing of their fondness for justice. That, I say, that alone is the true and primary cause of your growth. Without it neither the city itself nor the smallest home would either grow or even exist. Justice is the foundation of all cities on which, if one seeks the truth, your ancestors erected for you a most flourishing and powerful republic. If you allow this fact to be overlooked even through ignorance, what can you possibly expect other than a downfall?

Note that a band of infamous assassins appeared and (something that ought to have aroused the most widespread anger) ambushed a citizen of yours, an outstanding man, against whom it is believed they plotted from the day he left his home. They dared slay in your very midst, and they perpetrated under your very eyes on a public road and with cruel and intolerable insolence something that they would have feared even to think about in their very beds in the days of your forefathers. If you leave this crime unpunished, it will mean the end of your universal reputation, of your justice, and ultimately of your safety, of your liberty and of your glory. It will destroy the foundations from which you had sprung as high as the stars; and, dear God, by what hands they will be destroyed! A great portion of an offense is the violence of the perpetrator. A bunch of gallows-birds, murderers and cavemen, bestial in their nourishment but even more so in their hearts and in their ways, scarcely worthy of prison or chains or your hangman's rope, hasten to your bellies and ravenously feed upon the slaughter and blood of unfortunate people until they are full. They certainly would never have dared do this unless they had confidence either in your sluggishness or in their hiding places, a hope which would have proven completely useless to them if you, as was your custom, were truly men. I realize that fortune keeps you busy and preoccupied in times like these, but it does not scatter your forces nor weaken you to the point where you simply endure a few raging highwaymen freely circulating in your territories. True virtue rises higher and more clearly in adversity; and if I know your customs, nor has my opinion of you been wrong, you possess especially this one quality among the many that you have inherited from the Romans, namely, not to be cast down or crushed by the workings of fortune, but instead to let them exalt you and let your spirits spring forth in a more manly fashion amidst difficulties. I have become quite hopeful since hearing that, incensed by the atrocity of what has happened and inflamed with a noble indignation, you have turned to your usual arms of justice. If this is true, there is no place anywhere, I hope, no stronghold, no favor of wicked men that will turn the deserved thunderbolt of your wrath from the heads of the guilty.

I have indeed, illustrious men, spoken with you in a friendly fashion about many points concerning the loss of my dear and mourned friend over which I can be considered bitterly disturbed. But alas it has been in vain and too late! I realize that my loss cannot be recovered, not if I were to speak eternally with a thousand powerful tongues, or were to charm more sweetly than Orpheus the stone with my tearful plaints accompanied by the lyre. Never will my friend return to me. He entered upon a journey without return. It is now no longer a matter of his appearing again, but do not let your honor fall with him. His return is impossible, but maintaining your honor is very simple and within your power. To warn you that avengers of crimes do not look to the past but to the future is here not necessary. Of what benefit is it to concentrate on those things which cannot be undone? One must hasten to oppose such evils with their likes and contrain human rashness by means of frightful precedents. This is what produced that truly praised opinion of very learned men: "Punishments were invented not because evil exists, but to help avoid evil." Although such punishment is most appropriate because of the monstrous size of this crime, and although I can realistically expect it to be applied if I simply remain silent, I am nevertheless forbidden to demand it. Therefore let all these things I have said be understood as a reflection of my grief which by speaking out I am directing to friendly ears, and as a means of relieving my heavy heart of its weighty sadness, rather than as a means of inflaming your minds for bloody revenge. This would befit neither my profession nor my condition. I therefore declare (whatever I may say or have said) that I do not aspire to such vengeance, but rather request what I can ask in a more honorable fashion, namely, that mindful of your ancient glory and justice in which you flourished so uniquely, you do not allow them to perish in your day. And I beg even more firmly that at least your public roads over which there has always been much traveling both to your city and to the city of your ancestors, and over which there will now be even more traffic from every region since, as you know, we are about to celebrate the Jubilee, be purged of bandits and be open to pilgrims so that through justifiable apprehension they will not be compelled either to avoid undertaking the holy journey or to avoid taking the most direct route. Unless you see to this in a most expeditious manner (and I hope that you will be forward-looking), your reputation will be stained with eternal infamy. Among the first things, you must guarantee access to the pass over the Apennines where a greater number of travelers is expected. How I wish it had occurred to me to bring this to your attention earlier! The warning would perhaps have been more timely and the miserable fate of my unfortunate friend would not have provided others with a reason for being fearful. What was the reason for such a fear? Our age and our elders had always realized that the summit of the Apennines was naturally rough and demanding. Yet there was no place more safe for travelers nor more hospitable. What will happen, however, if the guardians become thieves and the dogs become wolves? When to the inherent terror of the woody mountain an external and additional fear is added, that entire tract of land will in a brief time be deserted by all and be viewed as more inhospitable than Mount Atlas or the Caucasian Mountains. Hasten to avoid this disgrace and this bane, oh powerful men; you see the rocks themselves still moist with your citizen's blood, which still has not dried. From this case learn how to provide for the safety of others. He who wishes to dry up streams must first dry up their source; he who wishes to destroy bandits must first insist that their protectors be rooted out. Go quickly, go happily back to what you began, and with the assistance of heaven destroy the foul hiding places of the criminals, and wipe this blot from before your eyes in order to leave to posterity the reputation for justice which you received from your fathers. God almighty will preserve you as victors and will protect you from so many evils in this world and keep you in a most happy state.

Parma, 2 June, hastily and deeply upset.

Bibliography

Bernardo, A. S. "Dramatic Dialogue in the Prose Letters of Petrarch."
Symposium V (1951): 302–316.
———. "Dramatic Dialogue and Monologue in Petrarch's Works."
Symposium VII (1953): 92–119.
———. "Letter-Splitting in Petrarch's *Familiares.*" *Speculum* XXXIII
(1958): 236–288.
———. "The Selection of Letters in Petrarch's *Familiares.*" *Speculum*
XXXV (1960): 280–288.
———. *Petrarch, Scipio and the 'Africa'.* Baltimore, 1962.
———. "Petrarch and the Art of Literature." In *Petrarch to Piran-
dello* (Toronto, 1973), 19–43.
Billanovich, G. *Lo Scrittoio del Petrarca.* Roma. 1947.
Bishop, M. *Petrarch and His World.* Indiana, 1963.
———. *Letters from Petrarch.* Indiana, 1966.
Bosco, U. *Francesco Petrarca.* Torino, 1946. 2nd ed., 1961.
———. "Francesco Petrarca." In *Letteratura italiana, I Maggiori*
(Milano, 1956), 111–163.
Calcaterra, C. *Nella selva del Petrarca.* Bologna, 1942.
Cornell University Library. *Catalogue of the Petrarch Collection.*
Bequeathed by Willard Fiske, compiled by Mary Fowler. Oxford
University Press, 1916. Revised and updated, 1974.
Dotti, U. "La formazione dell'umanesimo nel Petrarca." *Belfagor*
XXXIII (1968): 532–563.
———. *Francesco Petrarca Le Familiari, Libri I–IV* (Urbino, 1970).
New edition, vol. I, *Libri I–V*, vol. II, *Libri VI–XI* (Urbino, 1974).
Fracassetti, G. *Francisci Petrarcae epistolae de rebus familiaribus et
variae.* Florence, 1859.
———. *Lettere di Francesco Petrarca, delle cose familiari libri ven-
tiquattro, Lettere varie libro unico.* Florence, 1863–1867.
———. *Lettere senili di Francesco Petrarca.* Florence, 1869.
Garin, E. *Italian Humanism.* Translated by Peter Munz. New York,
1965.
Girardi, M. "La 'Nuova data' scoperta dal Nolhac nelle vita del
Petrarca." In *Atti e memorie della R. Accademia di scienze, lettere
ed arti in Padova* VIII (1892).
Kraus, F. X. "Francesco Petrarca in seinem Briefwechsel." In *Deutsche*

Rundschau LXXXV (1895), and LXXXVI (1896). Italian translation by D. Valbusa, *Francesco Petrarca e la sua corrispondenza epistolare*, Florence, 1901.

Magrini, Diana. *Le epistole metriche di Francesco Petrarca*. Rocca S. Casciano, 1907.

Nolhac, P. de. *Pétrarque et l'humanisme*. Paris, 1907.

Pasquali, G. "Le 'Familiari' del Petrarca." In *Leonardo* IV (1933).

Petrarca, Francesco. *Prose*. Ed. G. Martellotti, P. G. Ricci, E. Carrara, and E. Bianchi. Vol. VII in the series *La Letteratura italiana, storia e testi* (Milano and Napoli, 1955).

———. *Book without a Name*. Translated by P. Zacour. Toronto, 1973.

Raimondi, E. "Correzioni medioevali, correzioni umanistiche e correzioni petrarchesche nella lettera VI del libro XVI delle 'Familiares'." In *Studi petrarcheschi* I (Bologna, 1948).

Robinson, J. H. and Rolfe, H. W. *Petrarch, the First Modern Scholar and Man of Letters*. New York and London, 1898.

Rossi, V. "Nell'intimità spirituale del Petrarca (con tre lettere inedite)." In *Nuova Antologia* CCLXXVIII (July, 1931).

———. "Sulla formazione delle raccolte epistolari petrarchesche." In *Annali della cattedra petrarchesca*, 1932.

———. *Francesco Petrarca, Le Familiari*. Florence, 1933–1942.

Sapegno, N. "Le lettere del Petrarca." In *La Nuova Italia* VII (1936).

———. *Il Trecento*. Milano, 1942.

Seigel, J. E. *Rhetoric and Philosophy in Renaissance Humanism*. Princeton, 1968.

Studi petrarcheschi. Bologna, 1948–1966.

Tatham, E. *Francesco Petrarca, His Life and Correspondence*. London, 1926.

Tonelli, L. "Le raccolte epistolari." In his *Petrarca* (Milan, 1930).

Wilkins, E. H. "A Chronological Conspectus of the Writings of Petrarch." In *Romanic Review* XXXIX (1948): 89–101.

———. "Letters Addressed to Petrarch." *MLN* LXV (1950): 293–297.

———. "The Miscellaneous Letters of Petrarch." *MLN* LXV (1950): 374–377.

———. "Petrarch and Giacomo de'Rossi." *Speculum* XXV (1950): 374–377.

———. *The Making of the 'Canzoniere' and Other Petrarchan Studies*. Roma: Edizioni di Storia e Letteratura, 1951.

———. *A History of Italian Literature*. Cambridge, Mass.: Harvard University Press, 1954.

———. *Studies in the Life and Works of Petrarch*. Cambridge, Mass.: The Medieval Academy of America, 1955.

———. *Petrarch at Vaucluse*. Chicago: The University of Chicago Press, 1958.

———. *Petrarch's Eight Years in Milan*. Cambridge, Mass.: The Medieval Academy of America, 1958.

———. "A Survey of the Correspondence between Petrarch and Francesco Nelli." In *Italia medioevale e umanistica* I (1958), 351–358.

———. *Petrarch's Later Years.* Cambridge, Mass.: The Medieval Academy of America, 1959.